W9-CLG-169

COLLECTED WORKS OF ERASMUS

VOLUME 58

COLLECTED WORKS OF
ERASMUS

NEW TESTAMENT SCHOLARSHIP

General Editor Robert D. Sider

ANNOTATIONS ON GALATIANS
AND EPHESIANS

translated, edited, and annotated by

Riemer A. Faber

University of Toronto Press

Toronto / Buffalo / London

The research and publication costs of the
Collected Works of Erasmus are supported
by University of Toronto Press.

ISBN 978-1-4426-4193-8

Printed on acid-free, 100% post-consumer recycled paper with vegetable-based inks.

Library and Archives Canada Cataloguing in Publication

Erasmus, Desiderius, –1536
[Works. English]
Collected works of Erasmus.

Includes bibliographical references and indexes.
Contents: v. 58. Annotations on Galatians and Ephesians.
ISBN 978-1-4426-4193-8 (v. 58)

I. Title.

PA8500 1974   199'.492   C74006326X

University of Toronto Press acknowledges the financial assistance
to its publishing program of the Canada Council for the Arts
and the Ontario Arts Council, an agency of the Government of Ontario.

Canada Council   **Conseil des Arts**
for the Arts   **du Canada**

ONTARIO ARTS COUNCIL
CONSEIL DES ARTS DE L'ONTARIO
an Ontario government agency
un organisme du gouvernement de l'Ontario

Funded by the   Financé par le
Government   gouvernement
of Canada   du Canada

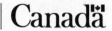

Collected Works of Erasmus

The aim of the Collected Works of Erasmus
is to make available an accurate, readable English text
of Erasmus' correspondence and his
other principal writings. The edition is planned
and directed by an Editorial Board, an Executive Committee,
and an Advisory Committee.

Contents

Illustrations
ix

Editor's Note
xi

Annotations on the Epistle of Paul to the Galatians
by Desiderius Erasmus of Rotterdam
In epistolam Pauli ad Galatas annotationes des. Erasmi Rot.
1

Annotations on Paul's Epistle to the Ephesians
by Desiderius Erasmus of Rotterdam
In epistolam Pauli ad Ephesios annotationes des. Erasmi Roterodami.
109

Works Frequently Cited
228

Short-Title Forms of Erasmus' Works
231

Index of Biblical and Apocryphal References
237

Index of Classical References
240

Index of Patristic, Medieval, and Renaissance References
241

Index of Greek and Latin Words Cited
244

General Index
249

Illustrations

Title-page of Erasmus Annotations,
Annotationes in Novum Testamentum
xiii

Title-page of Erasmus' translation of the commentary
on Galatians by John Chrysostom
xx

Title-page of Erasmus' edition of Cyprian,
Opera divi Caecilii Cypriani episcopi Carthaginensis
137

Title-page of Erasmus' edition of Hilary of Poitiers,
Divi Hilarii lucubrationes
186

Editor's Note

The series of volumes published as the New Testament scholarship of Erasmus is divided into two parts, the *Paraphrases on the New Testament* (CWE 42–50) and the *Annotations on the New Testament* (CWE 51–60).[1] The volumes containing the translation of the *Annotations* are arranged according to the order in which they appeared in Erasmus' edition of the New Testament, that is, the order of the Western canon of the Bible. Previously published in this part of the series are the *Annotations* on the Epistle to the Romans, CWE 56. The present volume contains Erasmus' *Annotations* on Paul's Epistles to the Galatians and the Ephesians. For a survey of Erasmus' New Testament labours, and for translations of the prefatory writings which accompanied the *Paraphrases* and *Annotations*, the reader is directed to the series' introductory volume, CWE 41.

THE PRODUCTION OF THE *ANNOTATIONS*

The origin of the *Annotations* may be traced to marginal comments which Erasmus wrote in his own copy of the Vulgate. We know that Erasmus began writing notes on the New Testament, and then brief commentaries on the Pauline epistles in particular, as early as 1514.[2] In May 1515, when he was completing the edition of the *Novum Instrumentum*, Erasmus wrote in a letter to Maarten van Dorp that he had appended 'annotations' to his version of the Greek text of the New Testament in order to show partly by argument and partly by appeal to ancient theologians that his emendations of the text were

* * * * *

1 For an overview of the New Testament scholarship in the *Collected Works of Erasmus* series see Robert D. Sider, 'Erasmus' Biblical Scholarship in the Toronto Project' in *The Unfolding of Words. Commentary in the Age of Erasmus* ed Judith Rice Henderson (Toronto 2012) 86–98.
2 CWE 2 300:164–6

not made haphazardly.³ And, in the dedicatory letter to Pope Leo X that prefaces the 1516 edition of the New Testament, Erasmus states that he appended annotations to it in order to show the reader what changes he had made to the text and to explain 'anything that may be complicated, ambiguous, or obscure.'⁴

Thus the first edition of the *Annotations* was published by Johannes Froben in Basel in February 1516 as a supplement to the *Novum Instrumentum*, which is the first printed edition of the Greek New Testament, accompanied by a new Latin translation. In *1516* the annotations were placed at the end of the volume. Subsequent editions authorized by Erasmus appeared in March 1519, February 1522, March 1527 and March 1535. With each new edition Erasmus made significant changes and additions to the text of the *Annotations*, including more evidence from the church fathers and supplemented by arguments in support of his text and translation. To accommodate the expanded notes, the *Annotations* were published as a separate volume in 1519. In *1527* three different texts of Scripture were brought together in three columns: the Greek text, Erasmus' Latin translation, and the Vulgate; the *Annotations* were appended.

When the fifth and final edition appeared in 1535, the *Annotations* presented a well-rounded work of New Testament scholarship, having been reinforced with numerous references to the Fathers of the church, scholastic exegetes, and the writings of more recent and contemporary scholars. As far as the Epistles to the Galatians and Ephesians are concerned, Erasmus favoured the patristic interpretations of Jerome, Origen, and Ambrosiaster (whom he calls Ambrose). In later editions he added references to Theophylact (especially *1527*) and Chrysostom (*1535*), and he further augmented these with references to Athanasius, Tertullian, Cyprian, and Augustine. Among the works of scholastic writers Erasmus used especially the commentary on the Pauline epistles by Thomas Aquinas, while among the products of more recent exegetes Erasmus engaged with the writings of Lorenzo Valla, whose *Collatio Novi Testamenti* he had published in 1505, and those of Jacques Lefèvre d'Etaples.⁵

Erasmus' controversies with the conservative critics of the edition, translation, and commentary of the New Testament also contributed to the production of the *Annotations*. Even before the *Novum Instrumentum* appeared in print in 1516, Erasmus had been warned that objections to his edition would arise. Erasmus wrote apologies in response to the attacks of several

* * * * *

3 CWE 3 138:907–11
4 CWE 3 223:64
5 For a survey of the sources Erasmus consulted for his *Annotations* to the Galatians and Ephesians see M.L. van Poll-van de Lisdonk in ASD VI-9 24–41. For Lorenzo Valla see the annotation on Gal 1:13 ('and was subduing') n1.

DES·ERASMI ROTE=

RODAMI IN NOVVM TESTAMENTVM ANNO,
tationes, ab ipso autore iam quintum sic reco,
gnitæ, ac locupletatæ, ut propemodum
nouum opus uideri possit.

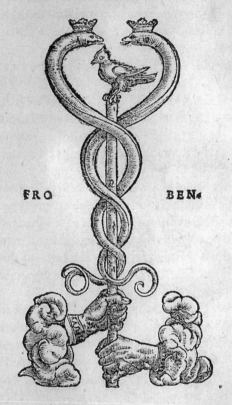

FRO   BEN

PLATO
Pulcherrimum uictoriæ genus est, seipsum uincere.

BASILEAE IN OFFICINA FROBENIANA
ANNO M. D. XXXV.

Cum priuilegio Cæsareo.

Title-page of Erasmus Annotations, *Annotationes in Novum Testamentum*
(Basel Froben 1535) Rotterdam Public Library

critics, and these are published as the *Controversies* in CWE 71–84. Though he rarely mentions his critics by name in the *Annotations*, Erasmus does respond to them by citing additional sources in support of his translation, or by expanding his explanations of the text. For example, in 1522 the commentary was expanded with responses to the objections published by Edward Lee and Diego López Zúñiga. In 1527 and 1535 the added commentaries contain Erasmus' reactions to the objections of Pierre Cousturier. Wherever possible, the editorial notes in the present edition identify the critics to whom Erasmus replies and give brief descriptions of the nature of the controversy. Several recent studies of Erasmus' interactions with his Catholic critics have done much to clarify the evolution of this part of the *Annotations*, and the notes provide suggestions for further reading where appropriate.[6]

THE CHARACTER OF THE ANNOTATIONS
ON THE GALATIANS AND EPHESIANS

Like Paul's letter to the Romans, the Epistles to the Galatians and Ephesians figured prominently in the movement of evangelical reform that took place during the first decades of the sixteenth century. These two texts were carefully studied and much discussed, for the doctrine of justification by faith – the key issue of the Reformation – is expressed emphatically in both Galatians and Ephesians. Two passages in particular stand out, namely Galatians 2:16, 'a man is not justified through works of the law but through faith in Jesus Christ' and Ephesians 2:8, 'for by grace you have been saved through faith; and this is not your own doing, it is the gift of God.'

Erasmus knew how important the letters of Paul to the Galatians and Ephesians were to the reform movement, and he explored their theological import in his interactions with Martin Luther over the freedom of the human will. In his *Assertion* of 1520, Martin Luther had quoted Ephesians 2:3 ('we were by nature children of wrath') in order to support his point that everything human beings do by nature deserves punishment (CWE 76 307–8). Erasmus responded in 1527 by stating that in this passage Paul is referring not to the original sin of all humanity, but to his own former life in Judaism (*Hyperaspistes* 2, CWE 77 372).[7] And it was not only in reaction to the writings

* * * * *

6 For a summary of Erasmus' interactions with his critics see Rummel 123–80; for a fuller treatment see Erika Rummel *Erasmus and His Catholic Critics* (Nieuwkoop 1989).

7 For a new English translation of the relevant writings by Erasmus and Luther on free will see C.H. Miller, P. McCardle *Erasmus and Luther: The Battle over Free Will* (Indianapolis 2012).

of others that Erasmus examined the theological teachings in Galatians and
Ephesians. For his own programme of religious reform, Erasmus was also
inspired by these two letters. In fact, for the popular *Enchiridion*, or *Handbook
of the Christian Soldier* (1503, revised in 1518) Erasmus was inspired by the
memorable image of 'the whole armour of God' in Ephesians 6:11–17 to paint
the picture of the Christian Soldier.[8]

It should be noted, however, that Erasmus does not use the *Annotations*
to engage in polemics with leaders of the reform movement, nor to advance
his own ideals of devotion and piety.[9] Instead, Erasmus employs his commentary to address matters of interpretation that have busied the Church since the
canon of Scripture was formed. Erasmus' deep interest in the history of biblical exegesis may be illustrated by his discussion of the so-called apostolic
conflict between Peter and Paul, recorded in Galatians 2:11–14. There we read
that in Antioch Paul openly resisted Peter for withdrawing from the company
of gentiles when members of the circumcision party arrived, together with
James. First, Erasmus provides a historical survey of the different patristic
interpretations of this passage, and then he relates in summary fashion
Thomas Aquinas' evaluation of the issues at stake. After weighing the evidence he presented, Erasmus concludes the annotation on Galatians 2:11 by
offering his own clear assessment: 'Paul's reprimand was nothing other than
a strengthening of those who were still not yet standing firm enough.'

In addition to summarizing and evaluating the history of textual exegesis, the *Annotations* have several other aims. One is to explain the Greek text
that Erasmus established.[10] On many occasions Erasmus mentions by name
the Greek and Latin manuscripts that he consulted in determining the correct
Greek text. He also cites the readings of early Christian writers, both Latin

* * * * *

8 For Erasmus' treatment of this image see *Enchiridion* CWE 66 30–46, and also
John W. O'Malley's note, xli–xlv.
9 Cf the annotation on Ephesians 1:6 ('unto the praise of his glory and grace') and
note 7 there, as well as the annotation on Eph 2:3 ('by nature children of wrath')
and note 7 there.
10 For a useful recent survey of Erasmus' involvement with the Greek text of the
New Testament, including the manuscripts consulted, his conjectural emendations, and other text-critical aspects of the *Annotations* the reader is directed to
Jan Krans *Beyond What Is Written: Erasmus and Beza as Conjectural Critics of the
New Testament* (Leiden 2006); for the Greek and Latin manuscripts consulted
by Erasmus see also Rummel 36–42. It is not known precisely what Vulgate
text(s) Erasmus used, but the Vulgate that Erasmus quotes in the *lemmata* of
his *Annotations* is, with some exceptions, identical to the Vulgate printed in the
1527 edition of his New Testament. For its similarity to the Clementine Vulgate,
see Jane Phillips 'Erasmus' Biblical Text' in CWE 72 (2005) xxvii–xxix.

and Greek. On two occasions Erasmus refers to the Septuagint version of the Old Testament to determine the reading: Galatians 4:27, which quotes Isaiah 54:1, and Ephesians 4:8, which quotes Psalm 68:18.

The *Annotations* seek also to explain the language of the New Testament, that is, the meaning of Greek (or Hebrew) idioms, the connotation of words, and aspects of syntax and style. Diction that conveys particular theological meaning had to be explained in light of classical Greek and Latin usage, and occasionally Erasmus documents instances of Greek and Latin words used by classical authors. Erasmus' interest in such matters of philology may be illustrated by his commentary on the word ἀρραβών ('guarantee'), which Paul employs in Ephesians 1:14 ('the guarantee of our inheritance' RSV). The Vulgate renders the Greek word as *pignus*, 'pledge.' Erasmus, who chooses to translate the Greek with the loan-word *arrhabo*, 'earnest,' points out that his translation is more accurate here because an earnest is a sign or assurance of future possession, while a pledge is given to a creditor until money owed is paid. In similar fashion Erasmus explains matters of sentence structure and syntax, and features of rhetorical or literary style. A full appreciation for the extensive and diverse range of Erasmus' involvement with the text and meaning of these two books of the New Testament will be gained best through a reading of the *Annotations* themselves.[11]

A NOTE ON THE TRANSLATION

The translation here offered is based on the fifth edition (1535) of the *Annotationes* as prepared by Ioannes Clericus for Volume VI of the *Opera Omnia* edition (Leiden 1705). The facsimile edition of the final Latin text by Anne Reeve and M.A. Screech, which is accompanied by marginal notes of information about all earlier editions, was employed to identify the additions, deletions, and alterations made in earlier editions. This edition was compared with an independent collation of the variants, and with the

* * * * *

11 Readers interested in a thorough introduction to the *Annotations* will wish to consult Erika Rummel *Erasmus' Annotations on the New Testament: From Philologist to Theologian* (Toronto 1986); the introductions to the *Annotations* by P.F. Hovingh in ASD VI-5 1–50, VI-6 3–10, and VI-7 1–29; and the introductions by M. van Poll-van de Lisdonk in ASD VI-9 3–50 and ASD VI-10.

recent critical edition by M.L. van Poll-van de Lisdonk in ASD VI-9.[12] In
cases of uncertain translation I have consulted the Dutch translation of the
Annotations by Jan Hendrik Glazemaker (1620–82), made available to me
from the Erasmuszaal of the Rotterdam City Library.[13]

A preliminary English translation of Erasmus' annotations on Ephesians
was prepared for CWE by the late Dr John J. Bateman; he very generously
permitted me to use it as a starting point for the translation here published.
In keeping with the series' goal of producing readable literal translations, the
English version of the *Annotations* reflects the original text as closely as is
possible with the modern reader in mind. Moreover, as Erasmus often merely inserted new material into the text of earlier editions without adjusting the
syntax, the reader may anticipate the sometimes uneven sentence structure,
evident also in the translation. As is the case for CWE 56, so too in this volume
the annotations are printed as separate units, each introduced by a cue
phrase, or *lemma*, representing a text of the Vulgate, preceded by the chapter
and verse numbers that are currently in use. For the sake of convenience,
Erasmus' Latin translation of the Greek text is presented first, together with
English translation, and then the text of the Vulgate, also in Latin and English.
Then follows Erasmus' annotation, accompanied by the editor's footnotes
immediately below each entry.

Throughout the annotations on Galatians and Ephesians Erasmus ascribes to Ambrose the commentaries by the fourth-century exegete now
known as Ambrosiaster. Initially Erasmus thought that these commentaries,
which were transmitted along with the writings of Ambrose, were by the
famous bishop of Milan. In preparing his 1527 edition of Ambrose, Erasmus
came to doubt the ascription to Ambrose, and he raised questions about their

* * * * *

12 Anne Reeve and M.A. Screech *Erasmus' Annotations on the New Testament:
   Galatians to the Apocalypse*. Facsimile of the final Latin text with all the earlier
   variants (Leiden 1993). For two reviews of this facsimile edition see H.J. de Jonge
   Novum Testamentum 29 (1987) 382–3 and *Nederlands Archief voor Kerkgeschiedenis*
   71 (1991) 111–13; see further M. van Poll-van de Lisdonk in ASD VI-8 12–13.
   Andrew Brown's critical edition of Erasmus' *Novum Testamentum*, and especially ASD VI-3 (containing the epistles to the Galatians and Ephesians), also
   served as an invaluable tool.
13 Jan Hendrik Glazemaker *Annotationes, of aantekeningen op't Nieuwe Testament*
   (Amsterdam 1663). An electronic version of this translation is now available
   from the Universiteitsbibliotheek Gent at: http://lib.ugent.be/en/catalog/rug
   01:001718559?i=0&q=glazemaker+annotationes (accessed 16 February 2017).

authenticity.[14] I have retained the name of Ambrose throughout the English translation. Erasmus also employed the original Greek and Latin translations of the commentaries of Theophylact, the archbishop of Ochrida, Bulgaria (died c 1108). In the first two editions of the *Annotations* Erasmus mistakenly refers to the author of them as 'Vulgarius'; by 1522 the authorship had been assigned to Theophylact, and this is the name that appears in our translation.[15]

Works cited frequently are referred to in abbreviated form in the footnotes. A list of these abbreviations along with full bibliographical information will be found on p 228 below. For a list of short-title forms used for Erasmus' works, see p 231. References to Erasmus' correspondence are to the English translation of the letters in CWE where these have been published, or to the Latin edition of P.S. Allen.

ACKNOWLEDGMENTS

There remains the pleasant task of thanking all who have assisted me in the course of preparing this volume. Beginning with the circle of experts who contribute to the *Collected Works of Erasmus*, I express my deepest appreciation first for the enthusiastic and generous support of the late Ron Schoeffel, who gave of his time, energy, and wealth of experience to guide me into the labyrinth of Erasmus' *Annotations*. I am grateful to Robert Sider, the general editor of the New Testament scholarship in CWE, for kindly answering many detailed editorial questions and for his encouragement, and to James McConica for his learned advice and unstinting support. I have benefited tremendously from regular contact with the other members of the Editorial Board.

A project of this nature requires access to both the earliest and the latest editions of Erasmus' works, and I would like to thank two librarians for their expert assistance in this regard. My thanks to Adrie van der Laan, secretary

* * * * *

14 The name 'Ambrosiaster' occurs first in the *Notationes* of Franciscus Lucas Brugensis (1580); see Jan Krans 'Who Coined the Name "Ambrosiaster"?' in *Paul, John, and Apocalyptic Eschatology* ed Jan Krans et al (Leiden 2013) 274–81. The commentaries on the Pauline Epistles that Erasmus ascribes to Ambrose are in large part, in fact, the work of Ambrosiaster; cf CWE 42 7 n13. English translations of the commentaries may be found in Gerald L. Bray *Commentaries on Galatians-Philemon. Ambrosiaster*. Ancient Christian Texts (Downers Grove, IL 2009).

15 See further H.J. de Jonge *Apologia ad annotationes Stunicae* ASD IX-2 92–3:64n, 192–3:493n, and 131:43n; also Rummel 36–7, 67–8, and P.F. Hovingh *Annotationes in Epistolam ad Romanos* ASD VI-7 6–7. See also the annotation on Gal 1:6–7 ('into another gospel, which is not another') n4.

of the Erasmus Center for Early Modern Studies and curator of the Rare Books Reading Room of the Rotterdam City Library, for giving access to the Erasmus collection, for providing digitized copies of unpublished works by and about Erasmus, and for answering several Erasmian queries. I owe a debt of gratitude also to Christine Jewell, Information Services and Resources Librarian at the University of Waterloo for her help in obtaining other materials that were difficult to access.

I would like to thank Dr P. Hovingh for generously sharing with me the results of his investigation into Erasmus' use of Ambrosiaster in the *Annotations* on Romans.[16] I am especially thankful to Dr M. Van Poll-van de Lisdonk, who not only shared with me the manuscript of her fine ASD edition of the *Annotations on the Galatians and Ephesians* before it appeared in print, but also answered several queries. I am indebted to Dr J. Trapman for providing me with several splendid volumes of the ASD series, thereby making my work so much more efficient. I also take the opportunity here to express my gratitude to David G. Hunter for his many useful tips and for sharing his work on Ambrosiaster; likewise to Andrew Cain, for giving me his translation of Jerome's commentary on Galatians before it went to press.[17] Stephen Cooper and Theodore de Bruyn kindly shared with me draft translations of the first seven chapters of Ambrosiaster's commentary on Romans, and their thoughts on the reception of Ambrosiaster.

The University of Waterloo generously provided funding through its President's Scholarship Award and the Research Assistantship Program so that I could obtain the assistance of four superb undergraduate students in the Department of Classical Studies. I am grateful to Tyler Flatt, and to April Ross, who assisted me in determining the differences in the Latin texts of the five editions of the *Annotations*, and in finding the biblical, patristic, and medieval sources mentioned in the *Annotations*. I am thankful also to Amanda Ross, and to Esther Knegt, who helped in implementing the editorial guidelines for this complicated text, and in preparing the indices. The University supported my research also via its Research Grant and Travel Programs, which allowed me to undertake several trips to obtain the resources necessary for the completion of this volume.

Riemer A. Faber

* * * * *

16 These results are summarized in ASD VI-7 7–9 and appear in editorial notes in the same volume.
17 *St. Jerome, Commentary on Galatians. The Fathers of the Church. A New Translation.* vol. 121. Tr. A. Cain (Washington 2010).

DIVI IOAN'
NIS CHRYSOSTOMI
Archiepiscopi Constantinopolitani
commentarius in epistolam ad
Galatas, Erasmo Roteroda
mo interprete.

AN. M. D   XXVII.

Opus nouum, & nunc primum natum atq; excusum.

Title-page of Erasmus' translation of the commentary on Galatians by John
Chrysostom, *Divi Ioannis Chrysostomi Archiepiscopi Constantinopolitani commentarius
in epistolam ad Galatas* (Basel Froben 1527) Rotterdam Public Library

ANNOTATIONS ON THE EPISTLE
OF PAUL TO THE GALATIANS BY
DESIDERIUS ERASMUS OF ROTTERDAM

IN EPISTOLAM PAULI AD GALATAS ANNOTATIONES[1]
DES. ERASMI ROT.[2]

Annotations on the Epistle of Paul to the Galatians
by Desiderius Erasmus of Rotterdam

From the First Chapter[3]

1 ANNOTATIONES] First here in *1519*; in *1516* this word was the first in
  the title.
2 DES. ERASMI ROT.] First in *1519* (as DES. ERASMI ROTERODAMI)
3 From the First Chapter] First in *1535*; in *1516*, simply 'Chapter One' (*1527*,
  'I')

1:1 [ER VG] *Paulus Apostolus* **'Paul**[1] **an apostle.'** Jerome points out that
'apostle' in Hebrew, which is 'silas,' has its own special nuance, that is
'sent' or 'commissioned' in Latin.[2] And just as though he had said 'sent'
[Paul] adds 'not by men'; 'not[3] by men' as if they were the ones who
authorized; 'not[4] through men' as if they were the ones who recom-
mended or endorsed [him].

1 'Paul ... endorsed.] With the exceptions noted in n3 and n4 below, this entire annotation was added in *1519*. On the meaning and usage of 'apostle'
  see the annotation on Rom 1:1 ('called an apostle') CWE 56 5, and n11
  there.
2 Jerome *Comm in Gal* 1 (on 1:1) CCL 77A 11:34–6. For Jerome's knowledge of
  Hebrew see the annotation on Gal 3:13 ('slandered is everyone who hangs
  on a tree') n6.
3 not] Added in *1527*
4 not] Added in *1527*

1:3 [ER *a deo Patre* **'from God the Father'**]
[VG] *a deo Patre nostro* **'from God our Father.'**[1] 'Our' should be applied
to 'Lord,' not to 'Father,' ἀπὸ Θεοῦ Πατρὸς καὶ Κυρίου ἡμῶν Ἰησοῦ Χριστοῦ
[from God the Father and our Lord Jesus Christ]. The two[2] codices of
Constance agreed with the Greek.[3]

1 Cf. the extended phrase:
  ER: *a Deo Patre et domino nostro Iesu Christo* 'from God the Father and our
  Lord Jesus Christ'
  VG *1527*]: *a Deo et Patre nostro et domino Iesu Christo* 'from God and our
  Father and the Lord Jesus Christ'

2 The two ... Greek.] Added in 1527
3 These codices contained the 'apostolic epistles' from the library of the cathedral at Constance. Erasmus, invited to Constance in the fall of 1522 by
John Botzheim, the canon of the cathedral of Constance (Allen Ep 1316),
evidently used the opportunity to view the New Testament manuscripts
housed in the chapter library. While preparing the fourth edition of his
New Testament in 1526, Erasmus acquired two manuscripts (now lost)
of the Pauline Epistles (Allen Epp 373 introduction; 1761:12–13 and 10n;
1858:82–5). See John Wordsworth *Old Latin Biblical Texts* 5 vols (Oxford
1883–1907) I (1883) 52–3.
Although the sequence Πατρὸς καὶ Κυρίου ἡμῶν 'of the Father and our
Lord' which Erasmus adopts here is supported by several witnesses, a
majority of modern scholars prefers the order Πατρὸς ἡμῶν καὶ Κυρίου
'of our Father and Lord' on the grounds that it accords with Paul's usage elsewhere, eg Rom 1:7; Metzger 520. Cf *a Deo Patre et Domino nostro*
(Weber 1802).
In the Argument to *Paraphrasis in Galatas*, Erasmus states that Paul had
received his authority for preaching the gospel 'from the already immortal Christ' (CWE 42 95).

1:4 [ER *ex praesenti seculo* 'out of the present age']
[VG] *de praesenti seculo* 'from the present age'; ἐκ τοῦ ἐνεστῶτος, that is
'out of the present,' although the Greeks sometimes use[1] the word to
mean 'threatening.' The word [the Translator] renders as 'depraved,'[2]
Ambrose[3] and Augustine[4] translate as 'depraved,' and[5] Jerome[6] as
'evil';[7] the Greek is πονηροῦ, which indicates 'wily' as well as 'wretched
and troublesome.' Moreover,[8] [Paul] calls this age evil in comparison
with the future age. Augustine[9] reads 'to remove' [*eximere*] in place of
'to deliver' [*eripere*] in the commentary on this Epistle.[10]

1 use] First in 1535; previously, subjunctive *appellent* 'they may use.'
2 In this annotation Erasmus goes on to comment on the entire phrase,
thus:
[ER *ex praesento seculo malo*: 'out of the present evil age']
[VG] *de praesenti seculo nequam*: 'out of the present wicked age'
Ambrosiaster (see n3 below) and Augustine use the adjective *maligno*
'evil' whereas the Translator of the Vulgate uses *nequam* 'wicked.'
For Erasmus' use of *instantia* as 'present' see the annotation on Rom 8:38
('nor things to come, nor might') in CWE 56 237.
3 Ambrosiaster *Comm in Gal* 1:4. On Ambrosiaster see the Introduction
and n14 there. For Ambrosiaster as biblical exegete and churchman
see David G. Hunter 'The Significance of Ambrosiaster' *Journal of Early
Christian Studies* 17 (2009) 1–26, and David G. Hunter and Stephen
Cooper 'Ambrosiaster *redactor sui*: The Commentaries on the Pauline
Epistles (Excluding Romans)' *Revue d'Études Augustiniennes* 56 (2010)
69–91.

4 and Augustine] Added in *1519*. For the reference see Augustine *Expos Gal* CSEL 84 58:8–11. On Erasmus' use of Augustine as biblical exegete see Hilmar M. Pabel 'The Authority of Augustine in Erasmus' Biblical Exegesis' *Erasmus of Rotterdam Society Yearbook* 29 (2009) 61–87.
5 and] Added in *1519*
6 Jerome *Comm in Gal* 1 (on 1:4–5) CCL 77A 14:2
7 So too Lefèvre *Pauli epistolae* fol 152 verso
8 Moreover ... future age.] Added in *1527*
9 Augustine ... Epistle.] Added in *1519*
10 Augustine *Expos Gal* CSEL 84 58:7–8

1:5 [ER *cui gloria* 'to whom (be) the glory']

[VG] *cui est gloria* 'to whom is the glory.' The word *est* [is] is not found in the Greek, but only *cui gloria* [to whom the glory];[1] it is [the expression][2] of a person in prayer.[3]

1 So too Lefèvre *Pauli epistolae* fol 153 verso
2 it is ... prayer] Added in *1527*
3 Erasmus expanded this annotation in *1527* in response to Edward Lee who had criticized the precise rendering of the Greek text. Lee (c 1482–1544), an English cleric and student of theology at Cambridge, had sent some notes to Erasmus when the latter was preparing the second edition of the New Testament. Erasmus incorporated some of Lee's notes, however without acknowledging their authorship, and the scholarly exchange turned personal, especially after Lee published his notes in *Annotationum libri duo* (February 1520); Erasmus replied with *Responsio ad annotationes Lei* (April 1520). For a history of the controversy and an introduction to the printed exchanges between Lee and Erasmus see Erika Rummel *Erasmus and his Catholic Critics* (Nieuwkoop 1989) 95–120; cf CWE 72 xix–xxv. See also Cecilia Asso 'Martin Dorp and Edward Lee' in *Biblical Humanism and Scholasticism in the Age of Erasmus* ed E. Rummel (Leiden 2008) 167–95. For Erasmus' defence of his text here see *Responsio ad annotationes Lei* 2 CWE 72 291.

1:6 [ER *quod adeo cito* 'that so quickly']

[VG] *quod sic tam cito* 'that thus so quickly'; οὕτως ταχέως [so quickly]. It is not *sic tam* [thus so] but *tam cito* [so quickly] or *sic cito* [thus quickly], for οὕτως means both.[1] It is astonishing that this reading, clearly absurd in itself, and one that disagrees with the Greek manuscripts, has gained such a currency that it is to be found both in Ambrose[2] and Augustine,[3] and in Tertullian.[4] But one can deduce from the commentary of St Jerome that the adverb *sic* [thus] had not been added by him.[5] But since some codices read *tam* [so], others had *sic*, some eager scholar had noted [the variation] in the margin and an inattentive copyist transferred it to the text.[6]

1 In objecting to the double rendering of οὕτως by both *sic* and *tam*,
Erasmus is following Lorenzo Valla, *Annot in Gal* 1 (I 875). Jacques
Lefèvre *Pauli epistolae* fol 153 recto translates οὕτως with *tam cito*.
Erasmus' point in this annotation is that a marginal gloss has been
adopted into the text of the Vulgate. On Valla and Lefèvre see the
annotation on Gal 1:13 ('and was subduing') n1.

2 Ambrosiaster *Comm in Gal* 1:6

3 Augustine *Expos Gal* CSEL 84 58:23

4 and in Tertullian] Added in 1522. For the reference see Tertullian *De praescribendis haereticis* CCL 1 208:9.

5 Jerome *Comm in Gal* 1 (on 1:6–7) CCL 77A 18:1

6 A footnote in the Patrologia Latina does indeed indicate variants: *Duo
mss. et vetus editio, quod sic tam cito, etc., hic atque infra, ubi locus iste recurrit*
'two manuscripts and the old edition (read) "that thus so quickly," etc,
here and below, where that passage occurs again' (PL 26 [1884] 342D n1).

1:6 [ER *transferamini* 'you are transferred']

[VG] *transferemini ab eo* 'you[1] will be transferred from him'; μετατίθε-
σθε. If one renders [the Greek] literally, the Latin equivalent is *trans-
ponimi* [you are being moved from one place to another]; the Translator
has rightly used a different word [*transferemini*]. Jerome's suggestion
seems likely, namely that Paul had made a play upon the Hebrew
word *Galatae*, which in that language means 'transported' [*translatus*]
or 'drawn away' [*deductus*], evoking an image taken from wheels or
spherical objects which are rolled easily from one place to another.[2]

1 'you ... another.] This entire annotation was added in 1519.

2 Cf Jerome *Comm in Gal* 1 (on 1:6–7) CCL 77A 20:61–3. Although Jerome
does link the Latin words *Galatia* and *translatio* 'a transporting,' Erasmus
appears to have gleaned his information about the Hebrew origins of
the 'image borrowed from wheels' from Johann Reuchlin *De Rudimentis
Hebraicis* (thus M. van Poll-van de Lisdonk in ASD VI-9 55:29–30n).

1:6 [ER *per gratiam* 'through grace'][1]

[VG] *in gratiam Christi* 'into the grace of Christ'; ἐν χάριτι, that is, 'in
grace.' In his exposition[2] Augustine reads 'into glory' instead of 'into
grace,' as his own interpretation of it confirms.[3] Without a doubt it is
clear that Jerome had the reading 'in grace,' in the ablative case, as
will be demonstrated easily from his own words. For he writes in his
commentary as follows: 'furthermore also the passage contains a hyperbaton;[4] the sentence arranged in its proper order can be read thus:
'I marvel that so quickly you are transferred from Christ Jesus, who
called you in grace, saying, "I have not come to call the righteous,"
et cetera.'[5] Yet here again another problem arises – that of ambiguity

– [in the expression] 'who called you through grace to another gospel.' For it can be construed that Christ has called them to another
gospel, as Ambrose takes it.[6] Consequently, by changing the order,
I express it as follows, 'I marvel that from Christ, who called you in
grace, or through grace, you are so quickly transferred to another gospel.' Now regarding what follows shortly thereafter, 'but even if we,
or an angel from heaven, should proclaim a gospel besides the one
we proclaimed to you,' Jerome also observes that this sentence can be
taken as hyperbole: not that an angel or Paul was about to proclaim
another gospel; he[7] means rather that one must absolutely not depart
from the gospel once it has been received.[8] For if anyone refuses to
admit figures of speech and patterned word order in the sacred writings, either he will get entangled on many occasions and be stuck in
difficulties, or he will be forced to extricate himself by means of the
most tedious explanations. Moreover, what Jerome adds – that Paul
acted thus so that Peter and John would not have an imposing authority, since not even he was permitted to proclaim another gospel –
I think this must be understood to imply, 'if Peter or John were com-
bining Judaism with Christ' (for the pseudo-apostles were attempting
to do just that on the authority of these two apostles). Otherwise Paul
would appear to esteem his own authority more highly than Peter's.

    And 'of Christ' can be referred either to 'grace' ['who called you
in the grace of Christ'] or to the preposition 'from,' so that in Latin it
would be the ablative case, 'from Christ [who called you in grace]'
or rather, 'from God [the one calling you].'[9] I would prefer the ablative case. Indeed, certain codices have the reading 'God' instead of
'Christ.'[10] For Paul always makes God the one who calls, but through
Christ. Also in the Gospels it is the Father who draws his own to Christ.
Now, when he said 'in grace' he meant 'through grace.'[11]

1 [per gratiam] First in 1519; in 1516 in gratia dei.
  In this annotation Erasmus goes on to comment on the entire main clause
  in Gal 1:6, as follows:
  ER: miror quod a Christo qui vos vocavit per gratiam adeo cito transferemini in
  aliud evangelium
  'I marvel that from Christ, who called you through grace, you are so
  quickly transferred to another gospel.'
  VG: miror quod sic tam cito transferemini ab eo qui vos vocavit in gratiam Christi
  in aliud evangelium 'I marvel that thus so quickly you are transferred from
  him who called you into the grace of Christ to another gospel.'
2 In his exposition ... more highly than Peter.] Added in 1519
3 Augustine Expos Gal CSEL 84 58:24, 59:1–2

4 Erasmus often notes this rhetorical figure. Hyperbaton is 'the separation of two syntactically very closely linked words by the insertion of a (one-word or two-word) sentence part which does not directly belong at this point' (Lausberg §716). Often it is used to mark excitement (Smyth 3028). For hyperbaton as an aspect of elegant style see Quintilian 8.6.62–7. Cf the annotation on Rom 1:4 ('from the resurrection of the dead of Jesus Christ') n21.

5 Jerome *Comm in Gal* 1 (on 1:6–7) CCL 77A 19:33–6. The Migne edition, however, reads '*into* grace.'
On Erasmus' usage of 'grace,' and on its occurrence with the preposition 'in' see R.D. Sider 'Χάρις and Derivatives in the Biblical Scholarship of Erasmus' in *Diakonia: Studies in Honor of Robert T. Meyer* ed Thomas Halton and Joseph P. Williman (Washington 1986) 245–6. Modern editions read ἐν χάριτι.

6 Ambrosiaster *Comm in Gal* 1:7

7 he ... received] Added in *1522*

8 Jerome *Comm in Gal* 1 (on 1:8–9) CCL 77A 20:5–9

9 or rather 'from God [the one calling you]'] Added in *1519*

10 Erasmus printed *dei* 'of God' in 1516, *Christou* 'of Christ' in *1519*; cf n1 above. Modern scholars are divided over which is the better reading; cf Metzger 520–1.

11 As in many other places, so too here Erasmus understands the Greek ἐν 'in' to be instrumental. Cf Allen and Greenough 121(16c). Erasmus changed the Vulgate's *in* to *per* about 180 times (in *1519*) throughout the Epistles alone (ASD VI-3 28:17n). Cf the annotation on Rom 1:4 ('in power') CWE 56 15–16.

1:6–7 [ER VG] *in aliud Evangelium, quod non est aliud* 'into another[1] gospel, which is not another.'** I see that the ancient expositors variously followed different readings. Jerome, as is clear from his own commentary, reads thus: 'because you are so quickly transferred into another gospel, which is not,' so that one would supply 'another.'[2] Or if you prefer, the word[3] 'another' has been added by him. Here [Jerome] places a comma, so that the sense is that [Paul] wonders about the fickleness of those who are being transferred, and further, are being transferred so quickly, finally, to another gospel – so much worse than the one they had received, that it really is no gospel. In astonishment the Apostle[4] wonders about the reason for this. But lest he appear to condemn the Gallic character, he casts the blame for the deed (in the manner of one making a conjecture) upon the overly Judaizing apostles, saying,[5] 'except there are some,' etc. So Jerome reads. Chrysostom and[6] Theophylact[7] agree with Jerome regarding the sense of the passage, except that they add 'another' and separate that which follows, 'except that [there are some]' from that which precedes. Ambrose has the following reading: 'from him who has called you into the grace of Christ, to a different gospel.'[8] He does not add 'which is not another'; nor can it be deduced from his exposition that he had read otherwise. Taking the phrase 'to another gospel' not with the verb 'you are transferred' but with 'he called,' Ambrose arranges the sentence as follows: 'I am astonished that so quickly you are transferred from him who has called you to another gospel, that is, to another one different from the one the pseudo-apostles preached to you when they called you back to Judaism.' What I am saying will be very clear to anyone who opens the commentaries of Ambrose. The reason I suspect Jerome had the reading, 'which is not' (without 'another' added), is that he adds 'because anything that is false does not subsist, and what is contrary to the truth does not exist' – like this example: 'do not, Lord, grant your sceptre to those who are not,' and 'God has called [into existence] the things which were not.' And immediately thereafter Jerome writes, 'if, however, it is said about those who believed in the same God and who had the same Scriptures, that they were transferred to another gospel, which is not the gospel, what about Marcion[9] and the other heretics,' etc.[10] But Ambrose by means of an interposed commentary separates 'but that there are some' from that which precedes, so that 'but that there are some' does not refer to 'not that there is another' but to 'I am astonished.'[11] Tertullian[12] in the fourth book against Marcion, seems to add 'another' – if the codices are free of error – but in such a way that the sense [as above] is the same as I have indicated.[13]

1 'into another ... am astonished.'] With the exceptions observed in nn3–7 below, this part of the annotation was added in *1519*.
2 Jerome *Comm in Gal* 1 (on 1:6–7) CCL 77A 18:22–19:49. For Erasmus' discussion of 'things that are' and 'things that are not' see the annotation on Rom 4:17 ('as those which are') CWE 56 119.
3 the word 'another'] Added in *1527*
4 Apostle] Added in *1527*
5 saying] Added in *1527*
6 Chrysostom and] Added in *1535*. For the reference see Chrysostom *Comm in Gal* 1.6 PG 61 622. In 1527 Erasmus published a Latin translation of Chrysostom's commentary on Galatians (LB VIII 266–318), but evidently he acquired this text too late for use in preparing *1527*.
7 Theophylact ... that which precedes] Added in *1527*. Theophylact *Expos in Gal* 1:7 PG 124 960A–C. Theophylact (died c 1108) was the archbishop of Ochrida (modern Ohrid, Yugoslavia), seat of the Bulgarian Orthodox patriarchate. For his first edition of the New Testament (*1516*) Erasmus had used a Greek manuscript of the Gospels containing the commentary of Theophylact, a manuscript he found in the Dominican library at Basel. As Erasmus refers on several occasions to 'Vulgarius' in the *1516*

annotations, he had read Theophylact's commentary also on the Pauline
Epistles. In 1518, when he was preparing his second edition (*1519*) in
Louvain, Erasmus used a Latin version of Theophylact's commentary that
was falsely attributed to Athanasius. The first edition of it was published
by the papal librarian Porsena in Rome in 1477, and subsequent editions
appeared in 1519 and 1529. Erasmus suspected that the work was a commentary of Theophylact, and when he returned to the Dominican library
in Basel in May of 1518 he was able to compare Porsena's translation with
the Greek and so determine that the Latin rendering by 'Athanasius' was
actually the commentary of Theophylact. In *1516*, Erasmus had referred
to the author of these commentaries as 'Vulgarius'; by *1522* the name
had been corrected in the annotations. See further H.J. de Jonge *Apologia
ad annotationes Stunicae* ASD IX-2 92–3:64n, 192–3:493n, and 131:43n;
also Rummel 36–7, 67–8, and P.F. Hovingh *Annotationes in Epistolam ad
Romanos* ASD VI-7 6–7.
8 Ambrosiaster *Comm in Gal* 1:6
9 Marcion was a radical Paulinist of the second century who sharply distinguished the 'God of law' of the Old Testament and the 'God of love' of
the New Testament, the redeemer God. On Marcion see the annotation on
Rom 16:25 ('now to him who is able') CWE 56 433, and note 8 there.
10 Jerome *Comm in Gal* 1 (on 1:6–7) CCL 77A 19:39–46. Jerome's quotation of
the sceptre of the Lord comes from the deuterocanonical Esther 14:11.
11 Ambrosiaster *Comm in Gal* 1:7
12 Tertullian ... indicated.] Added in *1527*
13 Tertullian *Adversus Marcionem* 5.2.4 CCL 1 666:24–5. Cf also 1.20.4 CCL 1
461.

1:7 [ER *et volunt invertere*[1] *Evangelium* **'and wish to turn the gospel
upside down'**]

[VG] *et volunt convertere Evangelium* **'and**[2] **wish to turn the gospel
around.'** I for my part would prefer *invertere* [to turn upside down, to
pervert], even though Ambrose,[3] Augustine,[4] and likewise Jerome[5] read
without exception *convertere* [to turn around]. However, the Greek word
is μεταστρέψαι, which means 'to turn away towards something else,' or
'to twist to the opposite.' The interpretation of Jerome, whose actual
words I shall quote, makes the word *invertere* [to turn upside down]
more appealing to me: 'everyone who expounds[6] the gospel in a spirit
and mind different from that in which it was written, confuses the believers, and overturns the gospel of Christ, so that he makes what is at
the front to be at the rear, and he puts things that are at the rear up front.
If someone follows only the letter, he places the less important matters
up front. If anyone concurs with the interpretations of the Jews, he puts
at the rear those things which by their own nature were ordained to
be at the front.'[7] Thus far Jerome. Yet all the same, *revertere* [to reverse]

strictly means to turn in the opposite direction and the wrong way around. Christ passed on this kind of teaching, so that there would be as much piety and as few ceremonies as possible. Those men conversely preferred there to be as many possible ceremonies and very little piety.

1 *invertere*] First in *1519*, in *1516 subvertere*
2 and] First in *1535*; previously *qui* 'who.' Erasmus corrects his own earlier misquotation of the Vulgate.
   Erasmus alters the Vulgate's *convertere* to *invertere* elsewhere too (eg Acts 13:10, and see the note in ASD VI-2 339:10(2)n). As he makes clear in this annotation, Erasmus thought that *invertere* more accurately conveyed the sense of inversion expressed in μεταστρέφω (LSJ: 'turn about, turn round').
3 Ambrosiaster *Comm in Gal* 1:7
4 Augustine *Expos Gal* CSEL 84 59:5
5 Jerome *Comm in Gal* 1 (on 1:6–7) CCL 77A 18:4 and 20:5
6 LB reads *interpretatus* while ASD, which we follow here, reads *interpretatur*.
7 Jerome *Comm in Gal* 1 (on 1:6–7) CCL 77A 20:54–60

1:8 [ER *praeter id quod* 'apart from that which']
[VG] *praeterquam quod* 'apart from that which'; παρ' ὅ, that is, 'besides that which,' and so it will be more precise.[1]

1 With this slight alteration, Erasmus seeks to avoid the sense of 'different from, beyond' which some may associate with *praeterquam*.

1:8 [ER VG] *anathema sit* 'let him be accursed.' St Jerome points out that *anathema* [accursed] is a word with meaning peculiar to the Jews, for by it they are accustomed to express extreme abhorrence.[1]

1 Jerome *Comm in Gal* 1 (on 1:8–9) CCL 77A 22:36–9. For other patristic interpretations of *anathema* see Lightfoot 78, who notes also that Paul means spiritual condition and not formal ecclesiastical censure. See also Erasmus' discussion of *anathema* in his annotation on Rom 9:3 ('for I myself wished') CWE 56 239–40.

1:10 [ER *nunc enim utrum hominibus suadeo* 'for am I now persuading either men[1]']
[VG] *modo enim hominibus suadeo* 'for am I just now persuading[2] men'; Ἄρτι γὰρ ἀνθρώπους πείθω, ἢ τὸν Θεόν; that is, 'for am I now persuading men, or God?'[3] That is, 'do I recommend matters of human, or divine nature?' Theophylact understands[4] it also in this sense.[5] And yet [the rendering in the Vulgate] *hominibus*[6] *suadeo* [I am persuading men] can be tolerated, since in Greek [the verb] πείθω[7] [persuade] when it has this meaning governs the accusative case on a number of occasions; this is not so when it means *confidere* [to put one's trust in], or *credere*

[to have faith in], or *morem gerere* [to gratify], as our friend Lefèvre
d'Etaples seems to think.[8] Even so, I know that Jerome,[9] Augustine,[10]
and Ambrose[11] follow a different line of interpretation.

But [in the Vulgate] the word *modo* [just now] was put in the place
of *nunc* [now]. For[12] [Paul] means[13] that ever since he became an apostle, he has been looking to nothing else than what is directed to the honour of God, although formerly in Judaism he had thought otherwise.

1　men] In *1516* and *1519 homines* ('men,' accusative case); in *1522* and later
　 editions *hominibus* ('men,' dative case)
2　persuading] First in *1535*; previously *persuadeo* 'I am convincing'
3　Erasmus follows a suggestion made by Valla, *Annot in Gal* 1 (I 875), in
　 allowing *persuadeo* to govern the accusative case.
4　Theophylact understands ... this sense.] First in *1519*; in *1516* this sentence
　 and the next appeared in reverse order.
5　Theophylact *Expos in Gal* 1:10 PG 124 961B
6　*hominibus*] Added in *1519*
7　in Greek πείθω] Added in *1527*
8　Lefèvre *Pauli epistolae* fol 32 recto and fol 153 recto. Jacques Lefèvre
　 d'Etaples (1460–1536) was a leading exponent of Christian humanism
　 in France; see *Contemporaries* II 315–18. Lefèvre published his commen-
　 tary on the Pauline Epistles in 1512. His correspondence with Erasmus
　 began in 1514 with a friendly letter to the latter (Allen Ep 315). Erasmus
　 disagreed with Lefèvre's biblical interpretation on Heb 2:7 ('you have
　 made him a little lower than the angels'), and the disagreement grew
　 into a public quarrel. See further H.J. de Jonge 'The Relationship of
　 Erasmus' Translation of the New Testament and that of the Pauline
　 Epistles by Lefèvre d'Etaples' *Erasmus in English* 15 (1987–8) 2–7; Erika
　 Rummel *Erasmus and his Catholic Critics* (Nieuwkoop 1989) 49–57; and
　 Guy Bedouelle 'Attacks on the Biblical Humanism of Jacques Lefèvre
　 d'Etaples' in *Biblical Humanism and Scholasticism in the Age of Erasmus* ed
　 E. Rummel (Leiden 2008) 117–41.
9　Jerome *Comm in Gal* 1 (on 1:10) CCL 77A 22:3–13
10　Augustine *Expos Gal* CSEL 84 59:25–60:4
11　Ambrosiaster *Comm in Gal* 1:10
12　For] Added in *1519*
13　means] First in *1535*; in *1516*, *significans* 'meaning'

1:10 [ER *nam si hactenus* 'for if until now']
　　　[VG] *si adhuc* 'if still'; εἰ γὰρ ἔτι, that is, 'for if until now.'

1:12 [ER VG] *accepi illud, neque didici* 'did I receive it, nor did I learn it';
παρέλαβον αὐτό, οὔτε ἐδιδάχθην. Jerome points out the difference in meaning between *accipere* [to receive] and *discere* [to learn]: we 'receive' what
is not our own but is given by someone else; we 'learn' something
when its secret is disclosed to us.[1] Yet all the same the Greek does not

state 'did I learn' but 'was I taught,' which can be taken simply as 'I was not taught but inspired,' or as 'I was not taught by man.'

As for the word ἀποκάλυψις [revelation], Jerome states that it is not found anywhere in the pagan writers, but like many other words it was newly devised by [the translators of] the LXX in order to explain more conveniently the newly revealed mysteries of God.[2]

1 Jerome *Comm in Gal* 1 (on 1:11–12) CCL 77A 26:45–51
2 Jerome *Comm in Gal* 1 (on 1:11–12) CCL 77A 26:52–8. As noted by BDAG, ἀποκάλυψις is here used for a particular kind of revelation, through visions, etc.

1:13 [ER *ac depopulabar* **'and was ravaging'**]

[VG] *et expugnabam* **'and was subduing'**; καὶ ἐπόρθουν. The word is used to characterize the action of people who despoil and demolish cities they have overtaken by force. And I do not see why Lorenzo [Valla] is upset on this point, as if it was said as a slander against the church of God that Paul would have captured it, and he prefers *oppugnabam* [I made an attack] to *expugnabam* [I was subduing].[1] And I do not deny that in Latin *expugnare* [to subdue] is one thing and *oppugnare* [to make an attack] another, even as *suadere* [to recommend] is one thing and *persuadere* [to prevail upon][2] another; *orare* [to plead] one thing, and *exorare* [to plead successfully] another. But what are you to do, when the Greek word πορθεῖν means nothing else than 'capture' or 'seize'? [Paul] actually calls that tiny flock of Christians the church, which he was subduing by all the means he possessed. For such was Paul's intention all along. Thus the expression 'I was ravaging' must not be taken to refer to the outcome of the action, but to his frame of mind and efforts. Quite fitting, too, would be the rendering of Jerome[3] and Augustine[4] in their commentaries on[5] the Sermon on the Mount: 'I was making desolate' [*devastabam*], or 'I was destroying' [*vastabam*], like an enemy or a wild animal that ruins everything.[6] And in fact[7] a little lower we read: '[he] who formerly was persecuting us, now preaches the faith which he once sought to destroy.'

The grammarians[8] think that the word [πέρθω] is derived from πρήθω, which means 'to set on fire,' by a reversal of merely two letters – πήρθω [pērthō], hence πέρθω [perthō], because by means of incendiary missiles a conqueror destroys his enemy.[9] Others prefer the explanation that πέρθω is pronounced like περθέω [pertheō], that is, to 'run around,' because that also happens in a captured city.

1 Valla *Annot in Gal* 1 (I 875). Lorenzo Valla (1407–57), professor of rhetoric and later secretary to Pope Nicholas V, wrote several important works that were influential in the sixteenth century. In 1443 Valla issued *Collatio Novi Testamenti*, a philological critique of the New Testament. Erasmus published this work in 1505, and he adopted and expanded Valla's methodology in producing his own annotations (Allen Epp 182, 2172). See further *Contemporaries* III 371–5; Raymond J. Schoeck 'Erasmus and Valla: The Dynamics of a Relationship' *Erasmus of Rotterdam Society Yearbook* 23 (2003) 45–63; and John Monfasani 'Criticism of Biblical Humanists in Quattrocento Italy' in *Biblical Humanism and Scholasticism in the Age of Erasmus* ed E. Rummel (Leiden 2008) 1–31.

2 *persuadere*] First in *1519*; in *1516*, *dissuadere* 'dissuade'

3 Jerome *Comm in Gal* 1 (on 1:13–14) CCL 77A 28:30

4 and Augustine] Added in *1519*

5 on ... Mount] Added in *1527*

6 Augustine *De sermone Domini in monte secundum Matthaeum* 1.7.18 CCL 35 19:412–13 (on Gal 1:23)

7 And in fact ... destroy.'] Added in *1519*

8 The grammarians ... in a captured city.] The remainder of this and all of the following annotation were added in *1527*.

9 It is not certain who are meant by 'the grammarians.' M. van Poll-van de Lisdonk in ASD VI-9 63:134 observes that the derivation of πέρθω from πρήθω occurs in the commentaries of Eustathius on the *Iliad* and *Odyssey*.

1:14 [ER *aequales* 'peers']

[VG] *coaetaneos* 'coevals.' I wish that this word [*coaetaneos*] was in established usage in Latin.[1] The Greek is συνηλικιώτας, that is 'peers' [*aequales*], that is, 'of the same age' [*eiusdem aetatis*], although both expressions are ambiguous. For these [also] are said to be 'of the same age' who have lived in the same time period (the Greeks call such συγχρόνους [contemporaneous]), and these [also] are called 'peers' who are matched in wealth or learning.

1 The word *coaetaneos* 'coevals' occurs in Apuleius *Metamorphoses* 8.7 and Tertullian *Adversus Hermogenem* 6.1 PL 2 (1844) 202C and 7.4 PL 2 (1844) 204A. The related verb *coaetaneo* is also used by Tertullian in *De resurrectione carnis* 45.5 PL 2 (1844) 858B. For συνηλικιώτης as 'a person of one's own age, a contemporary' see the word in BDAG.

1:14 [ER VG] *in genere meo* 'among[1] my people.' [Paul] calls the Jewish race *genus* [a people], just as in the previous Epistle, 'in danger from my own people.'[2]

1 'among ... from my own people.'] This entire annotation was added in *1519*.

2 Cf 2 Cor 11:26

1:14 [ER *studiosus* 'devoted to']

[VG] *aemulator* 'an imitator'; ζηλωτής.[1] For his excessive and over-scrupulous religious devotion and love [Paul] labels himself 'zealot.'

> 1 Erasmus prefers the translation *studiosus* to *aemulator* because it connotes zealous discipleship rather than imitation, which is denoted by the classical usage of *aemulator*. On Erasmus' translation of ζηλωτής elsewhere see Brown's note on Acts 21:20 (*studiosi sectatores*) in ASD VI-2 429 20(5) n, the annotation on Rom 10:2 ('that an emulation indeed') CWE 56 276–7, *Ciceronianus* CWE 28 379, and *Paraphrasis in Galatas* CWE 42 118 n14.

1:14 [ER *a maioribus meis traditorum institutorum* 'the precepts handed down by my ancestors']

[VG] *paternarum mearum traditionum* 'the traditions of my fathers';[1] πατρικῶν, 'of things handed down by one's fathers and ancestors.' [Paul] adds 'my' not because he reckoned the teachings to be his own, as Aquinas understands it,[2] but so that he may appear to with more justifiable reason to have gone astray, because born a Pharisee he followed the precepts of his own ancestors. However, he did not hesitate to abandon them when he acquired knowledge of sounder things.

> 1 'my fathers' ... sounder things.] This entire annotation was added in *1519*.
> 2 Thomas Aquinas *Super Gal lect* cap 1 lectio 3.37

1:15 [ER *ast ubi deo ... visum est* 'but when it seemed good to God']

[VG] *cum autem placuit ei* 'when it pleased him'; Ὅτε δὲ εὐδόκησεν ὁ Θεός, that is, 'but when it seemed good to God.'[1]

> 1 God's decision to call Paul to be an apostle provides the context for this annotation: it seemed good to God. In his annotation on Rom 1:1 ('called an apostle') Erasmus observes that 'calling' is a word Paul uses 'to remove from everyone trust in human works, and to transfer all the glory to the God who calls. Whoever heeds God when he calls is saved. Thus Paul soon obeyed after he had been called from heaven' CWE 56 6. Modern scholars are divided over the inclusion of ὁ Θεός in the text; while the reading appears to be a gloss, there is a preponderance of external support; see Metzger 521–2.

1:16 [ER *non contuli* 'I did not confer']

[VG] *non acquievi* 'I did not acquiesce in'; οὐ προσανεθέμην σαρκὶ καὶ αἵματι, that is, 'I did not confer with flesh and blood.' For thus Jerome translates the Greek in his commentary,[1] and the Greek scholia agree.[2] And in fact a little later the Translator himself renders it in this way. That is, 'I did not communicate my gospel with man, but my negotiations were with God.' Some have the reading προανεθέμην, that is, 'I conferred beforehand.'

Similarly, it is clear that Thomas[3] and Hugh of St Cher[4] achieve nothing when they interpret 'flesh and blood' as vices of the flesh, for nowhere do we read that Paul was prone to them – though indeed Thomas adds another explanation, interpreting 'flesh and blood' as feelings of attachment towards kinsmen. But Paul is saying not even this. Now it was the Translator who furnished the occasion for this misunderstanding, for he rendered προσανεθέμην as 'I did not acquiesce in,' although it should have been translated 'I conferred,' or 'I communicated with flesh and blood.'

Be that as it may, on this point St Jerome struggled very hard in his desire to unravel the problem arising from the fact that Paul addressed John and James as 'flesh and blood' in a rather insulting manner, especially since Porphyry hence slanders Paul of haughtiness, alleging that he did not deign to convey his own gospel to the other apostles.[5] Finally, [on this reading] it doesn't[6] make any sense that he who beforehand did not confer with flesh and blood, afterwards did confer with them, as though he lost confidence in himself once the enterprise was put to the test. Constrained by these difficulties,[7] Jerome finds an escape in this way. He does not take the adverb εὐθέως 'immediately' with the clause that follows: 'I did not acquiesce in flesh and blood [immediately]' [1:16c] (he thus avoids the implication that Paul, relying on revelation, should forthwith seem to have despised human intercourse). He instead takes the word with what precedes: 'When it pleased him who had set me apart from my mother's womb' [1:15a], then comes, 'to reveal his son to me' [1:16a], and finally, 'so that I might proclaim him among the gentiles immediately [1:16b]. Then, after these clauses a new sentence begins: 'I did not acquiesce in flesh and blood' [1:16c].[8] Thus the sense would be that Paul, having been ordered immediately and without delay to equip himself for preaching the gospel, did not linger or waste time by approaching the apostles and consulting them; instead, as soon as he was ordered, he proceeded to the task of proclaiming the good news. The Greek[9] commentaries also vary at this point.[10] However, further discussion does not belong to this enterprise. I merely make a note of what in my view pertains to the understanding of the text. Consequently, it also is not part of my work to explain the fact that Paul's account here appears[11] in many ways to disagree with that of Luke in the ninth chapter of the Acts of the Apostles – Jerome[12] has explained it thoroughly enough in his commentary.[13]

1 Jerome Comm in Gal 1 (on 1:16) CCL 77A 31:1–3
2 Cf Chrysostom Comm in Gal 1.9 PG 61 628; Theophylact Expos in Gal 1:16 PG 124 964D–965A. See also Lefèvre Pauli epistolae fol 153 verso, who translates the Greek here as contuli 'confer.'

With the words 'Greek scholia' Erasmus may be referring to the brief
exegetical comments in the form of catenae by the Eastern Fathers
which were being compiled towards the end of the patristic period. H.J.
de Jonge (*Apologia ad annotationes Stunicae* ASD IX-2 194:539n) identifies
these scholia with the anonymous commentary, incorrectly attributed to
Oecumenius, contained in ms 7 of the Pauline Epistles (A.N.III.11) in the
Basel University Library and accessible in Migne PG 118–19. See also the
note by M. van Poll-van de Lisdonk in ASD VI-9 62:154, and n1 on the annotation to Rom 1:4 ('who was predestined') CWE 56 10.

3 Thomas Aquinas *Super Gal lect* cap 1 lectio 4.44
4 Hugh of St Cher (c 1200–63) was a provincial of the Dominican order who
  taught at the Sorbonne. His best known work was the *Postilla in universa
  Biblia iuxta quadruplicem sensum*, a collection of exegetical notes on the
  Bible. Erasmus, who probably consulted the faulty 1504 Amerbach edition of this work, was highly critical of St Cher (see, for example, Allen
  Ep 456:138–40). See further Rummel 80–2 and C. Zeman 'Hugh of
  St Cher' *Dominicana* 44 (1959) 338–47.
5 For the reference to Porphyry see Jerome *Comm in Gal* 1 (on 1:16) CCL 77A
  31:3–6.
6 doesn't make any sense] First in *1519*; in *1516*, *videatur* 'doesn't *seem to
  make any sense*'
7 difficulties] Added in *1535*
8 In the text of the Greek New Testament the adverb εὐθέως 'immediately' is
  placed at the end of 1:16b and at the start of 1:16c, so that where punctuation is lacking the text can be read as either: 'proclaim him among the
  gentiles immediately,' or 'immediately I did not confer with flesh and
  blood.'
9 The Greek ... here.] Added in *1527*
10 Cf Chrysostom *Comm in Gal* 1.9 PG 61 628; Theophylact *Expos in Gal* 1:16
   PG 124 965A.
11 appears ... Apostles] First in *1522*; in *1516* and *1519*, *dissentit* '*differs* in
   many ways.' On account of Zúñiga's objection Erasmus altered the verb
   dissentit to *videtur dissentire* 'seems to disagree'; see *Apologia ad annotationes Stunicae* ASD IX-2 198:583–93.
12 Jerome ... commentary] Added in *1519*
13 Jerome *Comm in Gal* 1 (on 1:17) CCL 77A 33:6–36:72

1:17 [ER *redii Hierosolymam* 'I returned[1] to Jerusalem']

[VG] *veni Hierosolymam* 'I came to Jerusalem'; ἀνῆλθον, that is, 'I returned,'[2] or 'I went up.'

1 'I returned ... 'I went up.'] From *1516* to *1527* this and the next annotation
  appeared in the reverse order. The present order, first in *1535*, follows the
  order of the biblical text.
2 The rendering *redii* is adopted also by Valla *Annot in Gal* 1 (I 875) and
  Lefèvre *Pauli epistolae* fol 153 recto. Erasmus' comment concerns the force
  in the prefix ἀνά (cf 'going up to' NEB). For the chronology of Paul's visits
  to Jerusalem see Lightfoot 91–2 and 123–8.

1:17 [ER *ad eos, qui ante me fuerant Apostoli* 'to those[1] who before me were apostles']
[VG] *ad antecessores meos Apostolos* 'to my predecessor apostles'; πρὸς τοὺς πρὸ ἐμοῦ Ἀποστόλους, that is, 'to those who before me were apostles,'[2] and who seemed to some people to be greater because they had been called earlier.

  1 'to those ... called earlier.] Cf note 1 on 1:17 above.
  2 Erasmus follows Valla here, *Annot in Gal* 1 (I 875). Erasmus' translation is both simpler and follows the Greek more closely.

1:18 [ER *ut viderem Petrum* 'in order to see Peter']
[VG] *videre Petrum* 'to see[1] Peter'; ἱστορῆσαι: the Greek word means something more than 'to see,' namely: to see for the sake of making enquiries and being informed, although Jerome denies that [was Paul's intention].[2]

  1 'in order ... denies that was Paul's intention.] First in *1519*; in *1516*, this entire annotation was placed after the annotation on 1:21 ('parts of Syria and Cilicia') below.
  2 Jerome *Comm in Gal* 1 (on 1:18) CCL 77A 36:13–15. Cf BDAG ἱστορέω: 'visit for the purpose of coming to know someone.' Modern translations render the phrase as 'to visit Cephas' (RSV), 'to get to know Cephas' (NEB). Erasmus' translation implies that Paul did more than merely 'see' Peter. In *Paraphrasis in Galatas* (CWE 42 101) Erasmus states that Paul visited with Peter 'because he seemed to hold first place among the apostles.'

1:19 [ER VG] *Jacobum fratrem* 'James[1] the brother.' In his[2] commentary upon the Epistle to the Galatians, Jerome points out the error of those who think that this James was one of the twelve apostles, the brother of John, who is mentioned in the Gospel, even though in the[3] Acts of the Apostles one reads that it is he who,[4] soon after the murder of Stephen, poured forth his life-blood for the sake of the Lord.[5] But[6] [Jerome] supports[7] the view that this is the James with the byname 'the Just,' the son of Mary who was sister to[8] Mary, mother of Jesus. For also these [relatives] are called brothers in the established practice of the Jews. Theophylact[9] indicates that he was called brother of the Lord out of esteem.[10] This [James] was appointed the first bishop of Jerusalem, and many think that the Epistle which nowadays we also call 'James,' is from his hand. Moreover he is called an apostle in the same manner as all the others are called apostles, who preached Christ after they had seen him in the flesh.

  1 'James the brother.'] Added in *1519*. For a fuller discussion by Erasmus of the identity of James see *Peregrinatio Apostolorum Petri et Pauli* LB VI 425–6 and his annotation on James 1:1 ASD VI-10 387:4–388:21.

2 In his ... Galatians] Added in *1535*
3 in the Acts of the Apostles] Added in *1522*
4 it is he who] Added in *1522*
5 Jerome *Comm in Gal* 1 (on 1:19) CCL 77A 38:37–41. For the martyrdom of
   James the brother of John, cf Acts 12:1–2.
6 But] Added in *1522*
7 supports] Added in *1527*
8 who was sister to] From *1522*; in *1519*, *sororis* 'of the sister of'
9 Theophylact ... esteem.] Added in *1522*
10 Theophylact *Expos in Gal* 1:19 PG 124 965D–968A

1:20 [ER *non mentior* 'I do not lie']

[VG] *quia non mentior* 'that I do not lie.' Here the word ὅτι [that] could
have been omitted, as the clause has the force of introducing an emphatic statement, but in Greek only to a point – unless you prefer to
add [the words], 'behold I testify in the presence of God that I do not
lie.'[1] Actually the word was added to suggest that [Paul] was writing
under oath, which[2] clearly Jerome does not deny. But when he goes on
to suggest an interpretation at a higher level, adding [the words, what I
write to you, behold] they are before God, that is, worthy in the sight of
God – this seems to me somewhat too forced.[3] In fact the ancient commentators derive no small pleasure in musings of this kind, as they do
also with interpretations of the names 'Arabia,' 'Cilicia,' 'Damascus,'
and the rest. Ambrose[4] indicates that the expression reflects an oath;
Theophylact [thinks it conveys] a statement.[5]

1 Throughout the *Annotations* Erasmus frequently takes issue with the fact
   that the Translator renders the conjunction ὅτι 'that' with *quia* 'because,
   that,' especially in places where it is not needed. In classical Latin *quia*
   conveys the sense of cause, a sense not intended by the Greek text here.
   See the annotations on Rom 3:10 ('that there is not [anyone] righteous')
   CWE 56 98, Rom 9:7 ('nor who are the seed') CWE 56 254, and 4:17 ('that I
   have made you the father of many nations') CWE 56 117: 'If it is not right
   to omit anything, why did [the Translator] elsewhere omit the superfluous conjunction ὅτι [that]? But if it is permitted anywhere, surely it should
   have been omitted here.'
2 which clearly ... and the rest] Added in *1519*
3 Jerome *Comm in Gal* 1 (on 1:20) CCL 77A 39:1–4. The anagogical level of
   interpretation is one of four employed by medieval exegetes (the others
   being literal, allegorical, and moral or tropological); *anagoge* referred to
   the deeper, spiritual, or eschatalogical meaning of a text. On the four-
   fold method of interpretation (also known as the *quadriga*) see D. Baker-
   Smith's Introduction to CWE 63, on Erasmus' exegesis of the Psalms, and,
   more generally, H. de Lubac *Medieval Exegesis* 2 Vols (Grand Rapids MI,
   2000) II 179–226.

4 Ambrose ... statement.] Added in 1527. For the reference see Ambrosiaster
Comm in Gal 1:20.

5 Theophylact *Expos in Gal* 1:20 PG 124 968B

1:21 [ER *regiones Syriae Ciliciaeque* 'districts of Syria and Cilicia']
[VG] *partes Syriae Ciliciae* 'parts¹ of Syria and Cilicia'; Κιλικίας [of
Cilicia]. The [Greek] κλίματα is 'regions,' that is, 'districts.'

1 'parts ... districts.'] See the annotation on Gal 1:18 ('to see Peter') n1.
In employing the word *regiones* Erasmus probably is following Lefèvre,
Pauli epistolae fol 153 recto.

1:22 [ER VG] *quae erant in Christo* 'who were in Christ.' Why not rather,
'those who are in Christ,' ταῖς ἐν Χριστῷ [those in Christ]?¹

1 In the Greek text of 1:22 there is no verb in the phrase '[I was unknown]
to the churches of Judea in Christ.'

1:23 [ER *hic rumor apud illos erat* 'this report was circulating among them']
[VG] *auditum habebant* 'they were having it heard'; ἀκούοντες ἦσαν, that
is, 'they used to hear';¹ word for word it is 'they were hearing,' that is,
there was a report circulating among them. Very good Latin would be
auditum erat illis [it was reported to them], or rather² *hic rumor apud illos
erat* [this report was circulating among them], because³ the participle
ἀκούοντες [hearing] is in the present tense.⁴ Also in this passage it was
not necessary to translate [the conjunction] ὅτι [that], as the pronoun
nos [we] advises against it.⁵

1 'they used to hear'] First in 1519; in 1516, *audiebant* 'they were hearing.'
2 or rather ... against it] Added in 1519
3 because ... tense] Added in 1527
4 The participle 'hearing' forms part of a periphrastic expression with the
verb 'were' (ἦσαν) in order to convey the ongoing nature of the action in
time past.
5 Following the clause, 'they were having it heard,' the text of the Vulgate is
quoniam qui persequebatur nos 'that he who used to persecute us'; Erasmus
advises that with the removal of the conjunction *quoniam* 'that,' the direct
quotation in the remainder of the sentence will be clear. He means that
the use of the first-person pronoun 'us' (*nos*) in 'he who used to persecute
us' reveals that the remainder of the sentence is a direct quotation which
needs not be introduced by the conjunction 'that.' For Erasmus' criticism
of the Translator's penchant to translate the conjunction 'that' (ὅτι) see the
annotation on Gal 1:20 ('that I do not lie') n1.

1:23 [ER *quam quondam expugnabat* 'which formerly he sought to capture']
[VG] *quam aliquando expugnabat* 'which at some time past he sought
to capture'; ἐπόρθει [capture]. Again [Paul] used the same word as
above, as I have noted.[1]

> 1 Cf the annotation on Gal 1:13 ('and was subduing').

1:24 [ER *glorificabant in me deum* 'and they were glorifying God because
of me']
[VG] *clarificabant deum* 'and they were making God illustrious'; ἐδό-
ξαζον, that is, 'they glorified.' And so reads St Jerome;[1] Ambrose[2] [reads]
'they were magnifying.'

> 1 Jerome *Comm in Gal* 1 (on 1:22–4) CCL 77A 40:4–5
> 2 Ambrose ... magnifying'] Added in 1527. For the reference see
>   Ambrosiaster *Comm in Gal* 1:24.

From the Second Chapter

2:1 [ER VG] *post annos* 'after [fourteen] years'; διὰ δεκατεσσάρων ἐτῶν, that is,
'throughout fourteen years.' Nevertheless, the Translator has rendered
the meaning well.[1]

> 1 For Erasmus' defence, in face of Lee's criticism, of rendering the Greek
>   text as 'after fourteen years' see his *Responsio ad annotationes Lei* 2 CWE 72
>   291. In translating 'throughout' Erasmus recognizes the use of the geni-
>   tive to express the duration of time in Greek; see Smyth 1685.

2:2 [ER VG] *et contuli cum illis evangelium* 'and I shared the gospel with
them'; ἀνεθέμην [I set before]. St Jerome states that the strict meaning
of the Greek word is not 'to confer,' but to reveal what we know to the
confidence of a friend and to bring it into the open, so that by common counsel it may be approved or rejected.[1] Hence [the word] we
have met earlier in the text,[2] προσανεθέμην, means, 'I did [not] confer
with anyone,' that is, after [Paul] was called by Christ. Or if you read
προανεθέμην, that is, 'I conferred beforehand,' then doubtless it refers to
the time before he went into Arabia. In the former case it appears Paul
lacked no confidence in his own calling, while in the latter he seems not
to have needed the advice of others in order to teach Christ in Arabia.

What[3] Jerome observes about the special nuance in the word ἀνεθέμην, I think, points to the fact that in Greek [the verb] ἀνατίθεσθαι [to
put upon, to take up] is used equally of the person who takes up a burden and of the person who places it upon another. But he who confers

[*conferre*] with others, puts his own load down in their midst, as it were burdening those whom he makes judges of his deeds, and he intends to take up his own load again, whether they remove anything from it or add anything to it. Hence, also things that have been set aside and suspended aloft we call ἀναθήματα. Euripides in *Iphigenia at Aulis* uses the verb συνενέγκειν to express the same idea, as though in Latin one were to say *simul importare* [to bring in together]. Thus Clytemnestra says to Agamemnon: συνενέγκαι δ' ὅμως ['let them be brought together just the same'].⁴

1 Jerome *Comm in Gal* 1 (on 2:1–2) CCL 77A 41:9–13. Cf Lightfoot 102: 'to relate with a view to consulting.' In commenting on Galatians 2:1–16 Erasmus engages patristic exegesis, especially that of Jerome, whose commentary on this Epistle functioned as a key to his own interpretation of the Old Testament. See Giacomo Raspanti 'The Significance of Jerome's *Commentary on Galatians* in his Exegetical Production' in *Jerome of Stridon. His Life, Writings and Legacy* ed A. Cain and J. Lössl (Surrey 2009) 163–71.
2 Cf the annotation on 1:16 *non acquievi*.
3 What Jerome ... δ' ὅμως.] This remaining portion of the annotation was added in 1535.
4 *Euripidis Iphigenia Aulidensis* ASD I-1 310:981. It seems likely that Erasmus is citing the first Aldine edition of Euripides' tragedies (1503), the text on which he based his own Latin translation (1506). See further the Introduction to Erasmus' Latin edition of the *Hecuba* and *Iphigenia at Aulis* by J.H. Waszink in ASD I-1 195–212.

2:2 [ER *qui erant in pretio* 'who were in great repute']
[VG] *qui videbantur aliquid* 'who seemed something'; τοῖς δοκοῦσιν, that is, 'who seemed,' as Augustine reads,¹ or 'those approved.' But *aliquid* [something] was added by someone² to whom the clause appeared incomplete. Therefore those who read *qui videbantur aliquid* [who seemed something] are mistaken - but to add *qui sibi videbantur aliquid* [who seemed to themselves to be something] is a worse mistake. Among these is Ambrose – at least, if the codices are free of error.³ For it would be slanderous to state 'who seemed to themselves [to be] something,' as though of no repute⁴ save in their own opinion, whereas [the Greek expression] refers more to the esteem given to others. For in Greek only people who have great authority are called δοκοῦντες, just as they are ἀδοξοῦντες whose authority is slight. Thus Euripides in *Hecuba* says, Λόγος γὰρ ἔκ τ' ἀδοξούντων ἰὼν, κἀκ τῶν δοκούντων, αὐτὸς οὐκ αὐτὸ σθένει, that is, 'for⁵ the speech that issues from those of no esteem has an effect different from the speech of those who are esteemed.'⁶

In the Greek copies, in the first⁷ and third⁸ passage, the word τι, that is, 'something,' is not added; it is added only in the second passage, *ab iis autem qui videbantur esse aliquid* [from those who seemed to be something, Gal 2:6]. Perhaps it had been added by someone who thought that it should be supplied; yet all the same there is surprising uniformity in the copies. And indeed even Ambrose reads *qui existimabantur esse aliquid* [who were deemed to be something].[9] But to me Valla's conjecture seems likely – that[10] the word is an insertion.[11] And from Jerome's interpretation it seems virtually certain that he did not read *qui videbantur esse aliquid* [who seemed to be something], but only *qui videbantur* [who seemed]; for he writes, 'being uncertain about the expression *qui videbantur* [who seemed] I sought to know what it means; but now [Paul] has removed all doubt by adding [the phrase] *qui videbantur columnae esse* [who seemed to be pillars].'[12]And in the Pauline codex in the first passage there is only *qui videbantur* [who seemed].[13] What is more, since Paul believes that they were greatly esteemed – a point more clearly explicated in the expression *qui videbantur columnae esse* [who seemed to be pillars] [Gal 2:9] – how will this expression agree with the one under discussion, *qui videbantur aliquid* [who seemed something], the expression we use to bestow no value whatever?

Although Jerome agrees with me in that he does not add *aliquid* [anything], he does not seem to have given sufficient thought to the force of the Greek participle δοκοῦντες.[14] Therefore[15] I have translated it: *cum iis qui erant in pretio* [with those who were held in great repute]. Let me[16] be perfectly clear with the reader: since here the particle τι [something] is added once in the Greek copies [ie in 2:6a], it is possible that here [in 2:6a] [Paul] used the word 'something' with the same meaning in which Luke added 'someone' [Greek τίνα] in Acts 5 to mean [someone] 'great': 'for before those days Theudas arose, claiming that he was someone great [5:36].'[17]

In his commentary at this point, Ambrose[18] notes in passing what should rather have been noted in Acts. For when we read in the fifteenth chapter of that book the command to the gentiles that they must abstain from four things – from what has been sacrificed to idols, from unchastity, from blood, and from what is strangled – he observes that the apostles had commanded only three of them, and that the Greeks added the fourth.[19] For he ends his argument in this way: 'some clever Greeks knew the command to abstain from blood, but they did not understand it and they falsified scripture by adding a fourth command, to stay away from what has been strangled. I think that by God's will they are going to understand it, since what they added here had already been said above.'[20] And[21] [Ambrose] interprets the command to abstain from blood not as the order to refrain from murder (which had been forbidden by the laws of the pagans also) but to abstain from eating meat together with its blood,[22] as Noah had been commanded,[23] like the teaching of Pythagoras.[24] But those [Greeks] interpreted the command against[25] blood differently, and added something akin to it from the ceremonies of the Jews, that is, to abstain from what is strangled. But[26] it is pointless to forbid us to consume an animal that has been strangled, since we are ordered – in Ambrose's opinion at least – to abstain from eating all meat. Let[27] others see how much value must be ascribed to his interpretation; certainly Irenaeus makes no mention of 'things strangled' when he cites the passage in Acts on several occasions, specifically, in the third book *Against the Heretics*, chapter 12.[28]

1 as Augustine reads] Added in *1519*. For the reference see Augustine *Expos Gal* CSEL 84 64:23. Augustine's commentary actually reads *qui videntur* 'who seem' (present tense), although *videbantur* appears in certain codices, cf CSEL 84 64:23n. For a full treatment of this annotation in relation to Gal 2:6 see Jan Krans *Beyond What is Written. Erasmus and Beza as Conjectural Critics of the New Testament* (Leiden 2006) 122–4.

2 by someone ... (but] Added in *1519*

3 Ambrosiaster *Comm in Gal* 2:2

4 of no repute] First in *1522*; previously 'they were of no repute'

5 for ... are esteemed.] Added in *1519*

6 *Euripidis Hecuba* 294. On Erasmus' edition of Euripides see the annotation on Gal 2:2 ('and I shared the gospel with them') n4.
For δοκοῦντες meaning 'persons of repute' see also Erasmus' annotation on Rom 15:7 ('unto the honour') CWE 56 395.

7 That is, Gal 2:2

8 third] First in *1535*; previously 'second.' Erasmus here refers to Gal 2:6.

9 Ambrosiaster *Comm in Gal* 2:6. In Vogel's edition, Ambrosiaster actually reads *existimantur* 'are reputed.'

10 that ... Greek participle] Added in *1519*. The *1519* insertion continues at n15.

11 Valla *Annot in Gal* 2 (I 875)

12 Jerome *Comm in Gal* 1 (on 2:7–9) CCL 77A 49:68–74

13 Jerome *Comm in Gal* 1 (on 2:7–9) CCL 77A 49:69–70. John Colet, dean of St Paul's in London, had made available to Erasmus from the chapter house two ancient manuscripts of the Latin Bible, one containing the Epistles, the other the Gospels. Erasmus briefly describes the manuscripts in the preface to the *Annotations* for his first edition of the New Testament; they were written, he says, in a script so old that he had, as it were, to learn the alphabet all over again (cf Allen Ep 373:23–5). For a more detailed description of the manuscripts see ASD IX-2 165:997–1000n.

14 δοκοῦντες] Added in *1527*

15 Added in *1519*

16 Let ... that he was someone great [5:36].'] Added in *1527*

17 Cf Acts 5:36

18 Ambrose ... said above'] First in *1519*; in *1516* the substance of this passage was included in the annotation on Gal 2:6 ('they shared nothing'). See n8 there.

19 The 'Greeks' to whom Erasmus here refers have not been identified.
20 Ambrosiaster *Comm in Gal* 2:2
21 And ... what is strangled.] In *1516* these lines formed part of the annotation on Gal 2:6 ('they shared nothing'); see n8 there.
22 together with its blood] Added in *1519*
23 as Noah had been commanded] Cf Gen 9:4.
24 Ambrosiaster *Comm in Gal* 2:2. Ambrosiaster does not mention Pythagoras; this seems to be Erasmus' thought.
25 the command against] Added in *1519* .
26 But ... meat.] Added in *1519*
27 Let ... chapter 12.] Added in *1527*
28 Irenaeus *Contra haereses* 3.12.14 PG 7 908B

2:3 [ER *quum esset Graecus* 'although he was a Greek']
[VG] *cum esset gentilis* 'although he was a gentile'; Ἕλλην ὤν, that is 'although he was a Greek,' which[1] term he uses instead of pagan.

1 which ... pagan] Added in *1519*

2:4 [ER *propter obiter ingressos falsos fratres* 'on account of false brothers who entered surreptitiously']
[VG] *sed propter introductos falsos fratres* 'but on account of false brothers brought in'; παρεισάκτους [brought in secretly], as if to say, 'who entered surreptitiously.' For in Greek παρὰ often implies evil intent, and [the words] form a nominal phrase, not a participle, as if to say, 'brothers who have been led in secretly.' Accordingly it states, οἵτινες παρεισῆλθον, that is, 'who entered surreptitiously, while we were doing something else.' That is what spies and those who contrive plots do.[1] Soon [2:9] [Paul calls them] 'false brothers,' that is ψευδαδέλφους, or[2] falsely called 'Christians,' about which I commented somewhat earlier.[3]

St Jerome thinks that the conjunction *autem* [however] or *sed* [but] in this passage is superfluous and ought to be discarded; for one, because if it were kept there is[4] no phrase to which it would correspond.[5] In Greek [the particle] δέ [on one hand] always corresponds to μὲν [on the other]. Second, because it would be exceedingly incompatible with the general sense of this Epistle. For St Jerome understands that by no force could Paul have been compelled to circumcise Titus, although he was a gentile, and that the matter pertained to the truth of the gospel. But what follows, 'on account of false brothers brought in,' is joined together with [the preceding] to form '[Titus] was not compelled to be circumcised, on account of false brothers,' etc. Augustine[6] interprets it in this sense,[7] although Ambrose[8] has a different reading.

1 That is ... do] Cf Lightfoot 106: 'the metaphor is that of spies or traitors introducing themselves by stealth into the enemy's camp.'

2   or ... 'Christians'] Added in *1527*
3   See Erasmus' annotation on 2 Cor 12:26 (*in falsis fratribus*).
4   there is] Latin 'has.' First in *1519*; in *1516*, indicative *habet* 'it [the conjunc-
    tion] has'; in *1535*, subjunctive *habeat* 'it would have'
5   Jerome *Comm in Gal* 1 (on 2:3–5) CCL 77A 45:44–7
6   Augustine *Expos Gal* CSEL 84 65:25–66:1
7   in this sense] First in *1527*; previously the sentence began 'And thus
    Augustine interprets ...'
8   Ambrosiaster *Comm in Gal* 2:4

2:5 [ER *cessimus per subjectionem* 'we yielded through subjection']
[VG] *cessimus subjectioni* 'we yielded to subjection.' In the Greek copies ὑποταγῇ [submission] is in the dative case, but it should be translated
in the ablative, 'in subjection,' that is, 'so that we were made subject to
them.' And indeed[1] in the codex of St Paul's the first hand had written
'in subjection,' ablative case. Jerome indicates that in certain Latin codices οὐδέ [not even] does not occur, so that one would understand that
Titus did yield for an hour;[2] it does appear in the Greek manuscripts,
with the meaning that he had yielded in no way.[3] For if it is understood
that he did yield for an hour, then Jerome thinks this phrase does not
pertain to the circumcision of Titus, but only to the fact that he had
returned to Jerusalem to satisfy them. And yet[4] what Jerome states is
not found in the Latin codices, now appears written in all the Latin
copies, except Ambrose, who arranges the sentence differently even
from us, namely in the following manner: 'on account of false brothers secretly brought in, who slipped in to spy out our liberty which we
have in Christ Jesus, that they might subject us to slavery, we yielded
in submission for an hour.'[5] His commentary also makes it clear that
he read it in this order. He omits the pronoun *quibus* [to whom], which
if added makes the sentence seem incomplete, unless we arrange it in
this way: 'Titus was not compelled to be circumcised because of the
apostles, to whom we submitted on other occasions, but because of
false brothers secretly brought in, to whom we yielded not the slight-
est amount.' But in what way did he not yield who was compelled to
circumcise Timothy? Ambrose argues over this text with many words.
However I do not see how the text can be explained unless we grant
that Paul's writing is incomplete, so that we understand it in this way:
'the apostles were not compelling [us], but on account of false brothers
we appeared to be about to be compelled, because the pressure they
exerted was rather annoying, to whom on that occasion at least we did
not yield to the point that we circumcised anyone of the gentiles.'

1   And indeed ... case.] Added in *1519*
2   Jerome *Comm in Gal* 1 (on 2:3–5) CCL 77A 43:6–16

3 The omission of οὐδέ from the Greek text is limited to mainly Western witnesses (Metzger 522–3). As also Erasmus' explanation implies, the apostle's main point is that he did not yield in any way. The main point of Erasmus' annotation is to reconcile the behaviour of Paul recorded here with that in Acts 16:1–3, which recounts the circumcision of Timothy.
4 And yet ... of the gentiles.'] This remaining portion of the annotation was added in 1519.
5 Ambrosiaster *Comm in Gal* 2:4–5

2:5 [ER VG] *apud vos* 'towards[1] you'; πρὸς ὑμᾶς, that is, 'for you.'

1 towards ... 'for you.'] In 1519, 1522, and 1527, this entire annotation follows the annotation on 2:6 ('for to me those who were regarded to be something') below.

2:6 [ER VG] *ab iis autem qui videbantur* 'but from those who appeared.' Once again Paul does not complete the sentence he has begun, because he intersperses some words; thereupon, after changing the sentence structure, he returns to the point at which he had started. It seemed[1] that he was about to add, 'From those who were in repute I have benefited nothing.' Then as if by parenthesis he had interjected: 'what they once were makes no difference to me; God does not consider a person's standing.' For it seems that the thought entered his mind incidentally from what he had said, 'Who now seem to be great.' Soon he returns to the starting point, but with a different sentence structure: 'For to me those who seemed to be something added nothing.'

1 It seemed ... added nothing.'] This remaining portion of the annotation was added in 1519.

2:6 [ER *nam mihi qui videbantur esse in pretio* 'for to me those who were regarded to be of repute']
[VG] *mihi autem qui videbantur esse aliquid* 'for[1] to me those who were regarded to be something.' Once again, in this third passage it is not *esse aliquid* [to be something], but merely, οἱ δοκοῦντες, that is, 'who were regarded,' that is, 'held in esteem,' whom they commonly call 'reputed.'

1 for] In 1516 the cue phrase had *enim* for *autem*.

2:6 [ER VG] *nihil contulerunt* 'they shared nothing'; οὐδὲν προσανέθεντο, that is, 'imparted[1] nothing,' the same word which he more frequently renders *acquievi* [I acquiesced], as also St Jerome points out.[2] Paul had shared his gospel with them; they had not in turn shared their gospel with him, but had only approved Paul's gospel. Therefore in this passage *contulerunt* [they shared] does not mean the same as *addiderunt* [they added], as some think,[3] but it becomes clear from the following. For what could they who had not even shared their gospel with him have added to Paul? They could have received something from Paul, but they could not have added something [to him]. St Jerome considers this is a case of hyperbaton,[4] so that with the removal of the many words that have been interjected, we would read as follows: 'for those who were regarded to be [something] shared nothing with me, but on the contrary they extended to me and to Barnabas the right hand of fellowship.' Yet according to the earlier meaning we are able to read as follows, that free of any boastfulness[5] Paul subtly indicated that nothing had been conveyed by them to him, but rather by him to them. This interpretation is deduced more accurately from the facts, as I have just stated,[6] than from the meaning of the words. For here the same word προσανέθεντο occurs, which means 'to share for the sake of consulting upon a certain matter.' On this passage Valla[7] was not attentive enough, for he thinks that here *contulerunt* [they shared] has the same meaning as *addiderunt* [they added].[8]

1 'imparted] First in *1519*; in *1516*, *addiderunt* 'they added'
2 Jerome *Comm in Gal* 1 (on 2:6) CCL 77A 47:6–7. Migne notes that in old editions the Greek word προσανέθεντο was inserted next to the Latin *contulerunt* [they shared], PL 26 (1884) 360D n2. Jerome also seems to prefer *contuli* to *acquievi* elsewhere in his commentary, cf Jerome *Comm in Gal* 1 (on 1:16) CCL 77A 31:2. BDAG defines the use of προσανατίθημι here 'add or contribute something to someone.'
3 See, for example, Lorenzo Valla: 'They shared nothing. In fact they added nothing, lest anyone should think that the apostles had shared nothing with Paul,' *Annot in Gal* 2 (I 875).
4 For hyperbaton see the annotation on Gal 1:6 ('into the grace of Christ') n4.
5 boastfulness] First in *1519*; in *1516*, *iactationem* 'boasting'
6 as I have just stated] Added in *1519*
7 Valla *Annot in Gal* 2 (I 875)
8 In *1516* only, the annotation continued and concluded with the following: 'St Ambrose noted something on this passage (which in fact does not strictly relate to this passage, where we read in the Acts of the Apostles the decree that the gentiles should abstain from four [things] – from what has been sacrificed to idols, from unchastity, from blood, and from what is strangled), [namely] that scripture had been falsified by Greek sophists, who added the fourth [command to abstain] from what is strangled from their own [doctrine]. And from blood ... from what is strangled. But how much value should be ascribed to this Ambrosian argument is a question I leave to the judgment of the reader.'

2:7 [ER *quum vidissent mihi concreditum* 'when they saw that to me had been entrusted']

[VG] *cum vidissent quia creditum est* 'when they saw that to me had been trusted'; ὅτι πεπίστευμαι τὸ Εὐαγγέλιον [that I had been entrusted (with) the gospel], that is, 'to me had been entrusted, or committed, the gospel.' For thus[1] the Greeks speak, 'I am entrusted this matter,' and 'I am committed this matter.' ὅτι [that][2] either should have been omitted or rendered as 'that.'

1 For thus ... committed this matter.'] Added in *1519*
2 ὅτι ... as 'that.'] Added in *1527*

2:8 [ER *nam qui efficax fuit in Petro* 'For he who was effective in Peter']

[VG] *qui enim operatus est Petro* 'For he[1] who has worked Peter.' *In Petro* [in Peter] and *in me* [in me] would better suit the Greek text, ἐνεργήσας Πέτρῳ, ἐνήργησε καὶ ἐμοί, for the preposition is in the compounded verb. Nor is it simply *operatus* [worked], but *efficax fuit* [was effective], and manifested his own power. For Origen in [commenting on] the Epistle to the Romans thinks that ἐντελέχειαν [effect] and ἐνέργειαν [operation] have the same meaning, that is, 'action,' and 'an instrument that of itself brings about an effect.'[2] For [Paul] means that whatever was brought about through Peter was perfected not in his own strength but by God as its author. [Paul] himself, assisted by his strength and protection, performed no lesser deeds among the uncircumcised than [Peter] did among the circumcised. And here again there is need for parenthesis, so that we read in this way: 'yes indeed, to the contrary, when they saw that to me had been entrusted the gospel to the uncircumcised, in the same manner as Peter that to the circumcised,' then the following is separated by the parenthesis: 'for he who worked in Peter for the apostleship to the circumcised, worked also in me towards the gentiles.' What soon follows is linked to the preceding: 'and when they perceived the grace granted to me,' etc.

1 'For he ... etc.] This entire annotation was added in *1519*. In *1516*, parts of this annotation were included in the annotation on 2:9 ('among the gentiles') below; see n3 there.
2 Origen *Comm in Rom* 8.2 PG 14 1162C

2:9 [ER *dextras dederunt mihi ac Barnabae societatis* 'they gave to me and to Barnabas the right hand of fellowship']

[VG] *dextras dederunt mihi et Barnabae societatis* 'they gave[1] to me and to Barnabas the right hand of fellowship.' Either ἕνεκα [for the sake of] must be understood, or according to the Hebrew manner of expression he said 'right hands of fellowship,' like 'the kiss of peace,' instead of 'confederate right hands,' if I may express it that way.[2]

1 'they gave ... that way.] This entire annotation was added in 1519.
2 Erasmus is referring to the use of the genitive instead of an adjective. See F. Blass and A. Debrunner *A Greek Grammar of the New Testament and Other Early Christian Literature* trans and rev (from the 9th – 10th German edition, incorporating supplementary notes of A. Debrunner) Robert W. Funk (Chicago and London 1961) §165, which states 'The genitive of quality provides in many combinations an attributive which would ordinarily be provided by an adjective ... Hebrew usage is thus reflected, in that this construction compensates for the nearly non-existent adjective.'

2:9 [ER *in gentes* 'to the gentiles']
[VG] *inter gentes* 'among the gentiles'; εἰς τὰ ἔθνη, that is, *in gentes* [to the gentiles], as Ambrose reads.[1] On another[2] occasion he cites *ad gentes* [to the gentiles], or *erga gentes* [towards the gentiles], so that it corresponds to the preceding, εἰς ἀποστολὴν τῆς περιτομῆς [to the apostleship of the circumcision].[3]

1 Ambrosiaster *Comm in Gal* 2:9. Ambrosiaster actually reads *ad gentes* 'to the gentiles.'
2 On another ... *erga gentes*] Added in 1519. For the reference see Ambrosiaster *Comm in Gal* 2:8.
3 In 1516 only, the annotation continued with the following: 'It should be noted in passing on this passage that ὁ ἐνεργήσας [he who worked] means something different in Greek than *operatus* [worked] means to us. For ἐνεργεῖν [to operate] is to display his hidden power in some matter. Whence also ἐνέργεια [operation] is said, not *operatio* [working], but a certain power which, though hidden, is effective. For [Paul] showed that what was done through Peter was not done by his own strength, but by God as its author, and [Paul] was protected by His strength ...'

2:9 [ER VG] *ut nos in gentes, ipsi autem* 'so that we to the gentiles, but they.'[1] This sentence is not complete, but [after 'we'] one must supply 'should perform the apostolic duty.' For *in* [in] is put in place of *erga* [towards]. And [Paul] calls the Jewish race[2] 'the circumcision,' which he opposes to the gentiles, whom he[3] sometimes calls 'the foreskin.'

1 they'] First in 1519; in 1516, *illi* 'those [men]'
2 race] First in 1522; in 1519, *ipsam gentem Judaicam* 'the Jewish race itself'
3 whom he ... foreskin.'] Added in 1519

2:10 [ER VG] *tantum ut pauperum* 'only that the poor.' The adverb 'only' should be taken with what follows, not with what precedes.[1] I noted this because some [manuscripts] punctuate the sentence differently. Moreover² something must be understood: 'only they advised' or 'prescribed.'

> 1 Erasmus' point in this annotation is to observe that the adverb 'only' refers to 'they would have us remember the poor' (verse 11) and not to 'that we should go to the gentiles and they to the circumcised' (verse 10).
> In explaining the meaning of χρεῖαι 'needs' in his annotation on Rom 12:13 ('sharing in the needs of the saints') Erasmus refers to Gal 2:10.
> 2 Moreover ... 'prescribed.'] Added in 1519

2:11 [ER *palam illi restiti* 'openly I resisted him']

[VG] *in faciem ei restiti* 'to his face I resisted him'; κατὰ πρόσωπον αὐτῷ ἀντέστην, that is, 'I resisted him face to face,' or surely 'in his presence,' not 'in his face.'¹ That is, 'openly and in the full view of all.' For 'in his face' would have been too insulting. Nor is the Greek κατὰ προσώπου [into his face], but κατὰ πρόσωπον² [before his face]. With these also the Greek scholia agree,³ and Ambrose too, who interprets *in facie* as openly and in the presence of many.⁴ But St Jerome takes 'according to outward appearance' to be synonymous with 'not from the heart,' so that for those who were present [Paul] might put on a show of rebuke, whereby the falsehood of Peter, which he saw would be harmful to the gentiles, might be corrected by feigned rebuke.⁵ And he calls this hypocrisy of both men '(wise) management.' But according⁶ to this interpretation it would be rather feeble for Paul to frighten the Galatians from Judaism by means of this dishonest display, for he would be false in resisting him to his face, and even though the latter had committed no sin, [Paul] would have sought this opportunity to reprimand.

However, this interpretation of certain Greeks⁷ is for another reason also⁸ not approved by Augustine.⁹ And it is from this [cause] that the grand debate about the lie arose among them, although it is more a matter of falsehood¹⁰ and pretence than of lying. And Jerome does not so much abhor the word 'lie' that he is not afraid to ascribe hypocrisy of this sort even to the Prophets and indeed even to Christ himself.¹¹ For Peter, when the Jews came, rose from the table and pretended that he did not eat common foods, lest they who could not be persuaded that it was permitted should take offence, although [Peter]¹² knew that it was permitted. And again, when Paul realized that a serious scandal was arising from that pretence whereby Peter had been eager to cure the Jews – so much that he also feared for Barnabas – he did put up a sharp rebuke, but [one that was] 'according to outward appearance,' that is, to outward semblance and through falsehood. And this not because

he believed that Peter had sinned by his own pretence, but because he
saw that the thing which he believed Peter had done as a remedy for
his own race was tending towards the destruction of the gentiles, for
whom Paul was concerned. In explaining[13] this Epistle Augustine treats
Peter very harshly, in my opinion at least, speaking about him in these
terms: 'Now when Peter came to Antioch he was rebuked by Paul not
for observing the Jewish custom in which he had been born and raised
(although among the gentiles he did not observe it), but for wanting to
impose it on the gentiles.'[14] Thus far Augustine.[15] For it seems to smack
of certain wrong-headedness if anyone is eager to impose upon others
a burden which he thinks should not be assumed. But [Peter's] own
word is in the Acts of the Apostles chapter 15: 'Now therefore why do
you test God by putting a yoke upon the neck of the disciples which
neither our fathers nor we have been able to bear?' [Acts 15:10] How
does it make sense that the very person who says that anyone who
wishes to impose the yoke of the Law upon the gentiles is 'making a
trial of God' when he himself tried with so much zeal to impose [the
same yoke] that he employed falsehood for that purpose? And again
Augustine in the thirtieth chapter of the book *On the Christian Struggle*
calls this act of Peter a superstitious falsehood, and adds it to the mix-
ture of his other sins of untrustworthiness, quarrelling, and denial, and
even a little later in the same chapter calls it a crooked falsehood, saying, 'these the catholic church receives into her maternal bosom, like
Peter after he wept over his denial, when he was warned by the crow-
ing of the cock, or like the same [Peter] after his crooked falsehood,
having been set straight by the speech of Paul.'[16] But it is worth the
effort to see how much Jerome differs with Augustine's interpretation.
The latter is not afraid to lay a charge of crooked falsehood upon Peter,
the foremost of the apostles, and that after he had received the heavenly Spirit. The former does not permit even an error to be attributed to
Peter. For this is what he says in the Preface of the commentaries which
he published on this Epistle: 'Therefore [Paul] proceeds so cautiously
between the [extremes], and moderately, so that he would not betray
the grace of the gospel, being burdened by the weight and the authority
of his elders, while at the same time not injuring his predecessors when
he defends grace. But indirectly, and as if proceeding stealthily through
secret passages, in order to show that Peter acts on behalf of the people
of the circumcision that were entrusted to him. For if they deviated
suddenly from their ancient way of life, they might be scandalized at
the cross and so not believe. [Paul also wishes to show] that he himself
had been entrusted with preaching the gospel to the Gentiles, that he

is right to defend as true what the other was feigning as a matter of policy. The Batanean-born Porphyry[17] did not understand this at all; in the first book of the work against us, he objects that Peter was condemned by Paul for not walking uprightly in the preaching of the gospel. [Porphyry's aim] was to brand the former with the stain of error and the latter with impudence, and more generally to raise the false accusation of fabricated teaching, on the ground that the church leaders were disagreeing with one another.'[18] Thus far the words of Jerome that I have adduced.

But several, as they are not able to free themselves from these difficulties, have commented that this 'Cephas' whom Paul resisted to his face was not Peter the apostle, but some other person. The scholia of the Greeks cite Eusebius as the author of this interpretation in the *Ecclesiastical History*, who has made the case more probable by the following argument.[19] 'Why,' he states, 'was it necessary for Peter to withdraw himself from the table because of the intervention of the Jews, when already long before that time he had satisfied those who had complained about his fellowship with the uncircumcised Cornelius, and so satisfied them that once they understood the matter they gave thanks to God with one accord, especially since no mention was made of this matter in the Acts of the Apostles?'[20] But Jerome forcefully rejects this view as fabricated and unconvincing, since the matter itself teaches that the entire passage pertains to Peter and his companions.[21] And he denies that any other 'Cephas' is known to us besides [the one] of the apostles, who in the language of the Syrians is called 'Cephas,' which to them means the same as 'Peter' does to the Greeks and us Latins. Moreover [he continues] that it is a wonder that this fact is not mentioned by Luke, by whom so many other matters have been glossed over, such as the fact that Peter first occupied a seat in Antioch and thereafter transferred it to Rome. Lastly, [Jerome observes] that the sycophant Porphyry ought not to enjoy such esteem from us that for his sake we should make up a new 'Cephas.' Otherwise if we attempt to erase from Scripture whatever is subject to the false claims of the heretics, then many other passages would have to be removed.

Thomas Aquinas has cleverly compressed the very wordy dispute that occurs between Jerome and Augustine on this matter into a compendium, noting that the gist of the controversy is located especially in four points.[22] First, regarding the periods of time, which Jerome has divided into two, Augustine has divided into three parts, in such a way that observing the Law was valid before the gospel came, but shortly after Christ's death it was empty of life but not deadly for the Jews – so long as they did not place any hope of salvation in it.

Only when the gospel had been spread widely did keeping of the Law
bring death for all peoples. While Augustine has made these distinctions accurately, Jerome thinks that the gospel had been spread sufficiently already when it was revealed to Peter in a vision that nothing is
common, although he satisfied the Jews when they complained about
this matter, when he himself testified in a public meeting that the burden of the Law should be imposed upon no one, something neither
they themselves nor their own ancestors could bear. And shall we deny
that the grace of the gospel had been spread abroad when everywhere
among the nations so many thousands of people were holding to the
gospel? Especially when so much earlier Christ himself had said, 'The
Law and the Prophets right up to John,'[23] when the veil of the temple
was split into two from top to bottom. Even this action caused no harm
to the law, since it yielded to the truth because it was a shadow. And I
think that so much esteem was not owing to the Synagogue, for Christ
rejected it as murderous,[24] especially since the risk was very great that
only a very little esteem would be needed to draw the gentiles also
towards Judaism. Nor would there have been any distinction between
the sacrifices of the gentiles and the Jews, because while the former
would have to be detested always, the latter had enjoyed esteem for
a brief time. What distinguishing features shall we use to delineate
the boundary Augustine places between the two periods of time? Or
shall the sacrifices remain until the time when they must be respected?
Indeed there are many people of this sort among Christians, also in
our own times. But this entire argument which Augustine puts forth
about the dead but not deadly matters, about the middle time period,
about the Synagogue that must be carried respectfully to its grave,
rests more upon human reasoning than upon the testimony of sacred
Scripture. For what sane person would wish to adhere to those practices which offer no hope of fruit? But if the Jews were keeping the matters of Law with the understanding that they were neither useful nor
useless, why do they demand these things of Paul? Indeed, why from
the gentiles? Certainly those who were doing these things believed that
they served a purpose. Why do the apostles not rebuke these [Jews]?
But if no fruit came forth from these practices, certainly then for that
reason they ought be avoided, because those who keep them extend a
false picture to the weak, as if without these laws the gospel was not
sufficient. Indeed, it is surely from this misconception that the heresy of
the Ebionites arose, besides several others, which mix up [the teaching
of] Christ with [that of] Moses, although he [Christ] wished them to be
not at all confused.

Now on the second point of contention [Aquinas] states that in Jerome's view the apostles did not observe the finer points of the Law, except on a number of occasions, briefly giving the impression of doing so for some specific reason.[25] For example, they rested on the Sabbath day not out of superstition but for the sake of rest. They abstained from certain foods, not because these were forbidden, but because they disliked their taste. Unless I am mistaken, Thomas himself added these examples; as if today the same allowances actually would not be granted, or as if anyone is about to commit a sin, who, tired from a journey on a Sabbath-day, takes the occasional rest, or who having been served a capon, disdains rancid bacon. Or as if it is appropriate to ascribe to the apostles a haughty disdain of the sort that we observe in foolish, weak women. But, in keeping with Augustine's view, he states the apostles intentionally observed the Law without placing their trust in it. And this practice was permitted to them as Jews; if this was granted as a concession only to the weakness of a few individuals, what is that to the apostles, through whom alone the weakness of others was to be corrected? Furthermore, what difference is there between one who is forced to observe [the Law] lest he be a stumbling block to others and one who observes a useless custom for whatever reason? But what is his intention in doing this? Or does he have no purpose at all, who pretends to keep the Law in order to prevent anyone from being alienated from the gospel?

In the third place [Aquinas] states they differ in that Jerome absolves each of them of all sin, because each was conducting his own business, that is, the business of the gospel. Augustine does burden Peter with sin, but only with pardonable sin. Yet from the words of Augustine just quoted it does not seem that he considered this sin pardonable. Now the interpretation that frees both apostles of sin is more favourable than the one that places the burden of sin upon one of the two – but more will be said on this shortly. What Thomas adduces about the trustworthiness of the authors seems to me unconvincing. Thomas rejects four of the seven doctors[26] upon whose testimony Jerome relies, because they were disgraced by heresy: the Laodicean,[27] Alexander,[28] Origen, and Didymus.[29] For the explanation of Scripture, however, I would place one Origen ahead of ten orthodox teachers, except in a few doctrines of the faith. But if those whose books are found to contain heresy must be rejected, then perhaps also Cyprian and Ambrose are to be rejected. Now what kind of [argument] is it to bring Paul into the company of witnesses whose own writings are subject to debate? So that three may not be set against three; meanwhile not a word about the lie. For the pretence or the dissimulation, if it accords with the deed, cannot thus be labelled a lie, since that is always linked to sin. Moreover Paul's statement, *non recte incedunt ad Evangelium*[30] [they are not walking rightly to the gospel], is evidently said about others, not about Peter. And so one scruple remains, that Peter is called 'blameworthy' by Paul. For either it was said truly and it follows that Peter sinned, or falsely and Paul is held liable to a charge of falsehood. However, soon we shall show from the explanation of the ancients how also this knot can be undone.[31]

In the fourth place, lest I pursue each matter singly, Thomas recalls among the other remaining matters that Peter had sinned, because from his pretence a scandal arose; not so Paul, because from his rebuke no offence arose. But in truth how was Peter able to know that those who were reclining at table would be offended, when they knew that Peter was accommodating the Jews who perhaps were weak and fractious? If they knew that a Jew was permitted to eat and not to eat, why are they offended if he for a time does what he thinks is best? It was more likely to happen that the Jews would be offended than the gentiles. For if he had not made a pretence, he would have sinned more gravely because he would have caused more serious offence to his own people, for whom he should have more concern. But not every scandal is linked to sin. In fact, from such a sharp rebuke by Paul a serious offence could have been born. Firstly they could have inferred that some rancour was occurring among the leading apostles, since Paul on account of a petty matter thus confronted Peter to his face. Furthermore there was the danger that among the believers Peter's authority – which should have been inviolable – would be lessened. I deemed it worthy to include these [observations], because the common crowd of theologians thinks that the issue was handled well by Augustine, and that the issue was explained well by Thomas. Certainly the passage is unclear and it has tortured the most learned [men] of Greece. I do not see why out of hatred for the lie we should treat Peter as harshly as Augustine treated him. But the Parisian Articles are even harsher, as they state that Peter erred in the faith.[32] We read[33] that between Paul and Barnabas a disagreement arose.[34] But to suggest that the apostles erred in the doctrines of the faith, after the heavenly Spirit who would lead them into every truth had been received, – that is in my view an impious thing to say. However, I do think that Paul was incensed because this unsteadiness of Judaism had not yet been removed from among the Christians; [I think] that is what Paul [means when he] says, οὐκ ὀρθοποδοῦσιν [they did not walk straight], which refers to those who limp. For it would have been fitting, once every superstition was cast out, to profess Christ

candidly before everyone. But if Paul looked in vain for some steadfastness in this regard from Peter, it does not immediately follow that Peter
sinned, since indeed that limp started out from no other place than a
zeal for piety. Accordingly Paul's reprimand was nothing other than a
strengthening of those who were still not yet standing firm enough. I
have brought these matters forward to the best of my ability, and readily shall accept better explanations anyone may bring forward.[35]

1 Galatians 2:11–14 records the so-called apostolic conflict between Peter
and Paul at Antioch. Paul relates that he challenged Peter when the latter,
though he knew that the Old Law proscribing association with gentiles
had been replaced by the gospel and was no longer valid, withdrew
himself from the company of gentile converts out of concern for Jewish
Christians. On the right interpretation of the dispute recorded here
Augustine and Jerome exchanged twelve letters. Jerome's position was
that Peter's actions were a form of simulation, and moreoever that Paul
had rebuked Peter out of pretence, to strengthen the weak Christians.
Augustine objected on the grounds that attributing an act of pretence to
Paul made him guilty of a lie; in his view, Paul rebuked Peter because he
genuinely deserved it. Erasmus adopts a position similar to that of Jerome
(though not explicitly), and interprets Paul's behaviour as an instance
of simulation that is employed as a rhetorical and pedagogical device in
order to achieve a noble goal. On other patristic interpretations of this
passage see Lightfoot 128–32.
For a comparison of Erasmus' interpretation of this passage with those
of later exegetes see Pieter G. Bietenholz '"Simulatio": Erasme et les
interprétations controversées de Galates 2:11–14' in *Actes du Colloque
International Erasme* ed J.-C. Margolin (Geneva 1990) 161–9, and more
generally J. Trapman 'Erasmus on Lying and Simulation' in *On the Edge
of Truth and Honesty: Principles and Strategies of Fraud and Deceit in the Early
Modern Period* ed T. van Houdt, *Intersections: Yearbook for Early Modern
Studies* 2 (Leiden 2002) 33–46.
2 but κατὰ πρόσωπον] Added in 1522. On the use of κατὰ πρόσωπον (here 'opposed him to his face') see BDAG.
3 For the identity of the 'Greek scholia' see the annotation on Gal 1:16 ('I
did not acquiesce in') n2, and n1 on the annotation to Rom 1:4 ('who was
predestined') CWE 56 10.
4 Ambrosiaster *Comm in Gal* 2:11. Erasmus seems to overstate Ambrose's
testimony here. Perhaps he is anticipating 2:14, *dixi Petro coram omnibus*
'I said to Peter before them all.'
5 Jerome *Comm in Gal* 1 (on 2:11–13) CCL 77A 53:20–45
6 But according ... reprimand.] Added in 1519
7 By 'certain Greeks' Erasmus may be thinking of Theophylact and
Chrysostom; cf the note by M. van Poll-van de Lisdonk in ASD VI-9 62:154.
8 for another reason also] Added in 1519. Erasmus may have in mind
Theophylact *Expos in Gal* 2:11 PG 124 976A, and Chrysostom *Comm in Gal*
2.5 PG 61 641.

9 Augustine *Expos Gal* CSEL 84 69:6

10 falsehood ... Christ himself] Added in *1519*. In *1516*, 'This is not a lie that is expressed in speech, but merely dissimulation and the misrepresentation of a deed ...' Prompted in part by Lee's criticism of this interpretation, Erasmus expanded the annotation in *1519*. See also his *Responsio ad annotationes Lei* 2 CWE 72 292.

11 Jerome *Comm in Gal* 1 (on 1:11–13) CCL 77A 54:58–63. Jerome refers to the 'prophets' Jehu and David as examples.

12 (Peter)] Latin *ille* 'that man.' Added in *1519*

13 In explaining ... explanations anyone may bring forward.] This remaining portion of the annotation was added in *1519*.

14 Augustine *Expos Gal* CSEL 84 69:20–4

15 Thus far Augustine.] Added in *1522*

16 Augustine, *De agone christiano* 30.32 CSEL 41 135:2–8

17 Jerome identifies 'Bataneotes' as Porphyry, from the Syrian city of Batanea; see Jerome *Comm in Gal* Praefatio CCL 77A 8:92–9.

18 Jerome *Comm in Gal* Praefatio CCL 77A 8:83–99

19 Cf Pseudo-Oecumenius *Comm in Gal* 2:11–13 PG 118 1112B

20 Eusebius *Historia ecclesiastica* 1.12.2. Erasmus ascribes Pseudo-Oecumenius' argumentation to Eusebius.

21 Jerome *Comm in Gal* 1 (on 2:11–13) CCL 77A 55:90–56:108

22 For the substantial discussion which now follows see Thomas Aquinas' summary at *Super Gal lect* cap 2 lectio 3.86–9. For Erasmus' assessment of the biblical scholarship of Aquinas see the annotation on Eph 5:18 ('wherein is extravagance') n20.

23 Cf Matt 11:13, Lk 16:16

24 Matt 14:17

25 Jerome *Epistulae* 112.11 PL 22 923; *Epistulae* 112.17 PL 22 927

26 These doctors are identified in Jerome's letter to Augustine regarding this passage: six in Jerome's *Epistulae* 112.4 PL 22 918, and the seventh doctor, John Chrysostom, in *Epistulae* 112.6 PL 22 919. Augustine also lists these seven doctors in his reply to Jerome, Augustine *Epistulae* 82.23 PL 33 286.

27 The 'Laodicean' is identified as Apollinaris the Younger, bishop of Laodicea. Apollinaris (c 300–90) advanced the unorthodox teaching that Christ was divine but did not possess a human nature.

28 Alexander (c 244–337) was the first bishop of Constantinople.

29 Didymus, also called 'the Blind' (c 313–98), was made head of the catechetical school at Alexandria by Athanasius. Inasmuch as he had been influenced by Origen, he was condemned in 553, and much of his writing disappeared. In his view of the Trinity, however, he followed Nicene orthodoxy. In *Apologia adversus monachos* LB IX 1025E Erasmus cites these words from this annotation as evidence of his own orthodox Trinitarianism.

30 Cf Gal 2:14

31 By 'the explanation of the ancients' Erasmus is referring to the interpretations discussed in his annotation on Gal 2:11 ('because he was to be blamed') below.

32 On the Parisian Articles see Allen Ep 1841 ll.75–6; *Supputatio* ASD IX-V
500:796–7, and the note there by E. Rabbie explaining that Erasmus' reference is not to the Parisian Articles of 1277 but to a tract by Pierre d'Ailly
composed c 1388.
33 We read ... thing to say.] Added in *1535*
34 Cf Acts 15:36–40

2:11 [ER *eo quod reprehensus esset* 'because he was blamed']
[VG] *quia reprehensibilis erat* 'because he was to be blamed'; ὅτι κα-
τεγνωσμένος ἦν, that is, 'because he was blamed,' and condemned by
those who passed negative judgment concerning him – even though he
did not deserve to be blamed. And here the scholia of the Greeks are in
agreement.[1] Ambrose likewise has the reading, 'was blamed,' not 'worthy of blame.'[2] And he adds, 'was blamed.' By what? 'Clearly by the
gospel truth, to which this deed was opposed,' herein[3] disagreeing with
the Greek texts and agreeing with Augustine. The Greek scholia indicate yet another meaning.[4] [Paul] states, 'I was granted the opportunity
to withstand Peter openly, because on an earlier occasion he had been
censured by the apostles at Jerusalem for eating food with Cornelius
at Antioch.' If he had not been reprimanded previously he would not
have withdrawn now, but fearing lest an uproar should again arise he
was preparing to withdraw himself from the company. But Paul, making use of the opportunity, reprimands him openly not because he was
annoyed with him but to strengthen others who were wavering. For if
Peter actually had committed a sin, and Paul genuinely had been annoyed with him, he would have expostulated with him in private, not
in the presence of everyone. Nor, to be sure, does Paul relate these matters in a boastful tone, but out of concern for the Galatians' well-being.
Finally, it seems to me that James and those with him shared the view
that even after the gospel was spread abroad the Jews must observe the
Law also concerning the ceremonies, and also – as I have pointed out
in [the annotation on] Acts chapter 21[:24] – not because[5] they believed
that the grace of the gospel was not sufficient for salvation without
these [laws], but because of the inflexible superstition of certain people,
they thought it expedient not to disregard them entirely.

1 Cf Pseudo-Oecumenius *Comm in Gal* 2:11–13 PG 118 1113A
2 Ambrosiaster *Comm in Gal* 2:11
3 herein ... Acts chapter 21] Added in *1519*. See also Erasmus' explanation
in *Responsio ad annotationes Lei* 2 CWE 72 292.
4 Cf Pseudo-Oecumenius *Comm in Gal* 2:11–13 PG 118 1112C–D
5 not because ... entirely] Added in *1522*

2:13 [ER *ac simulabant una cum illo* 'and they were making a pretence together with him']
[VG] *et simulationi eius consenserunt* 'and they joined in his pretence'; συνυπεκρίθησαν αὐτῷ, that is, 'together with him they made a pretence,' and so reads St Ambrose.[1]

    1 Ambrosiaster *Comm in Gal* 2:13. Ambrosiaster actually reads *simulaverunt cum illo* [with him they put on a pretence], omitting *una* [together].

2:13 [ER *caeteri quoque Judaei* 'and also the other Jews']
[VG] *caeteri Judaei* '**the other Jews.**' *Et* [and] should be added, καὶ οἱ λοιποὶ, 'and the other,' or[1] 'and also the other.'

    1 or ... other'] Added in *1519*. The Vulgate reflects the omission of καί in some Greek manuscripts (cf *Novum Testamentum* 459 13(3)n).

2:13 [ER *in illorum simulationem* 'into their hypocrisy']
[VG] *ab eis in illam simulationem* '**by them into that hypocrisy.**' In Greek it is συναπήχθη αὐτῶν τῇ ὑποκρίσει, that is, 'likewise was carried away into their hypocrisy,' or, 'by their hypocrisy.' Lefèvre [d'Etaples] has the reading, ὥστε καὶ Βαρνάβας συναπεχθῆναι, that is, 'so that Barnabas abstained with them.'[1] But this neither appears in the Greek codices, nor is it read by anyone at all; nor do I think that ἀπέχθῆναι [to incur hatred] is shown anywhere to derive from ἀπέχεσθαι [to withdraw].[2]

    1 Lefèvre *Pauli epistolae* fol 33 recto, fol 154 recto, and fol 155 verso
    2 συναπήχθη is the first aorist passive of συναπάγω, which BDAG renders as 'cause someone in conjunction with others to go astray in belief, lead away with.' Unlike Erasmus, most modern interpreters take the dative τῇ ὑποκρίσει to express the means whereby, rather than the direction into which, Barnabas was led astray.

2:14 [ER *recto pede incederent* 'were (not) walking with straight feet']
[VG] *recte ambularent* '**were [not] walking rightly.**' In Greek the phrase forms one word, ὀρθοποδοῦσι [they are not walking straight].[1] St Jerome, [in his work] against Pelagius[2] and[3] likewise in the commentaries,[4] renders it *quod non recto pede incedunt* [because they are not proceeding uprightly], although he construes it as referring to the others and not to Peter. For these men deceived in one way, Peter in another way. Peter concealed[5] rather than deceived, lest he should cause a stumbling block to his own people. The others put on a pretence, thinking that something contrary to good morals had been introduced. Certainly Augustine in the letters[6] in which he clashes with Jerome about this passage reads

[the verb] in the plural number, and he quotes[7] it that way in the final chapter of [the treatise] to Consentius about the Lie.[8] Likewise Ambrose [reads] *recta via incedunt* [they walked by a straight road].[9] And again, [the text] is not *non recte ambulare* [to walk off course], that is, to wander from the road, but *claudicare* [to limp], and *vacillare* [to stagger], because they were not firm in what should be candidly guarded, for they inclined now this way and now that. And because the Mosaic law was located on the boundary, it could happen that even Peter was somewhat uncertain whether the Law should be openly disregarded. But actually this was hesitation, not an act of wickedness, since neither Paul nor Peter judged that keeping the Law was required for salvation, although Paul also was constrained to circumcise Timothy and to shave the head, not out of superstition but out of concession. To this point there has been no mention of a lie. Nor would anyone deny that a righteous man has the right to pretend or feign on occasion. And I have shown that from this passage it is not at all necessary to conclude that there was a lie. Nor did Peter compel the gentiles to be slavish Judaizers, as if to draw them into Judaism, but because certain individuals had seized an opportunity from his pretence.

1 LSJ defines ὀρθοποδοῦσι as 'walk straight or uprightly.' Erasmus interprets the word here to mean 'walk in a straight line'; the Galatians were deviating from the path of truth, though they did not err in a moral sense. Cf Erasmus' paraphrase of this verse: 'I saw that some were wavering, accommodating themselves now to the gentiles, now to the Jews, and that they were not straightly and constantly enough proceeding towards the truth of the gospel' CWE 42 105. The current edition of the Vulgate maintains the reading *non recte ambularent* (Weber 1804); modern English translations vary: 'they walked not uprightly' (AV), 'they were not straightforward' (RSV), 'they were not acting in line' (NIV).
2 Jerome *Dialogus adversus Pelagianos* 1.23 CCL 80 29:4–5
3 and ... commentaries] Added in *1519* ·
4 Jerome *Comm in Gal* 1 (on 2:14) CCL 77A 57:1
5 Peter concealed ... opportunity from his pretence.] This remaining portion of the annotation was added in *1519*.
6 Augustine *Epistulae* 82.4 PL 33 277; *Epistulae* 40.3 PL 33 155
7 and he quotes ... Consentius] Added in *1522*
8 Augustine *De mendacio* 1.21 CSEL 41 465:12–13
9 Ambrosiaster *Comm in Gal* 2:14. The word *ambulabant* [they were walking] was changed in a later revision of Ambrosiaster's commentary to *incedunt* [they are proceeding], with little difference in meaning.

2:14 [ER *dixi Petro* 'I said to Peter']
[VG] *dixi Cephae* 'I said to Cephas.' The Greek reads Πέτρῳ,[1] that is, 'to Peter,' although[2] it makes little difference for the meaning. For the

meaning of the Greek πέτρος is 'cephas' in Hebrew and Syriac, as Jerome notes.[3]

1 Current editions of the New Testament read Κηφᾷ; on the textual tradition see Metzger 524.
2 although ... notes] Added in 1519
3 Jerome *Comm in Gal* 1 (on 2:11–13) CCL 77A 56:111–15. For Jerome's knowledge of Syriac see Daniel King '*Vir Quadrilinguis*? Syriac in Jerome and Jerome in Syriac' in *Jerome of Stridon. His Life, Writings and Legacy* ed A. Cain and J. Lössl (Surrey 2009) 209–23.

2:14 [ER VG] *coram omnibus* **'in the presence of all.'** Here he explains what he had stated earlier, κατὰ πρόσωπον [face to face], that is, 'in the presence of all,' for whose[1] sake these things are being said.

1 for whose ... said] Added in 1519

2:16 [ER *quoniam scimus* **'since we know'**]
[VG] *scientes autem* **'but knowing.'** I do not find the conjunction *autem* [but] in the Greek copies, nor is it required, unless you supply the words 'we are' in the earlier passage,[1] so that we may read it thus: 'We [who] were born Jews, descended from venerable fathers, were born under the holy Law, but the gentiles were not – those who were produced from unholy and impious forebearers [who were] without the Law. Yet we ourselves who were born thus are also compelled, having despaired of our own Law, to take refuge in faith in Christ, if we would be saved, by which fact the gentiles are less likely to be persuaded that they should hope for salvation from the law of Moses.' Moreover, he said 'Jews by birth,' to the exclusion of converts [to Judaism].

1 Cf Gal 2:15

2:16 [ER VG] *nisi per fidem Iesu* **'except by faith in Jesus';** ἐὰν μή, that is, *si non* [if not]. This is an unusual form of speech; according to common practice one would say, 'not justified from works of the Law, but by faith only.'

2:16 [ER *in Christum Iesum*[1] *credidimus* **'we have believed in Christ Jesus'**]
[VG] *in Iesu Christo credimus* **'we believe in Jesus Christ';** ἐπιστεύσαμεν, that is, 'we have believed,' in the past tense, as Jerome also reads.[2]

1 Erasmus follows Valla here by using the accusative instead of the ablative. Valla reads *graece est credidimus*, ἐπιστεύσαμεν: *et in Iesum Christum*, εἰς Χριστὸν Ἰησοῦν; Valla *Annot in Gal* 2 (I 875).
2 Jerome *Comm in Gal* 1 (on 2:16) CCL 77A 59:2–3

2:16 [ER *propterea quod* 'because']

[VG] *propter quod ex* 'on account of which from'; *propterea quod* [because], if [Paul] had wished to say διότι in Latin.

2:18 [ER *rursum aedifico* 'again I build']

[VG] *reaedifico* 'I rebuild'; οἰκοδομῶ, that is, 'I build,' for πάλιν (that is, 'again') goes before it.

2:19 [ER *mortuus fui*[1] 'I was dead']

[VG] *mortuus sum* 'I am dead'; ἀπέθανον, that is, 'was dead': so that it is in the past tense, that is, 'through the law of faith I ceased to be bound to the Mosaic law.'

> 1 Erasmus employs the forms *fui/fueram* (for *sum/eram*) for the Greek aorist tense to refer more explicitly to a past action or a state of being; in this instance, 'was dead at that time.' Cf also Rom 4:2, where Erasmus wrote *nam si Abraham ex operibus justificatus fuit* 'for if Abraham was justified by works.'

2:19 [ER *crucifixus sum* 'I was crucified']

[VG] *confixus sum cruci* 'I was nailed to the cross'; Χριστῷ συνεσταύρωμαι, that is, 'I was crucified together with Christ,'[1] or 'I was crucified with Christ.'[2]

> 1 Cf Lefèvre *Pauli epistolae* fol 155 verso
> 2 Cf Valla *Annot in Gal* 2 (I 875)

2:20 [ER *vitam autem, quam nunc vivo* 'but the life which I now live']

[VG] *quod autem nunc vivo* 'since however I now live.' Once again ὅ [that] was preferable to ὅτι [because], just as I pointed out in [an annotation on] the Epistle to the Romans: 'For that he lives, he lives to God.'[1]

> 1 See Erasmus' annotation on Rom 6:10 ('for that which he died').

2:20 [ER *per fidem vivo Filii dei* 'I live by faith in the Son of God']

[VG] *in fide vivo Filii dei* 'I live in faith in the Son of God'; ἐν πίστει ζῶ τῇ τοῦ Υἱοῦ τοῦ Θεοῦ. The added article distinguishes faith in Christ from another faith, which could have been expressed as, 'I live in faith, in the faith, I say, in the Son of God.' It is remarkable that, as if forgetting the account and leaving it aside, he pursues the topic in such a way that it is not at all clear at what point he ceased rebuking Peter. Jerome,[1] with the agreement of Theophylact,[2] thinks Paul's reprimand continues until the end of this chapter, and he finishes the commentary on this chapter thus: 'If you yourself make this bold assertion, you see to what degree of impiety blasphemy will lead.'[3] Yet there are elements in this passage that better suit a teacher towards his student than Paul towards Peter. Therefore it is more probable that Paul had said the rest to those who were present, or that, having omitted what he had begun, Paul subtly turned aside to the Galatians. Otherwise [the comment] 'O foolish Galatians' would be too abrupt. From Ambrose's [commentary] nothing is sufficiently clear.[4]

1　Jerome *Comm in Gal* 1 (on 2:21) CCL 77A 65:19
2　Theophylact *Expos in Gal* 2:20 PG 124 981C
3　Erasmus appears to be mistaken, as this text is not found in Jerome.
4　Ambrosiaster *Comm in Gal* 2:21

2:21　[ER *non adspernor gratiam dei* 'I do not spurn the grace of God']
[VG] *non abjicio* 'I do not cast aside'; Οὐκ ἀθετῶ, that is, *non rejicio* [I do not reject], *non repello* [I do not push away], *non sperno* [I do not spurn]. Ambrose reads 'I am not ungrateful to the grace of God.'[1] Augustine [reads] 'I do not make the grace of God void.'[2] It seemed that [Paul] would spurn the grace of Christ if he received the Law of Moses as necessary for salvation.

1　Ambrosiaster *Comm in Gal* 2:21
2　Augustine *Expos Gal* CSEL 84 75:2

2:21　[ER *Christus frustra mortuus est* 'Christ died in vain']
[VG] *gratis Christus mortuus est* 'Christ died for nothing'; δωρεάν, which has the same meaning as *gratis* [for nothing]. It is an argument from the impossible,[1] since if no one is so foolish as to state that Christ died for nothing then it follows that salvation does not come by observing the Mosaic law.

1　*Ratiocinatio* is a form of inferential reasoning in which an inherent probability once exposed is thought to be convincing in itself. The inference may be explicated, as here, through questions posed and answered by the speaker. See Cicero *De inventione* 1.34.59; *Rhetorica ad Herennium* 4.16.23; Lausberg §367–72; for Erasmus' description see *Ecclesiastes* III ASD V-5 58:133–61:185. Erasmus tends to use the word *ratiocinatio* or 'syllogism' pejoratively; see CWE 44 7–8.

From the Third Chapter

3:1 [ER *O stulti* 'O foolish']

[VG] *O insensati* 'O senseless'; ἀνόητοι, that is, 'foolish.' And indeed this is how Augustine read it in the Commentary which he published on this Epistle.[1] Now the word 'senseless' is somewhat harsh and insulting.[2] The Greek word rather has the sense of 'rough' and 'endowed with too little intelligence,' especially because the Galatians had set forth from the wilder regions of the Gauls. Hilary, himself a Gaul, in the book of hymns, calls the Gauls undomesticated.[3] Jerome adds that he had seen the metropolis of Ancyra in Galatia, where many traces of its ancient wild character remained, and that prodigious heresies arose from the people of these regions, from those in Phrygia [τῆς κατὰ Φρύγας],[4] from the Ophitae,[5] Borboritae,[6] and Manichaeans.[7] He notes also that the language, with the exception of Greek which at that time almost all the Orient was using, was nearly the same as the one of the Treviri [inhabitants of Trier] at that time.[8] For Jerome dwelt among these people.[9] I do not[10] know whether the language which is now used by the Germans had once been that of the Gauls. The word the Translator here renders *insensatos* [senseless] he soon[11] translates *stultos* [foolish], in his[12] characteristic fashion indulging in [stylistic] variety.[13]

1 Augustine *Expos Gal* CSEL 84 75:10
2 Erasmus is following Valla here, *Annot in Gal* 3 (I 875).
  In his annotation on Rom 1:14 ('to the Greek and the barbarians') Erasmus defines ἀνόητος 'foolish' as 'unacquainted with philosophy and ... unlearned' (CWE 56 40). In the Argument to *Paraphrasis in Galatas*, Erasmus explains that by using this word Paul accommodates his discourse to the character of the Galatians, reproving and rebuking rather than instructing them (CWE 42 94). The change to the Vulgate's *insensati* is consistent with the word used in Gal 3:3.
3 Erasmus derived the reference to the (unidentified) book by Hilary from Jerome *Comm in Gal* 2 (on 3:1) CCL 77A 80:47–50.
  In *Hyperaspistes* 1 Erasmus mentions the Galatian people as an example of ignorant and feeble believers, 'unsuited to the study of the humanities' CWE 76 232. Scholarly evaluations of the culture and civilization of the Celts have changed considerably since Erasmus' time; for an assessment of the evidence see Stephen Mitchell 'The Galatians: Representation and Reality' in *A Companion to the Hellenistic World* ed A. Erskine (Oxford 2003) 280–93.
4 Phrygia] First in 1535; previously *Cataphrygum*. It appears Erasmus employed the Greek (Cata-Phrygum) as an etymological explanation for *Cataphrygum*. The followers of Montanus received the epithet *Cataphryges* from the name of the region in which Montanus was reported to have received his visions.

5 The Ophitae (literally: 'snake worshippers') were founders of a gnostic sect, first mentioned by Clement of Alexandria.

6 The Borboritae were founders of a gnostic sect.

7 Jerome *Comm in Gal* 2 (on 3:1) CCL 77A 82:109–17

8 at that time] Added in *1519*

9 On Jerome's correspondence with contacts in Gaul see Ralph Mathisen 'The Use and Misuse of Jerome in Gaul during Late Antiquity' in *Jerome of Stridon. His Life, Writings and Legacy* ed A. Cain and J. Lössl (Surrey 2009) 191–208.

10 I do not ... Gauls.] Added in *1519*

11 At 3:3 the Vulgate translates ἀνόητοι as *stulti* 'foolish.'

12 in his ... variety] Added in *1519*

13 Cf Erasmus' comment on Rom 15:7 ('unto the honour'). Titelmans complained about Erasmus' criticism of the Translator's variety, in *Responsio ad collationes* CWE 73 252–3; see further Rummel 96–7.

3:1 [ER VG] *quis vos fascinavit* **'Who has bewitched you?'** In Latin those who cause injury with an evil glance are said to 'bewitch' [*fascinare*], but in Greek βασκαίνειν, the word which Paul has employed here, bears also the meaning 'to envy' [*invidere*],[1] so that you would understand that certain people, moved by envy, wished to call the Galatians back to the slavery of the Law.[2] But Paul seems to have used the word instead of 'to enchant' [*incantare*], and he has applied it to the eyes as if with magic. For βασκαίνειν in Greek is said 'to make strange by means of the eyes' because the bewitcher inflicts harm through the eyes. Moreover, the words which follow immediately, 'before whose eyes Christ Jesus was condemned and among you crucified,' provide the evidence that Paul is thinking about eyes that have been deceived. Moreover, it is plainly a kind of magic when you do not see what is before your eyes, or when you think you are seeing that which is not. And yet Demosthenes, in the *Speech*[3] *in Defence of Ctesiphon*, employed the word to mean 'to accuse falsely,' 'to charge with a crime.'[4] Hesychius adds that [the word] is used especially of a thankless person.[5] Moreover, it was believed that an evil spell would harm especially boys, and for that he calls them foolish, fearing[6] not at all the gospel's statement: 'whoever says to his brother, you fool, shall be liable to the fire of Gehenna.'[7] For this reproach arises not out of anger but of love. What is more, he lightens their offence because he attributes such great blindness to an evil spell, casting[8] a large part of the blame upon other people.

1 BDAG defines βασκαίνειν as 'to exert an evil influence through the eye, bewitch someone.' For a discussion of the associations of this verb with the evil eye and jealousy see Lightfoot 133–4.

2 Law] In *1516* and *1519* the following sentence was added here 'In his second book *Against Jovinian* Jerome translates "he hindered."'

3 in the *Speech* ... thankless person] Added in *1519*

4 Ὑπὲρ Κτησιφῶντος [*In Defence of Ctesiphon*] was an alternate title for Περὶ τοῦ στεφάνου [*On the Crown*]. The passage cited is *de Corona* 18.252.

5 Hesychius 291 Latte. Hesychius, lexicographer probably of the fifth century AD, based his lexicon on the work of previous scholars. The abridged version that has come down to us is a valuable glossary of proverbs, biblical names, and Attic Greek. This lexicon was published first in 1514, edited by Marcus Musurus; see *Contemporaries* II 472–3 and Deno John Geanakoplos *Greek Scholars in Venice* (Cambridge 1962) 154–5.

6 fearing ... evil spell] Added in *1519*

7 Cf Matt 5:22.

8 casting ... people] Added in *1535*

[3:1] [ER *ut non crederetis veritati* 'so that you do not believe the truth']
[VG] *non credere veritati* 'not to believe the truth'; 'not to obey,' τῇ ἀληθείᾳ μὴ πείθεσθαι, that is, 'that you are not submissive to the truth';[1] although this phrase is entirely omitted by Jerome, because he states that it is not to be found in the copies of Adamantius.[2] In the oldest[3] and most emended copies of the Library of St Paul's [the phrase] is not added in the text, but someone in a more recent script notes it further down at a distance in the margin at the bottom. In the more[4] recent codex of Constance it does not occur at all; in the older codex it was read, 'who has bewitched you to not obey' – and 'the truth' was not added. They have added the same phrase also at another place further down [5:7], where instead of ἐβάσκαινον [bewitched] it was changed to ἐνέκοψεν [hindered]. This is[5] one of many places in which it is demonstrated that this edition was not entirely the work of Jerome.[6] For although he testifies that he had omitted this phrase on the grounds that it was not found in the codices of Adamantius, it is found consistently in our copies. Moreover, in the fifth chapter he states that the Translator in this passage had rendered 'not to believe the truth';[7] our codices have 'not to obey the truth.' Chrysostom reads nothing other than 'who has bewitched you.'[8] Nor does Theophylact have another reading, although the Translator characteristically follows our reading, while in the commentary there is not a word explaining this phrase.[9]

1 Erasmus is following Valla here, *Annot in Gal* 3 (I 875).
Modern editions of the New Testament leave out τῇ ἀληθείᾳ μὴ πείθεσθαι, which may have crept in here under the influence of Gal 5:7 (Metzger 524).

2 Jerome *Comm in Gal* 1 (on 3:1) CCL 77A 68:12–14. 'Adamantius' was an epithet for Origen.

3 In the oldest ... bottom.] Added in *1519*
4 In the more ... added.] Added in *1527*
5 This is ... this phrase.] This remaining portion of the annotation was
   added in *1535*.
6 Erasmus did not think that the Vulgate as he knew it was solely the work
   of Jerome; see Rummel 30.
7 Jerome *Comm in Gal* 3 (on 5:7) CCL 77A 160:1–7
8 Chrysostom *Comm in Gal* 3.1 PG 61 648
9 Theophylact *Expos in Gal* 3:1 PG 124 981C

3:1 [ER *quibus prae oculis* 'for whom before whose eyes']
[VG] *ante quorum oculos* 'in front of the eyes of whom'; οἷς κατ᾽ ὀφθαλ-
μοὺς ὁ Ἰησοῦς Χριστὸς προεγράφη, that is, 'for whom before[1] their eyes
Christ Jesus was portrayed.' I wonder why [the Translator] rendered
proscriptus [proscribed], since that word in Latin means something
quite different, except that the Greeks also call 'proscription' (which
was a kind of legal condemnation among the Romans) προγραφήν.[2]
Moreover there can be a double meaning: 1. the Galatians were so out
of their minds that what was most evident and placed before their eyes
they nevertheless did not see, having been completely blinded, or 2.
that they so saw absolutely nothing that they believed that Christ had
perished by [the] proscription, and that he had been crucified in the
common manner. Augustine[3] and Ambrose[4] follow the latter meaning.
To me the former meaning appeals as being simpler and less forced.
But Augustine seems to have the reading *praescriptus*, not *proscriptus*,
at any rate speaking about the appropriation of possessions which by
means of confiscation are transferred to the [legal] right of another.[5] If
anyone[6] should happen to require his words, I shall write them down:
'Before whose eyes,' he states, 'Christ Jesus was proscribed, after being
crucified. In other words, as they were watching, Christ Jesus lost his
inheritance and his possession to those who were taking it away and
banishing the Lord. They were calling those who had believed Christ
back to the works of the Law, back from the grace of faith whereby
Christ possesses the gentiles – in order to take away Christ's possession.' And a little later [he writes], 'In order to move them very deeply
when they considered the price Christ paid for the possession he was
losing in them. And so it is not enough to say (as the Apostle said earlier) "that Christ died for nothing." For that sounds as though Christ has
not attained to the possession for which he gave his blood; but when
Christ is also proscribed, what he was holding is taken away. However
this proscription does not harm Christ (who by his divinity is Lord of
all), but the possession itself, which is deprived of the care of his grace.'
Thus far Augustine.

From which words I think it is clear enough that [Augustine] is concerned with legal appropriation, and that in this entire passage *prae* has been replaced with *pro* in the word *proscriptione*. But Ambrose does have the reading *proscriptus*, making mention of condemnation in a court of law.[7] Nor is it a burden[8] to adduce his words for the lazy and untrusting reader: 'It is obvious,' he says, 'that to the eyes of the foolish, Christ appears to have been convicted [*proscriptus*], that is, to have been stripped of his goods or been condemned. But to the eyes and senses of the wise not only was he sold off, but he appears himself to have condemned death by means of his cross.' And shortly thereafter, 'but because these men began to entertain ignoble thoughts when they defected to the Law, [Paul] therefore laments that to their minds Christ appears convicted ...' Thus far I have passed in review the Ambrosian [commentary]. Theophylact has the reading *praescriptus*, that is, as though painted before their eyes.[9] For in Greek γράφειν is also 'to paint.' By means of this hyperbole he notes the very certain faith of those who more certainly have believed that Christ by his death had liberated the race of men than those who before their eyes had beheld him lifted onto the cross. And for this reason he is the more annoyed that they are falling back to Judaism as though deserting Christ. Jerome seems to have read *praescriptus*,[10] that is, 'written beforehand,' crucified on your behalf, before you read it in the gospel; in other words, for those who read and[11] believe[12] the predictions of the prophets who[13] much earlier had foretold that this was going to take place. It should be noted that the Greek word προεγράφη is common to writing and painting.

But if the prior interpretation is more appealing – it certainly commends itself more to me, and the Greek scholia agree[14] – it will better suit [the wording] *depictus ante oculos*[15] [portrayed before the eyes] than *praescriptus* [written beforehand]. The Donatian codex[16] had *praescriptus*, and so too[17] each codex of Constance, with no trace of erasure. However the wording[18] should be read as joined together, 'before whose eyes Christ was portrayed among you crucified,' as if he said, 'as though portrayed hanging on the cross, he has been manifested before your eyes.' For he had not been crucified among the Galatians, but through faith he was represented to them as crucified. This is what Chrysostom tacitly advises, making no mention of the prefix in προεγράφη, which Paul appears to have employed in place of *praescriptus est* [is written beforehand].[19] In Latin the preposition *pro* occasionally means something that is happening openly, as *prodere* [bring forward], *promulgare* [proclaim publicly], *proferre* [bring into the open], *proloqui* [speak out], *prostare* [expose to the public]. And long ago the names of those condemned were put on display publicly in the market, whence this kind of conviction was called *proscriptio* [advertisement].

1 before] First in *1519*; in *1516*, *in* 'in'
2 In his edition of the *Novum Testamentum* Erasmus translates the Greek προεγράφη as *depictus* 'portrayed,' following the variant *praescriptus* rather than the preferred *proscriptus* (Weber 1804). In his paraphrase Erasmus states that it is through the 'eyes of faith' that the Galatian believers saw the crucified Christ, *Paraphrasis in Galatas* CWE 42 108.
3 Augustine *Expos Gal* CSEL 84 75:12–19, 75:24–76:8
4 Ambrosiaster *Comm in Gal* 3:1
5 According to L&S, *praescriptus* does not have this technical meaning in court; only *proscriptus* does, which LSJ gives as a Latin equivalent for προγραφή.
6 If anyone ... in the word *proscriptione*.] Added in *1519*
7 Ambrosiaster *Comm in Gal* 3:1
8 Nor is it a burden ... as though deserting Christ.] Added in *1519*
9 Theophylact *Expos in Gal* 3:1 PG 124 984B
10 Jerome *Comm in Gal* 1 (on 3:1) CCL 77A 67:1–4
11 read and] Added in *1519*
12 believe] First in *1519*; in *1516*, *videlicet credentes* 'evidently those who believe'
13 who ... take place] Added in *1519*
14 Cf Pseudo-Oecumenius *Comm in Gal* 3:1–6 PG 118 1120B
15 *oculos*] First in *1519*; in *1516*, *oculus* (nominative singular)
16 The Donatian codex ... *praescriptus est*.] Added in *1522*. Erasmus visited Bruges in 1519 and 1521. While there, Erasmus was the guest of his friend, Marcus Laurinus, canon and later dean of the college at the church of St Donatian in Bruges. He thus acquired access to the cloister library, where he found several Latin manuscripts of the New Testament, two of which are described in his annotation on Matt 3:16 (*baptizatus autem Iesus*). These manuscripts, which date from the thirteenth century, appear as textual witnesses in the third edition of Erasmus' New Testament (1522). See Allen Epp 373 and 1223, and H.J. de Jonge *Apologia ad annotationes Stunicae* ASD IX-2 168:73–4n.
17 and so too ... erasure] Added in *1527*
18 However the wording ... *proscriptio*.] This remaining portion of the annotation was added in *1535*.
19 Chrysostom *Comm in Gal* 3.1 PG 61 648

3:1 [ER *inter vos crucifixus* 'among you crucified']¹

[VG] *et in vobis crucifixus* 'and in you crucified.' *Et* [and] is superfluous. And 'in you' can be accepted instead of 'among you,' so long as the first² meaning which I have enumerated finds favour. Not that Christ had been crucified among them, but that this³ was so noted and preached that they knew and believed⁴ it no less than if the act had been performed in their very presence.

1 These words do not occur in the modern edition of the Vulgate.
2 first] First in *1519*; in *1516*, *posterior* 'latter'
3 this] Added in *1522*
4 and believed] Added in *1519*

3:2 [ER *ex operibus legis* 'from the works of the Law']
[VG] *an ex operibus legis* 'or[1] from the works of the Law.' *An* [or] is superfluous here, and it is not added by St Jerome,[2] nor by Augustine,[3] and it is not found in the ancient copies. For he does not merely ask which it is of two, but he puts forward the former as though a foolish thing to say, and then for improvement he brings in what is true, as if to say, 'have you received the Spirit from works of the Law, or rather from hearing?' Furthermore that phrase, 'from the hearing of faith,' although it is understood by us, nevertheless strikes Latin ears as unusual. For the Greeks call reputation or gossip ἀκοήν [the hearing], but not so the Romans. Accordingly 'from the preaching of faith' would have been more clear, that is, 'from faith, which you have heard from us, you have not learned from the Law.'[4] For who would tolerate someone saying, 'the hearing of the slain king troubled the people,' instead of, 'the report of the slaying of the king?' I therefore translated 'preaching' instead of 'the hearing.'

1 or] Excised from Erasmus' reading of the Vulgate in *1535*.
2 Jerome *Comm in Gal* 1 (on 3:2) CCL 77A 68:1–2
3 nor by Augustine ... 'preaching' instead of 'the hearing'] This remaining portion of the annotation was added in *1519*. For the reference see Augustine *Expos Gal* CSEL 84 77:24–5.
4 In discussing this text in *Hyperaspistes* 2, Erasmus states that by 'Law' the apostle 'is speaking of ceremonial works' CWE 77 667.

3:3 [ER *quum Spiritu coeperitis* 'although you have begun in the Spirit']
[VG] *ut cum Spiritu* 'although with the Spirit.' *Ut* [that][1] is not in the Greek copies, but 'although you have begun in the Spirit, you are now being brought to completion in the flesh,' ἐναρξάμενοι πνεύματι νῦν σαρκὶ ἐπιτελεῖσθε, except[2] that the preposition is in the compound verb, just as [in] Horace, 'you sleep over [*indormis*] the coveted bags that have been piled together from all sides,'[3] and similarly [in] Virgil, 'having doubts about [*indubitare*] my powers.'[4] And the word *in* [in] is placed instead of *per* [through]. Therefore *Spiritu et carne* [through the Spirit and through the flesh] fits better. Chrysostom[5] has noted that the Apostle did not state τελεῖσθε, but ἐπιτελεῖσθε, as if one said, 'are you afterward being completed, disagreeing with the established teachings?'

1 Valla also omits '*ut*,' *Annot in Gal* 3 (I 875). He reads 'but without that *ut* [that] the meaning is more vivid.'

2 except ... fits better] Added in *1519*
3 Horace *Satires* 1.1.70
4 Virgil *Aeneid* 8.404. The current Oxford Classical Text has the reading
   viribus indubitare tuis 'having doubts about your powers.'
5 Chrysostom ... teachings?'] The remainder of this and all of the following
   annotation were added in *1535*. For the reference see Chrysostom *Comm
   in Gal* 3.2 PG 61 650.

3:4 [ER *frustra* **'in vain'**]
[VG] *sine causa* **'without reason'**; εἰκῇ, that is, 'in vain,' or 'rashly.'

3:5 [ER *subministrat vobis* **'supplies you'**]
[VG] *tribuit vobis* **'assigns**[1] **you'**; ὁ ἐπιχορηγῶν, that is, 'furnishes,' or
'supplies': ὁ ἐπιχορηγῶν [the one who supplies] and ὁ ἐνεργῶν [the one
who works] could be of the past tense, that is, 'who supplied,' and
'who worked,' so that one would assume that the next verb likewise
is of the past tense, *tribuerat* [had assigned], or something similar. But
Jerome quite rightly advises to read the verb in the present tense, because the Spirit has not ceased to supply his gifts;[2] so, too, Ambrose[3]
has the sound reading. Peter Lombard,[4] in the fourteenth chapter of
the first book of the *Theological Statements*, following the reasoning of
Augustine, thinks that this phrase, 'who offers [presents],' ought to be
referred to Paul personally,[5] although Jerome and Theophylact[6] refer it
to God, as is evident from their interpretation.

1 assigns] From *1527*; in *1516* and *1522*, *praebuit* 'offers'
2 Jerome *Comm in Gal* 1 (on 3:5) CCL 77A 73:2–5
3 so, too, Ambrose ... reading] Added in *1527*. For the reference see
   Ambrosiaster *Comm in Gal* 3:5.
4 Peter Lombard ... interpretation.] This remaining portion of the annotation was added in *1519*.
5 Peter Lombard *Sententiae* 2.35 PL 192 559
6 Theophylact *Expos in Gal* 3:5 PG 124 985A

3:5 [ER VG] *et operatur virtutes* **'and works miracles.'** *Operatur* [works] refers not to the Spirit but to [God] who does the supplying. This sentence[1] contains an ellipsis,[2] for one must assume *id facit* [does it]. This is
a Hebrew idiom, as I have already pointed out on numerous occasions.[3]

1 This sentence ... occasions.] Added in *1527*
2 Quintilian places the ellipsis (the omission of words necessary for the
   sense) among the faults of expression; cf 1.5.40 and 8.6.21. See Lausberg
   §504, 690–1.
3 For the other occasions on which Erasmus has noted the Hebrew idiom of
   verbal ellipsis see the note and discussion by M. van Poll-van de Lisdonk
   in ASD VI-9 107:770–1n.

3:6 [ER *quemadmodum*]

[VG] *sicut scriptum est* **'as it is written.'**[1] 'As it is written' is redundant. And Jerome has the reading, 'just as Abraham believed God.'[2] Nor does[3] it seem that Ambrose had a different reading, who further observes, 'he [Paul] shows with the example of Abraham, who is the father of faith, etc.'[4] Therefore he adduces an example, not proof from Scripture. Both codices[5] of Constance lend support to the correct reading.

> 1 The late Vulgate addition *scriptum est* 'as it is written' is not attested in most Greek manuscripts. In translating the Pauline epistles Erasmus frequently replaces the Vulgate's *sicut* with *quemadmodum* to render ὡς, ὥσπερ, and καθώς (thus Brown *Novum Testamentum* 26 13(8)n). Modern translations follow Erasmus; eg 'Thus Abraham "believed God, and it was reckoned to him as righteousness"' (RSV).
> 2 Jerome *Comm in Gal* 1 (on 3:7) CCL 77A 74:1
> 3 Nor does ... Scripture.] Added in *1519*
> 4 Ambrosiaster *Comm in Gal* 3:6
> 5 Both codices ... reading.] Added in *1527*

3:7 [ER *scitis igitur* **'for you know'**]

[VG] *cognoscite ergo* **'know therefore'**; Γινώσκετε ἄρα, that is, 'for you know.' And so St Jerome reads, 'for you have learned,'[1] and Ambrose[2] agrees with his reading, although the Greek word can have either meaning.

> 1 Jerome *Comm in Gal* 1 (on 3:7) CCL 77A 74:1
> 2 and Ambrose ... meaning] Added in *1519*. For the reference see Ambrosiaster *Comm in Gal* 3:7. In an earlier version Ambrosiaster's text read *intelligete* [understand], but was changed in a later revision to *cognoscitis* [you realize]. On the indicative rather than imperative mood in γινώσκετε see Lightfoot 137.

3:8 [ER *prius rem laetam nunciavit Abrahae* **'previously has announced the joyful matter to Abraham'**]

[VG] *praenunciavit Abrahae* **'has before announced to Abraham'**; προευηγγελίσατο, that is, 'has previously proclaimed the good news,' to express it thus for the sake of setting it forth in words. For εὐαγγέλιον in Greek means 'good and joyful tiding.' (Although in Homer Ulysses requests[1] an *evangelium*, that is, 'reward,' which is customarily given to those who had been the first to announce a happy matter.)[2] Accordingly that which had been displayed in the gospel of Christ had been promised to Abraham long before the gospel, which here he calls *praeevangelizavit* [has previously proclaimed the good news].

> 1 Ulysses requests] First in *1519*; in *1516*, *Penelope promittit* 'Penelope promises'
> 2 *Odyssey* 14.152

3:9 [ER *itaque qui ex fide sunt, benedicuntur* 'therefore those who are of
faith, are blessed']
[VG] *igitur qui ex fide sunt, benedicentur* 'therefore those who are of
faith, will be blessed'; εὐλογοῦνται, that is, 'are blessed,' in the present
tense. In a promise[1] the verb would be in the future tense, εὐλογηθή-
σονται [will be blessed]; here, in the present. I know that *benedicentur*
[will be well-spoken of] and *benedicuntur* [are being well-spoken of]
is improper Latin, but certain words of this sort can not be avoided
altogether. It could be said as *benedictionem consequentur* [they will obtain blessing]. But not even in this way would the shortcoming of the
language have been avoided. And it may be inferred that Ambrose had
this reading, although the passage is corrupt.[2] At any rate the scholia of
the Greeks accord with his text.[3] The verb[4] in the present tense accords
with what follows.

    1 In a promise ... his text.] Added in *1519*
    2 Ambrosiaster *Comm in Gal* 3:9
    3 Cf Pseudo-Oecumenius *Comm in Gal* 3:7–9 PG 118 1121A–C.
    4 The verb ... follows.] Added in *1527*

3:10 [ER *exsecratione sunt obnoxii* 'they are subject to the curse']
[VG] *sub maledicto sunt* 'they are under reproach'; ὑπὸ κατάραν εἰσί, that
is, 'under the condemnation,' or 'they are under the curse.' It could
have been rendered aptly, 'are subject to the curse.'

3:10 [ER *exsecrabilis omnis* 'cursed (is) everyone']
[VG] *maledictus omnis* 'condemned[1] [is] everyone.'[2] The passage is
the twenty-seventh chapter of Deuteronomy.[3] According to the LXX it is
read thus: *maledictus omnis homo, qui non permanserit in omnibus sermoni-
bus legis hujus, ut faciat illos, & dicet omnis populus, fiat* [cursed is every
man who will not continue in all the words of this law, in order to do
them, and all the people shall say, 'let it be so']. However in Aquila[4]
it says this: *maledictus qui non statuerit verba legis hujus, ut faciat ea, &
dicet omnis populus, vere* [cursed is he who will not have established
the words of this law, in order to do them, and all the people shall say,
'truly']. Symmachus[5] renders it in this way: *maledictus qui non firmaverit
sermones legis istius, ut faciat eos, & dicet omnis populus, amen* [cursed (is)
he who will not have confirmed the words of this law, in order to do
them, and all the people shall say, 'amen']. Theodotion[6] translated it
thus: *maledictus qui non suscitaverit sermones legis hujus facere eos, & dicet
omnis populus, amen* [cursed is the one who will not have stirred up the
words of this law to do them, and all the people shall say, 'amen'].

Jerome adds that just as with the other evidence so too in using this the Apostle was more concerned to convey the sense than the words.[7] Moreover, [he notes that] these words, *omnis homo* [every man] and *in omnibus* [in every man], because they are found only in the LXX have either been added by the LXX or have been erased by the Jews, especially since Jerome had discovered them in the Hebrew books of the Samaritans. But I do not see a reason so serious, why any Jew would wish to erase words that favour the Jews and do not oppose them. For they ought to have wished that the entire race of men be subjected to their Law. And they wished so much that everything which belongs to the Law ought to be observed that they even added many to them.

1 'condemned ... even added many to them.] This entire annotation was added in *1519*.
2 everyone] First in *1535*; previously *homo* 'man' was added to the cue phrase.
3 Cf Deut 27:26
4 Aquila, a Jewish proselyte of the early second century AD, made a very literal rendering of the Hebrew Bible into Greek. His version was included in the *Hexapla* of Origen.
5 Symmachus is known to us almost solely from the fragments of his Greek translation of the Hebrew Bible incorporated into Origen's *Hexapla*. Possibly of Jewish origin, he lived perhaps in the late second and early third centuries AD. The fragments have been edited by F. Field, *Origenis Hexaplorum quae supersunt; sive veterum interpretum Graecorum in totum vetus testamentum fragmenta* 2 vols (Oxford 1867–71).
6 Theodotion (second century AD) translated the Old Testament into Greek. His version is placed in Origen's *Hexapla* after that of the Septuagint.
7 Jerome *Comm in Gal* 2 (on 3:10) CCL 77A 83:17–84:21

3:10 [ER *qui non manserit* 'who has not remained']
[VG] *qui non permanserit* 'who will not have abided';[1] ὃς οὐκ ἐμμένει, that is, *qui non permanet* [who does not abide], even though[2] it does not affect the meaning.

1 In LB this annotation is not separated from the one above ('condemned [is] everyone').
2 even though ... meaning] Added in *1519*

3:11 [ER *quod autem* 'but that']
[VG] *quoniam autem* 'since that';[1] Ὅτι δέ, that is, 'but that.' And this is Ambrose's reading;[2] for 'since' is not fitting in this place.

1 'since that' ... place.] First in *1522*; in *1516* and *1519*, this entire annotation follows the annotation on 3:10 ('they are under reproach') above.
2 Ambrosiaster *Comm in Gal* 3:11

3:11 [ER *ex fide vivet* 'out of faith shall live']

[VG] *ex fide vivit* 'out of faith lives'; *vivet*, ζήσεται, 'shall live,'[1] as I have pointed out earlier in [an annotation on] the Epistle to the Romans.[2] Jerome[3] observes that it can be punctuated thus: 'the just out of faith,' and thereafter is supplied, 'shall live,' so that the sense is, 'who is truly righteous is going to live not from works of the Law, but from faith.' From his commentary it is obvious that he had the reading 'shall live,' not 'lives.' Moreover how differently this text reads in the Greek commentaries has been stated in [the annotation on] the Epistle to the Romans.[4]

1 Cf Valla *Annot in Gal* 3 (I 875): *vivet legendum est,* ζήσεται [it ought to be read as *vivet* 'shall live,' ζήσεται].

2 See the annotation on Rom 1:17 ('lives by faith').

3 Jerome ... Epistle to the Romans.] This remaining portion of the annotation was added in 1519. For the reference see Jerome *Comm in Gal* 2 (on 3:11–12) CCL 77A 86:27–8.

4 See annotation on Rom 1:17 ('lives by faith').

3:13 [ER *ab exsecratione legis* 'from the curse of the Law']

[VG] *de maledicto legis* 'from[1] the slander of the Law'; ἐκ τῆς κατάρας, that is, *ex maledictione* [from the condemnation], as Jerome reads in the second dialogue against the Pelagians, or *detestatione* [renunciation].[2] And a second time, *factus pro vobis maledictum* [having been made a slander for us]; κατάρα, that is, *exsecratio* [a curse]. I wonder why *maledictum* appealed [to the Translator] here, since that word in Latin means[3] something quite different, namely 'insult.'

1 from] In 1516, 1522, and 1527, *ex* 'out of.' In 1516 only, this entire annotation follows the annotation on 3:11 ('since that') above.

2 Jerome *Dialogus adversus Pelagianos* 2.9 CCL 80 66:19–20

3 means] First in 1519; in 1516, *significat* (indicative mood)

3:13 [ER *dum pro vobis*[1] *fact...us est exsecratio* 'when on your behalf he was made a curse']

[VG] *factus pro nobis maledictus* 'having been made slanderous for us'; κατάρα, that is, 'a curse,' as it appears[2] in the oldest copies, or *maledictio* [condemnation], or *exsecratio* [accursedness]. Just as we call someone who is pestilential a pest [*pestis*].

1 Erasmus alters the Vulgate's *nobis* 'us' to *vobis* 'you.'

2 as it appears ... copies] Added in 1519

3:13 [ER *exsecrabilis omnis qui pendet in ligno* 'cursed is everyone who hangs on a tree']

[VG] *maledictus omnis qui pendet in ligno* 'slandered is everyone who hangs on a tree.' The passage is the twenty-first chapter of Deuteronomy.[1] Paul wisely and knowingly, I think, avoided mentioning 'God' in this citation. For Aquila and Theodotion translate 'is the condemnation of God,'[2] the LXX, 'slandered of God.' Symmachus has *in blasphemiam dei suspensus est* [has been hung up to the blasphemy of God].[3] Hebion the arch-heretic, a half-Jew and half-Christian, explains it in this way, ὅτι ὕβρις Θεοῦ ὁ κρεμάμενος, that is, *injuria sive contumelia dei est qui pendet* [God's insult or affront is he who hangs].[4] Jerome adds that in the dispute of Jason and Papiscus, which had been written in Greek, he observed the reading, λοιδορία Θεοῦ ὁ κρεμάμενος, that is, *convitium dei qui pendet* [he who hangs is an insult to God].[5] The Jew Barhanina whom Jerome employed by night as a teacher suggests that the phrase may also be read thus, 'God has been outrageously hanged.'[6] Moreover I wonder why he is so concerned here not to call Christ 'cursed,' since Paul states that the same one has been made 'sin.' Surely just as Christ was sin, so he was also a curse. By a figure[7] of speech was he called sin, and by a figure of speech called curse.

1 Deuteronomy] In *1516* the following sentence was added here: 'The Hebrew has it thus: "he who is hanged is cursed of God."'
2 Aquila and Theodotion are found through Jerome *Comm in Gal* 2 (on 3:13–14) CCL 77A 89:14–19, 89:25–90:30.
3 Symmachus is found through Jerome *Comm in Gal* 2 (on 3:13–14) CCL 77A 89:19–25. He actually reads *quia propter blasphemiam dei suspensus est* [that he has been hung up as a blasphemy to God].
4 Hebion is found through Jerome *Comm in Gal* 2 (on 3:13–14) CCL 77A 90:34–7. Jerome translates the Greek as *quia injuria dei est suspensus* [because of an insult of God he has been hung up].
5 Jerome *Comm in Gal* 2 (on 3:13–14) CCL 77A 90:32–3. Jerome actually reads *maledictio dei qui appensus est* [he who has been hanged is the curse of God].
6 Barhanina's words are found in Jerome *Comm in Gal* 2 (on 3:13–14) CCL 77A 90:40–2. Barhanina was Jerome's instructor of Hebrew when he moved to Bethlehem; see Jerome *Epistolae* 84.3 PL 22 745. For Jerome's knowledge of Hebrew see Hillel Newman 'How Should We Measure Jerome's Hebrew Competence?' in *Jerome of Stridon. His Life, Writings and Legacy* ed A. Cain and J. Lössl (Surrey 2009) 131–40.
7 By a figure ... curse.] Added in *1527*

3:15 [ER *hominis licet testamentum* 'although the testament of a man']

[VG] *tamen hominis confirmatum testamentum* 'nevertheless the confirmed[1] testament of a man'; ὅμως ἀνθρώπου διαθήκην, which could have been rendered, *hominis licet testamentum* [although the testament of a man], so that one immediately assumes how much more that ought to be done in God; yet I observe[2] that what preceded can be joined with it, *secundum hominem loquor* [I speak according to men], that is, 'I shall introduce an example from human affairs, which should in no way be compared with divine affairs.' Yet even in a human testament no one annuls or alters anything – so strong is the force of a man's resolution and agreement.

1 confirmed] Added in 1535
2 yet I observe ... resolution and agreement] Added in 1519

3:15 [ER *tamen si sit comprobatum, nemo rejicit* 'provided it has been ratified, no one rejects']
[VG] *confirmatum testamentum nemo spernit* 'a confirmed testament no one spurns'; κεκυρωμένην διαθήκην οὐδεὶς ἀθετεῖ, that is, a confirmed [*confirmatum*] or ratified [*comprobatum*] testament no one rejects or rescinds [*rescindit*]. ἀθετεῖ a little above he translates *abjicit* [he casts aside]. Ambrose has the reading, *confirmatum auctoritate* [confirmed by authority].[1] Contrary to this is ἀκυροῦν, that is, 'to make ineffective and to rescind.' The participle [*confirmed*][2] is from a verb about which I have made mention in [an annotation on] a previous Epistle:[3] *confirmate in illo charitatem* [confirm in him the love].

1 Ambrosiaster *Comm in Gal* 3:15
2 The participle ... *in illo charitatem.*] Added in 1527. In 1516: '"to rescind." Jerome indicates that in this passage 'testament' means more 'treaty' in Hebrew than 'last will,' which [the Jews] call *Berith.*' For the reference see Jerome *Comm in Gal* 2 (on 3:13–14) CCL 77A 95:36–41.
3 Cf 2 Cor 2:8

3:15 [ER *aut addit* 'or adds']
[VG] *aut superordinat* 'or arranges [anything] above it'; ἐπιδιατάσσεται, that is, *adjungit* [attaches], and 'arranges anything in addition to it,' that is, neither 'removes, nor adds to or subtracts from, nor confers anything upon it.'

3:16 [ER *tanquam de multis* 'as concerning many']
[VG] *quasi in multis* 'as if in many'; ὡς, here *tanquam*, 'as,' would suit better.[1] St Jerome[2] notes in passing that Paul has employed this argument among the coarse Galatians, because he knew that it was not going to be accepted at all by wise and learned men and for that reason he forewarned the wise reader, 'brothers, I speak according to men.'[3]

For he states that in not any place in holy Scriptures does the word
seminis [seed] occur except in the singular.[4] However, the Apostle turns
it into an argument whereby to teach that this promise refers to Christ
alone. To me he seems more to have testified thus that he spoke in the
earthly manner because he was going to draw a comparison between
human affairs and divine matters for the sake of teaching. In this way
also Virgil states, 'if it is permitted to compare small with great things.'[5]

It ought to be known without a special note that the preposition *in*
[in] is used instead of *per* [through]; 'in your seed,' instead of 'through
your seed.' And he calls descendants *semen* [seed].

1 Cf Valla *Annot in Gal* 3 (I 875)
2 St Jerome ... descendants *semen*.] This remaining portion of the annotation
  was added in *1519*.
3 Jerome *Comm in Gal* 2 (on 3:15–18) CCL 77A 94:12–18, 94:34–6
4 Jerome *Comm in Gal* 2 (on 3:15–18) CCL 77A 95:33–6
  On the use of the singular 'seed' to indicate that the promised one is
  Christ, see Lightfoot 142: 'Avoiding the technical terms of grammar, he
  could not express his meaning more simply than by the opposition "not
  to thy seeds, but to thy seed."' For a more recent treatment of Paul's argument here see C. John Collins 'Galatians 3:16: What Kind of Exegete was
  Paul?' *Tyndale Bulletin* 54 (2003) 75–86.
5 Virgil *Georgics* 4.176; cf *Eclogues* 1.23.

3:17 [ER *testamentum ante comprobatum a deo* 'the testament previously
ratified by God']

[VG] *testamentum confirmatum a deo* 'the testament confirmed by
God'; διαθήκην προκεκυρωμένην ὑπὸ τοῦ Θεοῦ εἰς Χριστόν, that is, *testamentum ante confirmatum a deo in Christum* [the testament previously
confirmed by God unto Christ]. *In Christum* [unto Christ] is added in
the Greek copies, and likewise in Ambrose.[1] St Jerome[2] advises on this
passage that if one thoroughly weighs the evidence of the Hebrew volumes, that whenever the LXX translates διαθήκην, that is, 'testament,' the
Hebrew word is בְּרִית ['berith'], which means 'covenant' [treaty] rather
than testament. For faith[3] is required in covenants. But, according to St
Jerome, among the coarse Galatians Paul did not think that one has to
deal so precisely. As if in truth Paul did not follow the edition of the LXX
in numerous other places too.

But now[4] about the number of years, whether they actually accord with the account in Genesis, St Augustine clearly explains in the
twenty-fourth chapter of the sixteenth book of the *City of God* [5] – lest we
should burden this undertaking with more than enough appendices.

1 Ambrosiaster *Comm in Gal* 3:17. Ambrosiaster actually reads *in Christo* 'in Christ.'
The phrase εἰς Χριστόν is omitted in modern editions of the New Testament, on the grounds that it is a gloss; cf Metzger 525.
2 St Jerome ... rather than testament.] See the annotations on Gal 3:15 ('a confirmed testament no one spurns') n2 above. For the reference see Jerome *Comm in Gal* 2 (on 3:15–18) CCL 77A 95:36–41.
3 For faith ... covenants.] Added in *1519*
4 But now ... appendices.] Added in *1519*
5 Augustine *De civitate dei* 16.24 CCL 48 527:70–528:102

3:17 [ER *non facit irritum* 'does not make void']
[VG] *non irritum facit* 'does not void make'; οὐκ ἀκυροῖ,[1] which is the opposite to κυρόω, which is not so much 'to sanction' as 'to determine with authority,' and to perform a matter legally, so that thereupon what has been done is considered binding.

1 BDAG defines ἀκυρόω as 'make void.'

3:18 [ER *per promissionem donavit deus* 'through the promise God has granted']
[VG] *per repromissionem donavit deus* 'through the formal promise God has granted'; κεχάρισται [granted], a word from χάρις, a saying from *gratia* [grace], which Paul everywhere opposes to the works of the Mosaic Law.[1]

1 For a fuller discussion of the verb see Erasmus' treatment of it in his annotation on Eph 1:6 ('in which he has graced') and n1 there.

3:19 [ER *quid igitur lex? propter transgressiones* 'what then the Law? On account of transgressions']
[VG] *quid igitur lex, propter transgressiones* 'what then the Law, on account of transgressions?' Augustine in the Commentary bids that it be divided thus, *quid ergo?* [what then?], and that thereafter the reply be attached to it, *lex propter transgressores addita fuit* [the Law was added on account of the transgressors].[1] And this[2] division appears in each codex of Constance. But he withdraws [the suggestion], and he thinks it is better to divide it just as I have divided it: *quid ergo lex?* [what then the Law?]. And that thereupon Paul's reply to himself, *propter transgressiones addita fuit* [it was added on account of transgressions]. This division[3] he learned, as I think, from the Greek copies; for thus Theophylact: τί οὖν ὁ νόμος [what then the Law?].[4]

1 Augustine *Expos Gal* CSEL 84 86:8–11. Augustine actually reads *lex trans-gressionis gratia proposita est* 'the Law was promulgated for the sake of transgression.'
2 And this ... Constance.] Added in *1527*. For more information on the manuscripts from Constance see the annotation on Gal 1:3 ('from God our Father') n3 and CWE 56 xii.
3 This division ... ὁ νομός.] Added in *1527*
4 Theophylact *Expos in Gal* 3:19 PG 124 992A

3:19 [ER *addita fuit* 'it was added']

[VG] *posita est* 'it was placed';[1] προσετέθη, that is, 'it was added,' or 'it was applied to,' unless you read προετέθη [it was set up previously]; but Theophylact[2] has the reading προσετέθη, and explains it thoroughly enough. For [Paul] did not say 'placed,' but 'added,' lest anyone should hold it in special esteem, but that it was joined to it in passing between the first promise and the gospel.

1 'it was placed' ... the gospel.] In *1516*, this entire annotation and all of the next follow the annotation on 3:17 ('does not void make') above.
2 but Theophylact ... the gospel] Added in *1527*. Theophylact *Expos in Gal* 3:19 PG 124 992B

3:19 [ER *cui promissum fuerat* 'to whom the promise had been made']

[VG] *cui promiserat* 'to whom he had promised.' In a certain codex I read ὃ ἐπήγγελται, namely, 'that which had been promised.' In others[1] was [the reading] ᾧ [to whom]. For I do not think that in Greek the same happens in the nominative as in the oblique cases in construc-tions of this sort, namely that the postpositive article agrees with the preceding and not with its own verb, except that[2] in Greek they are said 'to be evangelized' to whom the news is brought. By this turn of phrase the sense would be the same whether one reads ὃ [who] or ᾧ [to whom]. Theophylact reads ᾧ.[3]

1 In others ... its own verb] Added in *1519*
2 except that ... reads ᾧ] Added in *1527*
3 Theophylact *Expos in Gal* 3:19 PG 124 992B

3:19 [ER *in manu intercessoris* 'in the hand[1] of an intercessor']

[VG] *in manu mediatoris* 'in the hand of a mediator'; μεσίτου. Perhaps this too is one of those words we cannot change as they are peculiar to divine Scripture, unless *conciliator* [intermediary], or *intercessor* [inter-cessary] is acceptable.[2] At this place[3] Jerome brings to mind hyperbaton[4] and he restored the mixed arrangement of the words in the following

way: 'The Law was laid down through angels by the hand of the mediator, on account of transgressions, ordained through angels, until the
seed should come to whom the promise was made.'⁵

1 'in the hand ... acceptable.] Added in 1519. The modern Vulgate maintains
the reading *iam pridem* (Weber 1806).
2 Perhaps ... acceptable.] Whereas most of the Fathers held that the 'intercessor' is Christ, modern scholars concur that it is Moses; see Lightfoot
146.
3 At this place ... *repromissum erat.*] Added in 1522
4 For hyperbaton see the annotation on Gal 1:6 ('into the grace of Christ') n4.
5 Jerome *Comm in Gal* 2 (on 3:19–20) CCL 77A 98:45–99:49. The order in the
Latin text is: *lex posita est per Angelos in manu mediatoris, propter transgressiones ordinata per Angelos, donec veniret semen, cui repromissum erat.*

3:24 [ER *paedagogus noster fuit ad Christum* 'was our pedagogue to Christ']
[VG] *paedagogus noster fuit in Christo* 'was our pedagogue in Christ.'
In Christum [unto Christ] or *ad Christum* [to Christ] would be better in
this passage: εἰς Χριστόν. And in fact this was Jerome's reading in the
second dialogue against the Pelagians.¹ For *paedagogus*² [pedagogue] in
Greek is a common word for the slave who is entrusted with the care of
a boy for a time, so that he does not do any mischief on account of his
young age, [a word] derived from the act of leading a boy, with which
'to Christ' (which follows) fits better.³

1 Jerome *Dialogus adversus Pelagianos* 2.9 CCL 80 66:23–4
2 For *paedagogus* ... fits better.] Added in 1527
3 In *Hyperaspistes* 2 Erasmus argues that the singular aim of the Law as tutor was to avoid baseness and promote honourable conduct. He explains
Paul's use of the tutor-metaphor thus: 'to keep the child from what is base
by means of shame or fear, lest he become so thoroughly spoiled that he
will not learn from philosophers or listen to his father's admonitions' CWE
77 363. In *Declarationes ad censuras Lutetiae vulgatas*, Erasmus adduces Gal
3:24 in support of the argument that unlike the gospel of love the Law
struck terror into people's hearts: when Paul 'calls the Law a tutor preparing for Christ, does he not attribute terror to it without charity?' CWE 82
91.

3:24 [ER *ut ex fide justificaremur* 'so that out of faith we would be justified']
[VG] *ut ex fide justificemur* 'so that out of faith we are justified.'
Ambrose has the reading, '[that] we would be justified,' ἵνα δικαιωθῶμεν.¹

1 Ambrosiaster *Comm in Gal* 3:24. Ambrosiaster actually reads *iustificemur*
'that we might be justified.'

3:28 [ER *non est masculus ac foemina* 'there is neither male and female']
[VG] *non est masculus neque foemina* 'there is neither male nor female.'** In the other phrases he used the conjunction[1] *neque* [nor]; in this final combination he employed καὶ [and], which conjunction nevertheless has the same force, ἄρσεν καὶ θῆλυ [male and female]. Jerome points out that here Ἕλληνα, that is, 'Greek,'[2] is put for 'gentile.'[3]

1 the conjunction] Added in *1519*
2 that is, 'Greek'] Added in *1519*
3 Jerome *Comm in Gal* 2 (on 3:27–8) CCL 77A 102:29–30

3:28 [ER *omnes enim vos unus estis* 'for you are all one']
[VG] *omnes enim vos unum estis* 'for you are all one thing.' Jerome[1] seems to have the reading *unum* [one (thing)], and so too Ambrose[2] and Augustine,[3] except[4] that one gets the impression Ambrose had read *unus* [one person], and not *unum* [one thing], from the following words he inserts, 'with God there is no discrimination of external status, but only of morals and life, so that men of one faith are distinguished according to their merits, not their external status.' But the Greek [texts] read 'one person,' in the masculine gender, εἷς ἐστέ [you are one (man)],[5] and Theophylact gives the interpretation: whether because we already[6] have put on the form of Christ,[7] or because[8] we are one body under one head, Christ.[9] Now Chrysostom[10] has the reading *unus* [one person], but the explanation is such that it even suits the reading *unum* [one thing]. And to me the reading we have commends itself more, except that with great consistency the Greek copies differ with it. However,[11] I do not see why we should shrink back from this turn of phrase by which we are all called one, since they are also called one or of one mind by this turn of phrase.

1 Jerome *Comm in Gal* 2 (on 3:27–8) CCL 77A 101:3–4; 103:44–6
2 Ambrosiaster *Comm in Gal* 3:28
3 Augustine *Expos Gal* CSEL 84 93:24, 94:2
4 except ... their external status'] Added in *1527*
5 Cf Valla *Annot in Gal* 3 (I 875): *Graece non est unum, sed unus homo, sive ut Graeci exponunt, una forma et unum corpus*, εἷς [in Greek it is not 'one,' but 'one man,' or as the Greeks explain, 'one form and one body,' εἷς].
6 already] First in *1535*; previously *tam* 'so, to such a degree'
7 of Christ] First in *1535*; previously *Christo* 'in Christ'
8 or because ... Christ] Added in *1527*
9 Theophylact *Expos in Gal* 3:28 PG 124 996B
10 Now Chrysostom ... *unum*.] Added in *1535*. For the reference see Chrysostom *Comm in Gal* 3.5 PG 61 656.
11 However ... by this turn of phrase.] Added in *1527*

3:29 [ER *quod si vos estis Christi* 'but if you are of Christ']

[VG] *si autem vos Christi* 'however if you [are] of Christ.' In this place
I observe that the ancients had three different readings. St Jerome reads
in the following way, which I have ascertained from the copies of the
Greeks: εἰ δὲ ὑμεῖς Χριστοῦ, that is, *quod si vos estis Christi* [but if you are
of Christ].¹ St Augustine reads with this arrangement, *omnes vos unum
estis in Christo Iesu* [all of you are one (thing) in Christ Jesus]; thereupon
he adds, *quod si* [but if], so that following an interposed break here one
assumes, *vos estis unum in Christo* [you are one in Christ], and thereafter
is added 'therefore you are the seed of Abraham.'² But now Ambrose
explains what Augustine thinks must be assumed, and reads in this
manner: 'If therefore you are one in Christ Jesus, then you are the seed
of Abraham.'³ Here Jerome explains that whenever mention is made
of Christ, the promises are placed in the plural number, just as in the
passage, 'but to Abraham the promises have been stated, and to his
seed, that is to Christ.'⁴ On the other hand when it concerns those who
through Christ are of Abraham, the singular number [obtains], as in
the text [Gal 3:29], κατ' ἐπαγγελίαν κληρονόμοι [according to the promise,
heirs].

1 Jerome *Comm in Gal* 2 (on 3:29) CCL 77A 103:1. Jerome actually reads *Si
autem vos Christi* 'if however you [are] of Christ.'
2 Augustine *Expos Gal* CSEL 84 93:24–94:5
3 Ambrosiaster *Comm in Gal* 3:29. Ambrosiaster actually reads *si igitur
omnes vos unum estis*, etc. [Therefore if you are all one, etc.].
4 Jerome *Comm in Gal* 2 (on 3:29) CCL 77A 103:13–16

From the Fourth Chapter

4:1 [ER VG] *dico autem* 'but I say.' Paul is accustomed to speak in this manner whenever he begins to explain what he has said.¹ Accordingly, 'what
I say is this' would be more clear, or, 'but this is what I am saying.'

1 Cf Rom 15:8; 1 Cor 1:12; 1 Cor 7:8; 1 Cor 15:50; Eph 4:17; Col 2:4.

4:1 [ER *haeres puer est* 'the heir is a boy']

[VG] *haeres parvulus est* 'the heir is a little child'; νήπιος, that is, 'boy'
or 'infant,' and of¹ that age which does not yet have good sense.²
However³ the Translator has translated it into Latin [well].

1 and of ... sense] Added in *1519*

2 have good sense] From *1522*; in *1519*, *sapiat* (subjunctive mood). Cf
Erasmus' annotation on Rom 2:20: '*νήπιος* when it refers to age means
"infant"; when it refers to the mind it means "insufficiently instructed,
not much developed in ability and experience"' cwe 56 85.

3 However ... Latin.] Added in *1527*

4:1 [ER VG] *nihil differt a servo* 'he differs nothing from a slave'; *διαφέρει*
has more than one possible meaning. For it means also 'to surpass';
but in this passage it makes no difference. In fact,[1] he is put under the
authority of the slave.

1 In fact ... slave.] Added in *1527*

4:2 [ER VG] *tutoribus et actoribus* 'guardians and stewards';[1] *ἐπιτρόπους καὶ*
οἰκονόμους, that is, under *curatores et dispensatores* [trustees and legal
guardians], that is, managers [*procuratores*] of the household affairs. But
Jerome[2] and Ambrose,[3] and likewise Augustine,[4] have the reading *sub*
actoribus [under agents], for *οἰκονόμοις*,[5] who manage the affairs of those
below the age of majority. But in fact *tutores* [guardians] are assigned to
orphans, while to the insane and to adolescents[6] *curatores* [trustees] are
assigned, who administer business on their behalf, although[7] I think
that these also are called *actores*. *Actor* is[8] a word with two-fold meaning; the first Greek[9] word is said of granted control or right, the latter of
the administration of household affairs.

1 stewards'] First in *1519*; in *1516*, *autoribus* 'authorities.' BDAG defines *ἐπί-*
τροπος here as 'guardian,' *οἰκονόμος* as 'manager of a household or estate.'

2 Jerome *Comm in Gal* 2 (on 4:1–2) CCL 77A 104:2–3

3 Ambrosiaster *Comm in Gal* 4:2

4 and likewise Augustine] Added in *1519*. For the reference see Augustine
Expos Gal CSEL 84 94:20.

5 for *οἰκονόμοις* ... majority] Added in *1527*. In *1516*, *1519*, and *1522*, (text in
boldface appeared in the *1516* edition only) ... *actoribus*, **vitiata ut opinor**
scriptura, *pro autoribus, sic enim vocantur, quorum autoritate res geritur.*
Nam quod tum egerit pupillus [*1516*: **pupillis**], *ratum non habetur.* Porro ...
'..."agents," as I think the scriptural text has been corrupted, in place of
"authorities," for thus are called the people by whose authority the affair
is managed. For that which an orphan does is moreover not considered
valid. But ...'

6 and to adolescents] Added in *1519*

7 although ... *actores*] Added in *1519*

8 *Actor* is ... meaning] Added in *1527*

9 the first Greek ... household affairs] Added in *1535*

4:2 [ER *tempus quod pater praescripserit* 'the time that the father had prescribed']

[VG] *praefinitum tempus* 'the fixed time'; προθεσμίας. This word means a prescribed [moment of time or day] to which someone's right is valid, beyond[1] which it is not permitted to act; such is the right of guardians [*tutores*].

    1 beyond ... guardians] Added in 1527

4:3 [ER *pueri* 'boys']

[VG] *parvuli* 'little children'; νήπιοι. About which [word] I have already very often commented.[1]

    1 Cf Erasmus' explanation of νήπιος 'boy' in the annotation on Gal 4:1 ('the heir is a little child'), and on Rom 2:20 ('master of infants') in CWE 56 85.

4:3 [ER *sub elementis mundi eramus in servitutem adacti* 'we had been forced into slavery under the elements of the universe']

[VG] *sub elementis mundi eramus servientes* 'we were serving as slaves under the elements of the universe'; δεδουλωμένοι, that is, 'driven to slavery,' which Ambrose reads 'made subject,'[1] and it seems the word should be applied to 'under the elements,' ὑπὸ τὰ στοιχεῖα, as if[2] one would say, 'under the elements into slavery driven.' The Latin[3] word *elementum* has a two-fold meaning, even as στοιχεῖον in Greek, which sometimes means the beginning or origin of something that is coming into being, and sometimes individual letters of the alphabet.[4] For also Aristotle, in *The Physics*, provides a review of στοιχεῖα among those things from which the understanding of things arises, that is, 'elements,' which he places under the category of principles and causes.[5] And Justinian calls his books of *Institutes* the 'Elements of the law,' as though primary lessons.[6] Paul employed the same word in the Epistle to the Colossians [2:8]: 'See to it that no one makes a prey of you by philosophy and empty deceit, according to human tradition, according to the elements of the universe,' κατὰ τὰ στοιχεῖα τοῦ κόσμου. And again in the same Epistle [2:20]: 'if with Christ you died from the elemental things,' ἀπὸ τῶν στοιχείων. And I do not perceive why St Jerome wishes *elementum* to have one meaning in this passage to the Galatians and another meaning in the Epistle to the Colossians.[7] Surely in both passages [Paul] is treating the ceremonies of the Jews, and the precepts of men, which have been granted as mere starting points to people still untrained and not able to grasp the teaching of the Gospel. Nor is what he writes to the Hebrews [5:12] different from these [usages], 'and though you ought to be teachers by this time, you again need to have someone to teach you what are the first principles of God's words,' τίνα τὰ στοιχεῖα τῆς ἀρχῆς. This meaning appears to me to be the true one, while the other ones, in my opinion, display the pedantry or tendency of the Translator rather than the mind of Paul. Nor is there any reason why Paul's addition 'elements of the universe' should affect our position. For he calls whatever may be seen and is transitory 'universe'; among matters of this sort is placed the superstitious belief in ceremonies: 'do not taste, do not touch, do not handle.'[8]

> 1 Ambrosiaster *Comm in Gal* 4:3. Erasmus' rendering *adacti* (perfect participle passive) reflects the tense in the Greek participle δεδουλωμένοι more accurately than the Vulgate's *servientes* (present participle).
> Erasmus' explanation of στοιχεῖον follows that of Ambrosiaster, who takes the word to mean the new moons and sabbaths observed by the Jews and which were granted to them as to children. Jerome relates two possible interpretations, namely that the 'elements' are the angels who have jurisdiction over the fundamental elements of the universe, or the Mosaic law and prophetic teachings. For a summary of the patristic interpretations of this expression see Lightfoot 167. See also the discussion of στοιχεῖον in BDAG, which reports the modern interpretations of the word as divided between elementary forms of religion and elemental spirits associated with the physical elements.
> 2 as if ... do not touch] Added in *1519*
> 3 Latin] From *1527*; in *1519* and *1522*, *Graeca* 'Greek'
> 4 For an explanation of this secondary meaning, cf the annotation on Gal 4:25 ('for it is joined to what is now Jerusalem') below.
> 5 Aristotle *Physica* 1 184a10–12
> 6 Justinian *Constitutio tanta* 23 (*Corpus iuris civilis* ed Th. Mommsen and P. Krüger, 3 vols [Berlin 1868–1895] I 23)
> 7 Jerome *Comm in Gal* 2 (on 4:3) CCL 77A 107:29–35
> 8 do not handle'] Added in *1527*. For the reference see Col 2:21.

4:4 [ER *emisit deus filium suum* 'God sent forth his own son']
[VG] *misit deus filium suum* 'God sent his own son'; ἐξαπέστειλεν, that is, 'sent forth,' or rather, 'commissioned,' namely, with orders. That is the strict meaning of the Greek word, for the other ['to send'] is πέμπειν.

4:4 [ER VG] *factum ex muliere* 'made from[1] woman.' The former 'made' in the Greek is γεννώμενον, the latter γενόμενον, so that one should translate the first one 'born,' the second 'was made' – although not all[2] the Greek codices make this distinction.[3] At any rate[4] Theophylact in both places has the reading γενόμενον [was made].[5] And Augustine, in the third chapter of the book *On the Trinity and Unity of God*, cites it this way: 'God sent his own son, born of woman, made under the Law,' and again in chapter six of the same work.[6] In this passage,[7] however, 'made' means nothing other than placed under the Law; in the same manner one who has turned pale is said to have been 'made pale' – lest on the basis of this passage anyone should moralize about what has been created.

1 from] Latin *ex*; in *1516, est*
2 all] Added in *1519*
3 The word γεννώμενον, with double ν, from γεννάω ('bring forth,' 'bear') means 'begotten,' while γενόμενον, with single ν, from γίγνομαι ('to become,' 'to be'). Cf Erasmus' annotation on Rom 1:3 ('who was made to him') n3 and n6. Edward Lee criticized Erasmus for making this distinction (fol LX[V]I). See further the annotation on Gal 1:5 ('to whom is the glory') n3.
4 At any rate ... γενόμενον.] Added in *1527*
5 Theophylact *Expos in Gal* 4:4 PG 124 997A–B
6 Pseudo-Augustine *De trinitate et unitate dei* 1.3 PL 42 1197
7 In this passage ... has been created.] Added in *1527*

4:5 [ER VG] *redimeret* **'redeem';** ἐξαγοράσῃ, which literally means 'to buy out,' that is, to lead out to freedom upon paying the price, which you[1] could express as 'to set free' [*eximere*].

1 which you ... free'] Added in *1527*

4:5 [ER *ut adoptione* **'so that by adoption'**]
[VG] *ut adoptionem* **'so that**[1] **(we might receive) the adoption.'**[2] In Greek there is only one word, υἱοθεσίαν, which the Translator, in order to express it more fully, has rendered by means of periphrasis [circumlocution],[3] because the meaning of 'adoption' seems to extend further.

1 'so that ... further.] First in *1519*; in *1516* this entire annotation was placed after the annotation on 4:6 ('into your hearts') below.
2 Erasmus' point in this annotation is that the Vulgate has rendered the one Greek word υἱοθεσίαν with two words, *adoptionem filiorum* 'the adoption of sons.' Erasmus maintains this periphrasis in his translation.
3 Periphrasis is the 'paraphrasing of one word by several words' (Lausberg §589).

4:5 [ER *acciperemus* **'we should receive'**]
[VG] *reciperemus* **'we should**[1] **get back';**[2] ἀπολάβωμεν. Augustine notes that it stated 'we should get back,' not 'we should receive,' so that we would understand it to mean that what had been lost is restored.[3] This interpretation would be more suitable if the Greek said ἀναλάβωμεν [we should regain].

1 'we should ... ἀναλάβωμεν.] This entire annotation was added in *1535*.

2 In LB this annotation is not separated from the one above ('so that we might receive the adoption of sons').

3 Augustine *Expos Gal* CSEL 84 96:11–13

4:6 [ER *quoniam autem estis filii* 'but because you are sons']
[VG] *quoniam autem estis filii dei* 'but because you are sons of God.'
'God' is redundant, according[1] to the unanimous reading of the Greek [texts], nor does it affect the sense very much,[2] since it pertains only to the nature of the children. However,[3] all the Latin [copies] which I have seen differ from this reading, with the exception[4] of the oldest Donatian codex.

1 according ... Greek] Added in *1527*
2 very much] Added in *1519*
3 However ... reading] Added in *1519*
4 with the exception ... codex] Added in *1522*

4:6 [ER VG] *in corda vestra* 'into your hearts'; ἡμῶν, that is, 'our,' and each[1] of the codices of Constance and Ambrose[2] and Jerome[3] are in agreement with the Greek ones. However, because 'you are' preceded, the insufficiently attentive reader corrupted Scripture. And[4] as was demonstrated somewhat earlier,[5] Ἀββὰ ὁ Πατήρ, 'Abba Father,'[6] is not ἀναδίπλωσις [repetition][7] according to Jerome,[8] with the agreement of Augustine[9] and, if I am not mistaken, Ambrose.[10] Now 'Abba' is a foreign word, common to Hebrew and Syrian which he explains by means of the added Greek word – a practice specific to divine Scripture, so that Bartimaeus is 'son of Timaeus' in the Gospel,[11] Aser is 'wealth,'[12] Tabitha is 'dorcas' [gazelle] in Acts;[13] and in Genesis[14] Mesech is 'native,' and [there are] other expressions like these.[15]

1 and each ... Scripture] Added in *1527*
   The reading ἡμῶν is attested by a variety of early witnesses, and so is preferred to ὑμῶν by most modern critics; cf Metzger 526. Cf A.J. Brown 'Whether Erasmus was correct to prefer ἡμῶν may be questioned. Although sudden changes of subject are fairly frequent in the Pauline epistles, the particular problem of ἡμῶν here is that it places in the mouth of the apostle a seemingly illogical inference: that because *you* (the Galatians) are sons, therefore God has sent the spirit of his son into *our* hearts. By adopting this reading, Erasmus in effect embraces the principle of *difficilior potior*, i.e. that the harder reading is more likely to be genuine' *Novum Testamentum* 473:6(3)n.
2 Ambrosiaster *Comm in Gal* 4:6
3 Jerome *Comm in Gal* 2 (on 4:6) CCL 77A 110:2
4 And] First in *1527*; previously *abba pater* 'Abba Father'
5 Cf the annotation on Mark 14:36 (*Abba Pater*) and also the annotation on Rom 8:15 ('Abba, Father') CWE 56 211.

6 'Abba Father' ... expressions like these] This remaining portion of the
annotation was added in *1519*.

7 Roman rhetoricians regarded *repetitio* [repetition] as a figure capable
of conveying important effects. See *Rhetorica ad Herennium* 4.13.19 and
Quintilian 9.1.33, and, for a noteworthy example, Cicero *Pro Caecina* 9.24.
Cf also *Ecclesiastes* III ASD V-5 108:74–88.

8 Jerome *Comm in Gal* 2 (on 4:6) CCL 77A 111:40–112:45

9 Augustine *Expos Gal* CSEL 84 97:3–4

10 Ambrosiaster *Comm in Gal* 4:6

11 Cf Mark 10:46.

12 Cf Gen 49:20.

13 Cf Acts 9:36.

14 Cf Gen 15:3. For Jerome's use of Mesech in this context, cf *Liber quaestionum hebraicarum in Genesim* PL 23 (1845) 999B–1000A.

15 Jerome *Comm in Gal* 2 (on 4:6) CCL 77A 112:45–6

4:7 [ER *iam non es servus* '**no longer are you a slave'**]
[VG] *iam non est servus* '**now he is not a slave.**' 'You are' (*εἶ*), in the
second person, not the third. In some[1] copies it is left out altogether;
there is only *οὐκέτι δοῦλος* [no longer a slave], so that one assumes 'he
is' or, if you prefer, 'you are.' And the Translator likes his *iam* [now] too
much, on other occasions deriving pleasure from variety even when it
is ill-suited.
οὐκέτι εἶ, that is, 'no longer are you,' 'no more are you.'

1 In some ... 'you are.'] Added in *1519*

4:7 [ER *et haeres dei per Christum* '**and heir of God through Christ'**]
[VG] *et haeres per deum* '**and heir through God'**; 'and heir of God
through Christ,' *καὶ κληρονόμος Θεοῦ διὰ Χριστοῦ*. Jerome[1] has the reading, 'and heirs through Christ,' leaving aside mention of God.[2] Ambrose[3]
and Augustine[4] have the same reading as our edition. To me the reading Jerome has commends itself more. Moreover 'of God' seems to have
been added by some Translator. For 'heir' would be more effective in opposition to 'slave' if you did not add another word. And finally, it is customary for Paul to add 'through Christ,' as he wishes all God's benefits
to emanate from the Father in such a way that they come through Christ
the Son to us, as if grafted into Christ. Through him[5] by adoption we
are both sons and heirs. At this point in the text Theophylact has more,
reading thus: *εἰ δὲ υἱὸς κληρονόμος, κληρονόμος μὲν Θεοῦ συγκληρονόμος δὲ
Χριστοῦ*, that is, 'but if a son then an heir, heir of God and fellow heir with
Christ.'[6] And as his reading is, so too is his explanation. But what was
added here appears copied from chapter 8 of the Epistle to the Romans.[7]

1 Jerome ... as if grafted into Christ.] Added in *1519*

2 Jerome *Comm in Gal* 2 (on 4:7) CCL 77A 112:1–2, and the apparatus there. Modern scholarship prefers the reading καὶ κληρονόμος διὰ Θεοῦ because it is attested by various early witnesses, accounts for the origins of the variant readings, and is not contrary to Pauline practice (eg 1 Cor 1:9); thus Metzger 526–7.
3 Ambrosiaster *Comm in Gal* 4:7
4 Augustine *Expos Gal* CSEL 84 99:7–8
5 Through him ... Epistle to the Romans.] This remaining portion of the annotation was added in 1527.
6 Theophylact *Expos in Gal* 4:6–7 PG 124 997C. Theophylact actually reads: εἰ δὲ υἱος καὶ κληρονόμος [but if a son then *also* an heir].
7 Cf Rom 8:17

4:9 [ER *posteaquam cognovistis* 'after you have come to know']
[VG] *cum cognoveritis* 'when you knew'; Νῦν δὲ γνόντες Θεόν, that is, 'but now, after you have come to know God.'[1]

1 Cf Valla *Annot in Gal* 4 (I 875). Erasmus used the adverb *posteaquam* more frequently than the Vulgate, as it allowed him to change a present participle in the Greek into a temporal clause (Brown *Novum Testamentum* 474:9(2)n).

4:9 [ER *quin potius cogniti estis a deo* 'nay rather, you have come to be known by God']
[VG] *imo cogniti sitis* 'yes and more, you have come to be known';[1] μᾶλλον δέ, that is, 'and what is more'; and thus reads Jerome.[2] But 'more' in this passage more precisely has the sense of correction [that is, 'rather'] than of comparison.

1 you have come to be known'] First in 1535; previously *cogniti estis* (indicative mood)
2 Jerome *Comm in Gal* 2 (on 4:8–9) CCL 77A 113:2–3

4:9 [ER *quibus iterum ab integro* 'to which a second time over again']
[VG] *quibus denuo* 'to which again.' For 'again' the Greek is πάλιν ἄνωθεν, that is, 'back from the beginning.' And the ἀναδίπλωσις [repetition][1] makes for a vigorous style. I rendered it[2] 'a second time over again.'

1 See the annotation on Gal 4:7 ('into your hearts') n7.
2 I rendered ... again.'] Added in 1527. For Erasmus' translation of ἄνωθεν elsewhere in the New Testament see Brown's note in ASD VI-2 37:3(2)n.

4:10 [ER VG] *et tempora* 'and times'; καιρούς, that is, 'opportunities.' For the word is not χρόνους [times of day]. These opportune times pertain to the festivals of the Jews, for whom[1] this or that was permitted or was not permitted.

1 for whom ... not permitted] Added in 1527

4:11 [ER *metuo de vobis* 'I am afraid concerning you']

[VG] *timeo ne* 'I fear lest'; φοβοῦμαι ὑμᾶς, that is, 'I fear [for] you.' And such is Ambrose's reading,[1] and likewise[2] Augustine;[3] nor does it occur differently in the ancient copies. It could be rendered, 'I fear about you.'

1 Ambrosiaster *Comm in Gal* 4:11
2 and likewise ... copies] Added in *1519*
3 Augustine *Expos Gal* CSEL 84 104:2

4:12 [ER *fratres, rogo vos* 'brothers, I ask you']

[VG] *fratres, obsecro vos* 'brothers, I beseech you'; δέομαι ὑμῶν, that is, 'I ask you.' St Jerome wishes that these words be referred to the preceding in the following way: 'brothers, I entreat you, be as I am, for I [was also] as you [now are].'[1] That is,[2] 'discard Jewish superstition, which you see I have discarded.' Or, 'make progress towards my perfection, seeing that I have modified my own behaviour to suit your weakness.' For Valla prefers *ut* [as] to *sicut* [just as], not only here but also in the next clause.[3]

1 Jerome *Comm in Gal* 2 (on 4:12–13) CCL 77A 121:5–8. Jerome actually reads *obsecro vos, fratres,* **estote** *sicut et ego,* **quia** *et ego* **sicut** *vos* [I beseech you, brothers, you shall be just as I am, because I was just as you are].
2 That is ... weakness.'] Added in *1519*
3 Valla *Annot in Gal* 4 (I 875)

4:13 [ER *prius* 'former']

[VG] *iam pridem* 'long ago.' The Greek is 'former,' πρότερον.[1]

1 LSJ defines πρότερον as 'former, earlier.' The modern Vulgate maintains the reading *iam pridem* (Weber 1806).

4:14 [ER *experimentum mei* 'my trial']

[VG] *tentationem vestram* 'your testing'; πειρασμόν μου, that is, 'my testing,' or 'the testing from me';[1] surely 'my testing,' so that you would understand that Paul had tested the pulse of the Galatians by means of his own simple and unrefined manner of speaking. But the Greek word is uncertain in meaning, and Jerome explains it in various ways.[2] Evidently[3] the testing of the Galatians was that a simple man who was also subject to human hardships preached Christ crucified and promised not a single splendid thing in addition to that except immortality. Or to be sure, that he laboured there with ill health, and although they saw that his wretched body was afflicted with ills, they still believed him when he preached eternal life. For there are those who think that Paul had been afflicted with a constant headache, and that this was called by him the thorn of Satan.[4] Or (what is actually closer to the truth),⁵ that they observed their own Apostle weighed down with insults, troubled by verbal attacks, scourged with whips, buried under rocks. These things were capable of diminishing their admiration of him. But we do not read⁶ that either the Lord or the apostles laboured under the burden of any illness.

1 Erasmus is following Valla here, *Annot in Gal* 4 (I 875): *nec tentationem vestram, sed meam, μοῦ* [not your (pl.) test, but mine].
Modern editions of the Greek New Testament prefer the reading *τὸν πειρασμὸν ὑμῶν* (see Metzger 527), which is followed by the Vulgate (Weber 1806), though modern translations are divided (AV 'my trial,' RSV 'a trial to you').

2 Jerome *Comm in Gal* 2 (on 4:14) CCL 77A 123:51–124:90

3 Evidently ... admiration of him.] Added in *1519*

4 See Erasmus' annotation on 2 Cor 12:7 (*et ne magnitudo*) for explanations of what this 'thorn' could be. See also Jerome *Comm in Gal* 2 (on 4:14) CCL 77A 124:79–82 *nam tradunt eum gravissimum capitis dolorem saepe perpessum; et hunc esse angelum Satanae, qui appositus ei sit, ut eum colaphizaret in carne, ne extolleretur* [for they relate that he often endured severe headaches; and that this was the messenger of Satan appointed to him, to buffet him in the flesh, lest he become conceited].

5 (what is actually closer to the truth)] Added in *1535*. Erasmus prefers the interpretation that Paul's affliction consisted in the persecutions he endured and not some physical malady. The former explanation is offered by Augustine *Expos Gal* CSEL 84 105:15–17. For a summary assessment of patristic interpretations of Paul's 'infirmity in the flesh' see Lightfoot 186–91.

6 But we do not read ... illness.] Added in *1535*

4:15 [ER *quae est igitur* 'what then is']
[VG] *ubi est ergo* 'where then is'; *τίς οὖν ἦν*, that is, 'what then was'; and this is the reading of Ambrose.¹ But *beatitudo* [blessedness] is not *μακαριότης* here, but *μακαρισμός*, which rather has the meaning *beatificatio* [beatification], from the verb *μακαρίζειν*, that is, *beatum dicere* [to call blessed], or [*beatum*] *judicare* [to consider blessed], what St Jerome quite clearly explains with these words: '"Although," he says, "at that time when you had received the gospel according to the flesh, I called you blessed because it was received warmly initially; but now because I do not see that a roof has been put on top of the building, and that the foundations have been laid almost to no avail, I am compelled to state, where is your blessedness, with which I previously deemed you blessed and praised you?"'² In a similar³ manner also Theophylact explains it, namely concerning the praise with which they had been celebrated by all, because they were *φιλοδιδάσκαλοι* [lovers of (their) teachers].⁴

1 Ambrosiaster *Comm in Gal* 4:15

2 Jerome *Comm in Gal* 2 (on 4:15–16) CCL 77A 125:21–6. The text of Jerome is slightly different from the one quoted by Erasmus: *Quamvis, inquit, vos eo tempore quo Evangelium juxta carnem susceperatis, beatos dicerem quod in initiis fervebatis: tamen nunc quia non video aedificio culmen impositum, et pene **nequaquam** jacta **fundamina**, cogor dicere: Ubi est **ergo** beatitudo vestra, qua vos beatos arbitrans ante laudabam?* '"Although,"' he says, "at that time when you received the gospel according to the flesh, I called you blessed because you were fervent initially, so now because I do not see that a top has been placed upon the building, and that hardly at all have the foundations been laid, I am compelled to state, where therefore is your blessedness, with which I previously deemed you blessed and praised you?"'
3 In a similar ... φιλοδιδάσκαλοι.] Added in 1527
4 Theophylact *Expos in Gal* 4:15 PG 124 1001B

4:17 [ER *ambiunt vos* 'they solicit you']
[VG] *aemulantur vos* 'they are envious of you'; Ζηλοῦσιν ὑμᾶς, 'They are envious of you'; although that word may have various uses, in this context it is correctly translated *diligunt* [they court], or *affectant* [they try to win over], or *ambiunt* [they solicit you], and¹ *zelotypia laborant erga vos* [with great envy they make attempts upon you], as also Jerome has noted subtly.² For he treats certain individuals who, under the pretext of love and zeal for the Galatians are behaving in this way in order to lure them into the slavery of the Mosaic law.³

1 and *zelotypia* ... subtly] Added in 1519
2 Jerome *Comm in Gal* 2 (on 4:17–18) CCL 77A 130:75–7
The Vulgate renders each of the three occurrences of ζηλοῦν in verses 17 and 18 as *aemulari* 'to emulate.' Erasmus prefers to make a distinction; he understands the first instance of the verb to mean 'to solicit,' and the next two 'to imitate.' BDAG renders the two occurrences of the verb in verse 17 as 'to be deeply interested in someone, court someone's favour'; it paraphrases verse 18 as 'it is fine to be zealously courted at all times in what is fine.' Cf NIV: 'zealous to win you over' (17) and 'be zealous' (17, 18). NEB renders the clause in verse 18 thus: 'it is always a fine thing to deserve an honest envy,' adding the note 'or to be honourably wooed.'

4:17 [ER *imo excludere vos* 'instead to shut you out']
[VG] *sed excludere vos* 'but to shut you out.' The Greek word is ἐγκλεῖσαι, that is, 'to confine.' However, the Greek codices have different readings here, since¹ in some there appears [the word] ἐκκλεῖσαι [to shut out]. *Includere* [to confine], that is, to entangle in the Law; *excludere* [to exclude], that is, from the freedom of Christ. Theophylact has the reading and also the explanation of *excludere*, ἐκβαλεῖν² [to cast out].³ For he is excluded who is not granted entry, and he is also excluded who is cast out. If only Paul's complaint did not apply to any of the Christians alive today!

1 since ... explanation of *excludere*] Added in 1519
2 ἐκβαλεῖν ... today!] Added in 1527
3 Theophylact *Expos in Gal* 4:17 PG 124 1001D

4:17 [ER *ut ipsos aemulemini* 'that you may envy them']
[VG] *ut illos aemulemiVni* 'that you may envy those'; ἵνα αὐτοὺς ζηλοῦτε,
'that them' or 'themselves¹ you may envy.'

1 or 'themselves] Added in 1522

4:18 [ER *bonum autem est aemulari in re bona* 'but it is good to be envious
in a good thing']¹
[VG] *bonum autem aemulamini in bono* 'but you imitate good in a good
thing'; καλὸν δὲ τὸ ζηλοῦσθαι ἐν καλῷ, that is, 'it is certainly good always
to be envious in a good thing'; it is good to wish to imitate others, but
not in any thing whatsoever, but only in a good thing. And Augustine²
reads in the following manner: '"but it is good," he states, "always to
imitate a good thing."'³ The Translator appears to have read, καλὸν δὲ
ζηλοῦσθε [be envious], so that⁴ the final syllable of the verb ends in epsi-
lon. For 'be envious' [imperative] and 'you are envious' cannot be distinguished by the sound of the word. Yes, even the infinitive could be
taken for the imperative, if the article [τό] had not been added. For in
the first passage [the word] 'to envy' means something different than in
the two later passages, in which it is not merely to imitate, but to imitate
with wonderment and with a desire to follow closely. For that is what he
states more openly a little later, 'but that they may glory in your flesh'
[Gal 6:13].

1 Cf Valla *Annot in Gal* 4 (I 875–6): *Quis sensus hic est nisi indignus Paulo? Ipse
ait: Bonum est aemulari, sive bona est aemulatio in bono, etsi non adest verbum
substantivum graece, sed subauditur,* καλὸν δὲ τὸ ζηλοῦσθαι [Who is judged
here by Paul if not the unworthy man? He himself said: 'It is good to
emulate,' or 'Emulation is good in a good thing,' even if the substantive
word is not present in Greek, but is understood, καλὸν δὲ τὸ ζηλοῦσθαι].
2 And Augustine ... glory in your flesh.'] This remaining portion of the annotation was added in 1519.
3 Augustine *Expos Gal* CSEL 84 106:8–9
4 so that ... epsilon] Added in 1522

4:18 [ER VG] *quum praesens sum apud vos* 'when I am¹ present among you.'
Although all [the codices] agree, the Greek word has more than one
meaning, which can have this meaning too: μὴ μόνον ἐν τῷ παρεῖναί με
πρὸς ὑμᾶς, 'not only in me being present among you,' because earlier
he stated, ἐν τῷ καλῷ [in the good thing]. For whatever² is honourable

should always be followed, even if the one who bestowed it is absent.
For he³ hints that his own absence was the reason they slipped⁴ into
another direction.

1 I am] Added in *1527*
2 For whatever ... absent.] Added in *1519*
3 ' For he ... direction.] Added in *1527*
4 slipped] Latin *delaberent*; in *1527*, *elaberentur* 'slipped away'

4:20 [ER *vellem autem adesse apud vos nunc* 'but I could wish to be in
your presence now']
[VG] *vellem autem esse apud vos modo* 'but I wished to be with you
a little while ago.' *Modo* [just now] is placed in this passage for ἄρτι
[now]. Nor is it *esse* [to be], but παρεῖναι, that is, *adesse* [to be present].

4:20 [ER *quoniam consilii inops sum in vobis* 'because I lack counsel
about you']
[VG] *quoniam confundor in vobis* 'because I am confused about you';
ἀποροῦμαι, that is, 'I am perplexed,' or 'I am in need,' for so St Jerome¹
explains it;² and yet in the Greek ἀπορεῖσθαι sometimes means 'to be
at a loss and wanting a plan.'³ Paul was so downcast, that he did not
know what to do with the Galatians, whom he perceived to be heading
towards slavery of the Law, and this while the great apostles, as it was
thought,⁴ were calling them to it. But the common⁵ man makes no distinction between 'confusion,' which in Greek is the word σύγχυσις, and
shame or feeling of guilt, which in Greek is αἰσχύνη [shame] or ἐντροπή
[modesty]. But it is one thing 'to be ashamed and to blush,' and another
'to be thrown into confusion in one's mind,' such that you do not know
what should be done. Although sometimes it may be directed towards
extreme modesty, which generally throws the soul into confusion and
spreads darkness, just as [it says] in Euripides: ὡς δ' ἄνολβον εἶχες ὄνομα
σύγχυσίν τε [and when you were both holding a wretched name and
being confounded].⁶ Nevertheless, here too 'confused' can be understood, rather than 'ashamed.' Nor was it because the word *confundere*
was altered in this passage, unless the Translator had used it willingly
and frequently elsewhere in place of 'to blush'; in any case he neatly
explains the Greek word ἀποροῦμαι.

1 St Jerome] Here in *1516* and *1519* Erasmus added the following phrase:
quem nos secuti sumus 'with whom we have agreed.'
2 Jerome *Comm in Gal* 2 (on 4:20) CCL 77A 134:14–16
3 LSJ defines ἀπορέω as 'to be at a loss, be in doubt, be puzzled.' Modern
English translations vary: 'I stand in doubt of you' (KJV), 'I am perplexed
about you' (RSV), 'I am at my wits end about you' (NEB).

4 as it was thought] Added in *1519*

5 the common ... But it is one thing] Added in *1527*. In *1516, 1519*, and *1522*, it reads: <u>Caeterum</u> *quantum ex Hieronymi verbis, licet conjicere, putat ille idem esse* σύγχησιν *et* αἰσχύνην, *quorum prius confusionem sonat, posterius erubescentiam, cum plurimum intersit inter haec duo. Nam* <u>aliud</u> ... 'But as much as one can conclude from the words of Jerome, he thinks σύγχησιν and αἰσχύνην are the same word, of which the first means "confusion," the second "blushing," since there is a very great difference between these two [words].'

6 Euripides actually reads ὡς <δ'> ἄνολβον εἶχες ὄμμα σύγχυσίν τ', *Iphigenia Aulidensis* 354. Cf the annotation on Gal 2:2 ('and I shared the gospel with them') n4.

4:21 [ER *legem ipsam non auditis?* 'do you not hear the Law itself?']

[VG] *legem non legistis?* 'do you not read the Law?' The Greek ἀκούετε is 'you hear.' Jerome has the reading 'you have heard,' unless there is a latent error;[1] for I think[2] that 'you hear' had been written. The figure of speech has special appeal, as if the Law itself were speaking, forbidding that it be obeyed from now on. And so in this matter they were resisting the Law, because they were striving to observe the Law.

1 Jerome *Comm in Gal* 2 (on 4:21) CCL 77A 136:1–2
2 for I think ... observe the Law] Added in *1527*

4:24 [ER *quae per allegoriam dicuntur* 'which things are spoken through allegory']

[VG] *per allegoriam dicta* 'through allegory spoken'; ἀλληγορούμενα, that is,[1] 'things that are spoken through allegory.' For it is an allegory when one thing is spoken and another thing is meant. Augustine,[2] in the ninth chapter of the fifteenth book of *Concerning the Trinity*, provides evidence that he had read 'things that are in allegory'; and that since 'allegory' is a Greek word, certain Latin translators have rendered it this way: 'things that signify something else.'[3] Chrysostom[4] points out that Paul employed this word 'allegory' in the place of [rhetorical] type and figure.[5] For allegory is actually a continuous metaphor.[6] But the Apostle is relating true history, which is the example for something else.[7]

1 that is] First in *1519*; previously *sunt quaedam* 'they are of a certain kind.'
2 Augustine ... something else.] Added in *1522*
3 Augustine *De trinitate* 15.9 PL 42 1068
4 Chrysostom ... for something else.] The remainder of this and all of the following annotation were added in *1535*.
5 Chrysostom *Comm in Gal* 4.3 PG 61 662

6 Metaphor is a comparison that is made by referring to one thing as another; see Lausberg §558–64. Erasmus says that 'nothing moves the emotions so forcefully, nothing brings so much distinction, beauty, and pleasure' as rhetorical metaphor (*Ecclesiastes* III ASD v-5 23–5). For Erasmus' view on metaphor, allegory, and allegorical interpretation see M. Hoffmann *Rhetoric and Theology: The Hermeneutic of Erasmus* (Toronto 1994) 95–133.

7 Cf *Hyperaspistes* 2 462, where Erasmus justifies Paul's use of the metaphor here thus: 'nothing in the historical sense is absurd or contrary to the articles of the faith.'

4:24 [ER *nam haec sunt duo testamenta* 'for these are two testaments']
[VG] *haec enim sunt duo testamenta* 'these in fact are two testaments.'
Chrysostom asks to what αὗται [these] refers.[1] It refers to the two mothers, the slave-girl Hagar and the freewoman Sarah, of whom mention had occurred earlier. In the Greek language the expression flows more smoothly, for in it 'testament' is grammatically of the feminine gender, διαθήκη. And again, the word 'they are' stands for 'they represent.'

1 Chrysostom *Comm in Gal* 4.3 PG 61 662

4:24 [ER *unum quidem a monte* 'one from the mountain']
[VG] *unum quidem in monte* 'one upon the mountain.' The Greek ἀπὸ ὄρους is 'from the mountain,'[1] and such is the reading of both Jerome[2] and Ambrose;[3] nor was[4] the reading of the Donatian codex different. In one[5] of the codices of Constance – the older one, to be sure – the genuine writing remained, while in the other an erasure bears witness to the deeds of a distorter. But the passage here has been corrupted in many ways. For the Greek has the following: ἀπὸ ὄρους Σινᾶ, εἰς δουλείαν γεννῶσα, ἥτις ἐστὶν Ἄγαρ. Τὸ γὰρ Ἄγαρ, Σινᾶ ὄρος ἐστὶν ἐν τῇ Ἀραβίᾳ, συστοιχεῖ δὲ τῇ νῦν Ἱερουσαλήμ, δουλεύει δὲ μετὰ τῶν τέκνων αὐτῆς. Ἡ δὲ ἄνω Ἱερουσαλήμ, ἐλευθέρα ἐστίν, ἥτις ἐστὶ μήτηρ πάντων ἡμῶν, that is, 'from Mount Sinai, bringing forth children to slavery; which is Hagar. For Hagar is Sinai, a mountain in Arabia, bordering upon present-day Jerusalem. Together with her children, she serves as a slave. But the Jerusalem from above is free; she is the mother of all of us.'[6] The scholia of the Greeks,[7] and together with them Theophylact,[8] observe that in the language of Arabia Mount Sinai is called Hagar: it is the same mountain under different names, although Jerome[9] makes no mention of this sort in his commentary on this Epistle. Augustine[10] and Ambrose[11] have the reading *quod est Agar* [which is Hagar], not *quae est Agar* [who is Hagar], although either reading expresses the same meaning, because the relative noun, being situated between the two nouns, usually agrees with whichever

of the two you wish. For *testamenta* [neuter plural] preceded it while the name of the woman 'Hagar' [feminine singular] follows it. If our reading, 'who is Hagar,' is not a case of ambiguity or should pertain to slavery, even so in this passage the sense has nearly the same effect. But the word *est* [is] has been put in place of *significat* [represents], in the same way as 'and the rock was Christ,' as Augustine observes in several places.[12] It matters very little indeed whether Hagar is an example of the testament that bears children unto slavery of the Law, or whether Hagar is an example of the actual service that the testament used to have. Consequently the word *generans* [bringing forth] must be taken with 'testament,' because he wishes that it had been represented in the type, Hagar. But the expression that follows, Τὸ γὰρ Ἀγὰρ [but Hagar], relates not to the slave girl but to the mountain, which can be ascertained from the gender, because 'mountain' in Greek is neuter. Ambrose seems to have left the Greek gender, when he states, 'bearing children for slavery, which is Hagar,' unless[13] someone prefers to take the relative pronoun with the context of the speech, that is, to bear children unto slavery. For whether mountain, or slave girl, or mountain that obtained its name from the slave girl, [the word] Hagar conveyed the example of this matter. And the fact that [Paul] adds, 'which now is Jerusalem,' pertains to the fact that once upon a time that city had been called by other names, first Jebus, then Salem, and then Jerusalem, as if a composite word from each of those names – and finally Aelia.[14] It ought not[15] to appear surprising if the common crowd said Jerusalem instead of Jebusalem, since it turned Salem into Solymam, and Hierusalem into Hierosolymam.

1 Cf Valla *Annot in Gal* 4 (I 876).
2 Jerome *Comm in Gal* 2 (on 4:25–6) CCL 77A 140:1–2
3 Ambrosiaster *Comm in Gal* 4:24
4 nor was ... different] Added in *1522*
5 In one ... distorter.] Added in *1527*
6 Erasmus and Valla follow the same Greek text, Valla *Annot in Gal* 4 (I 876). Valla also notes that the text was corrupt: *Non dicam quomodo sit deceptus interpres, quoque modo sit depravata scriptura. Tantum dicam, qualis esse debeat vera translatio* [I shall not say in what way the translator was deceived, and how Scripture was corrupted. I shall say only this much, what the true translation ought to be like].
7 Cf Pseudo-Oecumenius *Comm in Gal* 4:24–7 PG 118 1145B–C.
8 and together with them Theophylact] Added in *1519*. Theophylact *Expos in Gal* 4:25–6 PG 124 1005B–C
9 although Jerome ... testament used to have] Added in *1519*
10 Augustine *Expos Gal* (on 4:21–31) CSEL 84 108–12. Here Erasmus appears to follow a variant of the text (CSEL 84 108:12[*b*]). The connection however is uncertain, as the reading there (*quae est Agar* 'who is Hagar') conflicts

with Erasmus' argument. However, the reading *quod est Agar* occurs
in other works of Augustine, see for example *De civitate dei* 15.2 CCL 48
454:11–13; *Contra adversarium legis et prophetarum* 2.7 CCL 49 113:826–7;
Contra duas epistulas Pelagianorum 3.4.9 PL 44 593.

11 Ambrosiaster *Comm in Gal* 4:24

12 Cf Augustine *Contra adversarium legis et prophetarum* 2.6 CCL 49 107:635–6;
De civitate dei 18.48 CCL 48 646:22–6; *Contra Faustum Manichaeum* 16.17
CSEL 25 457:29–458:19.

13 unless ... of this matter] Added in *1535*

14 That is, Aelia Capitolina, founded on the ruins of Jerusalem by the
Emperor Hadrian in AD 135.

15 It ought not ... Hierosolymam.] The remainder of this and all of the following annotation were added in *1535*.

4:25 [ER *confinis est autem ei, quae nunc vocatur Hierusalem* 'for it is
neighbouring to what is now called Jerusalem']
[VG] *qui conjunctus est ei quae nunc est Hierusalem* **'for it is joined to
what is now Jerusalem'**; συστοιχεῖ δὲ τῇ νῦν Ἰερουσαλήμ; instead of 'joined
to' I have translated 'is neighbouring to.'[1] For St Jerome employed this
word in explaining the passage.[2] Nor is it a problem that Mt Sinai is
many days' journey away from Mt Sion, for here the apostle Paul is not
measuring the distance but is drawing a comparison of a spiritual sort.
For the things that correspond to each other in any similarity are said to
be neighbouring and bordering [upon each other], which Paul expresses in the Greek as συστοιχεῖν, as if to say that they were in one line. Hence
also the Grammarians call letters [of the alphabet] στοιχεῖα, because they
are connected to each other in a kind of row.[3] Philosophers label the
basic elements of matter στοιχεῖα, namely earth, water, air, and fire, because each of these exists in its own order. Similarly lines of poetry are
called στίχοι, and battle-ranks arranged in order are called στίχαι. These
words, and others like them, are derived from the verb στείχειν, which
means 'to proceed in order,' or 'to stand in a row.' Mt Sinai, although
separated from Jerusalem by a long distance, nevertheless is adjacent to
it through this likeness: just as on Sinai the Law was first revealed with
great terrors, so too on Mt Sion the same Law was proclaimed, and extended even to foreigners, in accordance with this prediction: 'the Law
shall go forth from Sion, and the Word of the Lord from Jerusalem' [Isa
2:3]. In this passage the Apostle states it because he wishes to show that
apart from grace the Law strikes terror through its threats and demands.
But to be forced by fear is slavery. But the Jews, who were keeping the
Law according to the letter and outward practices while lacking charity, although they had migrated from Mt Sinai to Jerusalem, they were
not moving on from their servile state, as though they were children of
Hagar and not of Sarah. The word συστοιχεῖν is found with this meaning

in the writings of reputed Greek authors; to be specific, in Theophrastus' *On Causes*,⁴ and Aristotle, ἐν τοῖς Μετὰ τὰ φυσικά [the Metaphysics].⁵ Nor is Suidas silent on the word σύστοιχα, [stating] that things of the same order and strength are so called.⁶ And a row of things that are similar to each other is called συστοιχία, for example when you place [the letters] π. κ. τ. together, there would be συστοιχία, for they have in common the fact that they are small. Another row is placed opposite it, and contains [the letters] φ. χ. θ. These elements, too, when gathered together are called σύστοιχα, but when compared to the earlier series, are called ἀντίστοιχα. St Chrysostom explains συστοιχεῖ as γειτνιάζει καὶ ἅπτεται, that is, 'neighbouring and adjacent.'⁷ Theophylact explains it more clearly, adding that this state of being adjacent is not in space but in likeness.⁸ And the *Glossa* known as *Ordinaria* explains the word *conjunctus* [joined] with the word *similis* [like].⁹ Aquinas, however, rejects this interpretation, because he reckons that it was not the meaning of Paul, and he prefers that Mount Sinai is said to be joined to Jerusalem because the Israelites had set forth from the one to the other, so that we must understand the mountain of Arabia to be bordering on Jerusalem not by the proximity of the location, but by the continuity in the journey.¹⁰ The fact that the verb συστοιχεῖ is in the present tense, which Ambrose renders, 'which is joined to,' militates somewhat against this comment.¹¹ For the journey had occurred many ages earlier. Whoever has collected the scholia on all the Epistles of Paul writes on this passage as follows: 'he [Paul] wishes that from the qualities of the locations the difference between the testaments be understood.'¹² Whoever he was, he seems to have realized that Sinai represents the old covenant, and Jerusalem the new. If we adopt this explanation, how can they be called συστοιχεῖν, 'neighbouring'? To me Paul seems to be equating Jews, Arabs, and people of Jerusalem, because each party equally served the Law, and [because] they belonged to the Synagogue, not the Church.¹³ Over against the earthly Jerusalem, which is no different from Mt Sinai, [Paul] places the heavenly Jerusalem, which is the Church. It is remarkable that the issue concerning the adjacency troubled neither Jerome nor Ambrose.

1 BDAG explains συστοιχεῖ ('correspond') in Gal 4:25 as members of the same category. Erasmus' main point in this annotation is that although physically removed from Jerusalem Sinai is similar to it and belongs in a series with it.
2 Jerome *Comm in Gal* 2 (on 4:25–6) CCL 77A 141:20–2
3 Cf also annotation on Gal 4:3 ('we were serving as slaves under the elements of the universe') above.
4 Theophrastus *De causis plantarum* VI.5.6 and VI.4.2

5 Aristotle *Metaphysica* 986a23; 1004b27; 1054b35; 1058a13
6 Suidas Σύστοιχα 1691 σύστοιχα λέγεται ἀλλήλοις καὶ τὰ ὁμοίως ἔχοντα πρός τινα, ἅ καὶ κατὰ ἀναλογίαν εἴη ἄν
7 Chrysostom *Comm in Gal* 4.4 PG 61 662
8 Theophylact *Expos in Gal* 4:25–6 PG 124 1005C
9 Cf *Biblia cum Glossa ordinaria et expositione Lyre literali et morali nec non Pauli Burgensis additionibus ac Matthiae Thoringi replicis* (Basel 1498) VI fol 27 verso. Originally known in the early Middle Ages simply as the *Glossa*, but later as the *Glossa ordinaria*, the Gloss consisted of marginal and interlinear notes and commentary extracted from the Fathers and early medieval writers, accompanying the text of the Bible. Compiled in the early twelfth century, it was the product of several collaborators, but the central figure was Anselm of Laon, who was principally responsible for the glosses on the Pauline letters. In the late fifteenth century the *Gloss* was printed in six volumes along with the *Postilla* of Nicholas of Lyra and the additions by Paul of Burgos and Matthias Doring. For the authorship, production, contents, and use of the *Glossa* see Lesley Smith *The Glossa Ordinaria: The Making of a Medieval Bible Commentary* (Leiden 2009). For Erasmus' attitude to the *Gloss* see n28 and n29 to the Translator's Note by John Bateman in CWE 44.
10 Thomas Aquinas *Super Gal lect* cap 4 lectio 8.262
11 Ambrosiaster *Comm in Gal* 4:25
12 In the ninth volume of the Froben edition of Jerome (1516) the commentaries on the thirteen epistles of Paul that had been transmitted under the name of Jerome were included, but Erasmus makes it clear that they were pseudonymous (see Souter 1 6). In his Introduction (1) Souter has demonstrated that the text of 'Pseudo-Jerome' is a commentary by Pelagius with interpolations. It appears Erasmus was unaware that Pelagius was the author of the primary text. See further CWE 56 155 n22.
13 Cf *Paraphrasis in Galatas* CWE 42 199, on Jerusalem: 'since this city is situated on a lofty hill, it represents the heavenly mother land into whose citizenship we have been received.'

4:27 [ER VG] *laetare sterilis quae non paris* '**rejoice you barren one who do not bring forth.**' The prooftext was taken from Isaiah chapter 54.[1] Jerome expressed the Hebrew[2] as follows: 'sing praise, o barren one, you who do not bring forth. Sing praise and whinny, you who were not in labour, for the sons of the abandoned woman are more than those of the one who has a man.'[3] But in accordance with the LXX we read as follows: Εὐφράνθητι[4] στεῖρα ἡ οὐ τίκτουσα ῥῆξον καὶ βόησον ἡ οὐκ ὠδίνουσα ὅτι πολλὰ τὰ τέκνα τῆς ἐρήμου μᾶλλον ἢ τῆς ἐχούσης τὸν ἄνδρα. That is, 'rejoice [o] barren one, who does not bring forth; break forth and shout, you who are not in travail, because the children of the desolate one are more numerous than those of her who has a man.' Symmachus renders it thus: 'be glad, o barren one who have not given birth, rejoice in exultation; and rejoice exceedingly you who have not been in travail, for the sons of the deserted woman are more than those of the one subject to a husband.' Theodotion and Aquila do not differ from this reading, except in a very few words. Therefore it is clear that in this passage Paul employed the text of the Septuagint, because in everything the sense accords with the Hebrew truth.

1 Cf Isa 54:1.
2 Hebrew] In 1516, 'the Hebrew has it as follows: "O barren one, who did not bear, break forth into singing, and cry aloud, you who did not labour, for more are the sons of the desolate one than the children of the married wife."'
3 Erasmus cites Jerome's translation as it appears in his commentary on Isaiah 54:1, CCL 73A 599:4–6. Jerome actually reads *laetare, sterilis, quae non paris: erumpe et clama, quae non parturis: quia multi filii desertae magis quam eius quae habet virum* 'rejoice, o barren one, you who do not bring forth. Spring forth and shout, you who are not in labour, because many more are the sons of the abandoned woman than those of the one who has a man.'
4 Εὐφράνθητι ... That is] Added in 1522

4:30 [ER VG] *cum filio liberae* '**with the son of the free woman.**' Jerome reads, 'with my son Isaac'[1] – and this,[2] to be sure, is the reading in Genesis chapter 21;[3] Ambrose has the same reading.[4] Therefore I wonder all the more from where this text made its way into the books of the Greeks and into our codices. From Theophylact's[5] explanation it is not sufficiently clear what his reading was, except[6] that the text agrees with our common [Latin] reading.[7] Chrysostom[8] has the same reading as the Latin;[9] nor does it matter much for the meaning. For the person Sarah the Apostle has placed the person of Scripture, so that the statement might have more weight, and he composed a suitable sentence for the matter he was dealing with. In this proof-text the Apostle followed neither the authority of the Hebrew nor the LXX, being content to express the meaning of Scripture with his own words.

1 Jerome *Comm in Gal* 2 (on 4:29–31) CCL 77A 144:4–5
2 and this ... our codices] Added in 1519
3 Cf Gen 21:10.
4 Ambrosiaster *Comm in Gal* 4:30
5 From Theophylact's ... reading was] Added in 1522
6 except ... reading] Added in 1527
7 Theophylact *Expos in Gal* 4:30 PG 124 1008C–D
8 Chrysostom ... his own words.] Added in 1535
9 Chrysostom *Comm in Gal* 4.4 PG 61 664

4:31 [ER VG] *qua libertate nos Christus* etc **'with what freedom Christ [has freed] us**[1] etc.**'**[2] The Greek states, *Τῇ ἐλευθερίᾳ οὖν, ᾗ Χριστὸς ἡμᾶς ἠλευθέρω-σε, στήκετε, καὶ μή,*[3] that is, 'for freedom, therefore, Christ has set you free; stand firm, and do not' so that the word 'freedom' pertains to that which follows and not to what precedes. But Jerome[4] renders it differently, and Augustine[5] and Ambrose[6] read differently, and begin a new sentence:[7] 'Stand fast therefore.' With me,[8] Chrysostom[9] and[10] Theophylact[11] make [the interpretation] very clear, as they[12] separate the word *στήκετε* [stand] from that which follows by means even of their interpretation. Nor could the Translator alter it; but it matters little to the sense.

1 us] Added in *1535*
2 In LB this annotation is not separated from the one above ('with the son of the free woman').
3 Cf Pseudo-Oecumenius *Comm in Gal* 4:28–31 PG 118 1148B.
4 Jerome *Comm in Gal* 2 (on 4:29–31) CCL 77A 146:66–7
5 Augustine *Expos Gal* CSEL 84 112:3
6 Ambrosiaster *Comm in Gal* 5:1
7 and begin a new sentence] Added in *1519*
8 With me ... very clear] Added in *1522*
9 Chrysostom *Comm in Gal* 5.1 PG 61 663
10 Chrysostom and] Added in *1535*
11 Theophylact *Expos in Gal* 5:1 PG 124 1009A
12 as they ... sense] Added in *1527*

From the Fifth Chapter

5:1 [ER *implicemini* **'be entangled'**]
[VG] *contineri* **'be enclosed';** *μὴ ἐνέχεσθε,* that is, *ne obnoxii sitis* [do not be bound up], or *implicemini* [entangled in], or *illaqueemini* [ensnared].

5:3 [ER *qui circumditur* **'who is circumcised'**]
[VG] *circumcidenti se* **'circumcising**[1] **himself';** *περιτεμνομένῳ,* that is, 'he who is circumcised.'

1 'circumcising ... circumcised.'] In *1516*, this annotation and the next appeared in reverse order.
Erasmus understands the Greek participle *περιτεμνομένῳ* to be passive, not active, and makes this clear by translating it into Latin with a finite verb in the passive voice.

5:4 [ER *Christus vobis factus est otiosus* **'Christ is made ineffectual for you'**]
[VG] *evacuati estis a Christo* **'you are**[1] **emptied from Christ';** *κατηρ-γήθητε ἀπὸ τοῦ Χριστοῦ.* The Translator regularly renders the word in

this way, whenever [Paul] says that an end is put to something and it becomes void and ineffectual, like something antiquated.[2] It is the same as what he stated a little earlier, 'Christ will be of no advantage to you' [Gal 5:2]. If you surrender yourself to the law of Moses, 'Christ is antiquated and ineffectual for you.' Jerome indicates that this word καταρ-γεῖσθαι [to be abolished] is not rendered correctly by the Translator since it means more to cease from working.[3] For ἀργός means 'ineffectual,' like ἀεργός [not working], from which comes the word καταργεῖσθαι.[4]

1 'you are ... comes the word καταργεῖσθαι.] See the annotation on Eph 5:3 ('circumcising himself') n1 above.
2 For example in Rom 3:3; 2 Cor 3:7, 11, 13, 14; Gal 3:17; Eph 2:15. See also the annotation on Rom 3:3 ('has made void').
3 Jerome *Comm in Gal* 2 (on 5:4) CCL 77A 153:10–17
4 BDAG defines the use of καταργεῖσθαι here as 'be estranged from Christ.' See also Erasmus' discussion of the verb in his annotation on Gal 5:11 ('therefore the scandal has been emptied').

5:6 [ER *per dilectionem operans* 'working through love']
[VG] *per charitatem operatur* 'is worked[1] through charity.'[2] Again here *operans* [working] does not mean what the common crowd imagines, but that which exercises its hidden power in us, which is peculiar to the Holy Spirit. For one feels his power, even though he himself is nowhere apparent. For [Paul] wants the Law to appear to be too ineffective, and faith, on the other hand, to be powerful. ἐνεργουμένη [being in action] could have been translated more accurately as *agens* [working].[3]

1 worked] Latin *operatur*; first in 1535. Previously, *operans* 'working'
2 charity'] Latin *charitatem*; first in 1535. Previously, *dilectionem* 'love'
3 Cf BDAG s.v. ἐνεργέω: 'work, be at work, be active, operate, be effective.'

5:7 [ER *quis vos impedivit* 'who has hindered you']
[VG] *quis vos fascinavit* 'who has bewitched you'; ἀνέκοψεν, which Jerome[1] and Ambrose[2] translate as 'has hindered.' And the *Glossa[3] Ordinaria* indicates that in the Latin codices there was a double reading, although in the Greek copies there is but one.[4] In the Donatian codex I have certainly found *fascinavit* [bewitched] written. It seems that *non credere veritati* [not to believe the truth],[5] about which I have made a note earlier, in chapter 3,[6] was added from this passage. And what [the Translator] there rendered as 'not to believe' is here translated 'not to obey.' In fact, Jerome made the observation that this entire phrase, *non obedire veritati* [not to obey the truth], is not found in the oldest codices, although the Greek codices are mixed up on this mistake.[7] At this point[8]

there is no difference between the Greek codices and the Latin ones, except that [the Greek ones] read 'hindered,' not 'bewitched,' while not even here would the added phrase make much difference for the meaning. For the full sense would be,[9] 'you were running well; who interrupted your course?' Here is[10] yet further proof that this edition is not entirely Jerome's, for with the Greek [codices] he has the reading *impedivit* [hindered].

1 Jerome *Comm in Gal* 3 (on 5:7) CCL 77A 160:1
2 Ambrosiaster *Comm in Gal* 5:7
3 And the *Glossa ... fascinavit* written.] Added in 1522
4 On the *Glossa Ordinaria* see the annotation on Gal 4:25 ('for it is joined to what is now Jerusalem') n9.
5 Cf Valla *Annot in Gal* 5 (I 876): *Praeterea ego transtulissem: Quis vos impedivit veritati obedire, sive quo minus veritati obediretis? Graece tamen est elegantius persuaderi, πείθεσθαι* [Moreover I had translated: 'Who has hindered you to obey the truth,' or '[hindered] you from obeying the truth?' In Greek, however, it is more elegantly 'to be persuaded,' *πείθεσθαι*].
6 in chapter 3] Added in 1535. Cf the annotation on Gal 3:1 ('not to believe the truth').
7 Jerome *Comm in Gal* 3 (on 5:7) CCL 77A 160:1–7
8 At this point ... not even here] Added in 1535; previously, the entire phrase was replaced by *nec* 'nor.'
9 For the full sense would be] Added in 1527
10 Here is ... *impedivit.*] Added in 1535. Modern editions of the Greek read *τίς ὑμᾶς ἐνέκοψεν [τῇ] ἀληθείᾳ μὴ πείθεσθαι* 'who hindered you from obeying the truth' (RSV), 'who cut in on you to keep you from obeying the truth' (NIV), 'who was it hindered you from following the truth' (NEB).

5:7 [ER omitted]

[VG] *nemini consenseritis* 'you consented[1] to no one.' This phrase also Jerome passes over on the grounds that it was an addition, since it can be found neither in the Greek codices, nor in any writing of those who have written commentaries on Paul.[2] And still[3] the translator of Theophylact has added [the phrase] in the text of his own doing, even though it does not occur in the Greek copies, and no mention is made of it in any commentary.[4] It certainly[5] was not added in the Donatian codex, nor[6] in either codex of Constance. And yet one can easily discern that Ambrose had added this [latter] phrase, though he had not added the previous one, *non credere veritati* [not to believe the truth], for he explains it as follows: 'he testifies that their regular practice in the works of faith was good, but by the wickedness of evil men they were held back from finishing their course through the exercise of perseverance. In order that they would recover from that, moreover, he admonishes those who put their faith in any persons who so prevented them from obeying the gospel truth that they were persuaded to keep the works of the Law.'[7] At any rate the phrase, *nemini consenseritis* [you consented to no one] is not added to the text in Ambrose, nor indeed in Augustine.[8]

1 'you consented ... commentaries on Paul.] In 1516, this entire annotation preceded the annotation on 5:7 ('who has bewitched you') above. In LB this annotation is not separated from the one above ('who has bewitched you'). See also Valla *Annot in Gal* 5 (I 876). The phrase *nemini consenseritis* is a late Vulgate addition that appears to have little or no support in the Greek manuscripts.

2 Jerome *Comm in Gal* 3 (on 5:7) CCL 77A 161:15–17

3 And still ... nor indeed in Augustine.] This remaining portion of the annotation was added in 1519.

4 Theophylact *Expos in Gal* 5:8 PG 124 1012C

5 It certainly ... codex] Added in 1522

6 nor ... Constance] Added in 1527. For more information on the manuscripts from Constance see the annotation on Gal 1:3 ('from God our Father') n3 and CWE 56 xii.

7 Ambrosiaster *Comm in Gal* 5:7. Ambrosiaster reads *exercitium illorum in* **opera** *fidei bonum fuisse testatur, sed nequitia malorum hominum detentos, ne cursum suum* **efficacia perseverantiae** *consummarent* [...] 'he testifies that their regular practice in the works of faith was good, but by the wickedness of evil men they were held back from finishing their course through the effectiveness characteristic of perseverance [...].'

8 Augustine *Expos Gal* CSEL 84 114:15

5:8 [ER *persuasio non ex eo profecta qui vocat vos* 'the persuasion did not proceed from the one who calls you']
[VG] *persuasio haec non est* etc 'this persuasion is not etc.' In the Greek there is neither *haec* [this] nor *vestra* [your], as Augustine reads,[1] but only ἡ πεισμονή, that is, 'persuasion'; but the sense is not in conflict, except that here it means the persuasion of the ones who are trying to persuade and not of those who obey, so that it refers to the previous question,[2] 'who hindered you while you were running well?' So obviously [it is] the persuasion of certain people who were summoning you away to the Mosaic ceremonies, a persuasion that did not proceed from Christ, who has called you elsewhere, namely[3] to the spiritual things.

1 as Augustine reads] Added in 1535. For the reference see Augustine *Expos Gal* CSEL 84 114:16.

2 'Question' here translates the Latin *interrogationem*. In *Ecclesiastes* III ASD v-5 948–68 Erasmus notes a distinction between *interrogatio* and *percontatio*: 'Certain people distinguish the two thus: *interrogatio* is [used] of one who wishes to learn and expects a reply; *percontatio* of one who is pressing a point to which no reply can be made.' Cf Lausberg §354, who

observes that the *interrogatio*, as an 'interplay' of question and answer, is called the *percontatio*.

3 namely] First in 1535; previously *nempe* 'naturally'

5:9 [ER *totam conspersionem fermentat* '**leavens the whole dough'**][1]
[VG] *totam massam corrumpit* '**spoils the whole lump'**; ὅλον τὸ φύραμα ζυμοῖ, that is, 'leavens the whole dough,' for so St Jerome translates it in his Commentary, openly denouncing[2] and rejecting the word *massa* [lump].[3] However he does not relate his reason for rejecting it, nor does he avoid using the denounced word in his commentary; nor indeed, can it be said that *massa* is not a Latin word, although *conspersio* [dough] in this sense is found in Columella,[4] and better expresses the Greek word, φύραμα [dough].[5] This passage demonstrates also that this translation is not by Jerome, for it contains a word that he testifies had been corrected by him. Jerome has the reading *fermentat* [leavens] in the place of *corrumpit* [spoils], for the Greek has ζυμοῖ [leavens]: since[6] what undergoes fermentation is not immediately spoiled. For Christ[7] compares his own teaching to yeast hidden in flour.[8]

1 Erasmus is following Valla here, *Annot in Gal* 5 (I 876). See also Erasmus' annotation on 1 Cor 5:6 (*modicum fermentum totam massam corrumpit*).
2 openly denouncing ... not immediately spoiled] Added in 1522
3 Jerome *Comm in Gal* 3 (on 5:9) CCL 77A 162:1–5. 'Openly denouncing' seems here to be an exaggeration; Jerome merely states that *conspersio* is a better reading than *massa*, which appeared in many codices ('*male in nostris codicibus habetur "Modicum fermentum totam massam corrumpit"* ...').
4 It appears that Erasmus is mistaken, as the word *conspersio* is not found in any of Columella's works. It may be found in Tertullian *Adversus Marcionem* 4.24.1.
5 Cf also Erasmus' discussion of *conspersio* in the annotation on Rom 11:16 ('but if the first portion') CWE 56 305.
6 since] From 1527; in 1522, *nec enim* 'nor indeed'
7 For Christ ... in flour.] Added in 1535
8 Cf Matt 13:33; Lk 13:21

5:10 [ER *quod nihil aliud sensuri sitis* '**that you will have no other view'**]
[VG] *nihil aliud sapietis* '**that you will discern no other'**; φρονήσετε [to think]. Better [is] Ambrose, who has the reading *sentietis*,[1] that is, 'you will not be of a different opinion, and you will not consider changing the accustomed way of life.' For it is nothing other, nothing different, nothing new. As we say [in Latin], *aliud*[2] *ab illo* [other (that is, 'different') than that].

1 Ambrosiaster *Comm in Gal* 5:10
2 *aliud*] First in 1519; in 1516, *ille* 'that'

5:10 [ER *quisquis fuerit* 'whoever he might be']
[VG] *quicunque est ille* 'whoever that man is'; ὅστις ἂν ᾖ, that is, 'whoever he might be,' or 'may be,' as St Ambrose reads.[1]

> 1 Ambrosiaster *Comm in Gal* 5:10. Ambrosiaster reads *quicumque fuerit* 'whoever he might be.'

5:11 [ER *abolitum est igitur offendiculum crucis* 'in that case the stumbling block of the cross has been destroyed']
[VG] *ergo evacuatum est scandalum* 'therefore the scandal has been emptied';[1] Ἄρα κατήργηται, that is, 'therefore it has ceased,' as St Jerome not inelegantly explained; [a stumbling block] is commonly said 'to have fallen over.'[2] He also makes the observation that here the Greek word expresses the mind of Paul more accurately than the Latin.[3] For what[4] is 'beginning to fall' has ceased to have strength.

> 1 Erasmus replaces the Vulgate's *evacuo* with *aboleo* elsewhere, too; see Brown's note *Novum Testamentum* 77:6(5)n.
> 2 Jerome *Comm in Gal* 3 (on 5:11) CCL 77A 165:2–3
> 3 Jerome *Comm in Gal* 3 (on 5:11) CCL 77A 165:2–3
> 4 For what ... strength.] Added in 1522

5:12 [ER *utinam et abscindantur* 'I wish that they also would be cut off']
[VG] *utinam abscindantur* 'I wish that they would be cut off.' *Utinam et abscindantur*,[1] with the particle, καὶ ἀποκόψονται, that is, 'would that even they be severed'; in the connective[2] particle more is implied than is actually stated [Latin *emphasis*], not only that they are judged but even that they become anathema, being utterly cut away from associating with you. Or, that those who wish you to be circumcised, are themselves cut off entirely, that is to say, Paul calls down a curse, that the entire male member of those who teach circumcision were cut off. Ambrose[3] approaches this interpretation, and so too Theophylact,[4] following Chrysostom;[5] but the other interpretation seems to me more befitting the solemnity of the Apostolic office.[6] Augustine turns the curse into a blessing when he interprets as follows: 'As if Paul were praying for the false teachers, not that they would be circumcised, but castrated, that is, that they become eunuchs for the sake of the kingdom of heaven.' For in this way it would happen that they would cease preaching Jewish circumcision.[7] He [Augustine] preferred[8] to accept this interpretation than to ascribe a curse to Paul.[9]

> 1 Erasmus is following Valla here, *Annot in Gal* 5 (I 876).
> 2 in the connective ... preaching Jewish circumcision] Added in 1519
> 3 Ambrosiaster *Comm in Gal* 5:12

4 Theophylact *Expos in Gal* 5:12 PG 124 1013C
5 following Chrysostom] Added in *1535*. For the reference see Chrysostom
   Comm in Gal 5.3 PG 61 666. Chrysostom calls Paul's words an *apostolica
   imprecatio* 'apostolic curse' and refutes those who have used the Apostle's
   words to justify their condemnation of the human body as inherently
   impure.
6 solemnity of the Apostolic office] From *1527*; in *1519* and *1522*, *apostolico
   sensu* 'attitude of the Apostolic office.'
   For a survey of the literal and metaphorical interpretations of this verse
   and its relevance to Galatian society see James R. Edwards 'Galatians
   5:12' *Novum Testamentum* 53 (2011) 319–37.
7 Augustine *Expos Gal* CSEL 84 116:12–14
8 He preferred ... Paul.] Added in *1527*
9 Augustine *Contra Faustum Manichaeum* 16.22 CSEL 25 465:11–20: 'For
   curses, when they are said from prophecy, are not from the ill will of
   calling down curses, but from the prescient spirit of warning. For those
   curses which are from ill will, are prohibited, since it is said, "Bless, and
   do not curse." (Rom 12:14) But this is often found in the discourse of the
   Saints, just as the Apostle Paul says, "Alexander the coppersmith says
   many abusive words to me; the Lord repay that man in accordance with
   his deeds." (2 Tim 4:14) For the Apostle seems to have wished it rather
   maliciously, just as if he was angry and indignant, "Would that those who
   disturb you also be severed." Especially because, if you were to consider
   the personality of the writer, you would understand him rightly to have
   prayed rather with the most ingenious ambiguity. For there are eunuchs,
   who sever themselves on account of the kingdom of heaven.' See also
   Contra adversarium legis et prophetarum 1.52 CCL 49:1486–92, 'For concerning a disgraceful curse even the Apostle Paul is able to be criticized
   because of impious wordy men, when he says, "Would that those who
   disturb you be severed!" (Gal 5:12) even if to those who understand it
   appears to be more elegantly a blessing, that they become eunuchs on
   account of the kingdom of heaven.'

5:12 [ER *qui vos labefactant* 'those who cause you to totter']
      [VG] *qui vos conturbant* 'those who upset you'; οἱ ἀναστατοῦντες ὑμᾶς,
      that is, 'those who remove you from your place.'[1] Consequently
      Ambrose has the reading, 'those who unsettle you.'[2] I have translated,
      'who cause you to totter.' For the word looks back to what he [Paul]
      had said before, 'stand.' For what[3] is being moved from where it stands
      is tottering. Theophylact[4] dutifully notes the emphasis in this word,
      and before him Chrysostom.[5]

      1 Cf BDAG ἀναστατόω 'to upset the stability of a person or group, disturb,
         trouble, upset.' Erasmus employs *labefacto* elsewhere in the New Testament
         only at Acts 15:24, for ἀνασκευάζοντες. Perhaps Erasmus used the verb here
         to avoid the repetition of *conturbo* in 5:10 (*qui autem conturbat vos*).
      2 Ambrosiaster *Comm in Gal* 5:12

3 For what ... this word] Added in *1519*
4 Theophylact *Expos in Gal* 5:12 PG 124 1013D
5 and before him Chrysostom] Added in *1535*. For the reference see
Chrysostom *Comm in Gal* 5.3 PG 61 666.

5:13 [ER *in occasionem detis carni* 'give (your freedom) as an opportunity
for the flesh']
[VG] *in occasionem detis carnis* 'give [your freedom] as an opportunity of the flesh.' The word *detis* [that you give] is not in the Greek copies,
and *carni* [flesh] is expressed in the dative case, not *carnis*, the genitive
case.[1] And *detis* must be assumed, as St Jerome points out, or something
else more suitable.[2] It seems that Valla takes the word *libertatem* [free-
dom] with the verb which follows, *serviatis* [serve] as if to say, 'do not
serve your freedom to the flesh.'[3] But besides the fact that it does not
suit all the sense, this [phrasing] is rather harsh and somewhat forced.
Theophylact thinks that the word ἔχωμεν, that is, 'we have,' must be
assumed.[4] At any rate, as I noted earlier, Jerome bears witness that the
word *detis* was added by the Translator, and not placed by Paul. Nor
do I know what special charm this aposiopesis[5] has in seeking to deter
those whom one doesn't wish to offend.

1 Erasmus is following Valla here, *Annot in Gal* 5 (1 876): *abest a graeca veri-
tate detis: nec legitur carnis, sed carni,* τῇ σαρκί ['that you give' is absent from
the Greek truth, nor is 'of the flesh' read, but 'for the flesh,' τῇ σαρκί].
2 Jerome *Comm in Gal* 3 (on 5:13) CCL 77A 169:1–4
3 Valla *Annot in Gal* 5 (1 876)
4 Theophylact *Expos in Gal* 5:13 PG 124 1016A
5 Aposiopesis is the rhetorical breaking off in the midst of a speech; see
Lausberg §887.

5:13 [ER *sed per charitatem servite vobis invicem* 'but through love be
servants to one another']
[VG] *sed per charitatem Spiritus* 'but through the love of the Spirit.'
Spiritus, 'the Spirit,' does not occur in the Greek codices, nor in Jerome[1]
and Augustine,[2] and I recall the reading only in Ambrose,[3] who interprets it so that it is placed opposite the flesh.

1 Jerome *Comm in Gal* 3 (on 5:14–15) CCL 77A 174:1
2 Augustine *Expos Gal* CSEL 84 117:21
3 Ambrosiaster *Comm in Gal* 5:13

5:14 [ER VG] *diliges proximum tuum* 'you shall love your neighbour.' The
Greek has ἐν τῷ, Ἀγαπήσεις τὸν πλησίον, that is, 'namely in this, that you
shall love your neighbour, etc.' wherefore I have so translated it. Here
Augustine[1] has a note of many words about the fact that no mention is

made of the love of God [that is, in the commandment to love the Lord and one's neighbour], because a pretense of it can more easily be fabricated, while in love for the neighbour one can be more easily proven guilty. And it follows that he who treats his neighbour harshly does not love God either. Ambrose implies as much, although more obscurely.[2] I thought this ought to be noted, lest someone add [something] of his own accord on the grounds that what had not been added by Paul was omitted.

1 Here Augustine ... was omitted.] This remaining portion of the annotation was added in 1519. For the reference see Augustine *Expos Gal* CSEL 84 119:1–120:3.
2 Ambrosiaster *Comm in Gal* 5:14

5:15 [ER *mordetis et devoratis* 'you bite and devour']
[VG] *mordetis et comeditis* 'you bite[1] and consume.' Instead of *comeditis* [consume] Ambrose has the reading *criminatis* [you make charges against], if the codex is free of error.[2] I do not know whether his copy had διαβάλλετε, that is 'bring false accusations.'

1 'you bite ... accusations.'] In 1516, this entire annotation and the next appeared in reverse order.
2 Ambrosiaster *Comm in Gal* 5:15

5:16 [ER *dico, autem* 'but I say']
[VG] *dico autem in Christo* 'but I say[1] in Christ.' 'In Christ' was not included in the Greek copies, nor in Jerome[2] and Ambrose,[3] and not[4] even in the oldest copy of St Paul's, with which[5] each codex of the church at Constance agrees; but there is only, 'but I say, walk by the Spirit.' For in this manner [Paul] indicates in what direction this entire speech is heading.[6]

1 'but I say ... heading.] See the annotation on Gal 5:15 ('you bite and consume') n1.
2 Jerome *Comm in Gal* 3 (on 5:16) CCL 77A 177:1
3 Ambrosiaster *Comm in Gal* 5:16
4 and not ... speech is heading] This remaining portion of the annotation was added in 1519.
5 with which ... agrees] Added in 1527
6 In the debate with Luther over the freedom of the will, the struggle between the flesh and the spirit that is described in Ephesians 5:16–24 played an important role. According to Erasmus, while Luther interprets this passage as referring to the righteous (whose flesh continues to struggle against the spirit), Erasmus contends that those who are regenerated by the Spirit are not entirely subject to 'wicked impulses of the flesh' but possess seeds of virtue and an innate horror of vice. For Erasmus' representation of the debate see *Hyperaspistes* 2, CWE 77 699–700.

5:16 [ER *et concupiscentiam* 'and strong desire']
[VG] *et desideria* 'and desires.' *Desiderium* [longing] in Greek is ἐπιθυ-
μίαν.[1] Ambrose[2] has the reading, *concupiscentiam carnis non perficietis*
[and do not perform the strong desire of the flesh], although it makes
little difference to the meaning.

> 1 Erasmus' translation is more precise, and moreover reflects the singular
> number in the Greek noun.
> 2 Ambrose ... *perficietis*] Added in 1519. For the reference see Ambrosiaster
> *Comm in Gal* 5:16.

5:17 [ER *haec autem inter se mutuo* 'but these things (are opposed) to each
other']
[VG] *haec enim sibi invicem* 'for these [oppose] each in turn.' In place
of *enim* [for], the Greek copies have δέ, 'but,' [the whole phrase being]
ταῦτα δέ, 'but these,' although it matters very little to the sense.

5:19 [ER *quae sunt haec* 'which are these']
[VG] *quae sunt* 'which are.' In reviewing the majority of terms such as
these the Latin manuscripts differ somewhat from the Greek ones, due
to the forgetfulness of the copyists. These are the terms in Greek, μοιχεία,
πορνεία, ἀκαθαρσία, ἀσέλγεια, εἰδωλολατρεία, φαρμακεία, ἔχθραι, ἔρις, ζῆλοι, θυ-
μοί, ἐριθεῖαι, διχοστασίαι, αἱρέσεις, φθόνοι, φόνοι, μέθαι, κῶμοι, that is, *adulterium, scortatio,*[1] *immunditia, lascivia, idolorum cultus, veneficium, simultates,
lis, aemulationes, irae, contentiones, factiones, sectae, invidiae, caedes, ebrietates; comessationes* [adultery, fornication, impurity, licentiousness, idol
worship, sorcery, quarrels, strife, rivalries, anger, dissensions, partisan-
ships, sects, jealousies, murders, drunkenness; riotous living]. And such[2]
is the reading also of Chrysostom, except that πορνείαν [fornication] occurs in the first place.[3] St Jerome reads as follows: *quae sunt fornicatio, immunditia, impudicitia, idolorum servitus, veneficia, inimicitiae, contentiones,
aemulationes, irae, rixae, dissensiones, haereses, invidiae, ebrietates, comessationes* [which are fornication, impurity, immodesty, service of idols,
sorceries, enmities, dissensions, rivalries, anger, brawls, disagreements,
heresies, jealousies, drunkenness, riotous living].[4] Ambrose reads in the
following way: *adulterium, fornicatio, impuritas, obscoenitas, idololatria,
veneficium, inimicitiae, contentiones, simulationes, irae, simultates, dissensiones, haereses, invidiae, ebrietates, comessationes* [adultery, fornication,
impurity, obscenity, idolatry, sorcery, enmities, dissensions, pretences,
anger, quarrels, disagreements, heresies, jealousies, drunkenness, riotous living].[5] Concerning each of these, if anyone wishes to be instructed
more fully, let him read the commentaries of Jerome at this point. In the

Epistle to the Romans I have already made note of the fact that there is a pleasant play upon the words φθόνοι [envies; 'phthonoi'] and φόνοι [murders; 'phonoi'], which the Translator was not even able to render into Latin.[6] The asyndeton[7] [omission of a connecting particle] and homoeoptota[8] [word-ending of similar inflection] possess a certain charm.

1 *scortatio*] First in *1519*; in *1516, fornicatio* 'fornication' (a synonym)
2 And such ... first place.] Added in *1535*
3 Chrysostom *Comm in Gal* 5.6 PG 61 672–3. Chrysostom's Greek list is accurately reported by Erasmus here, except that in the former's list εἰδωλολατρεία and φαρμακεία appear in reverse order and Chrysostom has ἔρις in the plural. The Latin translator of Chrysostom, however, uses words for the spiritual fruit that differ significantly from Erasmus' Latin rendering.
4 Jerome *Comm in Gal* 3 (on 5:19–21) CCL 77A 184:1–4. Erasmus seems to follow one of the manuscript variants mentioned at CCL 77A 184 n2, which reads *impudicitia* 'immodesty' instead of *luxuria* 'extravagance.'
5 Ambrosiaster *Comm in Gal* 5:19–21. Ambrose reads *veneficia* 'sorceries' in the plural, not *veneficium* (singular).
6 See Erasmus' annotation on Rom 1:29 ('[full of] envy, murders').
7 The asyndeton ... certain charm.] Added in *1527*
8 According to Quintilian (9.3.78–9), *homoioptoton* requires only similarity of cases, though similarity of sound is desirable. See Lausberg §729–31. Erasmus criticized the unrestrained use of this figure (cf *Ecclesiastes* III ASD V-5 134:589–95).

5:21 [ER *regni dei haeredes non erunt* 'they will not be heirs of the kingdom of God']
[VG] *non consequentur* 'they will not obtain'; οὐ κληρονομήσουσιν which Jerome [has translated] *possidebunt* [they will possess].[1] And with greater precision Ambrose [has], 'they will not obtain the inheritance of the kingdom of God.'[2]

1 Jerome *Comm in Gal* 3 (on 5:19–21) CCL 77A 184:1–192:202. BDAG defines the use of κληρονομέω here as to 'acquire, obtain, come into the possession of something.'
2 Ambrosiaster *Comm in Gal* 5:21

5:22 [ER *lenitas* 'gentleness']
[VG] *patientia* 'patience'; μακροθυμία, that is *longanimitas* [longsuffering], or *lenitas animi* [gentleness of soul][1] which that [Translator], as is his custom, virtually always renders as *patientia* [patience],[2] which word[3] is more frequently used of the body than of the soul – although St Jerome thinks that it makes little difference.[4] Ambrose renders 'gentleness.'[5] And here the catalogue of the fruits of the Spirit in the Greek copies is ἀγάπη, χαρά, εἰρήνη, μακροθυμία, χρηστότης, ἀγαθοσύνη, πίστις,

πραότης, ἐγκράτεια, that is *charitas, gaudium, pax, lenitas animi,*[6] *benignitas,*[7] *bonitas, fides, mansuetudo, temperantia* [love, joy, peace, gentleness of spirit, kindness, goodness, faithfulness, mildness, and self-control]. St Jerome, [in his work] *Against Jovinian,* has this reading: *charitas, gaudium, pax, longanimitas, benignitas, bonitas, fides, mansuetudo, continentia* [love, joy, peace, long-suffering, kindness, goodness, faithfulness, mildness, self-control].[8] And Ambrose reads this way: *charitas, gaudium, pax, longanimitas, benignitas, spes, lenitas, continentia, castitas, bonitas* [love, joy, peace, long-suffering, goodness, hope, gentleness, self-control, chastity, goodness] etc.[9] Obviously I think that the painstaking attention to detail of some whose practice it is to fret over the number in lists[10] of this sort ought not to praised here, and who superstitiously become entangled in drawing distinctions between each item, since it is likely that Paul had produced a certain collection of good and bad things, which they are accustomed to do, not because these are the only ones, but because this is a summary of them.[11]

1 or *lenitas animi*] Added in *1519*
2 The Vulgate translates μακροθυμία as *patientia* in Eph 4:2; Col 3:12; 1 Tim 1:16; 2 Tim 3:10; 2 Tim 4:2; 1 Pet 3:20, etc. In Rom 2:4, Col 1:11, 2 Cor 6:6, and 2 Tim 3:6 the Greek word is translated *longanimitas.*
3 which word ... soul] First in *1519*; in *1516, cum aliud quiddam sit* 'although it may be something different'
4 Jerome *Comm in Gal* 3 (on 5:22) CCL 77A 194:59–60
5 Ambrosiaster *Comm in Gal* 5:22–3. Ambrosiaster actually reads *longanimitas,* placing *lenitas* as a separate item later in his list.
6 *lenitas animi*] First in *1522*; previously, *longanimitas* 'long-suffering'
7 In his translation of the Epistle to the Romans Erasmus consistently renders χρηστότης as *bonitas* [goodness] and not *benignitas* [kindness], although in his annotations he notes that the latter is the better translation: Rom 2:4 ('the riches of his goodness' CWE 56 73) and Rom 15:14 ('you are full of love' CWE 56 402). See also Rom 11:22 ('goodness and severity') CWE 56 308 n1.
8 Jerome *Adversus Jovinianum* 1.38 PL 23 (1845) 276B
9 Ambrosiaster *Comm in Gal* 5:22–3
10 lists] First in *1519*; in *1516, catalogo* 'list'
11 Erasmus makes a similar comment in the annotation on Rom 1:29 ('with avarice'): 'I do not always approve of the too anxious care taken in these matters by certain people who think the number as well is to be observed in a thick forest of names' CWE 56 60–1.

5:24 [ER *qui vero sunt Christi carnem* 'but those who are of Christ (have crucified) the flesh']
[VG] *qui autem sunt Christi carnem suam* 'but those who are of Christ [have crucified] their own flesh.' In this passage Origen, by leaving out

the conjunction [connective particle] δέ [but], changes the entire sense, and reads as follows: Κατὰ τῶν τοιούτων οὐκ ἔστι νόμος, οἳ τοῦ Χριστοῦ τὴν σάρκα ἐσταύρωσαν σὺν τοῖς παθήμασι καὶ ταῖς ἐπιθυμίαις, that is, 'the law is not against such who have crucified the body of Christ [in their own flesh] with its vices and desires,' so that one takes it to mean not that those are of Christ who have crucified their own body, but rather that there is no law against those who have crucified the body of Christ in their own person, along with the vices and desires.[1] For the body of Christ is crucified in devout people with praise, in whom the impulses of the body have been mastered; but [the body of Christ] is badly recrucified,[2] as the Greek says it ἀνασταυροῦσθαι [crucified a second time], by those who have returned to their former lifestyle after they have once accepted Christ. But the Greek copies oppose this reading, even though Origen's understanding of it is approved by Jerome.[3] Ambrose appears to have had the reading, οἱ δὲ Χριστοί etc, so that christi [Christians] is in the nominative plural, not the genitive, for he adds that those who are dedicated to Christ are called 'Christians,' that is 'anointed.'[4]

1 Jerome Comm in Gal 3 (on 5:24) CCL 77A 197:2–4. Erasmus relies on Jerome as the source for Origen here, providing Jerome's Latin translation of Origen's Greek text. Origen's original Greek text no longer survives: his commentary on Galatians exists as a Latin translation from the Apologia pro Origene by Pamphilius. Consequently, Erasmus' Greek text is likely a translation from Jerome's Latin text. On the relationship between Jerome's commentaries on the Pauline epistles and those of Origen see Thomas Scheck St. Jerome's Commentaries on Galatians, Titus, and Philemon (Notre Dame, IN 2010) 8–14, and Ronald Heine The Commentaries of Origen and Jerome on St Paul's Epistle to the Ephesians (Oxford 2002) 1–71.
2 recrucified] First in 1519; in 1516, crucifigi 'crucified'
3 Jerome Comm in Gal 3 (on 5:24) CCL 77A 197:10–14
4 Ambrosiaster Comm in Gal 5:24

5:24 [ER cum affectibus et concupiscentiis 'with its feelings[1] and desires'] [VG] cum vitiis et concupiscentiis 'with its vices and desires'; παθήματα, that is, passiones [passions],[2] or as Augustine reads it, affectus [feelings].[3] In Against[4] the Manicheans concerning Genesis, he puts perturbationes [agitations] for affectus.[5] In Letter 39 he has the reading, cum passionibus et desideriis [with the passions and desires], although it[6] seems to be of Paul.[7] Although every pain or illness of the body can be called πάθημα [suffering], and therefore he has added ἐπιθυμίαις, which strictly speaking is for the longings of the soul, as also Jerome has observed.[8]

1 'with its feelings ... Jerome has observed.] In 1519, this annotation was followed by the chapter division title EX CAPITE SEXTO.
2 See also Erasmus' annotation on Rom 7:5 ('passions of sins').

3 It appears Erasmus is referring to some other work or is mistaken;
Augustine reads *passionibus* in his commentary, *Expos Gal* CSEL 84
128:24–5. Augustine translates πάθη as *affectus* in *De civitate dei* 9.4.1 CCL 47
251:1–4, though it is not in the context of Gal 5:24. Cf the note by Andrew
Brown on the text here: 'Erasmus attributed *affectus* to Augustine, though
the 1506 edition of Augustine's *Epistulae ad Galatas Expositio* had *passionibus* at this passage (edited as *perturbationibus*, in CSEL 84 128)' (*Novum
Testamentum* 488:24(3)n).

4 In *Against ... desideriis*] Added in *1519*
5 Augustine *De genesi contra manichaeos* 1.20 PL 34 188
6 although it ... Paul] Added in *1535*
7 Augustine *Epistulae* 243.11 PL 33 1059
8 Jerome *Comm in Gal* 3 (on 5:24) CCL 77A 198:26–40

5:25 [ER *Spiritu et incedamus* 'according to the Spirit let us also¹ proceed']
[VG] *Spiritu et ambulemus* 'by the Spirit let us also walk'; καὶ στοιχῶμεν,
which Valla corrects, *contenti simus* [let us be wholly dependent upon].²
But this suits the sense of Paul more than of the Greek word, στοιχῶμεν, which means 'to proceed in proper fashion,' so that you take it to
mean, 'let us hold ourselves fast to the Spirit, lest we cast our minds
back to the Law.' The action³ is a certain movement like that of a living
being. Yet the action proceeds from the same source from which the
life itself [proceeds]; consequently if our life depends upon the Spirit
and the Gospel, then we ought to conduct ourselves according to the
same [Spirit]. Nor do I perceive why [it] bothered Valla, unless he happened to have the reading στέγωμεν [let us contain ourselves] instead
of στοιχῶμεν; though I am aware of the fact that Theophylact interprets
the passage in the sense Valla does: στοιχῶμεν ἀντὶ τοῦ ἀρκεσθῶμεν, 'let us
be satisfied' instead of 'let us proceed.'⁴ St Augustine has the reading,
Spiritu vivimus, Spiritu et sectemur [we live by the Spirit, let us also aim
continually at the Spirit], interpreting⁵ it according to his reading – following whoever it was that translated or had the reading, or probably
dreamt up στοχῶμεν, from which is derived στοχάζω, which means 'to
focus one's eye upon the [archery] mark.'⁶ Moreover, the Greek⁷ verb
στοιχῶ is πολύσημον [multivalent], but is actually derived from [the word
for] order and direct course. Hence στίχοι, 'lines of poetry,' στοιχεῖα,
'principles' [*elementa*] or 'letters' [of the alphabet]; from it also derives
στοχάζω.

1 also] Added in *1535*
2 Valla *Annot in Gal* 5 (I 876)
3 The action ... from the same] Added in *1519*
4 Theophylact *Expos in Gal* 5:25 PG 124 1021B
5 interpreting ... reading] Added in *1519*
6 Augustine *Expos Gal* CSEL 84 129–30
7 Moreover, the Greek ... στοχάζω.] Added in *1527*

5:26 [ER VG] *inanis gloriae cupidi* **'desirous**[1] **of vain glory.'** In Greek there is
one word, κενόδοξοι, that is, 'vainglorious,' etc., or, as Ambrose reads,
'striving after vain glory.'[2]

1 'desirous ... after vain glory.'] In *1516*, this annotation was followed by the
chapter division title *EX CAPITE VI*.
2 Ambrosiaster *Comm in Gal* 5:26

From the Sixth Chapter

6:1 [ER *etiamsi occupatus fuerit* **'even if he will have been overtaken'**]
[VG] *si praeoccupatus* **'if anticipated'**; προληφθῇ [overtaken],[1] that is,
'overtaken'; this means stopped before he could take heed. With these
words he completely excludes premeditated malice and intention of
sinning.

1 Modern editions of the New Testament have the text προλημφθῇ. On the
element of surprise conveyed by the verb see Lightfoot 215. On Erasmus'
use of *occupo* to translate προλαμβάνω see Brown's note at ASD VI-2
145:35(2)n.

6:1 [ER *instaurate huiusmodi* **'restore one of this kind'**]
[VG] *huiusmodi instruite* **'instruct one of this kind'**; καταρτίζετε, that
is, *instaurate* [restore], *reficite* [rebuild], or *sarcite* [mend]. I suspect[1] that
a copyist altered the Translator's rendering, *instaurate*, to *instruite* [in-
struct]. Jerome, in explaining the sixteenth chapter of Ezekiel, reports
the reading *perficite huiuscemodi* [make perfect such a one].[2] Ambrose
has the reading, *humilitate* [cause to be disgraced], if at any[3] rate the text
is free of error, which seems very doubtful to me.[4] For from his commentary it cannot be gathered what the reading was; or, if anything can
be gathered, he has the reading *emendate* [correct], when he says, 'they
should be gently challenged to reform themselves.'[5] What Paul and the
sacred doctors are teaching here we ourselves hardly remember to do.
If there is anything that needs to be corrected, we immediately thunder
forth with such haughtiness and such ferocity. Behaviour of this sort
has caused many excellent men to be separated from the fellowship of
the church, which Jerome openly relates about Tertullian.[6]

1 I suspect ... Ambrose] Added in *1527*
2 Jerome *Commentarii in Ezechielem* 4 (on 16:15) CSEL 75 181:1433
3 if at any ... Tertullian] This remaining portion of the annotation was
added in *1519*.
4 Ambrosiaster *Comm in Gal* 6:1. Ambrosiaster actually reads *instruite* 'instruct'; see ASD VI-9 151:420n.
5 Ambrosiaster *Comm in Gal* 6:1–2
6 Jerome *De viris illustribus* 53 PL 23 (1845) 698B

6:1 [ER *considerans temetipsum* 'looking attentively to yourself']
[VG] *considerans teipsum* 'looking attentively to yourself.' Surprisingly
he has suddenly changed the number, σκοπῶν σεαυτόν, having regard
more for the sense than for the order of the words. And on the basis of
this text St Jerome comes to the conclusion that Paul's statement that he
was unskilled in speech was meant genuinely, and not so much from a
sense of modesty.[1] But to me he seems quite fittingly to have changed
the number suddenly, because the singular number was more suited
to reproaching the conscience of every one individually. Moreover
it would have been rather harsh to say to everyone, 'have regard for
yourselves, lest also you [pl.] are tempted.' And with marvelous care
[Paul] always behaves this way, lest anything should offend those
whom he is trying to correct. Moreover Theophylact[2] notes that σύ [you
(sg.)] was added to remind them of their human frailty.[3] At any rate this
statement applies not only to the Galatians, but also to each and every
human being individually. And it is for this reason that the number was
changed, something Paul does in other places, too, as I have pointed
out.[4]

1 Jerome *Comm in Gal* 3 (on 6:1) CCL 77A 206:65–71
2 Moreover Theophylact ... pointed out.] This remaining portion of the
annotation was added in 1527.
3 Theophylact *Expos in Gal* 6:1 PG 124 1021D–1024A
4 Cf the annotation on 1 Tim 1:9 (*scientes hoc*).

6:2 [ER *invicem alii aliorum onera* 'in turn one another's burdens (bear)']
[VG] *alter alterius onera* 'one the burdens of the other [bear]'; Ἀλλήλων
τὰ βάρη βαστάζετε. Ambrose[1] has rendered it in better Latin, and similarly[2]
Augustine[3] in the twenty-first sermon, *On the Words of the Lord*: *invicem
onera vestra portate* [in turn bear your burdens], quoting[4] it in the same
way elsewhere.[5] It could be rendered also in this way, *alii vicissim aliorum
onera bajulate* [carry one another's burdens in turn]. For *alter alterius* [each
other's] is said of two people in better Latin.[6]

1 Ambrosiaster *Comm in Gal* 6:2
2 and similarly ... *the Lord*] Added in 1519
3 Augustine, *On the Words of the Lord*, misquoted; in modern editions the
statement occurs in *De diversis quaestionibus* LXXI (CCL 44A 200–7, esp
200:1–2); see ASD VI-9.
4 quoting ... elsewhere] Added in 1519
5 Eg Augustine *De civitate dei* 15.6 CCL 48 458:5; *De trinitate* 8.7 PL 42 956;
Retractionum 1.26 PL 32 629. Ambrosiaster does not cite this phrase elsewhere in his works.
6 Erasmus follows Valla here, *Annot in Gal* 6 (I 876). He makes the same
change to the Vulgate at John 3:14 (cf ASD VI-2 149:14(2)n).

6:2 [ER *et sic complete* 'and so make complete']

[VG] *et sic adimplebitis* 'and so you will fulfil'; καὶ οὕτως ἀναπληρώσατε,
that is, 'and so fulfil' [imperative].¹ The Translator² reads ἀναπληρώσετε
[you will fulfil],³ nor does it matter very much for the meaning. [Paul]
again returns to the plural number.⁴ But the Greek word actually means
'fill up once more,' that is, 'fulfil a second time,'⁵ as if he is saying: 'what
was ruined by the neglect of one person in keeping the Law, let the love
of others restore.' Chrysostom⁶ carefully explains the rhetorical stress
[Latin *emphasis*]⁷ of this word.⁸

1 Erasmus is following Valla here, *Annot in Gal* 6 (I 876).
2 The Translator ... meaning.] Added in *1519*
3 In modern scholarship the reading ἀναπληρώσετε 'you will fulfil' is preferred on the basis of the textual evidence (cf Metzger 530); the Vulgate
   also has the verb in the future tense, indicative mood: *adimplebitis* (Weber
   1808). Modern English translations vary: 'and so fulfil' (AV and RSV), 'you
   will fulfil' (NEB).
4 plural number] In *1516, 1519,* and *1522* the following sentence was added
   here: *Quod autem dixit, ne et tu, hoc ad unumquemlibet retulit, ut admonuimus
   modo*, 'The fact that he said, "lest you [sg.] also," refers to each and every
   person, as we have already noted.'
5 In the 1516 *Novum Testamentum* Erasmus had used the non-classical
   verb *reimpleo*. He was criticized for this by the Spanish theologian
   Diego López Zúñiga (cf ASD IX-2 200–2), but nevertheless employed
   the non-classical verbs *readimplete* and *adimplete* in this annotation.
   Zúñiga or Stunica (d 1531) was a biblical scholar who taught at the
   University of Alcalá before moving to Rome in 1521. A collaborator
   on the Complutensian Polyglot Bible, Zúñiga began to collect notes on
   Erasmus' New Testament as soon as a copy reached him in 1516; he
   published a defence of the Vulgate in the *Annotationes contra Erasmum
   Roterodamum* (1520). Erasmus replied in the *Apologia ad annotatio-
   nes Stunicae* (October 1521). For a general introduction to Zúñiga see
   Contemporaries II 348–9 and H.J. de Jonge's Introduction to the *Apologia*
   in ASD IX-2, especially 14–34. For an account of the controversy between
   Erasmus and Zúñiga see Erika Rummel *Erasmus and his Catholic Critics*
   (Nieuwkoop 1989) 145–77, and Alejandro Coroleu 'Anti-Erasmianism in
   Spain' in *Biblical Humanism and Scholasticism in the Age of Erasmus* ed E.
   Rummel (Leiden 2008) 73–92.
6 Chrysostom ... word.] Added in *1535*
7 Erasmus uses here the transliterated Greek rhetorical term ἔμφασις
   [*emphasis*]. Quintilian defines 'emphasis' as 'words that mean more than
   they say' (8.2.11, and cf 9.2.64); Erasmus explains it in *Ecclesiastes* III as
   an expression that 'suggests more to the thought of the listeners than the
   words denote' (ASD V-5 148:859–81).
8 Chrysostom *Comm in Gal* 6.1 PG 61 675

6:3 [ER *si quis sibi videtur* 'if anyone appears to himself (to be something)']
[VG] *si quis existimet se* 'if anyone supposes himself [to be something]'
The Greek text is slightly different: Εἰ γὰρ δοκεῖ τις εἶναί τι, that is, 'for if anyone seems to be something,' assuming 'to himself.'[1] And the verb *seducit* [leads astray] in Greek is a compound verb, φρεναπατᾷ, that is, *mentem seducit* [he leads his soul astray] and deceives his own mind, as St Jerome explains.[2] For it is a very destructive kind of deception, when anyone fools himself.[3] Augustine,[4] in the second chapter of the book *On the Singularity of Clerics*, reads *seipsum implanat* [deludes himself], and as though commenting on the Greek word he adds, 'but a deceiver doubtless deceives especially his own mind.'[5] *Planus*[6] [deceiver] in Latin occurs as synonym for 'impostor'; I do not know whether [the verb] *implanare* [to deceive] is found.[7]

1 assuming 'to himself'] Added in *1519*
2 Jerome *Comm in Gal* 3 (on 6:3) CCL 77A 209:16–19
3 In his annotation on Rom 8:18 ('for I suppose') Erasmus cites this text to illustrate that *existimatio* means a false, not a fixed opinion.
4 Augustine ... his own mind.'] Added in *1519*
5 This treatise, thought by Erasmus to be by Augustine, and printed in CSEL 3/3 173–220 as spuria of Cyprian, may have been written by Macrobius or Novatian (ASD VI-9 154:453–4n).
6 *Planus* ... is found.] Added in *1522*
7 A. Souter *Glossary of Later Latin* (Oxford 1949) 188 defines *implanare* as 'deceive, lead astray.'

6:4 [ER *et tunc in semetipso* 'and then in himself']
[VG] *et sic in semetipso* 'and thus in himself'; καὶ τότε, that is, *et tunc* [and then], as Ambrose reads.[1] And *tantum* [so much] is not added in most[2] of the Greek copies, although[3] in a few μόνον [only] is added. Moreover, what in Greek is εἰς σεαυτόν,[4] that is, 'to himself,' and shortly thereafter likewise, καὶ οὐκ εἰς τὸν ἕτερον, that is, 'and not to another,'[5] [the Translator] perhaps would have rendered more accurately *apud seipsum* [to himself], and *non apud alium* [not to another]. However, I am aware that the sense of this preposition is unclear. Chrysostom[6] interprets, εἰς ἕτερον, καθ' ἑτέρου, that is, 'against another.'[7]

1 Ambrosiaster *Comm in Gal* 6:4
2 most] Added in *1519*
3 although ... added] Added in *1519*
4 In *Novum Testamentum* Erasmus prints εἰς ἑαυτόν.
5 Erasmus' translation of these Greek phrases does not follow the translation in *Novum Testamentum*. See also Valla *Annot in Gal* 6 (I 876); ASD VI-9 155:460–2n.
6 Chrysostom ... against another.'] Added in *1535*
7 Chrysostom *Comm in Gal* 6.1 PG 61 675

6:5 [ER *unusquisque enim propriam sarcinam bajulabit* 'for each one will bear his own load']
[VG] *unusquisque onus suum portabit* 'each one will carry his own burden'; φορτίον, which Ambrose reads as *sarcinam* [load].[1] And 'he will carry' is βαστάσει, which is appropriate to porters.

> 1 Ambrosiaster *Comm in Gal* 6:5; Erasmus is following the 1492 edition of Pseudo-Ambrose here; see further ASD VI-3 491:5n.
> In rendering the Greek word φορτίον [load] as *sarcina* in this passage, Erasmus implies that the Vulgate should have rendered it differently than *onus*, which it used for τὰ βάρη [burdens] in Gal 6:2. On the apparent paradox in bearing one another's burdens and each bearing his own load see Lightfoot 217.

6:6 [ER VG] *communicet autem qui* 'but let him share who.'[1] In Greek it is not *verbo* [in the word] but *verbum* [the word], accusative case, τὸν λόγον. Yet it could be accepted through synecdoche [a part representing the whole], so that the preposition κατὰ [according to] is assumed. Or he has said it in the following manner, *catechizatur verbum* [(he) is instructed in the word], just as we say, *docetur grammaticam* [he is taught grammar]. Ambrose expressed the Greek phrase in this way, ὁ κατηχούμενος τὸν λόγον, that is, 'he who is being catechized in the word.'[2] For *catechizare* is to teach the mysteries of the Christian religion.[3] However the phrase, *in omnibus bonis* [in all good things] ought to be taken with *commnunicet*, 'let him share,' and not with *catechizat*, 'instructs.' Marcion, as Jerome indicates,[4] takes λόγον ('speech, word'), in the accusative case, with the verb *communicet* [share], observing that believers ought to pray together with those who are being instructed, and that the instructor in prayer ought to share with the students. His interpretation is supported especially by the phrase that follows, *in omnibus bonis* [in all good things].[5] But if indeed the passage concerns prayer, the command ought to apply not to him who is being instructed but to him who instructs; that is, not to the student but to the teacher. However, the words which follow show that this interpretation is false: 'what a man will have sown that he will also reap.' Lorenzo Valla is somewhat upset that the Translator has maintained the Greek word *catechizatur*, although he has rendered it thus into Latin elsewhere. He thinks that [the sentence] ought to be translated thus: 'however let him who is taught the word share with the one who instructs him in all good things.'[6] For my part[7] I shall add the following, that λόγον [word] can be taken to mean a reckoning [*ratio*], so that we understand Paul is recommending there be a balance of giving and receiving between him who imparts the teaching of the faith and him who receives it, but only if in fact the teacher does so honestly. If not, the exchange would be unfair, when an act of kindness is offered in exchange for falsely transmitted teaching of the religion. And for this reason he added 'in all good things,' repeating what he has stated earlier [Gal 4:18], 'it is good always to be envious in a good thing.' But against those who dishonestly transmitted Christ for honour and profit he objects the following: 'God is not mocked' [Gal 6:7]. It appears Ambrose sensed this when he adds that regarding things that are not good one ought to dissent from such [teachers], so 'that the law rather than a human being should be our guide.'[8] Theophylact[9] explains the phrase about generosity from the point of view of those who are being instructed towards those who are instructing, and Jerome[10] is in agreement with him.

1 Cf *communicet autem is qui catecizatur verbum* (Weber 1808).
2 Ambrosiaster *Comm in Gal* 6:6
3 Christian religion] Here in *1516, 1519,* and *1522,* Erasmus added the following: *id quod scripto facere fas non erat* 'which it was not right to do by something written.' According to A. Souter *Glossary of Later Latin* (Oxford 1949) 47 *catechizare* means 'teach (by word of mouth) the elements of religion.'
4 as Jerome indicates] Added in *1519*
5 Jerome *Comm in Gal* 3 (on 6:6) CCL 77A 211:2–10
6 Valla *Annot in Gal* 6 (I 876)
7 For my part ... in agreement with him.] This remaining portion of the annotation was added in *1519*.
8 Ambrosiaster *Comm in Gal* 6:6. Erasmus here paraphrases Ambrosiaster, who reads *in his illis non communicandum, sed dissentiendum, ut magis lex tibi dux sit quam homo* 'in matters of this sort they should not share, but object, because the law is a better guide for you than a human being.'
9 Theophylact *Expos in Gal* 6:6 PG 124 1024D–1025A
10 Jerome *Comm in Gal* 3 (on 6:6) CCL 77A 211:15–19

6:7 [ER VG] *non irridetur* **'is not mocked'**; οὐ μυκτηρίζεται, which actually is 'to laugh at mockingly' [*scommate ridere*], and 'to smirk deridingly' [*subsannare*], and 'to thumb the nose at' [*naso suspendere*].[1] In Greek[2] μυκτῆρα means 'nose.'

1 See Erasmus *Adagia* I viii 22.
2 In Greek ... 'nose.'] Added in *1522*

6:8 [ER *quicquid enim seminaverit* **'for whatever he will have sowed'**] [VG] *quae enim seminaverit* **'for what things he will have sowed.'** In Greek [the word] is in the singular number, 'what thing a man will have sowed, this he will also reap.'[1] And so reads Ambrose,[2] and similarly Augustine.[3]

1 Erasmus is following Valla here, *Annot in Gal* 6 (I 876).
2 Ambrosiaster *Comm in Gal* 6:8
3 Augustine *Expos Gal* CSEL 84 136:4–5

6:8 [ER *per carnem* 'through the flesh']
[VG] *in carne* 'in the flesh.' The Greek is εἰς σάρκα,¹ that is, 'unto flesh':
even as a little later, εἰς τὸ πνεῦμα, that is, 'unto the Spirit' [Gal 6:8],² although the preposition εἰς is used in different ways.

> 1 It appears Erasmus inadvertently left out the article τήν; see ASD VI-3
>   491:8(2)n.
> 2 Erasmus is following Valla here, *Annot in Gal* 6 (I 876).

6:8 [ER VG] *metet corruptionem* 'will reap corruption'; θερίσει φθοράν, that
is, 'he will reap the source of corruption,' that is, 'fruit destined to bring
destruction,' for over against this [Paul] places eternal life.¹ The mortal
flesh bears mortal fruits; the eternal Spirit bears immortal fruits. But in
other places [the Translator] renders ἄφθαρτον as 'immortal,' and ἀφθαρσίαν as 'immortality.'²

> 1 In his annotation on Rom 8:21 ('will be freed from the servitude of cor-
>   ruption') Erasmus notes that φθορά 'corruption' has double meaning,
>   being used of a thing vitiated and of one who perishes.
> 2 ἄφθαρτος: 1 Tim 1:17; ἀφθαρσία: 1 Cor 15:54

6:9 [ER *defatigemur ... defatigati* 'let us grow weary ... grown weary']
[VG] *deficiamus et deficientes* 'let us fail, (and) failing.' In Greek the
words are different. For *deficiamus* [let us fail] is ἐκκακῶμεν, *deficientes*
[is] ἐκλυόμενοι, that is, 'grown weary.'¹ Ambrose has the reading *infati-
gabiles* [untiring] to render the tense also of the participle.² Tertullian³
in place of *ne deficiamus* [let us not fail], has the reading *ne taedeat* [let it
not be burdensome].

> 1 Erasmus is following Valla here, *Annot in Gal* 6 (I 876).
> 2 Ambrosiaster *Comm in Gal* 6:9
> 3 Tertullian ... *ne taedeat.*] Added in 1527. Tertullian *de resurrect.* 23.10 CCL 2
>   950:38–9.

6:10 [ER *erga omnes* 'towards all']
[VG] *ad omnes* 'to all.'¹ Why not rather 'towards all'?

> 1 'to all ... all'?] In 1516, this and the following annotation appeared in
>   reverse order.

6:11 [ER *quanta ... epistola* 'how great a letter']
[VG] *qualibus litteris* 'with what¹ letters'; πηλίκοις, that is, *qualibus* [with
what kind], but in such a way that it means size and cause for wonder.
This suits Paul's frame of mind more, since to him the matter was so
near to his heart that it was not a burden to write about these things

in his own hand. St Jerome thinks that the rest of the Epistle had been written by another hand, but that Paul, in order to avoid all suspicion of feigned words, had written this remainder of the Epistle with his own hand.[2] But why would it not be better, with all due respect to St Jerome, for us to conjecture from this passage that the entire Epistle had been penned by the hand of Paul? Jerome admits that the Greek word πηλίκοις means size rather than quality, which Hilary[3] also observes in [his commentary on] the Psalms, following Origen,[4] I think. The Greek word means size, but not so the Latin word; yet St Hilary refers the size not to the shape of the letters but to the lofty ideas, which seems to me to be somewhat forced. Moreover St Jerome struggles to explain how large these letters are, as if Paul had this in mind, that the Epistle had been written in very large letters. But the Greeks say 'letters' [*litterae*] in the plural number, and 'one letter' [or 'epistle'] in the singular, just as in Latin. Therefore the Apostle, in order to demonstrate to what extent this matter weighed on his heart, writes, 'you see how great an epistle I have written with my own hand,' for he had just now completed the Epistle. For in other Epistles he was accustomed merely to add the subscription, *mea manu Pauli* [with my own hand, Paul's]. Nor is there any reason why γράμμασι, in the dative case, not γράμματα [accusative], should offend anyone. For [we say] *loquimur multis* [we speak with many words] and *loquimur multa* [we speak many words], and likewise *scribimus paucis* [we write with few words] and also *scribimus pauca* [we write few words]. Ambrose[5] shares my point of view when he concludes from this passage that the Epistle was written entirely by Paul. Moreover I wonder why for *videte* [see] or *videtis* [you see] he should have the reading, *scitote* [know] unless he had a manuscript with the reading εἴδετε [know]. Augustine reads, *vidistis, qualibus litteris vobis scripsi* [you see with what letters I have written to you], as though Paul[6] gives his warnings[7] with recognizable handwriting lest they should be deceived by the faked letters of other men.[8] Theophylact,[9] following Chrysostom,[10] grants that it is clear from this passage that this Epistle had been written by Paul's hand. And also, the word *qualibus* [with what kind] pertains not to the size of the letters but to the ill-formed style, because Paul wishes to appear unskilled in writing, and yet it was not a burden for him to write the entire Epistle with his own hand.

1 'with what ... entire epistle with his own hand.] See the annotation on Gal 6:10 ('to all') n1 above. Erasmus' main point in this annotation is that γράμμασι means epistle and not, as Jerome thinks, letters of the alphabet.
2 Jerome *Comm in Gal* 3 (on 6:11) CCL 77A 218:8–10

3 which Hilary ... Moreover St Jerome] Added in *1527*. In *1516*, *et* 'also' in
    place of the entire phrase. Hilary *Tractatus super Psalmos* 118.19 CCL 61A
    179:19–23. Hilary's comments on Gal 6:11 are found in his Treatise on
    Psalm 118 [= 119]. For Erasmus' edition of the works of Hilary, see John
    C. Olin *Erasmus, Utopia and the Jesuits* (New York 1994), especially 27–37,
    'Erasmus and his Edition of Saint Hilary.'
4 Erasmus appears to err here, as Origen does not treat the matter.
5 Ambrose ... entire Epistle with his own hand.] This remaining portion
    of the annotation was added in *1519*. For the reference see Ambrosiaster
    Comm in Gal 6:11.
6 as though Paul] From *1527*; in *1519* and *1522*, *ceu* 'just as if'
7 gives his warnings] From *1527*; in *1519* and *1522*, *admonens* 'warning'
8 Augustine *Expos Gal* CSEL 84 137:23–5
9 Theophylact *Expos in Gal* 6:11 PG 124 1028B
10 following Chrysostom] Added in *1535*. For the reference see Chrysostom
    Comm in Gal 6.3 PG 61 678.

6:12 [ER *volunt iuxta faciem placere in carne* 'they wish according
to outward appearance to please in the flesh']
[VG] *volunt placere in carne* 'they wish to please in the flesh'; εὐπρο-
σωπῆσαι, that is, 'to please according to outward appearance'[1]; for the
Greek word is a composite of these elements, and that is 'in the flesh.'[2]

1 Erasmus' rendering *iuxta faciem* [according to outward appearance]
    more closely expresses the compound Greek verb εὐ-προσωπῆσαι than the
    Vulgate.
2 and that is 'in the flesh'] Added in *1527*. Valla did not read ἐν σαρκί, cf
    Valla *Annot in Gal* 6 (I 876): *Graece non legitur in carne* [In Greek 'in the
    flesh' is not read].

6:12 [ER *tantum ne ob crucem Christi persequutionem patiamur*[1] 'only that
on account of the cross of Christ we should not suffer persecution']
[VG] *tantum ut crucis Christi persequutionem non* 'only that the persecution of the cross[2] of Christ not.'[3] The Greek is as follows: μόνον ἵνα
μὴ τῷ σταυρῷ τοῦ Χριστοῦ διώκωνται, that is, 'lest they should be persecuted by the cross of Christ,' so that you take *persequantur* passively,[4]
that is, 'lest the cross of Christ should bring persecution to them.' In
Ambrose[5] the word *tantum* [only] is not added, although it is added
in Augustine.[6] Something must be added whereby the sentence is rendered more complete: 'they are doing this only in order to flee the hatred of the cross of Christ.'

1 Cf ASD VI-9 159:54 on *patiantur* 'they should not suffer.'
2 persecution of the cross] In *1516*, *persecuti crucis* 'of the persecuted cross';
    in *1519*, *1522*, and *1527*, *persecutionem crucis* 'persecution of the cross.'

3 of Christ'] Added in *1535*
4 For the rare, post-classical use of *patior* in the passive voice see L&S.
5 In Ambrose ... cross of Christ.'] Added in *1519*. For the reference see
  Ambrosiaster *Comm in Gal* 6:12.
6 Augustine *Expos Gal* CSEL 84 137:26–7

6:13 [ER *ipsi quidem legem servant* 'but they themselves keep the Law']
[VG] *legem custodiunt* 'they guard the Law.' *Ipsi* (αὐτοί), 'they them-
selves,' is missing, which also Ambrose added [to the Latin rendering].[1]
Jerome reads *hi* [these men], as if the Greek had read οὗτοι.[2]

  1 Ambrosiaster *Comm in Gal* 6:13. Ambrosiaster actually reads *hi* 'these men.'
  2 as if the Greek had read οὗτοι] Added in *1527*. For the reference see Jerome
    Comm in Gal 3 (on 6:13) CCL 77A 221:1.

6:14 [ER *absit ut glorier* 'far be it (from me) that I should glory']
[VG] *absit gloriari* 'far be it to glory.' 'Far be it that I should glory,' or
'let it not happen to me that I glory.'[1]

  1 Though more literal, the Vulgate rendering is rejected by Erasmus as
    inelegant.
    In his annotation on Rom 3:4 ('God forbid') Erasmus observes that this
    rhetorical expression of rejection is common in Paul's writing.

6:16 [ER *et quicunque iuxta regulam hanc incedunt* 'and all those who
walk according to this rule']
[VG] *et quicunque hanc regulam sequuti fuerint* 'and all those who will
have followed this rule'; καὶ ὅσοι τῷ κανόνι τούτῳ στοιχήσουσι. It is the
same word that he earlier[1] translated *ambulemus* [let us walk], στοιχῶμεν,
that is, 'whoever will walk by this rule.'

  1 Cf Gal 5:25. See the annotation there ('by the Spirit let us also walk').

6:16 [ER *et super Israelem*[1] *dei* 'and over the Israel of God']
[VG] *et super Israel dei* 'and over Israel of God'; τὸν Ἰσραήλ [the Israel],
so that you assume a man or people. And he adds, 'of God,' because of
the Synagogue of Satan.[2]

  1 On the declination of 'Israel' see ASD VI-2 23:31n.
  2 Synagogue of Satan] For this phrase cf Rev 2:9, 3:9.

6:17 [ER VG] *de caetero* 'concerning the other matter'; τοῦ λοιποῦ [genitive
case];[1] it is not τὸ λοιπόν[2] [accusative case], which elsewhere[3] he translates[4] as '[what] remains,' or, 'what is left.' But [Paul] appears here more
to be speaking about issues than about the time, so that[5] you assume

περί [concerning], περὶ λοιποῦ [concerning the other matter]:⁶ I have imparted what was to be imparted, I wish this to be certain, nor shall I
again allow it to be called into question.

1 Modern editions read τοῦ λοιποῦ.
2 it is not τὸ λοιπόν] Added in 1527
3 In fact, the expression does not occur elsewhere in the New Testament;
  see further the note by M. van Poll-van de Lisdonk ASD VI-9 161:554–555n.
4 he translates ... into question] Added in 1527. Previously, this entire
  phrase is replaced by solet 'is accustomed to.'
5 so that ... περὶ λοιποῦ] Added in 1519
6 περί, περὶ λοιποῦ] From 1527; in 1519 and 1522, τὸ λοιπόν. See also the annotation on Eph 6:10 ('brothers').

6:17 [ER *ne quis mihi molestias exhibeat* **'lest anyone produce trouble
for me']**
[VG] *nemo mihi molestus sit* **'let no one be a nuisance to me';**¹ κόπους μοι
μηδεὶς παρεχέτω, that is, 'let none produce hardships for me'; and in this
manner St Jerome both translates and explains [the words].² Augustine³
has the reading, 'let no one present trouble to me' – hardly hiding the
fact that in many codices the reading occurs, 'let no one be a nuisance to
me,' at the very opening of the book *On the Predestination of the Saints.*⁴

1 Erasmus' rendering is strictly classical; cf *exhibeant molestiam* in Plautus
  Captivi 817. See also Brown *Novum Testamentum* 494:17(2)n.
2 Jerome *Comm in Gal* 3 (on 6:17) CCL 77A 225:5–8
3 Augustine ... *the Saints.*] This remaining portion of the annotation
  was added in 1519. For the reference see Augustine *Expos Gal* CSEL 84
  140:15–16.
4 Augustine *De praedestinatione sanctorum* 1.1 PL 44 959–60

6:17 [ER VG] *stigmata* **'brand-marks.'** This is a Greek word, and it means
'a mark that is stamped.'¹ Slaves are commonly given a distinguishing mark by their masters, lest another² person be able to appropriate
them for himself. Therefore he wishes to indicate that he has certain
signs which show he is a servant of Christ, for whom he had suffered
so much. So many times³ beaten by rods, so many times stoned, so
many times thrown before wild beasts, so many times cast into chains:
from all these things he builds up his authority over against the false
apostles.⁴ They were glorying in the scars of circumcision, but Paul was
bearing in his own body the marks of the cross of Christ. Consequently
such a teacher ought to be believed rather than those self-indulgent
teachers who boast in the wounds borne by someone else.

1 On the appropriateness of the image of brand-marks in the service of Christ see Lightfoot 225.
2 lest another ... for himself] Added in *1519*
3 So many times ... someone else.] This remaining portion of the annotation was added in *1527*.
4 Cf 2 Cor 11:23–7.

ANNOTATIONUM IN EPISTOLAM AD GALATAS FINIS

The End[1] of the Annotations on the Epistle to the Galatians

1 The End ... Galatians] First in *1527*; previously, *Finis Epistolae Pauli ad Galatas*, 'The End of the Epistle of Paul to the Galatians'

ANNOTATIONS ON PAUL'S EPISTLE

TO THE EPHESIANS BY

DESIDERIUS ERASMUS OF ROTTERDAM

IN EPISTOLAM PAULI AD EPHESIOS ANNOTATIONES¹
DES. ERASMI ROTERODAMI.²

Annotations on Paul's Epistle to the Ephesians
by Desiderius Erasmus of Rotterdam

From the First Chapter³

In this Epistle of Paul there is the same fervour, the same depth of thought, the same spirit and feeling throughout, but nowhere else is the language more troublesome because of hyperbata,⁴ anadiploses,⁵ and other inconveniences. This was either due to the amanuensis whom he employed for this Epistle, or because his facility in expression did not match the sublimity of his thoughts.⁶ Certainly⁷ the style differs so much from the other Epistles of Paul that it might appear to be by someone else if the emotion and the genius of the Pauline mind did not claim it completely for him.

1 ANNOTATIONES] First in *1519;* in *1516* this word was the first in the title.
2 DES. ERASMI ROT.] First in *1519* (as DES. ERASMI ROTERODAMI)
3 From the First Chapter] Added in *1527*
4 Hyperbaton is the separation of words that naturally belong together, often to mark excitement; cf the annotation on Gal 1:6 ('into the grace of Christ') n4.
5 Anadiplosis is the immediate repetition of a word or phrase in order to add force to the argument (Smyth 3009). For anadiplosis as an aspect of rhetoric cf Quintilian 9.3.44.
6 In the letter to Domenico Grimani prefatory to the Paraphrases on the Epistle to the Romans (Allen Ep 710:1–35) Erasmus notes the obscurity, foreign flavouring, and other shortcomings in Paul's Greek style. For these observations he was criticized by Johann Eck, Diego López Zúñiga, and Noël Béda; cf Rummel 99–100.
7 Certainly ... for him.] Added in *1519*

1:1 [ER *qui agunt Ephesi* 'who live at Ephesus']
[VG] *qui sunt Ephesi* 'who are in Ephesus'; τοῖς οὖσιν ἐν Ἐφέσῳ.¹ This could also be read as the second person plural, 'You who are at Ephesus.' Ephesus² is the chief city of Asia, that³ is, properly speaking, Asia Minor.⁴

1 The words ἐν Ἐφέσῳ are lacking in several manuscripts, leading some commentators to suggest that the letter was intended as an encyclical to various churches in Asia Minor (Metzger 533).
2 Ephesus ... Asia] Added in *1519.* In *1522,* Erasmus amended the phrase to read 'Ephesus is the chief city of Asia *Minor.*' The 'Minor' was removed in *1527,* and replaced with the next clause, 'that is, properly speaking, Asia Minor.'

3 that ... Minor] Added in 1527
4 On Erasmus' understanding of what is meant by 'Asia' and 'Asia Minor'
   see the annotation on Rom 16:5 ('of the church of Asia') CWE 56 426 n7.
   For a depiction of the gospel spreading to Ephesus and the character
   of the people there see the Argument to *Paraphrasis in Galatas* CWE 43
   298–301.

1:2 [ER VG] *gratia vobis et pax* **'grace**[1] **to you and peace.'** Jerome observes
that grace and peace are referred alike to both the Father as well as to
the Son; however, it can be taken in such a way that grace is referred to
the Father, peace to the Son, so that the Father's grace is to be understood as his deigning to send the Son for our salvation; the Son's peace
as our reconciliation to the Father through him.[2] This idea has occurred
to Jerome because of the words which shortly follow, 'Unto the praise
of the glory of his grace, in which he has graced us in his beloved [Son]
[1:6].' For it is certain that these words pertain to the Father.

1 'grace ... Father.] Added in 1522. When this annotation was introduced in
   1522 it was wrongly placed before the preceding one; the error was corrected in 1535.
2 Jerome *Comm in Eph* 1 (on 1:2) PL 26 (1884) 473C–474A. For Erasmus' defi-
   nition of grace (*gratia*) as 'kindness' see the annotation on Rom 1:11 ('that
   I may impart some grace') CWE 56 35.

1:3 [ER VG] *benedictus*[1] *deus* **'blessed the God.'** These words can be punctuated in two ways: with a comma after 'God' so that the next words,
'and the Father of our Lord Jesus Christ,' are a separate addition; or
continuously without pause, 'God and Father of our Lord Jesus Christ'
– Father, because he begot; God in keeping with Jesus' assumption of
human nature. Jerome makes this point.[2]

1 On the use of the word *benedictus* see the annotation on Rom 1:25 ('who
   is blessed') CWE 56 55, where Erasmus expresses a preference for the term
   laudandus 'to be praised' because forms of *benedictus* may be wrongly
   associated with the bishop's blessing (*benedictio*) following the Lord's
   Prayer.
2 Jerome *Comm in Eph* 1 (on 1:3) PL 26 (1884) 475B–C

1:3 [ER *in caelestibus Christo* **'in heavenly places for Christ'**]
[VG] *in caelestibus in Christo* **'in heavenly places in Christ';** ἐν τοῖς
ἐπουρανίοις Χριστῷ. That is, in the heavenly or superheavenly places for
Christ, where 'Christ' is in the dative case. Ambrose omits the words
'in Christ';[1] Jerome does read the words 'in Christ.'[2] If you read, 'He
blessed us for Christ,' the meaning will be, 'He blessed us to the glory
of Christ.' If you read 'in Christ,' the meaning will be, 'He conferred

this blessing on us through the faith of Christ.' Theophylact,[3] who was recently made out to be Athanasius,[4] takes it in this latter sense. For[5] he reads ἐν Χριστῷ Ἰησοῦ [in Christ Jesus].

1 Ambrosiaster *Comm in Eph* 1:3. The commentaries on the Pauline Epistles that Erasmus ascribes to Ambrose are, in fact, the work of Ambrosiaster; see the Introduction and n14 there. Ambrosiaster is in fact missing the entire phrase *in caelestibus in Christo* 'in heavenly places in Christ,' see ASD VI-9 163:25n.
2 Jerome *Comm in Eph* 1 (on 1:3) PL 26 (1884) 474A
3 Theophylact ... sense.] Added in *1522*. See Theophylact *Expos in Eph* 1:3 PG 124 1036B. For the Greek text without the preposition 'in' see the note by Brown *Novum Testamentum* 495:3(2)n.
4 On Theophylact and Athanasius see the annotation on Gal 1:6-7 ('into another gospel, which is not another') and n7 there.
5 For ... Ἰησοῦ.] Added in *1527*

1:4 [ER *antequam iacerentur fundamenta mundi* 'before the foundations of the world were laid']
[VG] *ante mundi*[1] *constitutionem* 'before the foundation of the world'; πρὸ καταβολῆς. This phrase means something like 'before the foundations of the world were laid.' This is St Jerome's view, which he advances with abundant verbiage.[2]

1 *mundi* ('of the world')] Added in *1535*
2 Jerome *Comm in Eph* 1 (on 1:4) PL 26 (1884) 475C–476A

1:4 [ER *et irreprehensibiles* 'and without blame']
[VG] *et immaculati* 'and unspotted'; ἀμώμους, which means 'without fault' or 'without blame' rather than 'unspotted.' For μῶμος in Greek is fault-finding or the god of fault-finding.[1]

1 Cf Erasmus *Apologia ad annotationes Stunicae* ASD IX-2 202 and the notes on lines 653–64 by H.J. de Jonge. Momos (Greek Μῶμος) is the censorious offspring of the goddess Nyx. Like many of his siblings, Momos personifies a negative aspect of the human condition, in this case *disgrace* or *fault*. In literature he is often portrayed as one who constantly seeks to find faults, even insignificant ones, and becomes enraged when no faults are to be found.

1:4 [ER *per charitatem* 'through love']
[VG] *in charitate* 'in charity.' This phrase can be taken with the preceding words so that one understands that we are without fault and chosen in love, or with the words which follow so that you take it to mean that we have been predestined in love.[1] The Greek manuscripts, however, connect it with the preceding words. Jerome noted this.[2]

1 Although Erasmus does not comment on this point, his translation with the preposition *per* 'through,' not *in*, indicates that he took the phrase to be instrumental rather than circumstantial: we are chosen because of or through love. Cf Allen and Greenough 121(16c).
2 Jerome *Comm in Eph* 1 (on 1:5) PL 26 (1884) 478A–B. See Brown's note *Novum Testamentum* 496:4(5)n.

1:5 [ER VG] *qui predestinauit nos* 'who predestined us'; προορίσας. Jerome[1] and Ambrose[2] read 'in love predestining us.' But the verb 'predestining' is in the past tense in Greek, as if, allowing for a change in the voice, he had said 'having been predestined' or 'predetermined.' And in this passage the verb is actually 'predestine,' on which I touched somewhat in the Epistle to the Romans.[3] St Jerome thinks the difference between ὁρίζειν and προορίζειν to be this: the former attributes that quality to things which have always existed, the latter to things which at first did not exist but afterwards came into existence.[4] If anything had been determined or considered about them before they existed, then it is predestination. But if anything [had been determined] about the Lord Jesus Christ – who was always with the Father, nor was it ever the case that the Father's will preceded him – then it is destiny. Hence in the Epistle to the Romans when speaking about the Son of God [1:4], he said ὁρισθέντος 'destined,' not προορισθέντος 'predestined.'

1 Jerome *Comm in Eph* 1 (on 1:5) PL 26 (1884) 478A–B
2 Ambrosiaster *Comm in Eph* 1:5
3 See the annotation on Rom 1:4 ('who was predestined').
4 Jerome *Comm in Eph* 1 (on 1:5) PL 26 (1884) 478B–C
On the force of 'before, beforehand' in πρό see Smyth 1694.2.

1:5 [ER *ut adoptaret in filios* 'to adopt [us] as sons']
[VG] *in adoptionem filiorum* 'unto the adoption of sons.' This is a single word in Greek, υἱοθεσίαν, by which they mean that adoption whereby someone is adopted into the place of a son, as we advised above.[1] For[2] grandsons and granddaughters are also adopted.

1 See the annotation on Rom 8:15 ('the spirit of adoption of the sons of God') CWE 56 209–10.
2 For ... adopted.] Added in *1527*

1:5 [ER *in sese* 'to his own self']
[VG] *in ipsum* 'unto himself'; εἰς αὐτόν, that is, to his own self, so[1] that a reciprocal relation with the Father is made, although the phrase can be referred also to Christ, but by forcing the language.[2] For through adoption we are made brothers and not sons of Jesus Christ, in[3] keeping

with the proper meaning of the mystical way of speaking; [we are] sons of God the Father as members of the body of Christ and made one with him.

1 so ... is made] Added in *1519*
2 In replying to Edward Lee's criticism that the letter alpha in the personal pronoun αὐτόν must be aspirate for it to refer to God the Father, Erasmus argues that an error had occurred in the Greek manuscripts of this text; moreover, if the pronoun refers to Christ, then the syntax would be rather forced. See *Responsio ad annotationes Lei* 2 CWE 72 293; cf Erika Rummel *Erasmus and his Catholic Critics* (Nieuwkoop 1989) 102–3. For more on Lee see the annotation on Gal 1:5 ('to whom is the glory') n3.
3 in ... way of speaking] Added in *1519*

1:5 [ER *iuxta beneplacitum* 'in keeping with the good pleasure']
[VG] *secundum propositum* 'according to the purpose'; κατὰ τὴν εὐδοκίαν, that is, 'according to pleasure' or rather 'according to good pleasure.'[1] Jerome thinks the word is a neologism invented by the LXX[2] to be able to explain the Hebrew word רָצוֹן 'rason' [delight, pleasure].[3] Moreover, εὐδοκία is used properly not only when something has pleased, but has rightly pleased, too.[4] For pleasure is caused even by things which do not please rightly. Ambrose[5] reads 'according to the pleasure of the will.'

1 In altering the Vulgate's *secundum propositum* Erasmus is thinking of Romans 8:28, where he explains κατὰ πρόθεσιν ('according to the purpose') to mean the determining judgment of God. Paul's use of εὐδοκία here adds an element of pleasure to God's determining judgment. See the annotation on Rom 8:28 ('in accordance with the purpose') CWE 56 224.
2 On the 'Seventy' and the Septuagint see the annotation on Rom 1:17 ('lives by faith') n5; occasionally, Erasmus speaks of the 'Septuagint edition,' but more often he writes *Septuagint* 'the Seventy.' When the word 'Seventy' is the subject, Erasmus puts the verb in the plural, and in the past tense. The ambiguity in this use is reflected by the Roman numeral LXX, which suggests both the edition and the hypothetical seventy translators.
3 Jerome *Comm in Eph* 1 (on 1:5) PL 26 (1884) 478D. See Brown *Novum Testamentum* 497:5(4)n for Erasmus' use of various words and phrases denoting God's will. On Jerome's knowledge of Hebrew see the annotation on Gal 3:13 ('slandered is everyone who hangs on a tree') n6.
4 LSJ defines εὐδοκία as satisfaction or approval, and in particular that of God. Jerome specifies the additional meaning of 'rightly pleased': 'The word εὐδοκία ... is composed in Greek from two individual words, ἀπὸ τοῦ Εὖ, καὶ τοῦ Δοκεῖν, from *bene* [properly], and from *placitum* [that which pleases], which we are able to call *beneplacitum*, because not everything pleases immediately, and is able to please properly, but εὐδοκία, that is *beneplacitum* [properly pleasing], is said in the place where that which pleases is established as rightly pleasing.' See Jerome *Comm in Eph* 1 (on

1:5) PL 26 (1884) 478C–D, and Brown *Novum Testamentum* 497:5(4). For Erasmus' understanding of εὐδοκία as characteristic of God's gracious purpose and good will toward humanity, see *Paraphrasis in Lucam* (on 2:11–14) CWE 47 73 n19.

5 Ambrose ... will.'] Added in *1519*. See Ambrosiaster *Comm in Eph* 1:5.

1:6 [ER *ut laudaretur gloria gratiae suae* 'that the glory of his grace be praised']

[VG] *in laudem gloriae gratiae suae* 'unto the praise of his glory and grace.' Some manuscripts[1] wrongly add the conjunction 'and,' reading 'of glory and of his grace,' although [the Greek] is[2] δόξης τῆς χάριτος αὐτοῦ, that[3] is, 'the glory of his grace,' so that one understands that it is the glory of divine grace that is being praised. This[4] is exactly what Jerome reads.[5] Ambrose[6] has the reading 'unto the praise of his splendour,' without[7] any mention of grace. For he translated δόξα by 'splendour'; however, in his commentary he does mention 'grace.'[8] He usually translates δόξα by 'majesty' and majesty does fit better with the idea of power. Here he attributes it to grace. For God appeared more wonderful in redeeming humanity than in creating it. The Apostle everywhere extols grace while diminishing confidence in human works. Nowadays there are people who sin in both directions. The middle road is the safest. But if it is necessary to bend in one way or the other, it is better to bend to the side of grace where Christ is glorified than to the side of our works where humans are glorified.

1 This variant is not recorded in modern critical apparatuses of the Vulgate. It occurs in the Vulgate text of the 1527 edition of Erasmus' *Novum Testamentum*.
2 although the Greek is] Added in *1519*
3 that ... his grace'] Added in *1519*
4 This ... reads.] Added in *1522*
5 Jerome *Comm in Eph* 1 (on 1:6) PL 26 (1884) 479B
6 Ambrose ... splendour'] Added in *1519*. See Ambrosiaster *Comm in Eph* 1:6.
7 without ... humans are glorified] Added in *1527*. Those who sin on the side of grace are presumably the Lutherans with their claim of justification by faith alone, while the reliance on good works for salvation is the traditional Catholic position. See *De libero arbitrio* CWE 76 88.
8 LSJ defines δόξα as the outward appearance of splendour or magnificence. This meaning is usually found in the New Testament.

1:6 [ER *qua charos reddidit* 'wherein he rendered us dear']

[VG] *in qua gratificavit* 'in which he has graced'; ἐν ᾗ ἐχαρίτωσεν. Here 'has graced' means 'has made acceptable or dear,' ἐχαρίτωσεν;[1] from this verb comes the participle in κεχαριτωμένη Μαρία. But[2] if it was necessary there [Luke 1:28] to translate 'full of grace,' here he ought to have translated 'he filled with grace.' For the word *gratificare* strikes Latin ears as unusual; the deponent verb *gratificari* means to do something as a favour to another.

1 The Greek verb χαριτόω 'to show grace to someone, to favour' is not accurately translated by the Latin *gratificare*. As Mohrmann explains, *Études sur le Latin des Chrétiens* I (Rome 1961) 191, *gratificare* was a Christian neologism; in translating χάρις by *gratia* [grace], it formed a causative *gratificare* to render the Greek χαριτόω. In the common language, however, the deponent verb *gratificor* 'to show favour, to give liberally' already existed. Augustine also comments on the use of *gratificare* in this passage: '"In which he has graced us," it says, "in his own beloved son." Certainly in which he has graced us by his own favour. Thus it was said that *gratificavit* comes from *gratia*, just as it is said that *justificavit* comes from *justitia*.' Augustine *De praedestinatione sanctorum* 18.36 PL 44 987. For a summary of the different ways in which Erasmus translates χάρις see the note by P.F. Hovingh on *Annotationes in Epistolam ad Romanos* 1:5 ASD VI-7 46:247–51n. Erasmus' point in this annotation is that one has to understand the meaning of the Greek word χαριτόω to appreciate the force of the Latin *gratificare*.

2 But ... to another.] Added in *1527*. Erasmus' translation of κεχαρισμένη in the angelic greeting of Mary at Luke 1:28 as 'graceful' [*gratiosa*] instead of the traditional 'full of divine grace' [*gratia plena*] was not well received by Lee and other critics. In support of his reading, Erasmus interprets its use here in the conversational and not technical sense. See further Rummel 167–8.

1:6 [ER *per illum dilectum* 'through him the beloved']
[VG] *in dilecto filio suo* 'in his beloved son.' The words 'his son' are not added in the Greek or in Jerome:[1] ἐν τῷ ἠγαπημένῳ, that is, 'in him who was loved.'[2] For the word here is not ἀγαπητός [beloved]. Ambrose has the reading of the Vulgate edition and takes the meaning to be entirely about the Son.[3] But he preferred to designate him by the name 'the loved one' so that one would understand that we are loved by God, not because of our merits, but on account of the love which the Father bestows on the Son whose brothers he wanted us to be. Jerome[4] carefully observes that it does not say 'loved son.' For why is it a great thing if a father loves his son? Nor is he loved for one and all, but absolutely loved in all and before all and without whom no one else is loved.

1 Jerome *Comm in Eph* 1 (on 1:6) PL 26 (1884) 479B
2 Erasmus' point in this annotation is that the Vulgate has over-translated the Greek, and furthermore overlooked the force of the article in ἐν τῷ ἠγαπημένῳ 'in him who was loved.'
3 Ambrosiaster *Comm in Eph* 1:6
4 Jerome ... is loved.] Added in *1527*. See Jerome *Comm in Eph* 1 (on 1:6) PL 26 (1884) 479C–480A.

1:7 [ER *remissionem peccatorum* 'the remission of sins']
[VG] *in remissionem peccatorum* '**unto the remission of sins.**' The preposition *in* [unto] is not in the Greek nor in Ambrose[1] nor in Jerome.[2] It is necessary to connect the accusative case through an explanatory apposition. For to explain what that redemption is, he added 'remission of sins.' For it was from slavery that Christ redeemed us.[3] The[4] two manuscripts from Constance agree with this reading.

    1 Ambrosiaster *Comm in Eph* 1:7
    2 Jerome *Comm in Eph* 1 (on 1:7) PL 26 (1884) 480B
    3 For this notion see Gal 3:27–8 and 1 Cor 12:13. Cf Erasmus' paraphrase of this verse: 'But when his very precious Son at the price of his most sacred blood redeemed us from the slavery of vices and bonded us firmly to himself as members, it is impossible for the Father not to love those whom he has willed to share in the inheritance of the Son' *Paraphrasis in Ephesios* CWE 43 305.
    4 The ... reading.] Added in *1527*

1:8 [ER *nobis* 'to us']
[VG] *in nobis* '**in us**'; εἰς ἡμᾶς,[1] that is, 'unto us.'

    1 Erasmus' point here is that the preposition and accusative case in Greek mean that we are the objects of grace, not the sphere in which grace acts, as the preposition with the ablative in the Vulgate seem to imply.

1:8 [ER VG] *in omni sapientia et prudentia* '**in**[1] **all wisdom and prudence.**' These words can be referred to either the preceding statement or to the following one.[2] The meaning would be [the grace] which he abundantly poured out on us in all wisdom and prudence; or, making known to us the mystery in all wisdom and prudence. Jerome follows the latter punctuation.[3]

    1 'in ... punctuation.] This annotation was added in *1519*.
    2 The phrase 'in all wisdom and prudence' may be taken with what precedes 'that he lavished on us with all wisdom and understanding' (1:8 NIV) or with what follows 'for he has made known to us in all wisdom and insight' (1:9 RSV).
    3 Jerome *Comm in Eph* 1 (on 1:9) PL 26 (1884) 482A

1:9 [ER *patefacto nobis arcano'* 'the secret revealed to us']
[VG] *ut notum faceret* '**that he might make known**'; γνωρίσας ἡμῖν, that is, 'the mystery revealed or made known to us.' The Translator and Ambrose read, I think, γνωρίσαι [to make known].[1] Jerome reads, 'making known,' so that one realizes that the [Greek] verb is a participle, although it is a past tense.[2] Let me say this: even if it does not quite pertain to the meaning, nevertheless in my judgment it is not something

we should overlook. The others seem to me to have paid too little attention to the reading of the Greek manuscripts, for they have as follows: ἧς ἐπερίσσευσεν εἰς ἡμᾶς ἐν πάσῃ σοφίᾳ καὶ φρονήσει γνωρίσας ἡμῖν [wherein he has abounded to us in all wisdom and prudence, having made known to us]. The verb ἐπερίσσευσεν [he has abounded] placed here has a metaphorical[3] sense, 'he has caused to overflow.' Otherwise, the participle γνωρίσας has no verb on which to depend. It could be translated in the following way: 'Wherein he has abundantly imparted to us when the mystery was revealed to us, etc.' Certainly[4] it is clear that Chrysostom[5] and Theophylact understood it in this way, who in interpreting ἐπερίσσευσεν subjoined τοῦτ' ἐστίν [that is] to his interpretation, τοῦτ' ἐστὶν ἀφθόνως ἐξέχεεν, 'that is, he poured out amply.' He[6] [Paul] amplified the greatness of grace by a double sign[7] when he uses the noun πλοῦτον [wealth] and adds not the verb ἔδωκε [he gave] but ἐπερίσσευσεν [he abounded].

1 Ambrosiaster *Comm in Eph* 1:9. Ambrosiaster reads *notum faciat*.
2 Jerome *Comm in Eph* 1 (on 1:9) PL 26 (1884) 482A
3 Erasmus' term *transitive* [transferred] refers to a metaphorical sense of the verb under discussion. *Transitive* corresponds with the literal meaning of the Greek term μεταφορά 'transfer,' or rhetorically a 'transferred meaning.' According to Aristotle, any verb, noun, or phrase with a transferred sense is a metaphor. Quintilian states that metaphor should be used if there is no other suitable term, for clarity, or as ornamentation (Quintilian 8.6.4–18). See further the annotation on Gal 4:24 ('through allegory spoken') n6.
4 Certainly ... amply.'] Added in *1519*
5 Chrysostom and] Added in *1535*. See Chrysostom *Hom in Eph* 1.3 PG 62 14 and Theophylact *Expos in Eph* 1:7 PG 124 1040A.
6 He ... ἐπερίσσευσεν.] Added in *1535*
7 The rhetorical term αὔξησις or *augmentatio* refers to various methods of promoting or denigrating a subject matter through amplification. It is also generally used to further promote points that have already been demonstrated, hence the 'double sign' mentioned in this annotation. See Lausberg §400–2.

1:9 [ER *arcano* 'secret']

[VG] *sacramentum* 'sacrament.' In this passage μυστήριον means 'mystery';[1] Ambrose uses the Greek word here.[2] In Greek mystery is the word for something secret that should not be proclaimed to the public.[3] The term was then transferred to sacred matters which we venerate mostly in silence. Here it means the divine will to summon the gentiles to the faith that was unknown to the world in previous centuries when the Jews thought that this promise belonged to them in particular; but now what was hidden has become known.

1 For the translation *arcanum* see Brown *Novum Testamentum* 497–8:9(1)
  n. He notes that among classical authors the word *sacramentum* meant
  'oath,' and was therefore an unsuitable translation of the Greek μυστήριον.
  In changing *sacramentum* to *arcanum* Erasmus is following Valla *Annot in
  Eph* 1 (I 877), and so brings out the unrevealed nature of the mystery.
2 Ambrosiaster *Comm in Eph* 1:9
3 For the use of the word *mysterion* in Paul see Lincoln *Ephesians* 30–1.

1:9 [ER *iuxta beneplacitum suum* 'according to his good pleasure']
[VG] *secundum beneplacitum eius* 'according to the good pleasure of
him.'** Jerome reads 'according to good pleasure' or 'according to his
pleasure,' κατὰ τὴν εὐδοκίαν αὐτοῦ.¹

> 1 Jerome *Comm in Eph* 1 (on 1:9) PL 26 (1884) 483B. Jerome reads *secundum
>   placitum suum* 'according to his own pleasure.' Not occurring in classical
>   usage, *beneplacitum* is a close translation of εὐδοκία. Cf the annotation on
>   Eph 1:5 ('according to the purpose'). For Erasmus, God's 'good pleasure'
>   marks his reconciliation with sinful humanity through the incarnation of
>   Christ. For this see *Paraphrasis in Lucam* (on 2:14-15) CWE 47 73 n19.

1:9 [ER *quod proposuerat in seipso* 'which he had purposed in himself']
[VG] *quod proposuit in eo* 'which he has purposed in him.'** If one reads
ἐν αὐτῷ with the¹ [Greek letter] alpha aspirated, it means 'in himself.'
If one prefers αὐτῷ with the first syllable unaspirated,² it refers to the
Son in whom the Father has purposed to make us pleasing to himself.
And³ the commentators follow the latter meaning almost unanimously.
Jerome indicates the difference between προορισμός⁴ and πρόθεσις⁵, that
is, between 'predestination' and 'proposition' or 'purpose.'⁶ The former
refers to the things we decide in our mind long before they are done,
the latter when the execution is so close by that the effect follows right
after the thought.⁷

> 1 with ... aspirated] Added in *1519*
> 2 In Greek, an aspirated syllable was pronounced with an initial 'h,' and
>   an unaspirated syllable without. The difference is indicated by a rough
>   breathing mark (') for aspirated syallables, and a smooth breathing mark
>   (') for unaspirated syllables. The unaspirated Greek word αὐτός, -ή, -όν
>   can be a personal pronoun meaning 'him/her/it.' The aspirated Greek
>   word αὑτός, -ή, -όν, a contraction of the aspirated article and the unaspir-
>   ated personal pronoun, indicates a sameness, ie 'the same, the very one,'
>   from which Erasmus derives a reflexive meaning. See the annotation on
>   Eph 1:5 ('unto himself') n2.
> 3 And ... unanimously.] Added in *1522*
> 4 LSJ defines προορισμόν as 'an early determination.'
> 5 LSJ defines πρόθεσις as 'purpose.' On God's 'purpose' see the annotation
>   on Rom 8:28 ('in accordance with the purpose') CWE 56 224.

6 Jerome *Comm in Eph* 1 (on 1:9) PL 26 (1884) 483B

7 Erasmus is following Jerome here: 'There he placed προορισμόν, that is, "predestination [*praedestinatio*] for the adoption of sons through Jesus Christ." Here however it is πρόθεσιν, that is *propositio* "purpose." Moreover, those who are used to making distinctions between words, assert that the difference between "predestination" and "purpose" is that the "predestination" of something is prefigured in the mind of the one who destines what will happen, but "purpose" is when the execution is so close by that the effect follows right after the thought.' See Jerome *Comm in Eph* 1 (on 1:9) PL 26 (1884) 483B.

1:10 [ER *usque ad dispensationem* 'up to the dispensation']
[VG] *in dispensatione* 'in the dispensation'; εἰς οἰκονομίαν, that is, 'unto the dispensation.'[1]

1 See Brown *Novum Testamentum* 498–9:10(1)n for Erasmus' use here of *usque ad* 'up to.' The use of the ablative case following the preposition *in* in the late Vulgate is unsupported by the Greek manuscripts, and was a scribal alteration that occurred in the Latin tradition. The use of *usque ad* 'up to' corrects this error by ensuring that the noun that follows must be in the accusative case, which follows the Greek.

1:10 [ER *ut summatim instauret* 'to resume briefly']
[VG] *instaurare* 'to resume'; ἀνακεφαλαιώσασθαι, that is, 'to recapitulate,' that is, to bring together in a summary. For public speakers call it ἀνακε-φαλαίωσις, that is, 'recapitulation,'[1] when those things which have been said here and there and at length are repeated in a brief summary and at the same time renewed for the judge. St Jerome reads 'to recapitulate,' and believes that this verb is correctly used in Latin and wonders why *instaurare* is found in Latin manuscripts rather than *recapitulare*.[2] There are those, among whom are Theophylact[3] and Chrysostom,[4] who understand ἀνακεφαλαίωσις to mean that Christ was made the head [*caput*] of both angels and humans, both Jews and gentiles.[5] This notion fits the words which come a little later, 'and has made him head' [1:22]. And[6] the Greek word too has this meaning, as if one were to say 'to call back to the head.'[7]

1 The rhetorical term *recapitulatio* or ἀνακεφαλαίωσις has the primary function of refreshing the memory of points already made, but also acts upon the emotions of the audience by means of accumulation within a short space (Lausberg §434). Quintilian (6.1.1) states: 'The repetition and association of matters, which in Greek is called ἀνακεφαλαίωσις [anakeph-alaiosis], and by certain Latins "enumeration," restores the memory of the judge and places the whole case before his eyes at once, and, even if [each argument] had moved them less individually, rouses the crowd.'

2 Jerome *Comm in Eph* 1 (on 1:10) PL 26 (1884) 483C–D
3 among whom are Theophylact] Added in *1519*. See Theophylact *Expos in
   Eph* 1:10 PG 124 1040C.
4 and Chrysostom] Added in *1535*. See Chrysostom *Hom in Eph* 1.4 PG 62
   16.
5 both Jews and gentiles.] Added in *1535*. Erasmus' statement is incor-
   rect, though he, Chrysostom, and Theophylact are in good company; see
   Lincoln *Ephesians* 32–3.
6 And ... head.'] Added in *1527*
7 According to LSJ, the Greek verb ἀνακεφαλαιόω has the meaning 'to sum
   up the argument.' This derives from the metaphorical meaning of the
   Greek word κεφαλή, which literally translates as 'head,' but here refers
   to the 'sum' or 'total.' See also Erasmus' annotation on Rom 13:9 ('it is
   restored in this word') CWE 56 354.

1:10 [ER *quae in terra* 'which on earth']
     [VG] *quae in terra sunt* 'which are on earth'; τά τε ἐν τοῖς οὐρανοῖς καὶ
     τὰ ἐπὶ τῆς γῆς, that is, 'both¹ which are in the heavens and which on
     earth.' I do not find in either Ambrose² or in Jerome³ the addition of ἐν
     αὐτῷ, that is, 'in himself' found in the Greek manuscripts.⁴ Not⁵ even in
     Theophylact or in Chrysostom,⁶ at least in so far as their commentaries
     are concerned; for⁷ Theophylact adds it in the text. And 'in the same'
     would fit the context better than 'in himself.' For the Greek word has
     both meanings so that you may understand that everything is com-
     prehended in one and the same person, that the totality of everything
     is summed up in the one Christ, and that there is in one at once what
     was previously sought by many in several parts. Unless⁸ you prefer
     'through the same person' so that [the term] corresponds to what fol-
     lows, 'in whom etc' [1:11], or 'through whom' so that the meaning is:
     'All things have been reestablished through the same one in whom we
     too are allotted a share and communion.' For⁹ our reading 'all things in
     Christ' is in Theophylact πάντα τὰ ἐν Χριστῷ, that is, 'all things which are
     in Christ,'¹⁰ but I think this happened through a scribal error.

1 both] Added in *1519*
2 Ambrosiaster *Comm in Eph* 1:10
3 Jerome *Comm in Eph* 1 (on 1:10) PL 26 (1884) 483C. Jerome actually reads *in
   ipso* 'in himself' in the lemma, but not in his commentary.
4 Edward Lee, in criticizing Erasmus for not including ἐν αὐτῷ, claimed
   that the phrase does appear in Jerome's reading. Erasmus states that Lee
   erred in this claim; see *Responsio ad annotationes Lei* 2 CWE 72 293–4. For
   this reason also he invoked, in the *1535* edition, the additional support of
   Theophylact and Chrysostom.
5 Not ... concerned] Added in *1522*. See Theophylact *Expos in Eph* 1:10 PG
   124 1040C.

6 or in Chrysostom.] Added in *1535*. See Chrysostom *Hom in Eph* 1.4 PG 62
    15–16.
7 for ... text] Added in *1527*
8 Unless ... communion.'] Added in *1519*
9 For ... error.] Added in *1527*
10 See Theophylact *Expos in Eph* 1:10 PG 124 1040C.

1:11 [ER *in sortem asciti sumus* 'we have been received into the lot']
[VG] *sorte vocati sumus* 'we are called by lot'; ἐκληρώθημεν, that is, 'we
are chosen by lot.' Jerome indicates that this verb is derived partly from
[the word for] lot, partly from inheritance because κλῆρος [an allotment
of inherited land] can have either meaning.[1] Ambrose reads 'we are
allotted,' that is, 'we are received into the lot and share of the inheritance.'[2] In[3] [his] book *Exhortation to Virginity* he reads 'we are established by lot.'

    1 Jerome *Comm in Eph* 1 (on 1:11) PL 26 (1884) 484C
    2 Ambrosiaster *Comm in Eph* 1:11
    3 In ... lot.'] Added in *1519*. See Ambrose *Exhortatio virginitatis* 6.39 PL 16
        (1845) 347C.
        Cf BDAG s.v. κληρόω: '"in whom we have obtained an inheritance" Eph
        1:11 ... the point being that the nations are also included.'

1:11 [ER VG] *secundum propositum* 'according to the purpose.' The Greek[1]
here is not εὐδοκίαν [good pleasure], but πρόθεσιν [purpose].[2]

    1 The Greek] Added in *1519*. See the annotation on Eph 1:5 ('according to
        the purpose').
    2 In *De libero arbitrio* CWE 76 68, Erasmus uses this text to argue that every-
        thing must be attributed to the grace of God which, although it has
        no need of the assistance of mankind, enabled the human will to be co-
        worker with it.

1:11 [ER *cuius vi fiunt universa* 'by whose power everything is done']
[VG] *qui operatur omnia* 'who works all things'; τοῦ τὰ πάντα ἐνεργοῦντος [of him who accomplishes all things]. Ambrose reads 'of him who
created all things,'[1] if, that is, his text is free from error. But the Greek
word means rather 'of him by whose power and might all things are
done,' that[2] is, of the one who guides and controls all things, as I have
already often mentioned,[3] and I myself have accordingly so translated.

    1 Ambrosiaster *Comm in Eph* 1:11. Ambrosiaster actually reads *dei, qui uni-
        versa creavit* 'of God, who created all things.'
    2 that ... all things] Added in *1522*
    3 See the annotations on 1 Cor 12:6 (*divisiones operationum*) and Gal 2:8 ('for
        he who has worked Peter').

1:12 [ER *qui priores speravimus* 'who first hoped']

[VG] *qui ante speramus*[1] **'who before hope'**; προηλπικότας, that is, 'you[2] who before hoped.' St Jerome refers this to the divine foreknowledge in which we hoped, which existed before the world was restored,[3] obviously having been influenced by this preposition πρό.[4] Theophylact[5] has a different reference: we are even now hoping for what will happen to us in the age to come; or we began to hope when we earlier believed in Christ. Ambrose heads in another direction and refers it to the apostles, who, though they were still living in Judaism, nevertheless had their hope in Christ whom they were expecting from the oracles of the prophets.[6] Tertullian[7] in his *Against Marcion* V [17] follows this though he reads *praesperavimus* [we hoped beforehand] for *ante speravimus* [before we hoped].

1 The present tense *speramus* [we are hoping] is a typographical error in 1535; the earlier editions all have the perfect *speravimus* [we hoped], the reading of the Vulgate.
2 The 'you' is evidently a slip for 'we.'
3 Jerome *Comm in Eph* 1 (on 1:12) PL 26 (1884) 485B
4 According to LSJ, the Greek preposition πρό can be used to indicate time before. When combined with a verb as a prefix, it can also denote that the action took place beforehand.
5 Theophylact ... prophets.] Added in 1519. See Theophylact *Expos in Eph* 1:12 PG 124 1041B.
6 Ambrosiaster *Comm in Eph* 1:12
7 Tertullian ... *speravimus*.] Added in 1527. See Tertullian *Adversus Marcionem* 5.17.3 CCL 1 713:14–17.

1:13 [ER *in quo speratis et vos, audito verbo veritatis* 'in whom you too hope when the word of truth was heard']

[VG] *in quo et vos cum audissetis* **'in whom you too after you had heard'**; ἐν ᾧ καὶ ὑμεῖς ἀκούσαντες τὸν λόγον, that is, 'in whom you also who heard the word.' St Jerome quite elegantly reads 'in whom you also when the word of truth was heard.'[1] We should mention that the Greek text in some manuscripts[2] has the first person 'we,'[3] not the second person 'you.' Although Ambrose and Jerome seem to have had a different reading as may be gathered from their interpretations,[4] Theophylact does not reveal in his commentary what he read though his Greek text has the second person pronouns ὑμεῖς [you] and ὑμῶν [your].[5] The Aldine[6] edition had ἡμεῖς [we] and ὑμῶν [your], mixing the personal pronouns. The Spanish [edition][7] has the second person pronoun in both places. Others punctuate this passage: 'we who before hoped in Christ'; then they add separately 'in whom you also,' so that the first clause refers to the apostles or the Jews, the second to the Ephesians or gentiles. But it seems to me that Paul made a sudden change in the pronouns, paying more attention to the sense than to the rules of grammar.[8] For after he said, 'that we should be to the praise of his glory,' as though explaining whom he had called 'we,' lest anyone think that he was speaking only about Jews, he straightway added τοὺς προηλπικότας [who first hoped], as if one were to say, 'When I say "we," I mean all who hoped in Christ among whom we too are'; and he says 'we' so that he joins his own person with the person of the gentiles since he is the teacher of the gentiles. But the Greek preposition πρό, that is, 'before,' is something of an obstacle to this meaning. For if it is taken to mean all who had believed in Christ, who will be those who believed beforehand? Unless one is pleased to follow the meaning of Jerome, whom Rufinus[9] slanders as someone smacking a bit of Origen. However, if you prefer to change the pronoun and read 'in whom you also hoped' as Jerome does, which is clear from his interpretation, there is nothing in the preposition to offend us. For the 'before' refers to the Jews who were first to be called to the faith and the first to have believed in Christ; next the gentiles followed. But if one is completely satisfied with the first person pronoun, as some[10] Greeks read, then the preposition 'before' can be taken to mean others who will believe later. For they were the first among the gentiles to have believed. Unless one prefers to understand a kind of confused hope which savable pagans had even before the preaching of the gospel and if they did not yet know Christ, they nevertheless hoped in some way for salvation as though in a dream.

1 Jerome *Comm in Eph* 1 (on 1:13) PL 26 (1884) 486A
2 in some manuscripts] Added in *1527*
3 The actual pronouns 'we' and 'you' are added in the *1527* edition.
4 Although ... interpretations] Added in *1522*, in which it included the phrase 'Theophylact appears to have written "our".' For the confusion here and Erasmus' attempt to clear it up see Brown *Novum Testamentum* 500–1:13(1)n.
  On the readings of Ambrosiaster and Jerome, see Ambrosiaster *Comm in Eph* 1:13; Jerome *Comm in Eph* 1 (on 1:13) PL 26 486A.
5 Theophylact ... [your]] Added in *1527*
6 The Aldine edition, begun in 1501 by the famous Venetian printer Aldo Manuzio (Aldus), was completed in February 1518 and issued in 1520. According to Allen (Ep i 64:28on) this edition contains the Erasmian text of the New Testament. See further the annotation on Rom 11:6 ('otherwise grace is no longer grace') in CWE 56 296 n10.

7 The 'Spanish edition' refers to the Complutensian Polyglot Bible which was edited under the leadership of Cardinal Jiménez at Alcalá. Work on this Bible was begun in 1502 and completed in 1517, though it was not printed until 1522, that is, after the first edition of Erasmus' New Testament. For a description and assessment of this edition see Bentley *Humanists* 70–111.

8 Erasmus is commenting on his Greek text as it appeared in the editions before 1527. When he corrected 'we' to 'you' in the 1527 and 1535 editions, there is no sudden change in the pronouns. He evidently overlooked the discrepancy between the annotation and the revised text.

9 Rufinus, born in Italy near Aquileia c 345, lived for some time as a monk on the Mount of Olives while Jerome was in his monastery in Bethlehem. Rufinus returned to Italy in 397 and was asked to translate Origen's *On First Principles*. But Origen and Origenist doctrines had been severely attacked in the late fourth century. Consequently, in the preface to his translation Rufinus says he followed the method of Jerome, who had translated some of the homilies and commentaries of Origen but in such a way that everything offensive to orthodox faith had been removed. Rufinus had published his translation in Rome, but about 399 he moved to Aquileia where he was asked to continue his translations of Origen (CWE 56 95–6n14). Jerome and Rufinus engaged in a heated controversy over Origen's teachings after Jerome gave up his earlier allegiance to Origen as a result of the attack on Origenism that arose in Palestine in 393 (CWE 56 248n15). However, Rufinus maintained that Jerome still held to Origen's doctrine (ASD VI-9 175).

10 Some] Added in 1527

1:13 [ER *evangelio salutis* 'the gospel of salvation']

[VG] *evangelii salutis* 'of the gospel of salvation.' In the Greek, the word is joined by gospel in apposition: ἀκούσαντες τὸν λόγον τῆς ἀληθείας τὸ εὐαγγέλιον τῆς σωτηρίας, that is, 'you who have heard the word of truth, which is the gospel of salvation.' As[1] if the others, who teach anything but the gospel, promise no truth.

1 As ... truth.] Added in 1527. The point of the annotation is that the word 'gospel' is in apposition to the word 'the word'; as he rendered ἀκούσαντες τὸν λόγον [having heard the word] with an absolute construction in the ablative case, *audito verbo* [when the word was heard], Erasmus here puts 'gospel' also in the ablative.

1:13 [ER *in quo etiam posteaquam credidistis* 'in whom also after you believed.']

[VG] *in quo et credentes* 'in whom also believing.' In Greek the word for believing is in the past tense, πιστεύσαντες, that is, 'after you believed,' or 'because you believed,' or 'when faith was received,' or 'when having become believers.'

1:13 [ER *obsignati estis* 'you were sealed']

[VG] *signati estis* 'you were signed'; ἐσφραγίσθητε, which means 'you were sealed,' in the way that we seal pages in a contract, because thereafter mention is made of earnest-money to show that the hope is certain.[1] Didymus[2] in his work *On the Holy Spirit* refers to this passage in his argument that the Holy Spirit is holy and good not by virtue of participating in someone else but by his very own nature, because the mark that is imprinted upon a stamping-tool is an archetype[3] of the good. 'For,' he says, 'if some are signed by the Holy Spirit, they take on his form and appearance. The Holy Spirit accompanies these qualities that [people] have and they are nothing of themselves; those who have him are imprinted by his seal. Paul writes in the same way also to the Corinthians[4] when he says, "Do not grieve the Holy Spirit in whom you have been signed," attesting that the ones who are signed have experienced communion with the Holy Spirit.' I have brought these matters up here so that the reader may understand that my annotation of the Greek verb 'to seal' is not off the mark. Anyone who wants to philosophize in divine letters but is ignorant of Greek, is, as the Greeks would say, running ἔξω τῶν ἐλαιῶν [beyond the olive-trees].[5]

1 The verb *obsignare* is used to refer to the official sealing of a document such as a letter or will, and sometimes more particularly to the making of a pledge under one's seal. Such seals were legally binding in much the same way a personal signature is in the present day. See the note below on the annotation on Eph 1:14 ('who is the pledge') nn4–5, as well as the annotation on Rom 15:28 ('and have marked') CWE 56 418. At John 3:33 Erasmus similarly replaced the Vulgate's *signavit* with the more precise *obsignavit*.

2 Didymus ... ἐλαιῶν.] Added in 1519. Didymus of Alexandria, also called 'the Blind' (c 313–98), was appointed as head of the catechetical school at Alexandria by Athanasius. Influenced by Origen, he was condemned in 553, and much of his writing disappeared. Erasmus is citing Didymus from Jerome's Latin translation, *Interpretatio libri Didymi Alexandrini de spiritu sancto* PL 23 (1845) 113B–C.

3 According to scholastic theology, an archetype is an original pattern from which a copy, or ectype, is derived.

4 This is actually a citation from Eph 4:30. The reference to 2 Cor 1:22 occurs in Didymus from whom Erasmus may have taken it, evidently without noticing the mistake.

5 See Erasmus *Adagia* II ii 10. The proverb 'beyond the olive-trees' refers to a man overstepping the prescribed limits, or doing or saying things irrelevant to the matter at hand. The phrase originates from the running tracks for foot-races, where the prescribed course was bounded by rows of olive trees, which it was not permitted to cross. Anyone running 'beyond the olives' has gone outside of the course.

1:14 [ER *qui est arrhabo* 'who is the earnest']

[vg] *qui est pignus* 'who is the pledge'; ἀρραβών, that is 'arrabo.' St Jerome prefers to read it in this way, in[1] the belief that *arrabo* and *pignus* do not have the same meaning in Latin.[2] A *pignus* [pledge] is usually given to a creditor until money owed is paid; an *arrabo* is, as it were, a sign or assurance of future possession.[3] A pledge is given in a loan; an earnest [is given] in a contract between a seller and a buyer in order to ensure the obligation. But if the earnest that God gives to his own is so great, how great will be the actual property itself that he will provide in his time?[4] The Greeks[5] call an earnest ἀρραβών;[6] a pledge ἐνέχυρον[7] or security for a loan. The pronoun[8] 'who' does not refer to Christ, but to the Spirit, that is, the Spirit who is the earnest.

   1 in ... possession] Added in *1522*
   2 Jerome *Comm in Eph* 1 (on 1:14) PL 26 (1884) 487A–B
   3 possession] First in *1516*; in *1522* and *1527 emptioni* 'for purchase'
   4 A pledge ... time] First in *1527*; in *1516*, *1519* and *1522* and placed at the end of the annotation, 'Jerome thinks that the difference between a pledge and an earnest is that a pledge, which the Greeks call security, is given in a loan, while an earnest occurs in a contract for buying and selling in order to ensure the obligation.'
   5 The Greeks ... for a loan.] Added in *1522*
   6 LSJ defines ἀρραβών as an earnest or a pledge, particularly in the sense of a transaction whereby the purchaser places a deposit that is forfeited if the transaction is not carried through to completion.
   7 According to LSJ, ἐνέχυρον is a pledge or security offered in order to ensure the cooperation of those involved in a transaction or other matter, with the understanding that, unlike a deposit, the pledge will be returned upon the successful completion of the matter.
   8 The pronoun ... earnest.] In *1516* follows '... prefers to read it in this way,' and begins a new sentence.

1:14 [ER *in redemptionem acquisitae possessionis* 'unto the redemption of the purchased possession']

[vg] *in redemptionem acquisitionis* 'unto the redemption of acquisition'; εἰς ἀπολύτρωσιν τῆς περιποιήσεως, that is, 'unto the redemption of the acquisition' or 'possession,' as Jerome reads,[1] correcting the Vulgate edition which he had, *in redemptionem adoptionis* [unto the redemption of the adoption]. One may conjecture from this that the Vulgate which we now use was not same as the one which Jerome had at that time.[2] But that person, whoever he was, seems to me to have wanted to interpret the word as acquisition, which is in any case ambiguous. For the meaning is that the Holy Spirit was given by God to the faithful as an earnest so that they would have a sure knowledge that someday he would claim for himself his own possession which he had purchased

by redemption. Therefore,[3] I translated 'unto the redemption of the purchased possession.' For he calls property which was acquired and purchased an acquisition as we call something possessed a possession.

1 Jerome *Comm in Eph* 1 (on 1:14) PL 26 (1884) 487A–B
2 On Erasmus' assessment of Jerome as author of the Vulgate see Bentley *Humanists* 162.
3 Therefore ... possession.] Added in *1519*

1:15 [ER *cum audissem eam quae in vobis est fidem* 'when I heard of that faith which is in you']
[VG] *audiens fidem* 'hearing of faith'; ἀκούσας τὴν καθ' ὑμᾶς πίστιν, that is, 'when your faith had been heard of.'

1:16 [ER *non desino gratias agere* 'I do not cease to give thanks']
[VG] *cesso gratias agens* 'I stop giving thanks.' He is translating the Greek construction.[1] In Latin one ought to say '*non cesso gratias agere.*' And this is Jerome's reading.[2] Ambrose reads *gratias agendo* [in giving thanks].[3]

1 In Greek, verbs meaning 'to cease' or 'to stop' a current action are followed by a participle (Smyth 2140). In Latin such verbs are normally followed by an infinitive (Allen and Greenough 456).
2 Jerome *Comm in Eph* 1 (on 1:15–18) PL 26 (1884) 488A–B
3 Ambrosiaster *Comm in Eph* 1:16

1:16 [ER *mentionem vestri* 'mention of you']
[VG] *memoriam vestri* 'memory of you.' Why not 'mention of you,' μνείαν ὑμῶν, seeing that when we pray, we are conversing with God.[1]

1 Erasmus' objection to the Vulgate rendering is apparently to the use of the noun *memoria* as the object of the verb *facere* (to do, make). See Brown *Novum Testamentum* 25:9(6)n on Rom 1:9. The Vulgate rendering is in fact a literal translation of the Greek 'making remembrance.' Erasmus makes a similar annotation on Rom 1:9 ('remembrance of you'). On Erasmus' characterization of prayer as a colloquy or conversation with God see Hilmar Pabel *Conversing with God* (Toronto 1997) 35.

1:17 [ER VG] *deus domini nostri* 'the God of our Lord'; ὁ θεὸς τοῦ κυρίου ἡμῶν. Here it is clear that the Father is being called the God of Jesus Christ, which was ambiguous in other passages.[1]

1 The point here is that a distinction is made between God and Jesus; see Lincoln *Ephesians* 56. In his commentary on Rom 1:7 ('from God our Father and the Lord Jesus Christ') Erasmus observes that the apostles ascribe deity to God the Son as well as God the Father (CWE 56 31–2); see also his annotation on 2 Cor 2:15 '*bonus odor sumus deo*' (ASD VI-8 350:381–9).

1:17 [ER *per agnitionem* 'through the acknowledgment']
[VG] *in agnitionem* 'unto the knowledge'; ἐν ἐπιγνώσει, that is, 'in the knowledge,' as[1] Ambrose[2] reads and likewise Jerome, who notes the connotation of the word *agnitio* [knowledge, acknowledgment] by which we acknowledge something we have long known but at some point have ceased to know, while[3] γνῶσις [knowledge] is of those things which we have begun to know that were unknown previously.[4] And[5] he hints at something Platonic here from an opinion of Origen's, I suspect, about[6] the previously known Father whom we have begun to recall again through the revelation of the Spirit. But there was no need here for a Platonic fable. Philosophers knew God but did not acknowledge him, that is, they did not embrace him, just as many sons indeed know their father but do not acknowledge him.[7] And the words which follow, 'the eyes of your heart enlightened' [Eph 1:18], agree with this. For though seeing beforehand they did not see.

1   as ... ceased to know] Added in *1519*
2   Ambrosiaster *Comm in Eph* 1:17
3   while ... know] Added in *1527*
4   Jerome *Comm in Eph* 1 (on 1:15–18) PL 26 (1884) 488A and 489B. He reports that according to some γνῶσις is knowledge newly learned, while ἐπίγνωσις is knowledge of things once known, forgotten, and then recollected.
5   And ... I suspect] Added in *1519*
6   about ... see] Added in *1527*
7   Early Christian writers sometimes discuss Plato and Aristotle's views regarding a single god responsible for the creation of the world. See for example Lactantius: 'Indeed Plato spoke much about one God, by whom he said the world was made. But he said nothing about religion; for he dreamt of God, he did not know him' (Lactantius *De justitia* XV PL 6 597B); 'Plato alleged there was a monarchy, saying that there was one God, by whom the world was constructed and finished with miraculous reason. Aristotle, his student, acknowledged there to be one mind, which presides over the world' (Lactantius *Divinarum institutionum* 1.5.4 PL 6 1021C).

1:18 [ER VG] *illuminatos oculos* 'the eyes enlightened.' The entire sequence of the language here lacks coherence;[1] nevertheless, I am surprised at how Jerome labours to defend Paul against those who slander him because they thought him unskilled in the Greek language on the grounds that his language is full of solecisms, although elsewhere Jerome himself admits that Paul did not know Greek and he defends this against those who are unwilling to have what Paul wrote, 'though unskilled in language,' attributed to modesty but to true confession.[2] Jerome thinks the order of the words can be rendered as follows: 'Hearing of your faith in the Lord Jesus and to all his saints, and seeing the excellence of your faith regarding the Lord, I do not cease to give thanks and to make memory of you in my prayers that God the Father of our Lord Jesus Christ, the Father moreover of glory, give to you the spirit of wisdom and revelation.' And Jerome also thinks that the following expression, 'the eyes of your heart enlightened,' can be attributed to a hyperbaton[3] in this way: 'Wherefore I also hearing of your faith in the Lord Jesus, in the knowledge of him, the eyes of your heart enlightened, do not cease to give thanks for you, to make memory of you in my prayers that the God of our Lord Jesus Christ, the Father of glory, give to you the spirit of wisdom and revelation etc.' Ambrose, however, refers 'eyes enlightened' to the verb[4] 'give.'[5] For he adds 'to have' to the text, 'to have eyes enlightened.' It[6] is odd why Chrysostom and[7] Theophylact[8] felt no scruple here or if they did, they hid it.

1 See Lincoln *Ephesians* 47 note b on the syntactical problems of this phrase.
2 Jerome *Comm in Eph* 1 (on 1:15–18) PL 26 (1884) 488A–B. For Jerome's assessment of Paul's knowledge of Greek see the annotation on Eph 3:2 ('has been given to me in you') n4.
3 For hyperbaton see the annotation on Gal 1:6 ('into the grace of Christ') n4.
4 the verb] Added in *1519*
5 Ambrosiaster *Comm in Eph* 1:17–18
6 It ... hid it.] Added in *1527*
7 Chrysostom and] Added in *1535* with a consequent change in the verbs from singular to plural. See Chrysostom *Hom in Eph* 3.1 PG 62 24.
8 Theophylact *Expos in Eph* 1:17 PG 124 1045C

1:18 [ER *mentis vestrae* 'of your mind']
[VG] *cordis vestri* 'of your heart'; διανοίας ὑμῶν, that is, 'of your mind.'[1]

1 For the substitution of *mens* 'mind' for *cor* 'heart' see Brown *Novum Testamentum* 502:18(1)n. Most manuscripts replace διανοίας 'thought' with καρδίας 'heart,' in agreement with the Vulgate; and modern editions also read τῆς καρδίας. Cf 'understanding' (AV), 'heart' (NIV, RSV).

1:19 [ER *excellens magnitudo* 'exceeding greatness']
[VG] *supereminens*[1] *magnitudo* 'ever lofty greatness'; τὸ ὑπερβάλλον μέγεθος, that is, 'the sublime greatness,' as Jerome reads;[2] Ambrose has 'the lofty greatness.'[3]

1 The 1527 Vulgate reads *superveniens* [surpassing]. See Brown *Novum Testamentum* 502:19(1)n.
2 Jerome *Comm in Eph* 1 (on 1:18–20) PL 26 (1884) 489C
3 Ambrosiaster *Comm in Eph* 1:19

1:19 [ER *efficaciam roboris fortitudinis eius* 'the working of the strength of his power']

[VG] *operationem potentiae virtutis eius* 'the operation of the might of his power'; κατὰ τὴν ἐνέργειαν τοῦ κράτους τῆς ἰσχύος αὐτοῦ, that is, 'according to the working or force of the power of his firmness or strength,' for it is ἐνέργεια [energy, efficiency]. And [Paul] soon repeats it in [the verb] ἐνήργησεν [wrought], which I translated 'he exercised,' not as I wished but as I could, as the saying goes.[1]

1 See Brown *Novum Testamentum* 503:19(6)n for Erasmus' various translations of the Greek nouns meaning 'power, strength.'

1:20 [ER *cum suscitaret eum* 'when he raised him']

[VG] *suscitans illum* 'raising him up'; ἐγείρας αὐτόν, that is, 'after he was raised.'[1]

1 The point of this annotation is that the temporal clause more accurately reflects the aorist tense in the Greek participle ἐγείρας than the present tense participle *suscitans*.

1:20 [ER *et sedere fecit* 'and caused to sit']

[VG] *et constituens* 'and setting'; καὶ ἐκάθισεν, that is 'caused to sit.'[1] Jerome reads 'making him to sit';[2] Ambrose 'he placed.'[3] The[4] Greek word sometimes has an intransitive, sometimes a transitive meaning.

1 This rendering is probably taken, without acknowledgment, from Lefèvre
· *Pauli epistolae* fol 164 verso; see Brown *Novum Testamentum* 503:20(7)n.
2 Jerome *Comm in Eph* 1 (on 1:20–1) PL 26 (1884) 490B
3 Ambrosiaster *Comm in Eph* 1:20
4 The ... meaning.] Added in 1527

1:21 [ER *et virtutem et dominium* 'and might and dominion']

[VG] *et virtutem et dominationem* 'and[1] might and domination.' *Virtus* here is δύναμις [might], not ἀρετή [virtue]. And *dominatio* [domination] is κυριότης [lordship], which means authority and right of ownership. And this meaning is expressed better in Latin by 'dominion' than by 'domination.' For [Paul] is speaking not about angels only but about the entire universe.[2]

1 'and ... universe.] This annotation was added in 1522. Erasmus defends his translation here against Zúñiga, who considered the change unnecessary (*Apologia ad annotationes Stunicae* ASD IX-2 204).
2 See Brown *Novum Testamentum* 503:21(3)n, where it is observed that *dominium* better conveyed the sense of authority, while *dominatio* has pejorative connotations.

1:22 [ER *sub pedes* 'under his feet']

[VG] *sub pedibus* '**underneath his feet**'; ὑπὸ τοὺς πόδας, that is, 'under his feet.'[1]

> 1 Classical usage requires the accusative, *pedes*, since verbs of motion towards take the accusative case, sometimes preceded by a preposition (Allen and Greenough 388b). See Brown *Novum Testamentum* 87:14(4)n on Rom 7:14. Ps 8:7 in the Vulgate, which is being quoted here, has the ablative *pedibus*.

1:22 [ER *super omnia ipsi ecclesiae* '**over all things to the church itself**']

[VG] *super omnem ecclesiam* '**over all the church**'; ὑπὲρ πάντα τῇ ἐκκλησίᾳ, that is, 'over all things to the church,' so that *ecclesiae* is the dative case, not the genitive; in other words, 'He gave him to the church to be the head, the one in charge of all things.'[1] This is how Jerome reads in his commentary, in agreement with the Greeks,[2] although[3] Ambrose seems to have had a different reading.[4] Theophylact in his comment clearly shows that he read as I have edited [the text].[5] He adds that Christ is the head of the church in such a way that he excels not only his members, but also everything created in heaven and on earth. Chrysostom[6] takes it in the same sense but in two ways: above all things absolutely so that we understand that Christ is superior to all visible and intelligible creatures, or this is to be above all things which the Father made because he gave such a head to the church. The[7] older manuscript from Constance agreed with us. In it was written without any trace of an erasure 'above all things to the church.'

> 1 The addition of *ipsi* (itself), which has no equivalent in the Greek, serves to identify *ecclesiae* as the dative case. Modern English translations vary: 'for the church' (RSV, NIV), 'to the church' (AV).
> 2 Jerome *Comm in Eph* 1 (on 1:22–3) PL 26 (1884) 492B, 493A and 494C
> 3 although ... earth] Added in *1519*
> 4 Ambrosiaster *Comm in Eph* 1:22
> 5 Theophylact *Expos in Eph* 1:19–20 PG 124 1049A
> 6 Chrysostom ... church.] Added in *1535*; see Chrysostom *Hom in Eph* 3.2 PG 62 26.
> 7 The older ... church.'] Added in *1527*

1:23 [ER *complementum* '**the complement**']

[VG] *et plenitudo* '**and the fullness.**' The conjunction *et* [and] is not in the Greek manuscripts. It[1] was not added in the very old manuscript of St Donatian. Both[2] the manuscripts from Constance were in agreement. And it seems that τὸ πλήρωμα [the fullness] should be read in the accusative case so that it is referred to Christ. The words which follow support this.[3]

1 It ... St Donatian.] Added in *1522*. For the manuscript of St Donatian see
   the annotation on Gal 3:1 ('in front of the eyes of whom') n16.
2 Both ... agreement.] Added in *1527*
3 See Brown *Novum Testamentum* 504:23(2)n who notes that the use of the
   noun in the neuter gender retains the syntactical ambiguity of the Greek
   πλήρωμα, which is neuter in gender.

1:23 [ER *qui omnia in omnibus adimplet* 'who fills all in all']
[VG] *qui omnia in omnibus adimpletur*[1] 'who is filled all in all'; τὸ
πλήρωμα τοῦ πάντα ἐν πᾶσι πληρουμένου, that is, 'the fullness or fulfilment
[*impletio*] of him who fulfils all in all,' or, 'who is fulfilled.' The participle is in the middle voice. St Jerome seems to take it in two ways so that
one understands the body, that is, the faithful to be the consummation
of Christ himself, who is the head, who is so filled that he is all things
in all; or, he so fills that he is all to all things that have been bestowed,
sometimes on individuals and again differently on different persons.[2]
But if one understands πληρουμένου [being filled] as a passive, τὰ πάντα,
that is, 'in all' can be taken in such a way that one assumes the force of
the preposition κατά [according to] to be present so that the meaning is
that Christ is filled through all in all the members of his body collec-
tively at once. Chrysostom and[3] Theophylact[4] interpret it in the sense
that πλήρωμα [fullness] is the church and πληρουμένου [being filled] is in
the passive voice.[5]

1 The Vulgate has *adimpletur*, the passive, 'who is filled all in all.'
2 Jerome *Comm in Eph* 1 (on 1:22–3) PL 26 (1884) 494B
3 Chrysostom and] Added in *1535* with a change of the verb from singular
   to plural. See Chrysostom *Hom in Eph* 3.2 PG 62 26.
4 Theophylact *Expos in Eph* 1:23 PG 124 1049B
5 The meaning of verse 23 is still debated; see Lincoln *Ephesians* 72–8 whose
   conclusions support Erasmus' interpretation.

From the Second Chapter

2:1 [ER *et vos* 'and you']
[VG] *et vos convivificavit* 'and you he has quickened.' I do not find the
verb *convivificavit* in this position[1] [in the Greek codex] nor[2] in Jerome[3]
nor Ambrose[4] nor in the ancient manuscript of[5] St Donatian[6] nor in either of the manuscripts from Constance.[7] Hence[8] I wonder how it has
crept into the books now in circulation, unless perhaps it was taken
from the commentary of Thomas Aquinas or[9] of Jerome, who in his arrangement of the language of this passage thinks that *convivificavit* must
be understood here as though it has been put twice on account of the

extended hyperbaton.[10] He speaks as follows, 'And because you were dead through your trespasses and sins, God who is rich in mercy made you alive together with Christ on account of the great love with which he loved us; and because you were dead through the trespasses in which we at one time walked, according to the course of this world, according to the prince of the power of the air, the spirit which now works in the sons of disobedience among whom all of us too lived in the desires of our flesh, doing the wishes of our heart and minds and we were by nature sons of wrath, he brought us to life with Christ so that "and us he brought us to life with Christ" had to be understood as if they were spoken twice ἀπὸ κοινοῦ [in common].'[11] Thus far Jerome. Someone has put into the text what was to be understood. The Apostle himself has corrected the long circuit of the hyperbaton when he says, 'God who is rich etc.' For the rest, the accusative pronoun *vos* [you] could be referred to the preceding verb *dedit* [he gave]: 'he[12] gave him to be the head, you to be the members.' But it is closer to the truth that it was to be repeated here from the hyperbaton about which I shall speak a little below.

1 in this position] Added in *1519*
2 nor ... manuscript] Added in *1519*
3 Jerome *Comm in Eph* 1 (on 2:1–5) PL 26 (1884) 495A
4 Ambrosiaster *Comm in Eph* 2:1
5 of ... Constance] Added in *1527*
6 For the manuscript of St Donatian see the annotation on Gal 3:1 ('in front of the eyes of whom') n16.
7 For more information on the manuscripts from Constance see the annotation on Gal 1:3 ('from God our Father') n3 and CWE 56 xii.
8 Hence ... Aquinas] Added in *1519*. See Thomas Aquinas *Super Eph lect* cap 2 lectio 1.73.
9 or ... etc'] Added in *1535*
10 For hyperbaton see the annotation on Gal 1:6 ('into the grace of Christ') n4.
11 Erasmus uses the Greek grammatical term ἀπὸ κοινοῦ here; it is a construction that consists of two clauses or phrases that have a shared word with two functions in the syntax. See Smyth 3028e.
12 'he ... below] Added in *1519*

2:1 [ER VG] *cum essetis mortui delictis et peccatis* **'when you were dead in your offences and sins.'** One[1] could doubt whether the words 'offences and sins' are in the dative or ablative case, as if you would say, 'I am dead to you.' St Jerome[2] seems to understand it as though the Greek[3] is a dative of instrument, that is, 'dead through sin.' The word translated *delictum* [offence] here in Greek is παράπτωμα [trespass] which Jerome thinks is the first lapse towards the act of sinning.[4] For *peccatum* [sin] in Greek is ἁμαρτία which he thinks to be more serious when it has come to the evil act itself.[5]

1 One ... about] Added in 1522
2 Jerome *Comm in Eph* 1 (on 2:1–5) PL 26 (1884) 495A–C
3 Greek] Added in 1522
4 Jerome *Comm in Eph* 1 (on 2:1–5) PL 26 (1884) 495C–496A
5 Cf BDAG παράπτωμα 'a violation of moral standards, offense, wrongdoing, sin'; ἁμαρτία 'sin.'

2:1 [ER *peccatis* 'sins']

[VG] *peccatis vestris* **'your sins.'** *Vestris* [your] is redundant[1] according[2] to the manuscripts of the Greeks. For he is speaking generally about the sins which bring death to all. 'Dead because of sins' is a novel way of speaking since elsewhere [Paul] uses this phrase *mortuos peccato* 'dead to sin' of people in whom sin has been extinguished.[3] Here people whom sin has killed are called dead to sin. Moreover, the pronoun 'your' is superfluous in view of what follows, 'in which at one time you walked' [Eph 2:2].

1 Erasmus argues that the word *vestris* or ὑμῶν 'your' is redundant based on context. Brown suggests that the scribes of some early manuscripts may have experienced some interpretive additions. See Brown *Novum Testamentum* 505:1(3)n.
2 according ... walked'] Added in 1527
3 See the annotation on Rom 6:11 ('judge yourselves dead').

2:2 [ER *juxta principem cui potestas est aeris, qui est spiritus* **'according to the ruler to whom belongs the power of the air, who is the spirit'**]

[VG] *potestatis aeris huius spiritus* **'of the power of the air of this spirit'**; κατὰ τὸν ἄρχοντα τῆς ἐξουσίας τοῦ ἀέρος τοῦ πνεύματος [according to the ruler of the power of the air, the spirit] can be taken in two ways so that 'air' is connected with 'spirit' through apposition, 'of[1] the power of the air which is in fact the spirit.' And the article τοῦ, τοῦ πνεύματος [the spirit] invites us to take it in this way. For the Greeks are accustomed to understand the article in this way. But the words which follow, τοῦ ἐνεργοῦντος ['the one who is at work'], are somewhat opposed to this view. For it is not this air which does anything in the children of disobedience, but the instigation of the devil.[2] Therefore, it is better to read as follows: 'according to the ruler to whom the right and power of the air belong and the spirit of the one who is at work in the children of disobedience,' so that one understands the air to be the lowest part of the world alone in which he reigns, not as lord, since Christ is Lord of all, but as a tyrant who has power only because of our vice. Secondly, you may take spirit to be the worldly feeling, opposite to the heavenly spirit of Christ which loves nothing except heavenly things, and one may refer both nouns in the genitive, 'air' and 'spirit,' to the third noun which precedes them, 'power.'³ 'Power' here is not δύναμις [capability] but ἐξουσία [authority] so that we are to understand the term to mean right and authority. For the rest, the Translator adds the adjective 'this' [before 'spirit'] from his own initiative, since it is not in the Greek nor even in Jerome⁴ although⁵ the phrase 'this world,' κόσμου τούτου, came a little before.⁶

1 'of … spirit.'] Added in 1519
2 Cf the annotation on Eph 6:11 ('against the ambushes'). See Lincoln *Ephesians* 95–7.
3 See Lincoln *Ephesians* 96.
4 Jerome *Comm in Eph* 1 (on 2:1–5) PL 26 (1884) 495A and 496B
5 although … before] Added in 1527
6 The phrase 'this world' occurs earlier in Eph 2:2. The addition of 'this' in the Vulgate may have been prompted by a desire to prevent 'spirit' from being understood as referring to the Holy Spirit, as Brown notes *Novum Testamentum* 505:2(6)n.

2:2 [ER *in filiis contumacibus* 'in rebellious sons']
[VG] *in filiis diffidentiae* 'in the sons of unbelief'; ἐν υἱοῖς ἀπειθείας, that is, 'in the sons of disobedience' or 'unheeding' or¹, as Cyprian translates, 'rebellious.'² It is the proper duty of sons to be obedient and heedful of their parents. We³ have already advised about the trope several times:⁴ 'sons of disobedience' for 'disobedient sons' as a little before there was 'Father of glory' for 'glorious Father' [Eph 1:7]. In⁵ some manuscripts it was corrupted to 'on sons of disbelief.'

1 or … 'rebellious'] Added in 1522
2 Erasmus may be referring to Cyprian's use of *contumaciae* for ἀπειθείας at Eph 5:6. See Brown *Novum Testamentum* 505:2(5)n; Cyprian *Epistulae* 43.6 CSEL 3/2 595:18–19.
3 We … Father.'] Added in 1522
4 See the annotations on Luke 16:8 (*villicum iniquitatis*), Rom 1:4 ('through the spirit of sanctification') n3 and 1:26 ('to passions of shame') n4, and on Gal 2:9 ('they gave to me and to Barnabas the right hand of fellowship') n2.
5 In … disbelief.'] Added in 1527. Brown *Novum Testamentum* 505:2(5)n notes that the Vulgate word *diffidentia* 'meant a lack of confidence rather than a lack of belief.'

2:3 [ER *facientes quae … libebant* 'doing what pleased']
[VG] *facientes voluntatem* 'doing the will'; θελήματα, that is, 'wills,' for there are different kinds of feeling. But in many manuscripts they had corrupted *voluntates* 'wills' into *voluptates* 'pleasures.'¹

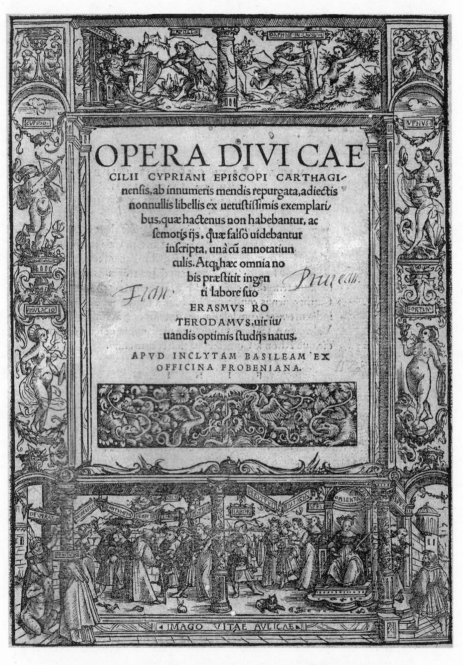

Title-page of Erasmus' edition of Cyprian, *Opera divi Caecilii Cypriani episcopi Carthaginensis* (Basel Froben 1520) Rotterdam Public Library

1 For the textual crux see A. Merk *Novum Testamentum Graece et Latine*
(Rome 1964) 636, which records that *voluptates* was written in three manuscripts of the Vulgate, as well as Tertullian and Ambrosiaster. Cf Weber
1809: *voluntates*. Cf *facientes voluntates* (Weber 1809).

2:3 [ER *ac menti* 'and the mind']
[VG] *et cogitationum* 'and of thoughts'; καὶ τῶν διανοιῶν.[1] It appears that
Jerome rather approves of *et mentium* [and of minds], distinguishing as
he does between sins of the flesh and sins of the mind.[2] The former are
cruder, such as lust, gluttony, drunkenness; the latter belong more to
the mind, like heresy. Ambrose reads *consiliorum* [of plans].[3]

> 1 BDAG defines διάνοια as 'understanding, intelligence, mind as the organ of
> νοεῖν.'
> 2 Jerome *Comm in Eph* 1 (on 2:1–5) PL 26 (1884) 497B
> 3 Ambrosiaster *Comm in Eph* 2:3

2:3 [ER VG] *natura filii irae* 'by nature children of wrath';[1] φύσει [by na-
ture], for which some, as Jerome indicates,[2] had translated 'totally' because the Greek word has more than one meaning.[3] And[4] Theophylact
advises that 'placed by nature' is said for 'truly' and 'properly,' as we
say a person is miserable by nature[5] who is so addicted to misery that
he is unwilling to escape it even if he could. Chrysostom[6] adds that
since nothing else than a human being is born from a human being, so
we are nothing else than children of wrath. I think that nature has been
opposed to grace because a little afterwards there follows 'by grace you
have been saved.' Wrath was part of our nature or birth; salvation was
part of grace and therefore it must be imputed to Christ and not to
ourselves.[7]

> 1 In the *1516* edition this annotation came before the previous one ('of
> thoughts').
> 2 Jerome *Comm in Eph* 1 (on 2:1–5) PL 26 (1884) 498C
> 3 For a fuller explanation by Erasmus of the ambiguity in φύσει see
> *Hyperaspistes* 2 CWE 77 372.
> 4 And ... could.] Added in *1522*. See Theophylact *Expos in Eph* 2:3 PG 124
> 1053A. Theophylact reads: τὸ δὲ 'φύσει', ἀντὶ τοῦ 'ἀληθῶς' καὶ 'γνησίως.'
> 5 by nature] Added in *1527*
> 6 Chrysostom ... wrath.] Added in *1535*. See Chrysostom *Hom in Eph* 4.1 PG
> 62 32.
> 7 In his *Assertion* Martin Luther adduced this text to argue that everything
> we do by nature merits wrath; see *Assertio omnium articulorum Martini
> Lutheri per bullam Leonis x novissimam damnatorum, articulus 36* CWE 76
> 307–8. In his discussion of Ephesians 2:3 in *Hyperaspistes* 2 (CWE 77 372)
> Erasmus responded by stating that Paul is not referring to original sin but
> to his own former life in Judaism.

2:4 [ER *propter multam* 'for his great']
[VG] *propter nimiam* 'for his exceeding'; διὰ πολλήν, that is, 'for his great' and this is the reading of Jerome[1] and Ambrose.[2] Otherwise, *nimium* [too much] is said of something which is beyond the mean.

1 Jerome *Comm in Eph* 1 (on 2:1–5) PL 26 (1884) 495A–B
2 Ambrosiaster *Comm in Eph* 2:4

2:5 [ER *etiam cum essemus* 'even when we were']
[VG] *et cum essemus* 'and when we were'; καὶ ὄντας ἡμᾶς, that is, 'even when we were.' The[1] conjunction 'and' which has a double meaning in Latin and Greek does not link here but emphasizes.[2]

1 The ... emphasizes.] Added in *1519*
2 The Greek conjunction καί, when followed by a participle (as here), represents καὶ εἰ 'although, even though,' which has an emphatic effect. Erasmus' use of the Latin *etiam* 'and even' reflects this meaning somewhat more accurately than *et* 'and moreover,' for the former is used to annex a more important idea to a preceding clause, while the latter is used to connect an idea that is either homogeneous or complementary to the preceding clause. See the relevant entries in LSJ (καί) and L&S (*et* and *etiam*). Modern English translations read 'even when we were dead' (AV, RSV, NIV).

2:5 [ER *mortui per delicta* 'dead through sins']
[VG] *mortui peccatis* 'dead in sins.' He would have avoided the ambiguity[1] if he had said *mortui per peccata* [dead through sins]. For otherwise Paul calls people 'dead to sin' who are no longer sinning, as[2] I advised a little earlier.[3] Ambrose did not add *peccatis* in this passage; he reads only 'when we were.'[4]

1 The ambiguity resides in the form *peccatis* which could be read either as a dative, 'to sins,' or an ablative, 'in sins.' On the literary and rhetorical figure of ambiguity (*amphibolia*) see Lausberg §222–3.
2 as ... we were] Added in *1527*
3 See the annotation on Eph 2:1 ('your sins').
4 Ambrosiaster *Comm in Eph* 2:5

2:4 [ER *sed deus qui dives est* 'but God who is rich']
[VG] *deus autem qui dives est* 'God[1] moreover who is rich.' Jerome advises that in *deus autem* the conjunction *autem* was either added by ignorant persons or was superfluously attached by Paul himself through inexperience in Greek.[2] For it interrupts the sequence of the thought. But I wonder why Jerome calls *autem* a causal conjunction. Perhaps he read *enim* [for] in place of *autem*. An adversative conjunction[3] is not otiose here, for it is opposed to the calamity which the Apostle exaggerates with many words, for great evils have need of rich mercy. But if one were to read *tamen* [however] for *autem*, the flow of the language is not impeded.

1 'God ... impeded.] This annotation was added in *1535*, and evidently misplaced in the text.
2 Jerome *Comm in Eph* 1 (on 2:1–5) PL 26 (1884) 495B. For Jerome's assessment of Paul's knowledge of Greek see the annotation on Eph 3:2 ('has been given to me in you') n4.
3 In coordinate clauses and similar constructions, a causal conjunction is used to introduce a cause or reason, whereas an adversative conjunction is used to imply a connection between the words, although there is a contrast in thought. See Allen and Greenough 223a.

2:5 [ER *convivificavit nos una cum Christo* 'he brought us to life together with Christ']
[VG] *convivificavit nos in Christo* 'he brought us to life in Christ.' Neither the pronouns *nos* [us] nor the preposition *in* [in] is in the Greek manuscripts; there is only[1] συνεζωοποίησε τῷ Χριστῷ so[2] that you are to understand that 'we rose again together with Christ.' So[3] reports Augustine in the eleventh book *Against Faustus*, chapter 8, in the manuscripts.[4] The[5] older manuscript from Constance retained the true reading, the two words *nos* [we] and *cuius* [whose] being erased by a not very recent hand. For the preposition *in* was added in neither [of the Constance manuscripts].

1 there is only] Added in *1527*
2 so ... Christ'] Added in *1519*
3 So ... manuscripts.] Added in *1522*. See Augustine *Contra Faustum Manichaeum* 11.8 CSEL 25 327:1–3.
4 In his letter to Maarten Lips of Brussels, Erasmus mentions the return of a manuscript of the *Contra Faustum*, and asks if there are any other older copies of the text (Allen Ep 1189:9–11). In a later letter, Erasmus again mentions an ancient codex that he used to correct the text of the *Contra Faustum* (Allen Ep 1309). Presumably it is to these manuscripts that Erasmus is referring in this annotation.
5 The ... neither.] Added in *1527*

2:5 [ER *per gratiam* 'through grace']
[VG] *cuius gratia* 'by whose grace.' *Cuius* [whose] is not added but only χάριτι ἐστὲ σεσωσμένοι, that is, 'by grace you have been saved.' And St Jerome[1] reads so that this particle is inserted as if a parenthesis,[2] as[3] Theophylact openly notes. Some[4] Latin texts added *enim* [for], but wrongly. But Jerome restored the order of the language, since it seems disturbed, in this way: 'And God, who is rich in mercy, since we were dead in trespasses and in our sins, has brought us to life with Christ on account of the great love with which he cherished us, he pitied us. And when we were dead in the sins in which we once walked according to the age of this world, the prince of the power of the air, [of] the

spirit, who now works in the children of unbelief, among whom we too
once dwelled in the desires of our flesh, doing the wills of the flesh and
mind, and we were by nature children of wrath, he brought us to life
with Christ.' Consequently, one twice repeats 'he brought us to life,' and
removes the causal conjunction 'for' in 'for God.' For Jerome seems to
have read ὁ γὰρ θεός [for God] because Jerome thinks this particle was
inserted by ignorant copyists or was added by Paul himself because
of his lack of familiarity with the Greek language,[5] although[6] in many
[manuscripts] there is a δέ, 'but.' And yet either conjunction keeps the
previous part of the sentence, 'when you were' etc, from being completed. But in my opinion Paul added the adversative conjunction δέ, that is
'but,' to create a contrast with the preceding words; that is, 'to have been
made alive' is contrasted with 'to be dead in sins.' Since many words
intervene, he added the preposition [sic] as though to start a new sentence. Moreover, it would have been better if the Translator[7] had said,
'Nevertheless, God has brought to life.' We[8] should note also that in this
passage Paul continuously varies the person, at one time addressing
them in the second person, at another including himself with them. The
following[9] needs to be added. In Ambrose the reading is different from
what we have,[10] but I do not know whether it was introduced by the
copyists. It is written in this way: 'God, however, who is rich in mercy,
had mercy on us because of his great love.'

1 Jerome *Comm in Eph* 1 (on 2:1–5) PL 26 (1884) 498D
2 A parenthesis (Latin *interpositio*) is the insertion of a clause, and thus an
   idea, that is foreign to the construction of the sentence; see Lausberg §860.
3 as ... notes] Added in *1522*. See Theophylact *Expos in Eph* 2:5 PG 124 1053C.
4 Some ... wrongly.] Added in *1527*
5 Jerome *Comm in Eph* 1 (on 2:1–5) PL 26 (1884) 495B. See also the annotation
   on Eph 2:4 ('God moreover who is rich') n3.
6 although ... 'but'] Added in *1519*
7 the Translator] Added in *1519*
8 We ... with them.] Added in *1519*
9 The following ... love.'] Added in *1522*
10 Ambrosiaster *Comm in Eph* 2:4

2:6 [ER *et simul cum eo resuscitavit et simul cum eo sedere fecit* 'and at
the same time he raised (us) up with him and at the same time made
(us) sit with him']

[VG] *et conresuscitavit et consedere fecit* 'and has raised [us] up together and made [us] sit together'; καὶ συνήγειρε καὶ συνεκάθισεν, that is,
'with him he raised and at the same time made to sit with him.'[1]

1 As Brown *Novum Testamentum* 507:6(1)n notes, the verbs *conresuscitare*
   and *consedere* in the Vulgate do not exist in classical usage.

2:7 [ER *benignitate* 'by his kindness']

[VG] *in bonitate* 'in[1] his goodness'; ἐν χρηστότητι, which Augustine in the eleventh book *Against Faustus* translates 'in kindness.'[2] For[3] it signifies the clemency and leniency of God towards us.[4]

> 1 'in ... kindness.'] This annotation was added in 1522.
> 2 Augustine *Contra Faustum Manichaeum* 11.8 CSEL 25 326:29. See also Lefèvre *Pauli epistolae* fol 165 verso.
> 3 For ... towards us.] Added in 1527
> 4 Cf *in bonitate* (Weber 1810).

2:8 [ER VG] *gratia enim* 'for by grace.' 'For' is not added in some manuscripts of the Greeks[1] just as it is not added a little below in the phrase 'for it is the gift of God,'[2] although this is how Ambrose reads.[3]

> 1 This omission is not recorded in the critical apparatuses. See Brown *Novum Testamentum* 507:8(1)n.
> 2 Erasmus is referring to the phrase *dei donum est* 'it is the gift of God,' which occurs later in Ephesians 2:8. The phrase lacks the Latin *enim* 'for,' just as the Greek manuscripts do not include the Greek counterpart γάρ.
> 3 Ambrosiaster *Comm in Eph* 2:8
> Ephesians 2:8–9 is a significant text in the evangelical movement of the sixteenth century: 'For by grace you have been saved through faith; and this is not your own doing, it is the gift of God – not because of works, lest any man should boast' (RSV). For Erasmus' understanding of this and related texts in 1519 see T.J. Wengert *Human Freedom, Christian Righteousness. Philip Melanchthon's Exegetical Debate with Erasmus of Rotterdam* (Oxford 1998) 50–1.

2:10 [ER *nam ipsius sumus opus* 'for we are his work']

[VG] *ipsius enim sumus factura* 'for we are his workmanship'; ποίημα. Ambrose reads *figmentum* [fashioning] as though something made from material.[1] And[2] this is how I translated because *factura* [workmanship] did not seem to be a good Latin word, but on the advice of some learned friends I changed *figmentum* to *opus* [work].[3] They were afraid the word *figmentum* would bother some ignorant person. But if it seemed a good idea to avoid with equal deliberation all the things that bothered those people, one would not change anything at all. Nevertheless, I for my part complied with the wishes of my friends rather than my own judgment.

> 1 Ambrosiaster *Comm in Eph* 2:10
> 2 And ... judgment.] Added in 1522. See Brown *Novum Testamentum* 507:10(2)n.
> 3 Weber (1810) reads *factura*; according to A. Souter *Glossary of Later Latin* (Oxford 1949) 147 *figmentum* means 'God's human creation; man.' Modern English translations have 'workmanship' (RSV), 'handiwork' (NIV).

2:10 [ER *ad opera bona* 'for good works']

[VG] *in operibus bonis* 'in good works'; ἐπ' ἔργοις ἀγαθοῖς, that is, 'for good works.'[1]

> 1 The Greek preposition ἐπί with the dative case can be used in a causal sense to indicate an end or purpose (LSJ s.v. ἐπί, B.III).

2:10 [ER VG] *quae praeparavit deus* 'which God has prepared'; οἷς, that is, *quibus* [for whom]. It should be referred, I think, to people. But in keeping with a grammatical feature of Greek[1] it can be referred to 'works,' so that the Greek dative case should be rendered in the accusative case [in Latin]; and thus Ambrose reads *quae praeparavit deus* [which God has prepared],[2] likewise Jerome.[3]

> 1 Erasmus is referring to the attraction of relative pronouns into the case of their antecedents, especially into the genitive or (as here) the dative (Smyth 2522).
> 2 Ambrosiaster *Comm in Eph* 2:10
> 3 Jerome *Comm in Eph* 1 (on 2:10) PL 26 (1884) 501A–B

2:11 [ER *ab ea quae vocatur circumcisio* 'by that which is called circumcision']

[VG] *ab ea quae dicitur circumcisio* 'by that which is called circumcision'; ὑπὸ τῆς λεγομένης περιτομῆς, [called], that is, by the Jews themselves, for the Greek is clearer [than the Latin]. The[1] Hebrew people is called the circumcision because of the cutting away of the foreskin; non-Hebrews were called the uncircumcision, but only by the Jews for whom the word circumcision was an honorific term while uncircumcision was a term of shame. And 'made by hands' has to modify 'circumcision,' not 'flesh.'

> 1 The ... shame.] Added in *1519*

2:12 [ER *quod inquam eratis* 'because, I say, you were']

[VG] *qui eratis* 'you who were.' One should read 'because' or 'since you were' as Ambrose read, in[1] agreement with the Greek, and Jerome,[2] with[3] the support of both manuscripts from Constance. [The Greek is] ὅτι ἦτε, so that the conjunction is repeated, as if he had put it, 'because, I say, you were.'

> 1 in ... Greek] Added in *1519*. See Ambrosiaster *Comm in Eph* 2:12.
> 2 Jerome *Comm in Eph* 1 (on 2:12) PL 26 (1884) 502B
> 3 with ... Constance.] Added in *1527*. The *qui* 'who' appears to be a scribal error for *quia* 'since, because.' Erasmus adds *inquam* 'I say' to mark a resumption from the previous *quod* 'because' in verse 11. See Brown *Novum Testamentum* 508:12(1)n.

2:12 [ER *abalienati a republica Israelis* 'alienated from the commonwealth of Israel']

[VG] *alienati a conversatione* 'being aliens from the conversation [of Israel]'; τῆς πολιτείας τοῦ Ἰσραὴλ, that is, 'from the polity' or 'from the commonwealth Israel' or 'of Israel.'[1]

> 1 or 'of Israel'] Added in *1519*. Valla also proposed this change (*Annot in Eph* 2 [I 877]). For the translation of the Greek see Brown *Novum Testamentum* 509:12(5)n. Weber 1810 retains *conversatione*.
> In response to Lee's criticism of his interpretation of πολιτεία as commonwealth and not, as Jerome takes it, communication, Erasmus states that 'in Greek citizens are called πολῖται because they are in communication with each other through their shared customs and laws' (*Responsio ad annotationes Lei* CWE 72 294).

2:12 [ER *et extranei a testamentis* 'and estranged from the testaments']

[VG] *et hospites testamentorum* 'foreigners to the testaments'; καὶ ξένοι τῶν διαθηκῶν, that is, 'sojourners or outlanders from the pacts or testaments.' He alluded to the commonwealth which he has just mentioned. Hence he calls 'strangers' people who are aliens without the right of citizens. And[1] he said the 'testaments of the promise' according to a Hebrew idiom.[2] Ambrose, however, adds a pronoun and reads 'their promise.'[3]

> 1 And ... 'their promise.'] Added in *1522*
> 2 Erasmus is referring to the use of the genitive instead of an adjective.
> See F. Blass and A. Debrunner *A Greek Grammar of the New Testament and Other Early Christian Literature* trans and rev (from the 9th – 10th German edition, incorporating supplementary notes of A. Debrunner) Robert W. Funk (Chicago and London 1961) §165, which states 'The genitive of quality provides in many combinations an attributive which would ordinarily be provided by an adjective ... Hebrew usage is thus reflected, in that this construction compensates for the nearly non-existent adjective.'
> 3 Ambrosiaster *Comm in Eph* 2:12

2:12 [ER *deoque carentes* 'and lacking God']

[VG] *et sine deo* 'and without God'; ἄθεοι [atheists], people who do not believe that there is a God; and ἀθεότης [atheism], which Plutarch shows to be less an evil than a superstition,[1] δεισιδαιμονία 'fear of the gods,' because[2] it imagines the gods to be bitter and vindictive although God is by nature beneficent.

> 1 See Plutarch *Moralia* 165B–C, 'On Superstition.'
> 2 because ... beneficent] Added in *1519*

2:12 [ER *in mundo* 'in the world']

[VG] *in hoc mundo* 'in this world.' 'This' is redundant except that I think the Translator wanted to convey the effect of the article τῷ [the].[1]

    1 Brown *Novum Testamentum* 509:12(9)n calls the *hoc* [this] a 'late Vulgate addition,' but it is found in some early manuscripts; see A. Merk *Novum Testamentum Graece et Latine* (Rome 1964) 637. The Latin demonstrative pronoun was frequently used to translate the Greek article. See W.E. Plater and H.J. White *A Grammar of the Vulgate* (Oxford 1926) §107.

2:14 [ER *et interstitium maceriae diruit, simultatem ... abrogans* 'and he has broken down the partition-wall, abolishing the hostility']

[VG] *et medium parietem maceriae solvens inimicitias* 'and breaking down the middle wall of partition, making void the enmities.' The Greeks punctuate so that the accusative *inimicitias* [enmities] is the object of the next participle καταργήσας[1] [having abolished], although it can be the object of both participles, λύσας [having broken down] which precedes and καταργήσας [having abolished] which follows, so that the noun 'enmity' is connected with 'the middle of the wall' or with 'the law of commandments.'[2] And it is odd that when he turned ὁ ποιήσας [the one who made] into a main verb, he did not also change the next participle λύσας [having broken down], that is, into 'who has broken down' or 'when the wall was broken down.' Furthermore, the Greek is τὸ μεσότοιχον τοῦ φραγμοῦ as if one were to say 'the intervening space of the barrier or fence.'[3] And in the comic poet, Micio 'orders the wall to be torn down to make one house.'[4] Therefore, that which separates house from house he calls μεσότοιχον. Nevertheless,[5] the translator's rendition is not bad except that it is not without ambiguity. For someone strikes the middle wall who hits the middle part.

    1 καταργήσας ... law of commandments'] Added in 1522
    2 See ASD VI-9 193:465–6n.
    3 For altering the Vulgate's *parietem* 'wall' to *interstitium* 'partition-wall' Erasmus was critized by Diego Zúñiga. He defended his rendering on the ground that it removed any ambiguity; see further Erasmus' *Apologia ad annotationes Stunicae* ASD IX-2 204 and H.J. de Jonge's note there (ASD IX-2 205:675n).
    4 See Terence *Adelphi* 908–9: *atque hanc in horto maceriam iube dirui quantum potest: hac transfer, unam fac domum* 'order a hole knocked in the garden wall right away. Bring her in that way and make one house.' The character who speaks these lines is Demea, not, as Erasmus has it, Micio.
    5 Nevertheless ... part.] Added in 1522

2:15 [ER *in decretis sitam abrogans* 'abolishing (the law) contained in ordinances']

[VG] *decretis evacuans* 'making void by decrees.' The omission of the preposition *in* overturns the whole meaning as if [Christ] abolished the Law by means of decrees. On the contrary, he abolished the Law that the precepts and decrees contained. Some edition which Jerome[1] cites had *in dogmatibus* [in decrees], using the Greek word. Ambrose reads *in decretis*;[2] elsewhere[3] he cites it with *edictis* [in edicts] in book two chapter six of *On Abraham the Patriarch*.[4] If[5] the article had been added in the Greek [before the phrase 'in decrees'] τὸν νόμον τῶν ἐντολῶν τὸν ἐν δόγμασι [the law of commandments found in decrees], there would have been no problem. As it is, the language is ambiguous. For [the phrase] ἐν δόγμασιν can be taken with the preceding words as well as with the words that follow. If [taken] with the preceding words, the meaning will be 'he abrogated the law of commandments which is contained in decrees'; if [taken] with the following words, the meaning will be, 'he made obsolete the law of ceremonial commandments through evangelical decrees,' taking the preposition ἐν [in] as placed instead of *per* [through]. The Translator seems to have followed the latter when he omitted the preposition ['in'] as superfluous to us in Latin. I find this interpretation in one Theophylact,[6] who[7] seems to have followed Chrysostom.[8] He thinks the decrees are the faith by which we are saved, or evangelical commandments such as 'but I say to you not to be angry at all.'[9] Ambrose[10] follows a different path and I shall append his words: 'he eliminated the Law which had been given to the Jews regarding circumcision – new moons, food laws, sacrifices and sabbaths; for he now ordered an end to be put to what would be a burden, and in this way he made peace. Hence the apostle Peter says in the Acts of the Apostles, "Why do you place a yoke upon the neck of the brothers which neither our fathers nor we have been able to bear?"'[11] In these words of Ambrose there is no mention of the decrees through which the Law had been abrogated. Ambrose implies, moreover, that circumcision and similar observances of the Law were an obstacle to the union of the Jews and the gentiles. Therefore, when these were abrogated through Christ, we were reconciled by faith which conferred salvation on Jews and gentiles alike without the observance of the Law. Jerome [comments] in the following way: 'The Law was also overturned in the decrees after circumcision and sabbath observance remained for the people of God; and not to appear empty in the sight of God, Easter and Pentecost are understood more deeply than the words sound, and we, withdrawing from the letter which kills, begin to follow the Spirit

which makes alive.'¹² From these words of Jerome it is quite clear that
he means that it was not through the decrees that the Law was abrogated, but through the spiritual understanding of those things which
he discerned. Nor does the comment of the scholiast to whom they attribute the name Jerome shrink from this.¹³ He says, 'Justifying through
faith alone, discerning only behaviour.' Now elsewhere too Paul calls
the prescriptions of the Law decrees, as in Colossians 2:[14], '... the
handwriting of the decree which was against us.'¹⁴ In this passage the
Greeks read τοῖς δόγμασιν in place of ἐν δόγμασιν. For the preposition
was added from an idiom of the Hebrew language.¹⁵ In another passage there is τί ἔτι δογματίζεσθε [why are you still bound to decrees].¹⁶
Moreover, nowhere do we read in Paul that evangelical precepts are
called decrees. Therefore, that question [above] about the article should
be ignored. I think it was omitted because of the heaping up of articles
which would happen if he had said τὸν νόμον τῶν ἐντολῶν τὸν [ἐν δόγμασι]
or τῶν ἐν δόγμασι. For I think 'in decrees' belongs rather with the closest
word, otherwise the same thing would seem to be said twice τὸν νόμον
τῶν ἐντολῶν τὸν ἐν δόγμασι. As it is, to show that the Law is overbearing,
he calls it τῶν ἐντολῶν [of commandments], as if you were to say ἐντέλ-
λουσας, that is, 'commanding.' How? Not by persuasion and gentleness
or by promises, but by commands, which he here calls 'decrees,' in
Latin 'decisions.' For if one were to ask why God ordered us to abstain
from such and such foods, the Jew would answer, 'because it was his
pleasure.' And 'abolishing' is in the past tense, as if one were to say,
'when the law had been made obsolete.'

1 Jerome *Comm in Eph* 1 (on 2:15–18) PL 26 (1884) 504A
2 Ambrosiaster *Comm in Eph* 2:15
3 elsewhere ... chapter six] Added in *1519*
4 Ambrose *De Abraham* II 6.28 CSEL 32/1 585:22
5 If ... Theophylact] Added in *1527*
6 Theophylact *Expos in Eph* 2:15 PG 124 1061B
7 who ... angry at all'] Added in *1535*
8 Chrysostom *Hom in Eph* 5.2 PG 62 39
9 Cf Matt 5:22.
10 Ambrose ... pleasure.'] Added in *1527*. See Ambrosiaster *Comm in Eph* 2:15.
11 Cf Acts 15:10.
12 Jerome *Comm in Eph* 1 (on 2:15) PL 26 (1884) 504C–505A
13 Pelagius *Expos in Eph* 2:15 (Souter II 355:5)
14 Erasmus' point here is to draw a parallel between 'the decrees' in Eph
    2:15 and those in Col 2:14, where 'decrees' represents the old, bygone
    order. See further the note by M. van Poll-van de Lisdonk ASD VI-9
    196:502–4n.

15 Erasmus apparently has in mind the use of the preposition ἐν which can have a positional, locative meaning; see further Brown *Novum Testamentum* 510:15(1)n.

16 Cf Col 2:20.

2:15 [ER *ut duos conderet* 'that he might make the two']

[VG] *et* [sic][1] *duos condat* 'that he may make the two.' The meaning here is 'he might create' or 'he might prepare,' κτίσῃ [he might create], explaining, as it were, the thought.

> 1 *et* 'and' is a typographical error for *ut* 'that.' The imperfect subjunctive *conderet* retains the secondary sequence of tenses set by the preceding past tense verbs. See Brown *Novum Testamentum* 510:15(3)n.

2:15 [ER *in unum novum hominem* 'into one new man']

[VG] *in uno novo homine* 'in one new man.' The Greek is εἰς ἕνα καινὸν ἄνθρωπον, 'into one new man.' Augustine[1] reports it thus in the twenty-second book *Against Faustus*, chapter 89. Both[2] manuscripts from Constance agree. The Greek[3] ἀποκαταλλάξῃ translates into Latin as *reconciliet* [he may reconcile]. Augustine translates *commutaret* [he changed].[4] It seems that the one who translates in this way had read ἀλλάξῃ [he changed].

> 1 Augustine ... chapter 89.] Added in 1522. See Augustine *Contra Faustum Manichaeum* 22.89 CSEL 25 696:16.
> 2 Both ... agree.] Added in 1527
> 3 The Greek ... ἀλλάξῃ.] Added in 1522
> 4 Augustine *Contra Faustum Manichaeum* 22.89 CSEL 25 696:17

2:16 [ER *perempta inimicitia per eam* 'the enmity having been done away with through it']

[VG] *inimicitias in semetipso* '[killing] the enmities in himself'; ἐν αὐτῷ [thereby]. Jerome reads *in ea* [in it] so that the pronoun refers to 'cross,' not to 'Christ.'[1] In Greek also the word 'cross' is masculine in gender. But if it were a reflexive pronoun, that is, *in se ipso* [in himself], [the pronoun] would have the initial alpha aspirated, ἁ, ἐν αὐτῷ.[2] However, this is not observed by Greek authors. Lastly, Ambrose has a different reading.[3]

> 1 Jerome *Comm in Eph* 1 (on 2:15-18) PL 26 (1884) 504B and 504C. Erasmus understands the Greek ἐν 'in' to be instrumental; cf Allen and Greenough 121(16c). See further the annotation on Gal 1:6 ('into the grace of Christ') n10.
> 2 The reflexive pronoun ἑαυτῷ does occur in a few late manuscripts; thus Brown *Novum Testamentum* 511:16(3)n.
> 3 Ambrosiaster *Comm in Eph* 2:16

2:17 [ER *et iis qui prope* 'and to them who were nearby']
[VG] *et pacem iis qui prope* 'and peace to them who were nearby.' 'And peace' is not repeated in the Greek.[1]

1 'And peace' here is the reading of the older Greek manuscripts. Its omission is restricted almost entirely to the medieval manuscripts. See Brown *Novum Testamentum* 511:17(3)n, and Metzger 534, who suggests the words may have been removed for seeming redundant.

2:18 [ER *habemus aditum* 'we have entrance']
[VG] *habemus accessum* 'we have access'; προσαγωγήν, that is, entrance or introduction as when someone is introduced into the presence of a prince.[1]

1 See Brown *Novum Testamentum* 511:18(3)n and 67:2(1)n on Rom 5:2. Erasmus frequently replaces *accessus* [access] with *aditus* [entrance], feeling that the Greek προσαγωγή implies that someone is introduced into the presence of God. The Latin *aditus* is more frequent in classical usage than *accessus*.

2:19 [ER *hospites et incolae* 'strangers and sojourners']
[VG] *hospites et advenae* 'strangers and foreigners'; ξένοι καὶ πάροικοι, that is, foreigners and sojourners or migrants, that is, people who migrate from some place into a foreign state.[1] Augustine[2] sometimes reads *inquilini* [tenants] for *advenae* [strangers].

1 According to LSJ, a πάροικος is one who dwells nearby, or a neighbour. The meaning of a sojourner became common in New Testament Greek.
2 Augustine ... *advenae*.] Added in 1519. See for example Augustine *Contra Faustum Manichaeum* 12.24 CSEL 25 352:14 –15, *Contra Adversarium Legis et Prophetarum* 2.2 CCL 49 93:183, *Enarrationes in Psalmos* 86.2 CCL 39 1199:38.

2:19 [ER *sed concives* 'but fellow citizens']
[VG] *sed estis cives* 'but you are citizens'; ἀλλὰ συμπολῖται, that is, 'fellow citizens,' to[1] translate verbatim.

1 to ... verbatim] Added in 1519. Erasmus means that the Latin prefix *con-* (*cum*) translates the Greek prefix συν- (syn- or sym-). Both mean 'with, together,' or 'fellow' (AV).

2:20 [ER *superstructi super fundamentum apostolorum ac prophetarum* 'built upon the foundation of the apostles and prophets.']
[VG] *superaedificati super fundamentum apostolorum et prophetarum* 'built[1] upon the foundation of the apostles and the prophets.' The followers of Marcion erased the phrase *et prophetarum* [and prophets], doubtless from their hatred of the Old Testament.[2]

1 'built ... Testament.] This annotation was added in 1527.
2 For Marcion see Tertullian *Adversus Marcionem* 5.17.16 CCL 1 716:22–7.
Erasmus is following Tertullian here, but his statement is erroneous since
the 'prophets' here meant are New Testament prophets. Apostles and
prophets are mentioned later in Ephesians 3:5 and 4:11, where they are
clearly New Testament prophets (Lincoln *Ephesians* 153).

2:20 [ER VG] *angulari lapide* **'corner stone.'** In Greek it is a single word, ἀκρογωνιαίου, which denotes the highest stone in the corner of a building,
which usually is also the strongest.[1] [In Latin] it is an ablative absolute
construction as if[2] one were to say 'in which building Christ is the highest point in the corner stone.' And[3] for this reason Augustine, citing this
passage in his commentary on Psalm 81, adds the participle 'existing,'
for the sake of clarity rather than good Latin. Also[4] in *Against Faustus*,
book 12, chapter 24.

1 According to LSJ, the adjective ἀκρογωνιαίος refers to something at the
farthest corner. In stonemasonry, therefore, the stone that is ἀκρογωνιαίος is
a corner foundation-stone.
2 if] Added in 1522
3 And ... Latin.] Added in 1519. See Augustine *Enarrationes in Psalmos* 81.5
CCL 39 1139:29. In adding the participle *existente* 'is,' Augustine makes it
clear that Christ is to be identified with the corner stone.
4 Also ... 24.] Added in 1522, See Augustine *Contra Faustum Manichaeum*
12.24 CSEL 25 352:17. For the modern debate over the meaning of 'corner
stone' see Lincoln *Ephesians* 152–4.

2:20 [ER *summo angulari lapide ipso Iesu Christo* **'the highest corner stone
(being) Jesus Christ himself'**]
[VG] *in ipso summo angulari lapide Christo Iesu* **'Jesus Christ himself
being the chief corner stone.'**[2] Here too it is an absolute construction[1] as
if one were to say *Christo duce* 'with Christ as leader,' ὄντος ἀκρογωνιαίου
αὐτοῦ Ἰησοῦ Χριστοῦ, that is, 'Jesus Christ himself being the highest corner
stone.'

1 The preposition *in* and the word order *Christo Iesu* (for *Iesu Christo*) were
added in 1535. The *in* is probably a typographical error. On the word
order of *Iesu Christo* in the manuscripts see Brown *Novum Testamentum*
513:20.
2 The ablative absolute is a construction that is grammatically independent from the rest of the sentence, used to indicate the time or circumstances under which the action of the main clause takes place. In its
most common form, it consists of a noun or pronoun in the ablative case,
with a participle in agreement. In Greek this construction is rendered
with a noun or pronoun in the genitive case, independent of the main
clause, with a participle in agreement, and can be used to indicate time,

opposition or concession, cause, condition, or attendant circumstance in relation to the main clause (Smyth 2070; Allen and Greenough 419).

2:21 [ER *coagmentatur* 'is fitted together']
[VG] *constructa* 'constructed.' The Greek word συναρμολογουμένη [framed together] is more meaningful, that is, 'fitted together' or 'put together' or 'joined together.' Jerome reads *compaginata* 'fashioned together,'[1] Ambrose *compacta* 'joined together.'[2] Nor does [Paul] mean that every building has been joined together by this corner stone, but whatever building is being held together by that stone, that building rises into a temple of the Lord. For συναρμολογουμένη is a present participle. However,[3] πᾶσα [all] could be translated 'the entire building' so that one understands that it is not some part but the whole structure, and that is how Theophylact takes it.[4]

1 Jerome *Comm in Eph* 1 (on 2:19–22) PL 26 (1884) 506B
2 Ambrosiaster *Comm in Eph* 2:21
3 However ... takes it.] Added in *1522*
4 Theophylact *Expos in Eph* 2:21 PG 124 1065B–C

2:22 [ER *per spiritum* 'through the spirit']
[VG] *in spiritu sancto* 'in the Holy Spirit.' 'Holy' is redundant according to the Greek and Ambrose,[1] and[2] likewise Jerome.[3] Their commentary shows what they read. For Paul opposes spirit to carnal Judaism which he everywhere assails.

1 Ambrosiaster *Comm in Eph* 2:22. On the instrumental use of *per* see the annotation on Gal 1:6 ('into the grace of Christ') n10.
2 and ... assails] Added in *1519*
3 Jerome *Comm in Eph* 1 (on 2:19–22) PL 26 (1884) 506B

From the Third Chapter

3:1 [ER *vinctus sum Christi Iesu* 'I am the prisoner of Christ Jesus']
[VG] *vinctus Christi Iesu* 'the prisoner of Christ Jesus.' 'Prisoner' is a noun in Greek, δέσμιος [prisoner],[1] and[2] for this reason it goes more easily with the genitive 'of Jesus Christ.'[3]

1 An attributive participle may become a substantive participle when the substantive noun or adjective is omitted (Smyth 2050).
2 and ... Christ'] Added in *1519*
3 The Latin word *vinctus* 'having been imprisoned' is a perfect passive participle and would not normally be construed as here with a noun in the genitive case. Following Lefèvre *Pauli epistolae* fol 166 recto Erasmus adds the verb *sum* 'I am.'

3:1 [ER VG] *pro vobis gentibus* 'for[1] you gentiles.' I think this is an error because in the manuscripts of Ambrose the reading is 'for you brothers.'[2]

> 1 'for ... brothers.'] This annotation was added in 1522.
> 2 Ambrosiaster *Comm in Eph* 3:1. Modern editions of the New Testament
> read ὑπὲρ ὑμῶν τῶν ἐθνῶν 'for you gentiles.' Cf *gentibus* (Weber 1810), 'gen-
> tiles' (AV, RSV, NIV).

3:2 [ER VG] *dispensationem gratiae* '**the dispensation of the grace**';
οἰκονομίαν, that is, dispensation or administration.[1]

> 1 BDAG s.v. 2b explains the meaning of οἰκονομία here as God's 'plan of
> salvation, his arrangements for redemption of humans.' Cf the annotation
> on Eph 1:10 ('in the dispensation').

3:2 [ER *data est mihi in vos* '**has been given to me towards you**']
[VG] *data est mihi in vobis* '**has been given to me in you**'; εἰς ὑμᾶς, that
is, 'towards you.' Here too Jerome renders the anacoluthon[1] in this passage as follows: 'For this cause I, Paul, the prisoner of Jesus Christ and
the prisoner for you, who are gentiles, knew the mystery in order that
I might pass it on to you too, as I remarked a little earlier in this same
epistle.[2] Moreover, you must hear the dispensation of the grace of God,
which has been given to me in you who are gentiles for whom I am
even a prisoner of Jesus Christ.'[3] However, Jerome thinks it is simpler
to admit that Paul has stumbled in a foreign language and he should be
judged more by the meaning than by the words.[4] The awkwardness of
the imperfect manner of speaking could also be removed by supplying
the verb 'I am' here: 'I, Paul, am the prisoner of Jesus Christ.'

> 1 Anacoluthon, or grammatical inconsistency, 'is inadvertent or purposed
> deviation in the structure of a sentence by which a construction started at
> the beginning is not followed out consistently' (Smyth 3004).
> 2 See Jerome *Comm in Eph* 1 (on 1:9) PL 26 (1884) 482A. Cf the annotation on
> Eph 1:9 ('that he might make known').
> 3 Jerome *Comm in Eph* 2 (on 3:1–4) PL 26 (1884) 508C–D
> 4 Jerome *Comm in Eph* 2 (on 3:1–4) PL 26 (1884) 508C. See also Jerome *Comm
> in Gal* 3 (on 6:1) CCL 77A 206:71–4, 'Therefore the Hebrew of Hebrews,
> and the one who was very learned in his native tongue, was not able to
> express deep thoughts in a foreign language, nor did he care very much
> about words, since he safely grasped their meaning.'

3:3 [ER *notum mihi fecit* '**he made known to me**']
[VG] *notum factum mihi est* '**has been made known to me**'; ἐγνώρισέ
μοι τὸ μυστήριον, that is, 'he has made known to me the mystery.'[1] The
Translator has again rendered *mysterium* as 'sacrament.'[2]

1 Erasmus alters the passive voice in *notum factum est* of the Vulgate to the
active *fecit* in order to reflect the active voice in the Greek verb ἐγνώρισε.
On *notum facere* 'to make it known' see OLD *notus* 4.c. Modern editions
have ἐγνώρισέ μοι.

2 Cf Eph 1:9 and 5:32. In his annotation on Rom 11:25 ('brothers this mystery') Erasmus defines 'mystery' as 'something hidden, and known to
few, and which is to be shared only with initiates.'

3:3 [ER *quemadmodum ante scripsi* 'as I wrote previously']
[VG] *sicut supra scripsi* 'as I have written above'; καθὼς προέγραψα, that
is, 'as I wrote before.'¹ So Ambrose.² St Jerome reads *praescripsi* [I wrote
beforehand].³

1 Erasmus implies that the prefix προ- is temporal in force, not locative, as
the preposition *supra* in the Vulgate suggests. According to this interpretation, Paul had written a previous letter. On the meaning 'before,
beforehand' in verbs compounded by προ- see LSJ s.v. D.III.5 and Allen
and Greenough 1694.2. Cf also Erasmus' long note on προγράφειν in Rom
15:4 ('for whatever things have been written'). In adding the verb *sum* 'I
am' Erasmus is following Lefèvre *Pauli epistolae* fol 166 recto.

2 Ambrosiaster *Comm in Eph* 3:3

3 Jerome *Comm in Eph* 2 (on 3:1–4) PL 26 (1884) 507D

3:3 [ER *paucis* 'in a few words']
[VG] *in brevi* 'in brief'; ἐν ὀλίγῳ, that is, 'in a little,'¹ so Jerome² and
Ambrose.³ He means that he has written about these things in a few
words, as the Greek scholia explain.⁴ The sense here can also be 'as I
wrote⁵ a little earlier.' For he has in mind those who were afar, meaning
the gentiles. Theophylact⁶ comes close to this sense.

1 On the spatial or temporal force in ἐν ὀλίγῳ see LSJ s.v. ὀλίγος A.IV.3.

2 Jerome *Comm in Eph* 2 (on 3:1–4) PL 26 (1884) 507D

3 Ambrosiaster *Comm in Eph* 3:3

4 Pseudo-Oecumenius *Comm in Eph* 3:1–6 PG 118 1201C. For the identity of
the 'Greek scholia' see the annotation on Gal 1:16 ('I did not acquiesce in')
n2 and the annotation to Rom 1:4 ('who was predestined') n1 CWE 56 10.

5 be 'as I wrote] Added in *1519*

6 Theophylact ... sense.] Added in *1519*. See Theophylact *Expos in Eph* 3:3 PG
124 1068B.

3:4 [ER *in mysterio Christi* 'in the mystery of Christ']
[VG] *in ministerio Christi* 'in the ministry of Christ'; ἐν τῷ μυστηρίῳ,
that is, 'in the mystery,' a word he usually translates as 'sacrament.'¹

1 *ministerio* appears to be an error in the medieval or later Vulgate for
mysterio. It does not appear in the earlier manuscripts of the Vulgate,
Ambrosiaster, Jerome, Manetti and Lefèvre (Brown *Novum Testamentum*
514:4[3]n). See also Erasmus' comment on Eph 1:9 ('sacrament') above,
and on Eph 3:3 ('has been made known to me'). Mystery is a predominant
concept in the letter to the Ephesians: cf 1:9, 3:9, 6:19.

3:5 [ER *in aliis aetatibus* 'in other ages']
[VG] *aliis generationibus* 'in other generations.' Ambrose's reading,
aliis seculis [other times], is clearer because [Paul] is talking about ages,
not about peoples.[1]

  1 Ambrosiaster *Comm in Eph* 3:5

3:5 [ER *non innotuit* 'did not become known']
[VG] *non est agnitum* 'was not known';[1] οὐκ ἐγνωρίσθη, that is, 'not made
known,' or 'unlocked.'[2]

  1 According to OLD, the intransitive verb *innotesco* means 'to become
    known,' *agnosco* 'to recognize.'
  2 or 'unlocked'] Added in *1519*

3:5 [ER *per spiritum* 'through the Spirit']
[VG] *in spiritu* 'in the Spirit.' 'Holy' is added in the Greek. Not[1] only is
the reading different but so too is the punctuation. Theophylact arranges the wording thus: 'as it has now been revealed to his holy apostles
in the Holy Spirit,' so that we understand that this has been revealed
to them through the Holy Spirit.[2] Ambrose on the other hand connects
'Spirit' with the words which follow: 'As has now been revealed to his
saints and prophets, that by the Spirit the gentiles are co-heirs.'[3] His
commentary proves this clearly when he teaches that the gentiles are
co-heirs not by the ceremonies of the Mosaic Law but by the Spirit, that
is, by evangelical teaching. St Jerome follows the punctuation of the
Greeks.[4] I approve rather what Ambrose follows.[5]

  1 Not ... follows.] Added in *1519*
  2 Theophylact *Expos in Eph* 3:5 PG 124 1068D. Erasmus has modified
    Theophylact's rendering by adding *sancto* 'holy' to modify *spiritu* 'Spirit,'
    and by omitting *et prophetis* 'and prophets' following 'his holy apostles.'
    See ASD VI-9 203:585n.
  3 Ambrosiaster *Comm in Eph* 3:5–6
  4 Jerome *Comm in Eph* 2 (on 3:5–7) PL 26 (1884) 509C, 510D, and 511B–C
  5 In the Latin text of Erasmus the comma appears after, not before *per spiri-
    tum*; so too in the corresponding Greek text and the current Greek New
    Testament. See further A. Merk *Novum Testamentum Graece et Latine* (Rome
    1964) 639.

3:6 [ER *ut sint gentes* **'that the gentiles should be'**]
[VG] *esse gentes* **'that the gentiles are'**; εἶναι τὰ ἔθνη, that is, 'that the gentiles should be.'[1]

> 1 Though also in AV, this is a questionable interpretation of the Greek which is an indirect statement, not an indirect command. It is correctly translated in the Vulgate and the reading is maintained in Weber 1811. Modern English translations vary: 'that the gentiles should be fellow heirs' (AV), 'that the gentiles are heirs' (NIV), 'that is, how the gentiles are fellow heirs' (RSV).

3:6 [ER *eiusdem corporis* **'of the same body'**]
[VG] *concorporales* **'fellow comrades'**; σύσσωμα, as if one were to say, 'of one body.'[1] The piling[2] up of the prefix *con* in this passage offended the ears of Jerome,[3] in his view through a lack of harmony, *cohaeredes* [fellow heirs], *concorporales* [fellow comrades], *comparticipes* [fellow partakers]. It is strange that he is bothered by so trivial a matter when he so often makes Paul ignorant of the Greek language, though he admits that Paul was not ignorant in knowledge.[4] Secondly,[5] although he admits that *comparticipes* is to be read and without doubt in a good sense, nevertheless, in the fifth chapter of this Epistle he says that this word is not read in Sacred Scripture except in a bad sense.[6] But more will be said about this matter there.[7]

> 1 Erasmus replaces the word *concorporales* in the Vulgate because it does not occur in classical usage.
> 2 The piling ... knowledge.] Added in *1519*
> 3 Jerome *Comm in Eph* 2 (on 3:5–7) PL 26 (1884) 512A
> 4 Jerome *Epistolae* 121.10 PL 22 1029. For Jerome's assessment of Paul's knowledge of the Greek language see the annotation on Eph 3:2 ('has been given to me in you') n4.
> 5 Secondly ... matter there.] Added in *1527*
> 6 Jerome *Comm in Eph* 3 (on 5:7) PL 26 (1884) 555D
> 7 See the annotation on Eph 5:7 ('partakers with them'). Brown notes that Erasmus also substituted *consortes* for *participes* at Eph 5:7, due to the pejorative sense of the word (*Novum Testamentum* 515:6[4]n).

3:6 [ER *promissionis eius in Christo* **'of his promise in Christ'**]
[VG] *promissionis in Christo Iesu* **'of the promise in Christ Jesus.'** The Latin text[1] lacks αὐτοῦ, that is 'his own' or[2] 'his' so that it refers to the Spirit, as Ambrose appears to have thought when he writes, 'This is what he says, "By the Spirit the gentiles are fellow heirs and fellow comrades and partakers of his promise in Christ." For who worships God in the Spirit has no need of the work of the Law.'[3]

> 1 The Latin text] Added in *1527*
> 2 or ... the Law'] Added in *1519*
> 3 Ambrosiaster *Comm in Eph* 3:6

3:8 [ER VG] *omnium sanctorum* **'of all the saints.'** The word[1] 'of men' is added in some Greek manuscripts but wrongly unless I am mistaken. And so too ἐλαχιστοτέρῳ, which Jerome translates by *infimo* [lowest].[2] But Paul in order to depreciate himself the more fashioned a comparative out of the superlative, as if one were to say *infimiori* [more lowest] for *infimo* [lowest] or *postremiori* [more last].[3]

  1 The word ... mistaken.] Added in *1519*. The *1516* version of the annotation read, 'In the Greek ἀνθρώπων, that is, "men," is also read.' Erasmus has apparently made a mistake in revising the note for the *1519* version of the annotation. Brown suggests that Erasmus may have meant that some manuscripts replace ἁγίων by ἀνθρώπων (*Novum Testamentum* 515–16:8[2]n).
  2 Jerome *Comm in Eph* 2 (on 3:8–9) PL 26 (1884) 513B
  3 According to L&S, *postremior* 'more last' is the comparative degree of *postremus* [last], which is itself a superlative degree of *posterus* 'next.' This is rendered in English as a double comparative, whereby the word 'more' (often used to create comparatives) is used with an adjective already inflected in the comparative or superlative degree; see *Merriam-Webster's Dictionary of English Usage* (Springfield Mass. 1995) 363.

3:8 [ER *impervestigabiles* **'untraceable'**]
[VG] *investigabiles* **'unsearchable'**; ἀνεξιχνίαστον πλοῦτον, that is, 'untraceable riches.' I[1] do not know whether the reading in Ambrose, 'inestimable,' was made through an error of a copyist.[2] Certainly Ambrose understood the word to mean 'incomprehensible.'

  1 I ... incomprehensible.'] Added in *1519*. Though *investigabilis* normally describes something that can be searched into, in the Vulgate it means 'untraceable' (eg Prov 5:6, Rom 11:33). Cf the reading *ininvestigabiles* (Weber 1811). Erasmus' *impervestigabilis* is a neologism, literally 'something that cannot be searched through.' See also the annotation on Rom 11:33 ('untraceable'). Modern English translations vary: 'unsearchable' (AV, RSV), 'boundless' (NIV).
  2 Ambrosiaster *Comm in Eph* 3:8

3:9 [ER *et in lucem proferam omnibus* **'and I am bringing into the light for all'**]
[VG] *et illuminare* **'and to enlighten'**; καὶ φωτίσαι πάντας [and to make all men see]. Ambrose does not add 'all men' though the words are quite useful.[1] Nor is there any mention of this additional phrase in Jerome, but[2] there is only 'to enlighten.'[3] Paul is not enlightening men, but bringing into the light, and is making what was previously hidden visible to all.

  1 Ambrosiaster *Comm in Eph* 3:9
  2 but ... to enlighten'] Added in *1519*

3 Jerome *Comm in Eph* 2 (on 3:8–9) PL 26 (1884) 513B. In Migne's edition
Jerome actually does read *illuminare omnes* 'to enlighten all,' but Migne
notes that in other manuscripts the word *omnes* is absent, although the
Greek requires it. Cf Jerome *Comm in Eph* 2 (on 3:8–9) PL 26 (1884) 513D
n1. On the textual tradition of πάντας, for the inclusion of which there are
several important witnesses and manuscripts, see Metzger 534.

3:9 [ER *quae sit communio* 'what is the fellowship']
[VG] *quae sit dispensatio* 'what is the dispensation';[1] ὁ πλοῦτος, that
is, 'the riches' is also read.[2] Again, he translates μυστήριον [mystery] as
sacramentum [sacrament].[3]

1 Metzger 535 notes that some witnesses replace οἰκονομία with the inter-
pretative κοινωνία 'fellowship'; it appears Erasmus followed this reading,
and with him AV ('fellowship'). The reading οἰκονομία is followed by RSV
('plan') and NEB ('purpose').
2 No surviving Greek manuscript contains this reading.
3 See the annotations on Eph 1:9 ('sacrament') and Eph 3:3 ('has been
made known to me'). With the rendering *mysterii* Erasmus is following
Ambrosiaster and Lefèvre.

3:9 [ER *qui universa condidit* 'who founded the universe']
[VG] *qui omnia creavit* 'who created all things';[1] διὰ Ἰησοῦ Χριστοῦ,
that is, 'through Jesus Christ' is added in this place in the Greek although Jerome[2] does not have it nor does Ambrose[3] nor[4] the old Latin
manuscripts.

1 The Greek text is τὰ πάντα κτίσαντι, 'who created all things' (RSV). Erasmus
translates κτίζω by *condo* elsewhere too (eg Rom 1:25).
2 Jerome *Comm in Eph* 2 (on 3:8–9) PL 26 (1884) 513B
3 Ambrosiaster *Comm in Eph* 3:9
4 nor ... manuscripts] Added in 1527. As Brown observes, the textual issue
is whether a corrector inserted the mention of Christ's role in creation
or whether these words, which have doctrinal significance, were part of
the original text (*Novum Testamentum* 517:9[7]n). Modern editions of the
New Testament leave out διὰ Ἰησοῦ Χριστοῦ (Metzger 535). In making this
change Erasmus is following Lefèvre (*Pauli epistolae* fol 166 verso).

**3:10 [ER *ut nota fiat nunc* 'that it (the wisdom of God) be now made
known']**
[VG] *ut innotescat* 'that [the wisdom of God] may be made known'; ἵνα
γνωρισθῇ νῦν, that is, 'that it may be made known now.'[1] Jerome reads
et nunc [even now] with the addition of the conjunction [*et*], so long as
there is no error in the manuscript.[2]

1 On the manuscript tradition followed by the Vulgate in omitting *nunc*
here see Brown *Novum Testamentum* 517:10(2)n. On *innotesco* see the annotation on Eph 3:5 ('was not known') n1.

2 Jerome *Comm in Eph* 2 (on 3:10–11) PL 26 (1884) 514C. Erasmus appears to be mistaken here, as Jerome actually reads *ut innotesceret* 'that [it] may be made known,' with no mention of *et*.

3:10 [ER VG] *potestatibus in*[1] *caelestibus* '**powers in heavenly places**'; ἐν τοῖς ἐπουρανίοις, that is, 'in heavenly places.'

1 In the editions from *1516* to *1527*, the word *in* [in] occurred prior to *potestatibus* [powers].
As is evident from his paraphrase, Erasmus regarded the 'powers' here to refer to principalities obedient to God (*Paraphrasis in Ephesios* CWE 43 323 and n14 there). Cf the annotation on Eph 1:3 ('in heavenly places in Christ').

3:10 [ER VG] *per ecclesiam* '**through the church**'; διὰ τῆς ἐκκλησίας [through the church]. The preposition 'through' in this place signifies instrument as if one were to say 'by the work of the church.'[1] Though,[2] to speak frankly, the Greek clearly would be ambiguous if the article τῆς [the] had not been added, in which case the meaning would have been 'on account of the congregations' or 'the churches.'[3]

1 The Latin preposition *per* [through] with a noun in the accusative case indicates an instrumental meaning, whereas the Greek preposition διά [through] takes a noun in the genitive case to indicate the instrumental meaning (LSJ and L&S).
2 Though ... churches.'] Added in *1519*
3 In Greek, the form of the word ἐκκλησίας can be genitive singular [of the church] or accusative plural [the churches]. The article is necessary to distinguish the number and case, τῆς for the genitive singular and τάς for the accusative plural.

3:10 [ER *vehementer varia sapientia* '**the extremely varied wisdom**']
[VG] *multiformis sapientia* '**the multiform wisdom**'; πολυποίκιλος [much variegated] or elsewhere παμποίκιλος [all variegated], that is, 'very greatly variegated' and 'variegated in every way.' For πᾶν [all] in compound adjectives serves to add intensification.[1]

1 For Erasmus' use of *vehementer* [extremely] see Brown *Novum Testamentum* 517:10(5)n. See also his note on Gal 1:14 ('an imitator') *Novum Testamentum* 463:14(2). The Latin adverb *vehementer* [extremely, very much] intensifies the meaning (L&S).

3:11 [ER VG] *secundum praefinitionem* '**according to the prior determination**'; κατὰ πρόθεσιν, that is, 'according to the purpose,' in Jerome's reading.[1]

1 Jerome *Comm in Eph* 2 (on 3:10–11) PL 26 (1884) 514C

3:11 [ER VG] *quam fecit* 'which he made'; ἣν ἐποίησεν [which he made]. The Greek is ambiguous. For the Greek relative pronoun can refer either to 'wisdom' or to 'church,'[1] or to 'prior determination,' which Ambrose[2] and Jerome[3] call 'purpose.' If the reference is to 'purpose,' the meaning is 'according to the time he purposed or previously determined in Christ'; if[4] to 'church,' the meaning would be 'the church made in Christ Jesus'; if to 'wisdom,' you understand that 'wisdom was made,' that is, created in Christ. Jerome especially approves this last meaning.[5] And *fiduciam* [3:12] is παρρησίαν [boldness] which Ambrose translates 'freedom.'[6] It is the boldness to speak freely.[7] Nothing[8] is more fearful than a bad conscience, as nothing is more confident than innocence.

1 or to 'church'] Added in *1519*
2 Ambrosiaster *Comm in Eph* 3:11
3 Jerome *Comm in Eph* 2 (on 3:10–11) PL 26 (1884) 514C. Cf the annotation on Eph 3:11 ('according to the prior determination').
4 if ... Christ Jesus'] Added in *1519*
5 Jerome *Comm in Eph* 2 (on 3:10–11) PL 26 (1884) 515C–D
6 Ambrosiaster *Comm in Eph* 3:12
7 Cf BDAG s.v. παρρησία 3b: 'joyousness, confidence' that is the result of faith.
8 Nothing ... innocence.] Added in *1522*. Erasmus may have added this statement in *1522* in self-defence against Lee and Diego López Zúñiga (ASD VI-9 207:638–9n). For more on Lee see the annotation on Gal 1:5 ('to whom is the glory') n3; for Zúñiga see the annotation on Gal 6:2 ('and so you will fulfil') n5.

3:13 [ER *ob afflictiones meas quas pro vobis tolero* 'on account of my afflictions which I endure for you']
[VG] *in tribulationibus meis pro vobis* 'at[1] my tribulations for you'; αἰτοῦμαι μὴ ἐκκακεῖν [I ask you not to faint]. St Jerome advises that the Greek is ambiguous because the verb ἐκκακεῖν [to faint] could take any one of the three persons as its subject:[2] I ask that I not faint, that you not faint, that they not faint. Jerome at least understands it in either the first or second meaning: 'I ask that I not faint, that the powers of the air attacking from every direction do not overcome me.'[3]

1 'at ... overcome me.'] The annotation was added in *1519*. For the several textual changes in Erasmus' translations of this sentence see Brown *Novum Testamentum* 517:13(3,4)n. Modern scholars generally prefer the view that Paul is asking his readers not to be discouraged. See Lincoln *Ephesians* 191.
2 Jerome *Comm in Eph* 2 (on 3:13) PL 26 (1884) 516B–C
3 Jerome *Comm in Eph* 2 (on 3:13) PL 26 (1884) 516C–D and 517A. Erasmus does not accurately quote Jerome here. Jerome states 'I ask that I not faint in my tribulations for you.'

3:13 [ER VG] *quae est gloria* 'which is glory.' Some Greek manuscripts have 'which will be,' ἥτις ἔσται.[1] Jerome[2] tortures himself a fair amount in this passage, nor do I fully understand why he does so, for he thinks that the grammar of this phrase cannot be consistent unless we admit that Paul spoke ignorantly when he attached a singular relative pronoun – *quae est gloria* [which is glory] – to a plural antecedent 'tribulations.' As if grammar does not teach that in speaking in this way we are more correct than if we were to say 'in the tribulations which are your glory.'[3] Jerome finds the grammar so bad that he tries through a hyperbaton[4] to connect the clause, 'which is your glory,' to the earlier clause 'in whom we have confidence and access and faith' etc.[5] This confidence, access, and faith is your glory. But since he sees that this is too harsh, he prefers to accuse Paul of ignorance of the language. But what will they do to Jerome in the meantime, who want the knowledge of languages to have affected all the apostles by the gift of the Holy Spirit, and this gift to them to have been perpetual? One of their number seems to be even Aquinas in [his lectures] on the Epistle to the Galatians. But Jerome is not afraid again and again to accuse Paul of ignorance of Greek.[6] But in this particular passage I do not see what might seem to be said ignorantly except that he said 'in tribulations' for 'on account of tribulations' in a more Semitic than Greek manner.

1 For this reading, found apparently in only one of Erasmus' Greek manuscripts, see Brown *Novum Testamentum* 517:13(5)n.
2 Jerome ... on account of tribulations.'] Added in *1519*. See Jerome *Comm in Eph* 2 (on 3:13) PL 26 (1884) 516D–517A.
3 Erasmus frequently comments on ambiguous relative pronouns; cf the annotation on Eph 3:11 ('which he made') and Gal 4:24 ('one upon the mountain').
4 For hyperbaton see the annotation on Gal 1:6 ('into the grace of Christ') n4.
5 Jerome *Comm in Eph* 2 (on 3:13) PL 26 (1884) 516D–517A
6 See previous footnote on Eph 3:2 ('has been given to me in you') n4.

3:14 [ER VG] *ad Patrem domini nostri Iesu Christi* 'to[1] the Father of our Lord, Jesus Christ.' St Jerome indicates that the four words, 'of our Lord Jesus Christ,' were added in the Latin manuscripts while the genuine text remains in the Greek.[2] For [Paul] is not speaking here specifically about the Father of the Lord Jesus Christ, but generally he is bending his knees before[3] that father whom all rational creatures acknowledge as their creator and source. Nevertheless, it is odd that what Jerome writes was added in the Latin manuscripts is now found in the Greek. And yet Chrysostom and[4] Theophylact[5] in their commentaries on the passage do not touch on this phrase. Hence one must conjecture that it was added to the Greek from our [Latin] manuscripts or the Greek manuscripts once upon a time varied.[6]

1 'to ... varied.] This annotation was added in 1522.
2 Jerome *Comm in Eph* 2 (on 3:14) PL 26 (1884) 519A–B. On the textual tradition see Metzger 535.
3 he is bending his knees before] Added in 1527
4 Chrysostom and] Added in 1535. See Chrysostom *Hom in Eph* 7.1 PG 62 51.
5 Theophylact *Expos in Eph* 3:14–15 PG 124 1073C–D
6 For the textual problem discussed here see Brown *Novum Testamentum* 518:14(1)n.

3:15 [ER *omnis a communi patre cognatio* 'every kinship from a common father']

[VG] *omnis paternitas* 'all paternity'; πᾶσα πατριά, that is, 'every family,' as also St Jerome indicates in his commentary.[1] In writing against Helvidius he also states that what the Greeks call πατριάι speakers of Latin call *parentelas* [family relationships] when a large number of descendants flow from a single root.[2] But in the Greek there remains a verbal connection which the Latin tried to preserve.[3] As for those questions which Thomas Aquinas advances in this passage:[4] whether there is any 'paternity' in heaven and whether 'every paternity in heaven and on earth' is derived from that paternity which exists in divine beings, let the theologians see how aptly the questions relate to this passage, inasmuch as he did not understand the word from which he draws the entire matter. Certainly the Translator elsewhere renders it by 'family,' as in Psalm [22:27], *omnes familiae gentium* [all the families of the gentiles], πατριαί [families].[5] Likewise[6] in Luke [2:4], 'from the house and family of David.' The translator of Origen's second homily on Numbers noted this.[7] Chrysostom[8] explains it as meaning φυλαί, that is 'tribes.' But the Translator, as[9] I had started to say, affected to render the affinity of the words *pater* and *paternitas*. And yet this was not so important that the meaning had to be lost. *Parentela*[10] [family relationship] would be an adequate explanation of the matter, so long as that was an acceptable word.[11] Nevertheless[12] Jerome testifies that in his own day it was in common use and for this reason more endurable than *paternitas*, especially since analogy[13] casts a vote of support.[14] For as *clientela* [clientele] is from *cliens* [client], so *parentela* is from *parens* [parent]. I have rendered it as best I could by a circumlocution.[15]

1 Jerome *Comm in Eph* 2 (on 3:14) PL 26 (1884) 519B
2 Jerome *Adversus Helvidium de Mariae virginitate perpetua* 14 PL 23 (1845) 207B

3 A connection between πατήρ (father) and πατριά (paternal family) in Greek, *pater* (father) and *paternitas* (fatherhood). See Brown *Novum Testamentum* 518:15(1)n for Erasmus' struggles with these words.

4 Thomas Aquinas *Super Eph lect* cap 3 lectio 4.168

5 Following '[families],' the clause 'which in Hebrew is "all the families of the nations"' occurred in *1516* only.

6 Likewise ... noted this.] Added in *1519*

7 Origen *Homilia in Numeros* 2.2 PG 12 593A–C

8 Chrysostom ... tribes.'] Added in *1535*. See Chrysostom *Hom in Eph* 7.1 PG 62 51.

9 as ... say] Added in *1527*

10 *Parentela* ... acceptable.] Added in *1519*

11 Cf Erasmus' defence against the criticism of Lee (*Responsio ad annotationes Lei* 2 CWE 72 295): 'In common speech it may be called *parentela*, but to scholars the term *paternitas* means either nothing or something different, namely the concept of fatherhood.' A. Souter *Glossary of Later Latin* (Oxford 1949) 286 defines *parentela* as 'relationship.'

12 Nevertheless ... circumlocution.] Added in *1522*. See Brown *Novum Testamentum* 518:15(1)n, who notes that the annotation may have been expanded in response to a criticism by Zúñiga. On Zúñiga see the annotation on Gal 6:2 ('and so you will fulfil') n5.

13 For the distinction between *similitudo* and *analogia* as forms of argument see Quintilian 5.11.22 and 5.11.34; see also *Ecclesiastes* II ASD V-4 414:165–418:256 for Erasmus' definitions.

14 Erasmus appears to be mistaken, since the word *parentela* does not appear either in Jerome's commentary on Ephesians or in his discussion of Jesus' family in *Adversus Helvidium*. Jerome, in *Adversus Helvidium de Mariae virginitate perpetua* 14 PL 23(1845) 207B, does use *paternitates* 'paternities.'

15 Circumlocution, or periphrasis, is the use of an entire phrase for a single word, even if that word is included in the phrase itself (Smyth 3041).

3:16 [ER *ut fortitudine corroboremini* 'that you be strengthened with might']
[VG] *virtute corroborari* 'to be strengthened with power'; δυνάμει, that is, 'with might.' The meaning would be clearer if he had translated the Greek infinitive by a verb in the subjunctive, *ut corroboremini* [that you be strengthened].[1]

1 As elsewhere (eg Eph 1:10, 3:8; Gal 5:7) so here Erasmus often replaces the Vulgate's infinitive construction with a subordinate clause. On replacing *virtute* with *fortitudine* see the annotation on Eph 1:19 ('the operation of the might of his power') and n1 there.

3:18 [ER *profunditas et sublimitas* 'depth and height']
[VG] *sublimitas et profundum* 'height and deepness'; καὶ βάθος καὶ ὕψος, that is, 'both the depth and the height.'[1] Jerome has *et profundum et altitudo* [both the deep and the height].[2]

1 For the difference in the text see Brown *Novum Testamentum* 519:18(3)n.
2 Jerome *Comm in Eph* 2 (on 3:16–19) PL 26 (1884) 521C

3:19 [ER *cognoscereque* 'and come to know']
[VG] *scire etiam* 'to know also.' It is not the beginning of a new heading
so that there is a need for an *etiam* [also]. γνῶναί τε, that is, *scireque* [and
to know] or *utque sciretis* [and that you might know].

3:19 [ER *praeeminentem cognitioni dilectionem* 'the love surpassing
knowledge']
[VG] *supereminentem scientiae charitatem* 'the charity which exceeds
all knowledge.' In Latin[1] it is uncertain whether *scientiae* [knowledge]
is a dative case or genitive so that one may either understand that the
charity of Christ is known to be greater than could be learned and[2] as
Ambrose puts it, 'which surpasses our knowledge,'[3] or that one may
understand that the love of knowledge is outstanding. But the second meaning fits better with the Greek. Jerome follows this meaning.[4]
Moreover,[5] that Ambrose meant what I said above is made clear from
these words of his, 'After the infinite and incomprehensible knowledge
of God the Father and his indescribable mercy he wants us to acknowledge also Christ's love which is of surpassing knowledge – the word
"human" is understood – so that Christ's love is considered beyond
the knowledge of humans. For who can infer the basis of the mystery
of this love that even God was born a human for the sake of humans,
etc.'[6] However, I suspect that this text is not without error. For the biblical text has 'and to come to know the surpassing knowledge of Christ's
love,' as[7] Augustine too cites it in his one hundred and twentieth letter.
This reading differs considerably from the Greek. Besides what is in
[the text of] the commentary, 'is of surpassing knowledge,' I suspect
he actually wrote, 'is surpassing of knowledge.'[8] However, Jerome's
discussion of this passage seems to me to be somewhat harsh.[9] Nor[10]
does he connect the word 'knowledge' with 'surpassing' but with 'charity.' Certainly Theophylact interprets the meaning in the same way as
Ambrose.[11] Augustine[12] agrees with Ambrose when he cites this passage
in the nineteenth chapter of *On Grace and Free Will*, saying, 'Likewise
when the Apostle says "the love of Christ surpassing knowledge," what
is more insane than to think that there is knowledge from God which is
to be subjected to love and from humans there is a love which surpasses knowledge.' There would be no doubt at all, however, if ὑπερβάλλω
[surpass] would allow the genitive case to be joined to it as do ὑπερα-
σπίζω [defend] and ὑπεραπολογοῦμαι [defend] and[13] ὑπερέχω [exceed],
which have the same meaning as ὑπερβάλλω. I have no interest in saying
that Paul misused the case because of either his neglect or ignorance of
the Greek language.[14] Theophylact[15] expresses the following opinion,
saying, 'So that you can come to know the love of Christ, excelling all
knowledge. How shall we come to know? First of all, he says it excels

knowledge, that is, human knowledge. However, you will come to know it not through human knowledge but through the Spirit. Secondly, he did not say this, "you will know how great it is," but the very fact that it is great, that it excels all knowledge. I pray for this, that you learn from the Spirit. And he says, who do not know this? All, even those who are annoyed by what befalls them and those who prefer Mammon[16] to God. But if we were to come to know it, we would never murmur against divine providence or pay attention to our present circumstances, rebelling against the God who loved us so. Attend also to the following point: if love excels all knowledge, how much more does the substance of it.' Thus far Theophylact, from whose words it appears that he believed love to be more excellent than knowledge. Chrysostom[17] does not touch on this question.

1 In Latin] Added in 1522. Erasmus means that *scientiae* can be taken as an objective genitive with *dilectionem* or *charitatem*, or as a dative governed by *praeeminentem* or *supereminentem*. For the ambiguity of the Latin and Erasmus' replies to critics (especially Zúñiga) who questioned his interpretation see Brown *Novum Testamentum* 519:19(3)n.

2 and ... knowledge'] Added in 1522

3 Cf Ambrosiaster *Comm in Eph* 3:19. This quotation does not match the current critical editions of Ambrosiaster since Erasmus' edition contained many small variations. See ASD VI-9 212:699n.

4 Jerome *Comm in Eph* 2 (on 3:16–19) PL 26 (1884) 523B

5 Moreover ... Greek language.] Added in 1522

6 Ambrosiaster *Comm in Eph* 3:19

7 as ... letter] Added in 1535. See Augustine *Epistulae* 140.25.62 PL 33 565 and 140.26.63 PL 33 566.

8 Ambrosiaster *Comm in Eph* 3:19. The alternate reading *supereminens est scientiae*, 'is surpassing of knowledge,' is present in two codices: the codex Florentinus Laur. Ashb. 60 and the codex Oxoniensis Bodl. Lyell Empt. 9.

9 Jerome *Comm in Eph* 2 (on 3:16–19) PL 26 (1884) 522B–523C

10 Nor ... charity.'] Added in 1527

11 Theophylact *Expos in Eph* 3:19 PG 124 1076D–1077B

12 Augustine ... surpasses knowledge.'] Added in 1527. See Augustine *De gratia et libero arbitrio* 19.40 PL 44 905.

13 and ... ὑπερβάλλω.] Added in 1527

14 In the 1522 edition the following passage appeared, but was removed in subsequent editions: 'When I wrote this the Greek codex of Theophylact was not at hand; either the translator did not interpret the Greek faithfully enough, or the author read something other than what we read, or he thought the genitive case rightly adjoined the participle ὑπερβάλλουσαν.'

15 Theophylact ... more excellent than knowledge.] Added in 1527. See Theophylact *Expos in Eph* 3:19 PG 124 1076D–1077B.

16 Mammon is a Semitic word for 'riches.' Cf Erasmus' *Life of Jerome* (CWE 61 35), where he implies that the word is of Syrian origin.

17 Chrysostom ... question.] Added in 1535. See Chrysostom *Hom in Eph* 7.2 PG 62 52.

3:20 [ER *ei vero qui potest cumulate facere ultra omnia* 'to him truly who can do abundantly above all']

[VG] *ei autem qui potens est omnia facere* 'now to him who is able to do all things.' The Greek is ὑπὲρ πάντα ποιῆσαι, that is, 'to do above all things.' And this is how Ambrose[1] and Jerome[2] read it, but[3] in such a way that ὑπέρ seems to be an adverb, not a preposition, to be powerful to an extent as to be equivalent to extraordinarily.[4] Certainly when it is repeated in the next passage, ὑπὲρ ἐκπερισσοῦ [overabundantly], it cannot be anything except an adverb.[5] There is, moreover, a two-fold emphasis[6] as noted by Chrysostom[7] and Theophylact.[8] God can do all things, something which no human can do, and he can offer most abundantly whatever he wills, even[9] beyond our requests. Now, dear reader, even unadvised you notice that this is a flourish of the kind that Paul, as though carried away and inspired, sometimes attaches to the end of his argument.[10]

1 Ambrosiaster *Comm in Eph* 3:20.
2 Jerome *Comm in Eph* 2 (3:20–1) PL 26 (1884) 523C
3 But ... argument.] Added in *1519*
4 Cf BDAG s.v. ὑπέρ 2B: '"More than" also takes on the sense more exalted or excellent or glorious than.'
5 Lexicographers consider ὑπερεκπερισσοῦ 'overabundantly' to be a single word. In the *Annotations* it is printed as two words, ὑπέρ and ἐκπερισσοῦ, hence Erasmus' view of ὑπέρ as an independent adverb. In his *1535* Greek text the word appears as three separate words ὑπὲρ ἐκ περισσοῦ.
6 Quintilian defines 'emphasis' as 'words that mean more than they say' (8.2.11, and cf 9.2.64); Erasmus explains it in *Ecclesiastes* III as an expression that 'suggests more to the thought of the listeners than the words denote' (ASD V-5 859–61).
7 Chrysostom] Added in *1535*. See Chrysostom *Hom in Eph* 7.2 PG 62 52.
8 Theophylact *Expos in Eph* 3:20–1 PG 124 1077C
9 even ... requests] Added in *1535*
10 From *1519* to *1522*, a passage was included after 'argument': *Necque enim suspicari lubet ab aliis additas ad lectionis intervallum* 'To suppose that words have been added from elsewhere to fill a gap in the reading is also appealing.' Erasmus here has in mind the doxology of Rom 16:25–7, on which he comments on the possible transposition of the text; cf the annotation on Rom 16:25 ('now to him who is able').

3:20 [ER *ultra omnia quae petimus* 'above all that we ask']

[VG] *superabundanter quam petimus* 'over abundantly than we ask'; ὑπὲρ ἐκπερισσοῦ ὧν αἰτούμεθα, that is, 'from abundance beyond that which we ask.'[1]

1 The main reason Erasmus changed the Vulgate's *superabundanter* is that it does not occur in classical Latin.

3:20 [ER *quae petimus aut cogitamus* 'that we ask or think']

[VG] *quam petimus aut intelligimus* 'than we ask or understand'; ὧν
αἰτούμεθα ἢ νοοῦμεν, that is, 'beyond[1] all that we ask or think.' Lorenzo
[Valla] makes this correction although[2] as far as the meaning is concerned it does not matter much.[3] The[4] reader with only a rudimentary
knowledge [of Greek] needs to be advised that the [relative] pronoun
ὧν is congruent with the preceding words though it does not agree with
its own verb, in keeping with the propriety of the Greek language.[5]

1 'beyond all] Added in 1519
2 although ... much] Added in 1519
3 Valla *Annot in Eph* 3 (I 877). On Lorenzo Valla see the annotation on Gal
  1:13 ('and was subduing') n1.
4 The reader ... language.] Added in 1527
5 Erasmus is describing the rule whereby the case of the relative pronoun
  is attracted to the case of its antecedent, here an implicit genitive. A direct
  object of the verb 'ask' would otherwise be in the accusative case. Cf
  Smyth 2522.

3:21 [ER *in ecclesia per Christum Iesum* 'in the church through Christ Jesus']

[VG] *in ecclesia et in Christo* 'in the church and in Christ Jesus.' The
conjunction 'and' is redundant. Ambrose[1] reads in the reverse order, 'in
Christ Jesus and in the church,' and interprets in accordance with this
order. In[2] the one place the preposition is used absolutely, 'in church,'
as if one were to say 'in the senate,' in the other it is a Hebraism.[3] For
he prays that the Father be glorified in the congregation of the saints
through his Son, Jesus Christ. In this meaning there is no need for a
preposition.[4]

1 Ambrose ... this order.] Added in 1522. See Ambrosiaster *Comm in Eph*
  3:21.
2 In ... for a preposition.] Added in 1527
3 In his annotation on Acts 10:38 (*quomodo unxit eum*) Erasmus made this
  observation about the influence of Hebrew upon the writing style of the
  New Testament: 'Even if the apostles wrote in Greek, they introduced
  much from their own language ... for the apostles learned their Greek not
  from the orations of Demosthenes, but in talking with the common folk'
  (ASD VI-6 250:666–71).
4 For the text see Brown *Novum Testamentum* 521:21(2)n. Erasmus' Greek
  text omits the 'and' between 'church' and 'Christ Jesus.' Hence his view
  that the second 'in' is a Hebraism is probably misguided though others
  have followed him; cf AV 'by Christ Jesus.' For the meaning of 'in Christ
  Jesus' see Lincoln *Ephesians* 217.

From the Fourth Chapter

4:1 [ER *ita ut dignum est vocatione* '**in such a way as is worthy of the calling**']

[VG] *digne vocatione* '**worthily of the calling**'; ἀξίως τῆς κλήσεως [in a manner worthy of the calling]. He made a noun the object of an adverb as if one were to say, 'he sings similarly to you.'[1] And again,[2] the relative pronoun corresponds to the case of its antecedent in disagreement with its own verb. Otherwise one would have to say ᾗ ἐκλήθητε [by which you were called].

> 1 For the use of the genitive following adverbs derived from adjectives that govern the genitive case see Smyth 1437, Allen and Greenough 418.
> 2 And again ... ᾗ ἐκλήθητε.] Added in *1527*. For the grammatical attraction see the annotation on Eph 3:20 ('than we ask or understand') n5.

4:2 [ER *cum omni submissione* '**with all lowliness**']

[VG] *cum omni humilitate* '**with all humility**';[1] ταπεινοφροσύνης. It denotes a mental attitude that is the opposite of arrogance.[2] For 'humility' as translation of ταπείνωσις [humble status] has a different meaning.[3] For this reason Ambrose adds 'humility of mind' to keep us from taking the word to mean of humble circumstance.[4]

> 1 Weber 1811: *humilitate*. Cf modern English translations: 'with all lowliness and meekness' (AV, RSV), 'be completely humble and gentle' (NIV).
> 2 The Greek word ταπεινοφροσύνη is composed of two elements, 'humble-mindedness.'
> 3 Erasmus is here following Valla *Annot in Gal* 1 (I 877).
> 4 Ambrosiaster *Comm in Eph* 4:2

4:2 [ER *cum animi lenitate* '**with gentleness of mind**']

[VG] *cum patientia* '**with patience**'; μακροθυμίας, that is, 'longsuffering,' if[1] someone wants to translate verbatim. Ambrose[2] reads as follows: 'with all humility of mind and modesty, with magnanimity.'[3] He[4] translates μακροθυμία by *magnanimitas* [magnanimity] though the [Greek] word means rather the gentleness of mind and self-control[5] by which it happens that we are not easily stirred up and carried away to a desire for revenge.[6] *Longanimitas* [long-suffering] expresses the meaning of the Greek word[7] better than *magnanimitas*. Still a 'long mind' is something different from one that is gentle and slow to anger. *Patientia* [patience] would be correct except that it is ambiguous and refers more to physical endurance than to mental gentleness.[8]

> 1 if ... verbatim] Added in *1519*
> 2 Ambrosiaster *Comm in Eph* 4:2

3 In the 1516 edition, this sentence continued as follows: *ut autem exprimeret ταπεινοφροσύνης, usus est circumitione* 'but to express ταπεινοφροσύνης he uses circumlocution.'

4 He ... mental gentleness.] Added in 1519

5 and self-control] Added in 1527

6 Cf BDAG s.v. μακροθυμία: 'patience, steadfastness, endurance; forbearance, patience towards others.' See also the annotation on Gal 5:22 ('patience') and n2.

7 of the Greek word] Added in 1527

8 Cf OLD s.v. *patientia* 2: 'ability or willingness to endure hardship, pain, etc., endurance, hardiness.'

4:3 [ER *studentes servare* 'endeavouring to keep']

[VG] *solliciti servare* 'careful to keep';¹ σπουδάζοντες, that is, 'endeavouring,' which Augustine,² in the sixty-ninth chapter of the second book *Against the Letter of Petilianus*, translates 'acting carefully,' and shortly thereafter in the seventy-eighth chapter he translates 'endeavouring to keep,' just as I do. Ambrose [translates] 'carefully keeping.'³

1 Weber 1811 retains *solliciti*. Erasmus' rendering reflects the present tense in the Greek participle.

2 which Augustine ... as I do] Added in 1522. See Augustine *Contra litteras Petiliani* 2.69.155 PL 43 308 and 2.78.174 PL 43 312.

3 Ambrose ... keeping.'] Added in 1527. See Ambrosiaster *Comm in Eph* 4:3.

4:3 [ER *per vinculum pacis* 'through the bond of peace']

[VG] *in vinculo pacis* 'in the bond of peace'; ἐν τῷ συνδέσμῳ, as though one were to say 'the binding and chaining together.'¹ Augustine² in the same passage translates it by 'conjunction.' For³ a bond can be said of one thing. It is a σύνδεσμος when one thing is bonded to another.

1 As BDAG s.v. σύνδεσμος observes, the expression means 'the bond that consists in peace (epexegetic gen.).' Cf Erasmus' paraphrase of this text: 'By harmony and concord you have been connected and cemented together with the bonding of peace' *Paraphrasis in Ephesios* CWE 43 327.

2 Augustine ... conjunction.'] Added in 1522. See Augustine *Contra litteras Petiliani* 2.69.155 PL 43 308.

3 For ... to another.] Added in 1527

4:6 [ER *qui est super omnia et per omnia* 'who is above all things and through all things']

[VG] *qui super omnes et per omnia* 'who [is] above all and through all things.'¹ It would be better to continue in the same gender and not to mix things with persons: *super omnia et per omnes* [above all and through all] or *super omnia et per omnia* [above all things and through all things].

In the Greek the gender is uncertain.² Jerome seems to embrace the neuter when he cites the well-known Virgilian phrase,³ *Deum namque ire
per omnes/ terrasque tractusque maris caelumque profundum* ['for god goes
through all lands and tracts of the sea and the deep sky'].⁴ Though⁵ the
copyists cram in an *omnes*, the sense is against it, for Jerome explains
thus: 'For God the Father is "over all" because he is the creator of all'
things. The Son is "through all" because he traverses all things and goes
through all things. The Holy Spirit is "in all things" because nothing
exists without him.'⁶ Thus far Jerome. Since the word *omnium* in the
initial phrase covers all three genders, it is not clear whether it refers to
all humans or to all existing things. When in the next phrase he adds the
reason – because he traverses and goes through all things – he reveals
that he did not read *per omnes* but *per omnia*. *In omnibus* is ambiguous,
but when he attaches the explanation, 'nothing exists without him,' he
makes clear that *in omnibus* is the neuter gender. Otherwise he would
have said, 'no one exists without him.' This leads to a question which
Jerome immediately takes up. 'However, one ought not to think,' he
says, 'that he is the one God and Father of all in a shared way so that
the name 'father' could be applied to irrational animals' etc.⁷ There
is no point in advancing this scruple if he reads 'to be Father over all
persons.' A further statement points in the same direction, 'something
such as Zeno with his Stoic followers suspects about creatures and
God.'⁸ Jerome is thinking of the dogma of Zeno reported by [Diogenes]
Laertius:⁹ θεὸν δὲ εἶναι ζῷον ἀθάνατον λογικὸν ἢ νοερὸν ἐν εὐδαιμονίᾳ κακοῦ
τινος ἀνεπίδεκτον, προνοητικὸν κόσμου τε καὶ τῶν ἐν κόσμῳ· μὴ εἶναι δὲ μέντοι
ἀνθρωπόμορφον, εἶναι δὲ τὸν δημιουργὸν τῶν ὅλων, ὥσπερ καὶ πατέρα πάντων,
κοινῶς τε καὶ τὸ μέρος αὐτοῦ διῆκον διὰ πάντων, ὃ πολλαῖς προσηγορίαις προ-
σονομάζεται κατὰ τὰς δυνάμεις. Δία μὲν γάρ φασι δι᾽ ὃν τὰ πάντα, Ζῆνα δὲ κα-
λοῦσι, παρ᾽ ὅσον τοῦ ζῆν αἴτιός ἐστιν, etc, which means 'God is an immortal
living thing, endowed with reason or intellect, so fortunate that he is
incapable of receiving evil, having the providence and care of the world
and of everything in the world. Still he is without human form, but is
the maker of all, even as he is the father of all in common, but in such a
way that he is part of the world itself who or what penetrates through
all things. He is called by various names according to diverse powers.
For, that is, they call him Δί, that is Jove, because all things exist through
him, but they call him Ζήν [Zeus], that is Jove, because he is the source
of life.' So Laertius. I suspect there is a mistake in his wording here
which the translator seems to have followed. What has been written δι᾽
ὃν τὰ πάντα should, I think, have been written διῆκον τὰ πάντα [passing
through all things] so that you supply the word ζῷον [life] or διήκοντα

πάντα [traversing all things] or at least δι' οὗ τὰ πάντα [through whom all things]. For δι' ὃν τὰ πάντα does not mean 'through whom all things,' but 'on account of whom all things.' Therefore, Jerome[10] with his eye on this view of Zeno's adds 'whom Virgil followed when he says: "For God passes through all / the lands and the tracts of the sea and the deep heavens."[11] And "in the beginning heaven and earth,"'[12] etc. These citations do not fit together unless we read 'through all things.' The observation he then tacks on agrees with this: 'Some think the words "above all, through all, and in all" should be referred to the Father and the Son and the Holy Spirit so that "above all things" belongs to the Father because he is greater[13] than all things, "through all" is the Son's because all things were created through the Son, and "in all" pertains to the Spirit because he is given to believers and we are a temple of the Holy Spirit, and the Father and the Son dwell in us.'[14] Here again you see that with the exception of the last phrase 'all things' is put in the interpretation, not 'all men.' And yet that the neuter 'all things' fits in the third phrase is shown by the testimony of the Psalm: 'The Spirit of the Lord has filled the earth and that which contains all things has knowledge of his voice.'[15] Likewise at the beginning of Genesis,[16] 'The Spirit of the Lord is spread above the waters.' What important things would the Apostle be saying if he were to teach that God the Father is above all humans since the angels are superior to the human race? The scruple which disturbs Jerome could be removed in another way, namely since all things are said absolutely to be from God the Father, it would not be absurd to call him Father of all things with the generic use of the noun 'father,' just as the devil is called the Father of Lies because he was the first to teach how to lie. I would not be burdening the reader with notes of this kind if some persons with a great show of disdain had not criticized me because I said Jerome's commentary seemed to show a preference for the neuter gender.[17] Chrysostom in his commentary on this passage informs that ἐπὶ πάντων [above all] is said for ἐπάνω πάντων [up above all].[18] The position of God is superior not only to humankind but to the whole of creation. Secondly, when he explains 'through all things' as the governance of God, it is because God governs all things. In his commentary Chrysostom adds in the third phrase the pronoun 'you,' ἐν πᾶσιν ὑμῖν, that is, 'in all of you.' But the pronoun is not added in the citation of the text. Ambrose prefers the masculine gender throughout, 'above all humans, through all humans, and[19] in all of you,'[20] the last of which cannot not be masculine. Theophylact in both places refers to us in the masculine gender.[21]

1 Weber 1811 retains the text of the Vulgate. On the textual tradition see Metzger 536.

2 The word for 'all' in the Greek can be either masculine or neuter. In his paraphrase of this verse Erasmus takes all three pronouns ('all') as masculine (*Paraphrasis in Ephesios* CWE 43 327n9). In order to supply a verb for the clause, Erasmus adds the word *est* ('is').

3 Jerome *Comm in Eph* 2 (on 4:5–6) PL 26 (1884) 529A

4 Virgil *Georgics* 4.221–2

5 Though ... citation of the text.] Added in *1535*

6 Jerome *Comm in Eph* 2 (4:5–6) PL 26 (1884) 528C–D

7 Jerome *Comm in Eph* 2 (on 4:5–6) PL 26 (1884) 528D

8 Jerome *Comm in Eph* 2 (on 4:5–6) PL 26 (1884) 529A

9 Laertius *Vitae Philosophorum* 7.147. Erasmus' point in quoting Diogenes Laertius is to demonstrate the Stoic teaching of god as a force that permeates all things. The popular etymology of Δί (related to διά 'through') and Ζῆν (related to the infinitive of ζῶ 'to live') illustrates this teaching.

10 Jerome *Comm in Eph* 2 (on 4:5–6) PL 26 (1884) 529A

11 Virgil *Georgics* 4.221–2

12 Virgil *Aeneid* 6.724–7

13 Jerome actually states *auctor* 'creator.'

14 Jerome *Comm in Eph* 2 (on 4:5–6) PL 26 (1884) 529A–B

15 Book of Wisdom 1:7, which reads *hoc* for *hic*

16 Gen 1:2. Erasmus paraphrases the text, substituting *expanditur* 'is spread out' for the Vulgate's *ferebatur* 'is moved.'

17 Cf n3 above. It is uncertain which critic Erasmus has in mind here; M. van Poll-van de Lisdonk (ASD VI-9 220:832–3) suggests Pierre Cousturier, on whom see *Contemporaries* I 352–3 and the annotation on Eph 4:29 ('the edification of the faith') n7.

18 Chrysostom *Hom in Eph* 11.1 PG 62 80

19 and ... masculine gender] Added in *1519*

20 Ambrosiaster *Comm in Eph* 4:6

21 Theophylact *Expos in Eph* 4:6 PG 124 1081C

4:6 [ER VG] *et in omnibus vobis* 'and[1] in you all.' Ambrose reads in place of this 'in all believers.'[2] The pronoun 'you' is not added in Jerome, there is only 'in all.'[3] Nor can another reading be extracted from his commentary. From[4] this passage the Greeks[5] refute heretics who make the Son less than the Father and the Holy Spirit less than both because they said the preposition διά [through] belonged properly to the Son and the preposition ἐν [in] to the Holy Spirit while the preposition ἐξ [above] is attributed to the Father. Here both prepositions, διά [through] and ἐν [in], are attributed to the Father. Nor do they have a force of diminishing [him].

1 'and ... commentary.] This annotation was added in *1522*.

2 Ambrosiaster *Comm in Eph* 4:6

3 Jerome *Comm in Eph* 2 (on 4:5–6) PL 26 (1884) 527C

4 From ... diminishing [him].] Added in *1527*

5 Theophylact *Expos in Eph* 4:6 PG 124 1081C–D

4:8 [ER *cum ascendisset in altum* 'when he ascended up on high']

[VG] *ascendens in altum* 'ascending on high';[1] ἀναβὰς εἰς ὕψος, that is, 'after he ascended on high,' past tense. Now the testimony which he adduces here is in Psalm 67[68][2] which the LXX[3] translated as follows: ἀνέβης εἰς ὕψος ᾐχμαλώτευσας αἰχμαλωσίαν· ἔλαβες δόματα ἐν ἀνθρώποις [having ascended on high, you took captivity captive; you received gifts from among humans]. Paul knowingly and prudently changed one word from the Hebrew as Jerome indicates in his discussion of this passage. For while it reads in the Hebrew 'he received gifts from among humans,' Paul changed it to 'he gave gifts among[4] humans.' Nor is this variation any obstacle to the meaning inasmuch as the Psalm makes a promise for the future which had not yet happened and on account of this he is said to have received gifts which will be handed out later. Since the Apostle is here describing what had now been done through the foundation of churches everywhere in the world, he wrote 'has given,' not 'has received.'

1 Weber 1812 keeps the Vulgate text.
2 Ps 68:18. The author of Ephesians modifies the text of the LXX to suit his purpose. See Lincoln *Ephesians* 243 who observes, '[the author] integrates his exposition of its meaning in the light of fulfilment in Christ into the actual quotation, a procedure which is, of course, not unusual in the contemporary Jewish exegetical techniques elsewhere in the use of the OT in the NT.' For a treatment of the explanation by Erasmus and others of the use of Psalm 68 here see Bernard Roussel, 'Biblical Paraphrases of the Sixteenth and Seventeenth Centuries' in *Holy Scripture Speaks* ed H. Pabel and M.Vessey (Toronto 2002) 67–8.
   In the *1516* edition, the following passage occurred: 'here the Hebrews have only "you have ascended on high, you have led captivity captive, you have received gifts among men."' This is the Hebrew version of Psalm 67(68):18. Erasmus frequently omitted the Hebrew text in later editions. See ASD VI-9 221:850n.
3 Though Erasmus sometimes speaks of the 'LXX edition' he more frequently writes simply *septuaginta*, 'the seventy,' as in this note. See further the annotation on Rom 1:17 ('lives by faith') n5.
4 to] Added in *1519*. Erasmus changes the simple dative form *hominibus* 'to humans' into the phrase *in hominibus* 'among humans.' In his paraphrase of Eph 4:8 Erasmus interprets the image of gift-giving in light of the custom of scattering gifts by Roman generals celebrating a military triumph (*Paraphrasis in Ephesios* CWE 43 329 and n17 there).

4:9 [ER *caeterum illud ascendit, quid est* 'but as for the 'he ascended']

[VG] *quod autem ascendit* 'now that he ascended'; τὸ δὲ ἀνέβη τί ἐστιν, that is, 'but that which was said, he ascended, what is it?'

4:11 [ER *alios autem pastores ac doctores* 'and others pastors and teachers']
[VG] *alios autem pastores et doctores* 'and[1] others pastors and teachers.' Jerome[2] remarked and,[3] following him, Augustine[4] in his fifty-ninth
Letter, that although he had distinguished among the other kinds, here
he joined two together. For it does not say, 'some pastors, some teachers,' but 'other pastors and teachers,' that is, whoever the pastors are,
the same men have to be teachers, though[5] Ambrose, failing, I think,
to notice this, takes them separately, as if pastors and instructors are
different. Further, he does not seem to have noticed that in the Greek
the word for 'instructors' is διδάσκαλοι, that is, 'teachers.' For he takes
the instructors to be ushers who in church keep in check and lash dis-
turbers. And[6] Theophylact after proposing the meaning I have shown
brings this also to bear on deacons.

    1 'and ... have to be teachers] Added in *1519*
    2 Jerome *Comm in Eph* 2 (on 4:11–12) PL 26 (1884) 532B
    3 and ... 59] Added in *1535*
    4 Augustine *Epistulae* 149.2 PL 33 635
    5 though ... disturbers] Added in *1522*. See Ambrosiaster *Comm in Eph* 4:11.
    6 And ... deacons.] Added in *1527*. See Theophylact *Expos in Eph* 4:11 PG 124
      1085B–C.

4:12 [ER *ad instaurationem sanctorum* 'for the renewing of the saints']
[VG] *ad consummationem sanctorum* 'for the perfecting of the saints';
πρὸς τὸν καταρτισμόν [for the completion]. Jerome reads 'for the instruction.'[1] The word means also the remaking or the rebuilding or[2] the re-
newal of something that has fallen down.[3] For teachers bring help to
the fallen and downcast. But[4] special proof is given by the fact that
Ambrose translates with us 'for the perfecting of the saints,' for this too
is the meaning of the Greek word καταρτίζεσθαι [to bring to completion].
This fits well with what follows, 'for the building up of the body of
Christ,' namely[5] so that the body is made perfect on every side.

    1 Jerome *Comm in Eph* 2 (on 4:11–12) PL 26 (1884) 531D
    2 or ... fallen down] Added in *1519*
    3 Cf BDAG καταρτισμός 'equipment, equipping'; the noun does not occur else-
      where in the New Testament.
    4 But ... the body of Christ'] Added in *1519*. See Ambrosiaster *Comm in Eph*
      4:12.
    5 namely ... side] Added in *1522*

4:13 [ER *et agnitionis filii Dei* 'and of the knowledge of the Son of God']
[VG] *in agnitione*[1] *filii Dei* 'in the knowledge of the Son of God.' 'And
of the knowledge of the Son of God,' καὶ[2] τῆς ἐπιγνώσεως [and of the

knowledge]. For it is grammatically dependent on the noun ἑνότης [union] just as is the noun 'faith.' And this is the reading of St Jerome who elsewhere advises that the verb *agnosci* [to acknowledge, to know] properly means to acknowledge what had previously been known.[3]

1 The reading *in agnitione* is not recorded in the apparatuses of editions of the Vulgate. It is presumably a late medieval corruption. The 1527 Vulgate reads with Erasmus *agnitionis*.
2 καὶ ... faith'] Added in 1527
3 Jerome *Comm in Eph* 2 (on 4:13–15) PL 26 (1884) 533A

4:14 [ER VG] *et circumferamur* **'and carried about.'** The Greek is a participle, περιφερόμενοι, that is, 'driven about.' Augustine[1] reads 'carried about,' which would be satisfactory in all other respects if the tense corresponded.[2] And 'children' [literally, 'little ones'] is [in Greek] νήπιοι ['silly children'] which denotes a child as someone who is not prudent.[3] And 'every wind' would more correctly be 'any wind at all.' For the Greek word παντί [all, every, any] shifts in meaning.

1 Augustine ... respects] Added in 1519. See Augustine *De civitate dei* 22.18 CCL 48 836:11.
2 Erasmus means if the tense of the perfect passive participle is appropriate. The Greek present participle means 'being carried about,' but Latin does not have a corresponding present passive participle; hence the translation with the present passive subjunctive, 'we are being carried about.'
3 See also the annotation on Gal 4:1 ('the heir is a little child') and n2 there.

4:14 [ER *per versutiam hominum* **'through the cunning of people'**]
[VG] *in nequitia hominum* **'in the wickedness of people';** ἐν κυβείᾳ [by dice-playing]. This word is said from the game of dice in which whoever can imposes and deceives the opponent. Lefèvre, though[1] only in the first edition, substituted 'confusion and disturbance' for 'wickedness,' but was deceived, apparently, by the similarity of the letter kappa to beta. Therefore, he reads κυκείᾳ [confusion][2] for κυβείᾳ, though the consonant is really a 'β' [beta]. He changed[3] this passage in the second edition, but in such a way that not even there do I agree with him. I have touched on this matter in my Apology.[4] The word seems to be formed from κυβεύω, which means 'I play with dice,' because in games of this kind there is need for craft and each person strives to deceive his fellow player if he can, looking solely to his own advantage, so that one could call κυβεία gambling, that is, cleverness and deceptive artifice or rather artful deception. Hesychius[5] also gives witness that κυβεῦσαι [to play at dice] in addition to other things also means χλευάσαι which

means to laugh at or to mock. Jerome compares it to the cunning of dialecticians and to their insidious sophisms.[6] After I had published this conjecture, though quite probable, of my own mind, I obtained Bishop Theophylact's commentaries on the Pauline Epistles which are to be in nowise disregarded, and I discovered that he also thinks the same as I. I shall not hesitate to quote his words so far as it pertains to the issue: κυβευταὶ λέγονται, οἱ τοῖς πεττοῖς κεχρημένοι, τοιοῦτοί εἰσιν οἱ ψευδο-διδάσκαλοι μετατιθέντες τοὺς ἀφελεστέρους ὥσπερ πεττοὺς ὡς βούλονται,[7] that is, 'Dice-players are said to be those who make use of dice; such are the false teachers shifting the simple around like dice as they wish.'[8] My conjecture, which squares with the truth, would satisfy me. But because authority has more effect on some people than facts,[9] I added the vote of the Greek interpreter. Theophylact[10] followed Chrysostom[11] as he usually does. It is odd that neither makes any difference between the two words for dice, κύβους καὶ, πεττούς, except that in both there is room for deception. Jerome makes the point that the entire passage is quite clear if someone reads the Greek,[12] but when it is rendered verbatim into Latin it becomes quite obscure.[13] It[14] could be explained by a paraphrase as follows: 'Until we all reach the point where all have the same faith and the Son of God is known and acknowledged by all alike.' That is, 'that we attain a perfect, firm, and adult age, namely to that measure of age which will make us fully adult in Christ so that we are not afterwards like infants who are carried and tossed about by any random wind of doctrine as the craftiness of men imposes on us. Men whose aim is not to teach us Christ sincerely, but attacking us with clever stratagems ensnare and take us captive.' On the contrary, let us neglect those wretched ideas and let us pursue things which are true and worthy of Christ and let us grow in all things to adulthood in him who is the head of all. That one, however, is Christ, not Moses, for Moses is but a member, not the head.[15] Jerome has 'in the deception of men, in cunning, etc.'[16]

1 though ... first edition] Added in 1519. See Lefèvre *Pauli epistolae* fol 38 recto and fol 169 recto. On Lefèvre and the nature of his controversy with Erasmus see the annotation on Gal 1:10 ('for am I just now persuading men') n8.
2 There is no such word as κυκεία, which was supposedly derived from the verb κυκᾶν 'to stir, mix up,' hence 'to confuse.'
3 He changed ... Apology.] Added in 1519. Lefèvre's second edition appeared in 1516.
4 Erasmus *Apologia ad Fabrum* CWE 83 99–100
5 Hesychius ... mock.] Added in 1519. See Hesychius κυβεῦσαι (vol. 2).
6 Jerome *Comm in Eph* 2 (on 4:13–15) PL 26 (1884) 533C

7 Theophylact *Expos in Eph* 4:14 PG 124 1088C
8 Erasmus' translation of *pessos* or *tettos* by *talus* 'die' is not quite accurate. *Pessoi* were oval-shaped stones or the like used as pieces in board games whereas *tali*, literally, 'ankle bones' of animals, were marked on four sides and thrown like dice. *Tesserae* were six-sided cubes and marked on all six sides like modern dice. The idea of skill or craft in moving pieces around to deceive an opponent is more appropriate to board games than to games of chance.
9 M. van Poll-van de Lisdonk (ASD VI-9 225:907–8) suggests that Erasmus may be referring here to Maarten van Dorp (1485–1525) with whom he enjoyed an uneven relationship, as numerous letters reveal (see especially Allen Epp 304.98–101 and 337.713). On Dorp's life and career see *Contemporaries* I 398–404, and Cecilia Asso 'Martin Dorp and Edward Lee' in *Biblical Humanism and Scholasticism in the Age of Erasmus* ed E. Rummel (Leiden 2008) 167–95.
10 Theophylact ... deception.] Added in *1535*
11 Chrysostom *Hom in Eph* 11.4 PG 62 83
12 Jerome *Comm in Eph* 2 (on 4:13–15) PL 26 (1884) 534C
13 On Erasmus' principle of achieving a lucid translation by means of a non-literal rendering see Rummel 93–4.
14 It ... not the head.] Added in *1519*
15 Jerome *Comm in Eph* 2 (on 4:13–15) PL 26 (1884) 533A
16 etc] Added in *1519*

4:14 [ER *qua nos adoriuntur ut imponant nobis* 'by which they spring upon us to deceive us']
[VG] *ad circumventionem* 'for the deception'; πρὸς τὴν μεθοδείαν. The word is derived from μεθοδεύειν which means to attack a person from ambush.[1]

1 Cf LSJ μεθοδεύω 3: 'defraud, get round.' The word μεθοδεία occurs again elsewhere in the New Testament only in Eph 6:11, where Erasmus translates the plural form as *assultus* 'attacks.' See the annotation on Eph 6:11 ('against the ambushes').

4:14 [ER *ut imponant nobis* 'to deceive us']
[VG] *erroris* 'of error';[1] τῆς πλάνης [error, deception]. He would have translated it better with *imposturae* 'deceit, imposture.' For πλάνη [deceit] is the part of the one who deceives, 'error' of the one deceived. What Ambrose followed when he read 'for the remedy of error'[2] is strange unless,[3] perhaps, he wrote *methodum* [deception] and someone transformed it into *remedium* 'remedy.'[4] Augustine translates it by 'machination.'[5]

1 In LB this annotation is not separated from the one above ('for the deception').
2 Ambrosiaster *Comm in Eph* 4:14
3 unless ... machination'] Added in *1519*

4 An interesting conjecture, but *remedium* is found in several Old Latin manuscripts and Latin church fathers besides Ambrosiaster. See A. Merk *Novum Testamentum Graece et Latine* (Rome 1964) 641.
5 Augustine *De civitate dei* 22.18 CCL 48 836:12

4:15 [ER *sed veritatem* 'but (pursuing) truth']
[VG] *veritatem autem* 'however'[1] [doing] the truth.' 'But' or 'but rather' would be clearer than 'however,' for he is correcting what has preceded.

1 'however ... preceded.] This annotation was added in 1527.

4:15 [ER *sed veritatem sectantes* 'but pursuing truth']
[VG] *veritatem autem facientes* 'however, doing the truth';[1] ἀληθεύοντες, that is, 'pursuing the truth.'[2] ἀληθεύειν means either 'to do what one has said' or 'to speak what is true.' For he has opposed this to τῇ κυβείᾳ καὶ τῇ πλάνῃ, that is, 'to cunning and deception.'

1 In LB this annotation was part of the previous annotation ('however [doing] the truth').
2 For Erasmus' treatment of this Greek verb see Brown *Novum Testamentum* 524:15(1)n. Cf BDAG s.v. ἀληθεύω: tell the truth 'in such a way that the spirit of love is maintained (Eph. 4:15).'

4:15 [ER *adolescamus in illum* 'we may grow up into him']
[VG] *crescamus in illo* 'we may increase in him'; αὐξήσωμεν εἰς αὐτὸν τὰ πάντα, is, 'we may grow into him in everything.' This is Lorenzo's correction of the text.[1] I for my part think it can be correctly translated 'let us grow up into him in all things,' so that one supplies the preposition κατά 'in' with τὰ πάντα 'all things.' But Jerome reads 'that we may grow in him in all respects.'[2] So does Ambrose, provided the manuscripts are free from error.[3] Theophylact does not differ from them when[4] he interprets, 'all things must be increased in us, both life and doctrines.'[5] Chrysostom[6] interprets in three ways: first, that we understand that the body makes an increase when the Spirit works in individual members in accordance with the manner of each; secondly, that we understand the individual members acquire increase from the underlying service of the Spirit; thirdly, that we understand the spirit is increased when it flows from the head and passes through all the members, touching and connecting each one. The pronoun[7] 'we' can be understood in the transitive verb, although the verb αὐξάνω 'I grow' has an intransitive meaning in Greek; and I do not recall having found it as having any other significance. Therefore, the reader may follow what he most approves even if my reading differs very little from their interpretation, especially since [the phrase] τὴν αὔξησιν τοῦ σώματος 'the increase of the body' follows shortly thereafter.

1 Valla *Annot in Eph* 4 (I 877). As the annotation makes clear, Erasmus' choice of *adolescamus* over *crescamus* is in order to preserve the biological metaphor in this verse. See also the annotation on 4:16 ('through every juncture') and n1.
2 Jerome *Comm in Eph* 2 (on 4:13–15) PL 26 (1884) 533A
3 Ambrosiaster *Comm in Eph* 4:15. Ambrosiaster actually reads *augeamus in ipsum omnia* 'that we grow up in every way into him.'
4 when ... doctrines'] Added in *1527*
5 Theophylact *Expos in Eph* 4:15 PG 124 1089A
6 Chrysostom ... significance.] Added in *1535*. See Chrysostom *Hom in Eph* 11.3 PG 62 84.
7 The pronoun ... transitive verb] Added in *1519*

4:16 [ER *si coagmentetur* 'if it is fastened together']
[VG] *compactum* 'having been compacted'; συναρμολογούμενον [being fitted together]. Earlier he had translated this by *constructum* 'built together.'[1]

   1 See the annotation on Eph 2:21 ('constructed'). Cf *conpactum* (Weber 1812).

4:16 [ER *compingatur* 'is fitted together']
[VG] *connexum* 'joined together'; συμβιβαζόμενον, that is, 'fitted together.' Jerome reads *conglutinatum* 'cemented together.'[1]

   1 Jerome *Comm in Eph* 2 (on 4:16) PL 26 (1884) 534C

4:16 [ER *per omnem commissuram* 'through every joint']
[VG] *per omnem iuncturam* 'through every juncture'; ἀφῆς. One could not translate this word more aptly than by 'joint.' For ἀφή is a joining together in such a way that from each side there is a mutual touching as limb connected to limb.[1] Therefore,[2] Augustine in [his commentary on] Psalm 10 reads 'through every touch.'[3] In the twenty-second book, chapter 18 of the *City of God* he draws on this passage with the following words: 'He himself is the one who descended and who ascended above all the heavens to fill all things. And he himself gave some to be apostles, some to be prophets, others again to be evangelists, and others to be pastors and teachers in order to perfect the saints for the work of ministry to build up the body of Christ until we all attain to the unity of faith and the knowledge of the Son of God, to a perfect man, to the mature measure of the fullness of Christ, so that from now on we are no longer children, tossed to and fro and carried about by every wind of doctrine in the deceit of men, in craftiness to contrive error; but doing the truth in love, we may grow up in all things in him who is the head, Christ, from whom the whole body, joined and fitted together, through every joint of

the system according to the working in due measure of each part makes increase of the body for the building up of itself in love.'[4]

1 LSJ cites Eph 4:16 as an instance in which ἀφή means 'ligament.' In Col 2:19 the word occurs again, and there too Erasmus' translation is *commissura*, which OLD defines as 'the place where two parts of a structure, etc., come together.' The point of this annotation is to show that *commissura* 'joint' better conveys the image of the human body.
2 Therefore ... in love.'] Added in *1519*
3 Augustine *Enarrationes in Psalmos* 10.7 CCL 38 79:5–6
4 Augustine *De civitate dei* 22.18 CCL 48 836:3–837:17

4:16 [ER *iuxta actum* 'according to the working']
[VG] *secundum operationem* 'according to the operation'; κατ᾽ ἐνέργειαν [effectual working]. Again it is the word, encountered so many times,[1] which signifies action and hidden power. He has in mind the life-giving Spirit which, proceeding from the head, imparts its power, not in equal amounts to all parts, but to the extent that it is beneficial, to the whole body. Chrysostom,[2] and Theophylact,[3] interpret it in such a way that ἐνέργεια, which he here translates 'operation,' relates to the action of the spirit of Christ in his members, not to our works, as Lyra[4] explains it. Thomas modifies the interpretation so that it seems to have both in mind.[5]

1 BDAG defines ἐνέργεια as 'working, operation, action ... always of transcendent beings.'
2 Chrysostom] Added in *1535*. See Chrysostom *Hom in Eph* 11.3 PG 62 84.
3 Theophylact *Expos in Eph* 4:16 PG 124 1089B–C
4 Nicholas of Lyra *Postilla ad loc. Biblia sacra* VI col. 552. Nicolaus Lyranus (c 1270–1349) was a Franciscan theologian whose commentaries on the Bible (1323–32) were widely read, especially after the publication of the first five-volume edition appeared in Rome in 1471. For a brief introduction to his life and writings see P.D.W. Krey and L. Smith *Nicholas of Lyra. The Senses of Scripture* (Leiden 2000) 1–16. On Erasmus' critical attitude towards Lyra see Rummel 82–4.
5 Thomas Aquinas *Super Eph lect* cap 4 lectio 5.225–8

4:16 [ER *in mensura* 'in the measure']
[VG] *in mensuram* 'unto the measure'; ἐν μέτρῳ, that is, 'in the measure' (although the Latin manuscripts vary), so that you understand that in the body physical life and nourishment are imparted to each member in keeping with its own small measure. For[1] when he said 'in the measure' it is as though he had said 'through the measure' or 'in keeping with the measure.'[2]

1 For ... measure.'] Added in *1527*
2 In making this change to the Vulgate Erasmus is following Lefèvre.

4:16 [ER *uniuscuiusque partis* 'of every part']
[VG] *uniuscuiusque membri* '**of every member**'; μέρους, that is, 'part.'
However, in Greek the difference between μέλος [member] and μέρος
[part] is slight. Chrysostom[1] reads μέλους [member].

> 1 Chrysostom ... μέλους.] Added in 1535. See Chrysostom *Hom in Eph* 11.3
> PG 62 84. The translation 'member' in the Vulgate may reflect, as Erasmus
> suspects, the reading μέλους [member, limb] found in several Greek manu-
> scripts which were probably unknown to Erasmus. See Brown *Novum
> Testamentum* 525:16(4)n.

4:16 [ER *in aedificationem sui ipsius* '**for the building up of its own self**']
[VG] *in aedificationem sui* '**for the building up of itself**'; ἑαυτοῦ, that is,
of its own self.[1]

> 1 There is no essential difference in meaning between *sui* and *sui ipsius*
> except that the addition of *ipsius* [self] intensifies the reflexive meaning
> of the pronoun. See Lincoln *Ephesians* 264, who comments, 'The ἑαυτοῦ,
> "of itself," adds ... the note of the Church's active participation and is in
> line with the earlier emphasis of the verb on the Church's promotion of
> its own growth, though ultimately the source of that growth is Christ,
> the head.' Lefèvre likewise added *ipsius*; see Brown *Novum Testamentum*
> 525:16(9)n.

4:17 [ER *per dominum* '**by the Lord**']
[VG] *in domino* '**in the Lord**.' Some Greek manuscripts have ἐνώπιον τοῦ
Θεοῦ, that is, 'in the sight of God.'[1]

> 1 For this apparently unattested reading see Brown *Novum Testamentum*
> 525:17(3)n.

4:17 [ER *quemadmodum et reliquae gentes* '**as also the other gentiles**']
[VG] *sicut et gentes* '**as also the gentiles**.' Some manuscripts have 'as
also the other gentiles,' τὰ λοιπὰ ἔθνη.[1]

> 1 For the variants in the Greek manuscripts see Metzger 537.

4:17 [ER *in vanitate mentis suae* '**in the vanity of their mind**']
[VG] *in vanitate sensus* '**in the vanity of [their] feelings**'; νοός, that is,
'mind' rather than 'feeling.'[1] And that is how the Translator renders it a
little later: 'be renewed in the spirit of your mind' [4:23]. Valla[2] rightly
criticizes those who take *sensus* [feeling] to mean sensuality because
νοῦς in Greek is that part of the soul which is most removed from bodily
matter and which alone is thought to do something without the aid of
bodily organs.

1 Weber (1812) reads *in vanitate sensus*; cf modern English translations: 'in the vanity of their mind' (AV), 'in the futility of their minds' (RSV), 'in the futility of their thinking' (NIV).
2 Valla *Annot in Eph* 4 (I 877)

4:18 [ER *dum mentem habent obtenebratam* 'while they have their mind darkened']
[VG] *obscuratum habentes intellectum* 'having their understanding obscured'; ἐσκοτισμένοι τῇ διανοίᾳ, that is, 'obscured in their thinking or in their mind.' Jerome reads 'obscured in their mind.'[1] Ambrose 'obscured in their understanding.'[2] But our Translator in this passage more clearly expressed the [word] ὄντες [being].[3]

1 Jerome *Comm in Eph* 2 (on 4:17–19) PL 26 (1884) 536A
2 Ambrosiaster *Comm in Eph* 4:18
3 The Greek text reads literally 'being darkened in their understanding,' using separate participles for 'being' and 'darkened.' Erasmus means that the use of the present participle *habentes* [having] with the perfect passive participle *obscuratum* [darkened] renders the Greek more closely than the translations of either Jerome or Ambrosiaster. L&S defines the meaning of *obtenebro* as 'to make dark, to darken.'

4:18 [ER *abalienati a vita* 'estranged from the life']
[VG] *alienati a vita* 'alienated from the life.' *Abalienati*. ἀπηλλοτριωμένοι, that is, 'estranged.' This is the reading of St Jerome.[1]

1 Jerome *Comm in Eph* 2 (on 4:17–19) PL 26 (1884) 536B. There is no essential difference in meaning between the two verbs, but Erasmus probably thought that the compound verb with the prefix *ab-* [from] was a closer equivalent to the Greek verb with its prefix ἀπ- [*ap-* 'from'].

4:18 [ER VG] *a vita Dei* 'from the life of God.' Some manuscripts have *a via Dei* 'from the way of God,' but incorrectly. It is definitely 'from the life,' τῆς ζωῆς [the life]. Ambrose reads *a fide Dei* 'from the faith of God.'[1] The sense here can also be 'from the life that is God.' For this is what the articles added to both nouns suggest, τῆς[2] ζωῆς τοῦ Θεοῦ, 'from[3] the true life that is God.'

1 Ambrosiaster *Comm in Eph* 4:18
2 τῆς ζωῆς τοῦ Θεοῦ] Added in 1519
3 'from ... God'] Added in 1522. Erasmus' grammatical analysis is rather forced, but for the meaning see Lincoln *Ephesians* 277–8 who quotes Westcott, 'The life of God is that life which answers to the nature of God and which he communicates to his children.' Lincoln (*Ephesians* 278) observes that '"separated from the life of God" is ... equivalent to the earlier description of the readers' former condition as "dead" (2:1, 5) and "without God" (2:12)' (B.F. Westcott *St. Paul's Epistle to the Ephesians* [London 1906]).

4:18 [ER *propter ignorantiam* 'because of the ignorance']
[VG] *per ignorantiam* 'through the ignorance'; διὰ τὴν ἄγνοιαν, 'because of ignorance.'[1]

> 1 In making this change Erasmus is following Valla *Annot in Eph* 4 (I 877).

4:18 [ER *(propter) ... et excaecationem* 'and because of the blinding']
[VG] *propter caecitatem* 'because of the blindness'; πώρωσιν. This word really means 'blinding.' It is odd where Ambrose got his reading *duritiam* 'hardness'[1] instead of *caecitatem* 'blindness' unless his manuscript perhaps had σκλήρωσιν 'hardening' for πώρωσιν 'blinding.'[2]

> 1 Ambrosiaster *Comm in Eph* 4:18
> 2 Erasmus was evidently not aware of the medical use of πώρωσις to describe the hardening of bone or flesh as in a callus (thus LSJ), which is in fact the meaning of the term in the present context, 'the hardening of the heart.' Cf Mark 3:5 and see Lincoln *Ephesians* 278. BDAG defines πώρωσις as a 'hardening, dulling,' in the figurative sense of 'dullness, insensibility, obstinacy.'

4:19 [ER *qui posteaquam pervenerunt eo ut dolere desierint* 'who after they came to the point of ceasing to grieve']
[VG] *qui desperantes semetipsos* 'who despairing, have given themselves up to'; οἵτινες ἀπηλγηκότες ἑαυτοὺς παρέδωκαν, that is, 'who, being engaged in indolence gave themselves up to,' as Valla emends it.[1] But St Jerome believes the correct translation can be *indolentes* [being indolent] in place of *desperantes* [despairing][2] because the Greek[3] word seems to be derived from the situation where someone lacks sorrow and the awareness of his own wickedness and for this reason is stolidly borne into every vice. The Greek Scholia interpret in the same way.[4] Marcus[5] Tullius, to be sure, uses the word *indolentia* [insensitive to pain] but out of a desire to explain the Greek word ἀναλγησία [absence of pain]. For ἀλγεῖν in Greek means 'to feel pain,' ἀπηλγηκώς [having ceased to feel grief or pain] who, so to speak, 'has been pained out,' or,[6] as the Comic poet[7] says, 'has borne pain to the ultimate,' and who has become so callous that he has become deaf to any feeling of wrongdoing. Just so in Latin someone who has ceased to boil is said to have boiled dry and who has ceased to be wise is said to be witless. I do not know whether the Translator may have read ἀπηλπικότες [having despaired]. A slip in one little letter is very easy. Still, Ambrose reads and interprets 'despairing.'[8] Chrysostom[9] takes the words to mean ἀπεγνωκότες ἑαυτῶν [having despaired of themselves] although his biblical text has ἀπηλγηκότες ἑαυτούς and in his commentary he mentions ἀναλγησίας

[insensitivity to pain] because those two go together, desperation and insensitivity to pain. And in my opinion 'despairing' is more in accordance with the tenor of the meaning. For the pleasures of this life most eagerly carry away people who despair of the existence of life after death and gorge themselves with them as if when they are lost they will have nothing pleasant. Nor[10] do I think Greeks speak in this way, ἀνήλγηκεν ἑαυτόν, 'he made himself insensitive to pain.'

1 Valla *Annot in Eph* 4 (I 877). On Lorenzo Valla see the annotation on Gal 1:13 ('and was subduing') n1.
2 Jerome *Comm in Eph* 2 (on 4:17–19) PL 26 (1884) 537A–B
3 Greek] Added in 1527
4 Pseudo-Oecumenius *Comm in Eph* 4:17–19 PG 118 1225C
5 Marcus ... nothing pleasant.] Added in 1519. See Cicero, *De finibus* 2.4.11; 2.6.19; *De officiis* 3.3, 12; *Tusculan Disputations* 3.6, 12.
6 or ... ultimate'] Added in 1527
7 See Terence *Eunuchus* 74.
8 Ambrosiaster *Comm in Eph* 4:19
9 Chrysostom ... insensitivity to pain.] Added in 1535. See Chrysostom *Hom in Eph* 13.1 PG 62 93.
   Modern translations vary: 'they have become callous' (RSV), 'having lost all sensitivity' (NIV), 'dead to all feeling' (NEB).
10 Nor ... pain.'] Added in 1535

4:19 [ER *immunditXiam omnem cum aviditate* 'all uncleanness with greediness']

[VG] *immunditiae omnis in avaritiam* 'of[1] all uncleanness unto covetousness.' Greed seems to have little connection with uncleanness or lust and for this reason Jerome advises that the Greek is not φιλαργυρία [love of silver] or φιλοχρηματία [love of money], words denoting a greed for money, but πλεονεξία [desire for gain],[2] a word meaning to have more than is fair.[3] Moreover, a person who is excessively eager for pleasure is not satisfied with his own wife, but commits fornication also with the wife of another and then goes on to assault a third, so as to put off satisfying his pleasure. [Jerome] thinks that this understanding of the text should also refer to the passage of Paul in the first epistle to the Thessalonians, chapter 4 [verses 3–6]: 'For this is the will of God, your sanctification; that you should abstain from sexual immorality; that each of you know how to control his own body in holiness and honour, not in the passion of desire like the gentiles who do not know God; and that no man transgress nor circumvent his brother in this matter, because the Lord is the avenger of all these things.' For[4] there too the verb the Translator renders by 'circumvent' is πλεονεκτεῖν [to take advantage of]. It seems to me that ἐν πλεονεξίᾳ [in greediness] can also be taken to mean 'avidly.' Theophylact[5] refers to every uncontrolled covetousness, for this is what draws people into mental blindness; Chrysostom refers to 'greed.'[6]

1 'of ... avidly.'] Added in *1519*
2 Cf BDAG πλεονεξία: 'the state of desiring to have more than one's due, greediness, insatiableness, avarice, covetousness.'
3 Jerome *Comm in Eph* 2 (on 4:17–19) PL 26 (1884) 537C–538A
4 For ... πλεονεκτεῖν.] Added in *1527*
5 Theophylact ... blindness] Added in *1527*. See Theophylact *Expos in Eph* 4:19 PG 124 1092D.
6 Chrysostom 'to greed'] Added in *1535*. See Chrysostom *Hom in Eph* 13.1 PG 62 94.

4:19 [ER *cum aviditate* 'with greediness']
[VG] *in avaritiam* 'unto covetousness.' 'In covetousness,' ἐν πλεονεξίᾳ, as[1] if one were to say 'through greed' or 'coveting someone else's property.'

1 as ... property'] Added in *1527*. This sentence replaces one found in the first three editions: *quod proprie dicitur quoties alio fraudato plus sibi vindicat aliquis quam per est* 'which is properly said whenever someone defrauds another and claims more for himself than is right.'

4:21 [ER *siquidem illum* 'if indeed [you have heard] him']
[VG] *si tamen illum* 'if, however, [you have heard] him'; εἴγε, that is, 'if indeed' or 'if truly.' Theophylact[1] advises that it is the sign of one who affirms, not one who doubts. Yet the addition of 'however' [in the Vulgate] makes the utterance doubtful.[2]

1 Theophylact ... doubtful.] Added in *1519*. See Theophylact *Expos in Eph* 4:20–2 PG 124 1093A.
2 J.D. Denniston *The Greek Particles* (2nd edition Oxford 1954) 146 observes that εἴγε 'emphasizes the hypothetical nature of a statement.'

4:22 [ER *deponere* 'to put off']
[VG] *deponite vos* 'you put off.' The Greek has ἀποθέσθαι ὑμᾶς τὸν παλαιὸν ἄνθρωπον, ἀνανεοῦσθαι δὲ τῷ πνεύματι, καὶ ἐνδύσασθαι τὸν καινὸν ἄνθρωπον, that is, 'that you put off the former man, to be renewed by the Spirit and to put on the new man.' Or as St Jerome reads, 'you to put off' is to be referred to 'you have learned,'[1] but in that case the pronoun 'you' has to be omitted. Jerome arranges the sentence in this way: 'you have not so learned Christ, if indeed you have heard him, and you have been taught in him to put away in accordance with your prior way of life the old self who is corrupted according to the desires of error.'[2] Ambrose[3]

reads in this way: 'That you put off in accordance with the prior way of life the old man'; but then he changes the infinitives into imperatives, 'be renewed, put on.' Theophylact thinks the infinitives can depend on the words 'you have been taught' or on 'as the truth is,' as though you were to ask: what have you been taught, namely to put off the old man; or, what is the truth, namely to put off, etc.[4] Chrysostom[5] follows the second view, 'so that,' he says, 'life accords with the teachings.'[6]

1 Jerome *Comm in Eph* 2 (on 4:22) PL 26 (1884) 539D
2 Jerome *Comm in Eph* 2 (on 4:22) PL 26 (1884) 539D
3 Ambrose ... to put off etc.] Added in *1519*. See Ambrosiaster *Comm in Eph* 4:22.
4 Theophylact *Expos in Eph* 4:20–2 PG 124 1093B
5 Chrysostom ... teachings.'] Added in *1535*. See Chrysostom *Hom in Eph* 13.1 PG 62 95.
6 For a survey of the arguments over the syntax of the infinitives in this sentence see Lincoln *Ephesians* 283–4. Cf *deponere* (Weber 1812).

4:22 [ER *iuxta concupiscentias erroris* 'according to the lusts of error']
[VG] *secundum desideria erroris* 'according[1] to the desires of error.'[2]
Hilary in the twelfth book of *On the Trinity* adds a pronoun: 'According to the lust of his deception.'[3] Perhaps he was eager to express the force of the article, τῆς ἀπάτης [the deception].

1 'according ... τῆς ἀπάτης.] This annotation was added in *1527*.
2 Erasmus prefers to render κατά as *iuxta*, and alters the Vulgate's *secundum* to *iuxta* elsewhere also; cf his annotations on Rom 2:6 ('according to the works of him'), Rom 5:6 ('according to the time'), Rom 8:28 ('in accordance with the purpose'), Rom 12:6 ('in accordance with the rule of faith') in CWE 56.
3 Hilary *De Trinitate* 12.48 PL 10 464B, where one reads *secundum concupiscentias deceptionis*; cf ASD VI-9 233:48n, which notes that the 3 pronoun *eius* occurs in Erasmus' 1523 edition of Hilary. For Hilary see the annotation on Gal 6:11 ('with what letters').

4:23 [ER *renovari* 'to be renewed']
[VG] *renovamini autem* 'but be renewed.' Here too there are infinitives which, as we mentioned,[1] can depend upon the same verb, 'you have been taught.'

1 See the annotation on Eph 4:22 ('you put off').

4:24 [ER *et sanctitatem veritatis* 'and (through) the holiness of truth']
[VG] *et sanctitate veritatis* 'and in holiness of truth'; ἐν ὁσιότητι τῆς ἀληθείας [in holiness of truth].[1] Ambrose reads 'in truth and righteousness.'[2] [The Greek] could be translated 'in the religion of truth.' For[3]

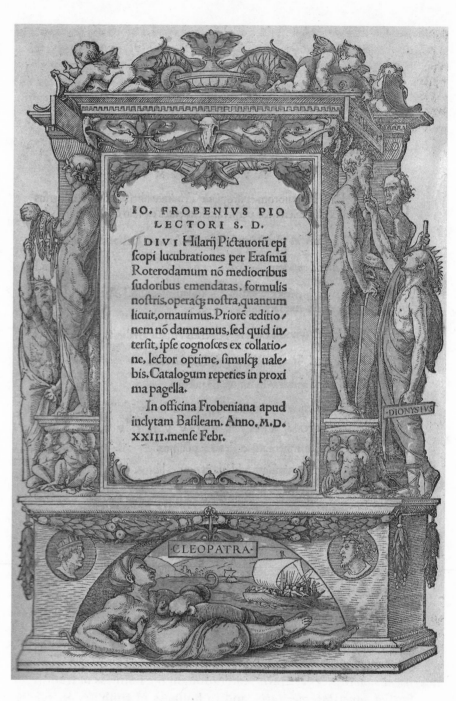

IO. FROBENIVS PIO
LECTORI S. D.

DIVI Hilarij Pictauorũ epi
scopi lucubrationes per Erasmũ
Roterodamum nõ mediocribus
sudoribus emendatas, formulis
nostris, operacʒ nostra, quantum
licuit, ornauimus. Priorẽ æditio=
nem nõ damnamus, sed quid in=
tersit, ipse cognosces ex collatio=
ne, lector optime, simulcʒ uale=
bis. Catalogum reperies in proxi
ma pagella.

In officina Frobeniana apud
inclytam Basileam. Anno. M.D.
XXIII. mense Febr.

DIONYSIVS

CLEOPATRA

Title-page of Erasmus' edition of Hilary of Poitiers, *Divi Hilarii lucubrationes*
(Basel Froben 1523) Rotterdam Public Library

Greek lexicographers[4] think the adjective ὅσιος is a variant form of ἅσιον [reverential] from the verb ἅζω, which is 'I reverence as a divine power.'

1 Erasmus' main point in this annotation is to convey the instrumental use of ἐν clearly in Latin.
2 Ambrosiaster *Comm in Eph* 4:24
3 For ... divine power.'] Added in 1527. There is no Greek adjective ἅσιος.
4 Erasmus may here have in mind Hesychius, among others, whose lexicon was transmitted in abridged form and first edited by Marcus Musurus and published in 1514; see *Contemporaries* II 472–3, and E. Dickey *Ancient Greek Scholarship* (Oxford 2007) 88–90.

4:25 [ER *proximo suo* 'to his neighbour']
[VG] *cum proximo* 'with his neighbour'; μετὰ τοῦ πλησίον, that is, 'to the neighbour'; although the Translator has rendered it correctly. For[1] we are said to speak with him whom we are speaking to, as we are said to fight with him against whom we are fighting.

1 For ... are fighting.] Added in 1522

4:26 [ER *irascimini et non peccetis* 'be angry and sin not']
[VG] *irascimini et nolite peccare* 'be angry and do not sin.' As this is taken from a Psalm,[1] so is it expressed in Hebrew fashion.[2] For the meaning is, 'if you happen to get angry, do not sin,' that is, 'check your anger.' Paul is not telling us to get angry, but he does not want anger to be continuous nor to progress to the point of injury. In Greek it is not *iracundia* [proneness to anger],[3] a word which in Latin signifies not so much anger as a natural vice or at least the habit of a mind that easily gets angry.[4] The Greek word is παροργισμῷ, that is, 'anger' or 'emotional disturbance' or 'irritation'[5] so that we understand that for the person who is wounded by some injury, even if he is pained to some extent, nevertheless the pain ought to last briefly and between Christians it should end without retaliation for the injury. I do not know whether 'devil' here [4:27] can be understood as 'slanderer.' Be of the same mind, he says, so that even if you rightly punish, you do not give an opportunity to the gentiles for slandering, to whom[6] you will seem to be eager for vengeance. For[7] the devil also slanders through his instruments. Nothing in Latin prevents a slanderer from being called the devil himself, seeing that my translation[8] of this passage has not lacked its own devil. Chrysostom[9] touches on both meanings. Discord opens the way to an enemy, to Satan and the slanderer.

1 Ps 4:5 in LXX and the Vulgate; Ps 4:4 in AV
2 For the syntax and analysis of the meaning see Lincoln *Ephesians* 301 who agrees in essence with Erasmus.

3 *iracundia* is the translation in the Vulgate. Cf Eph 6:4 where Erasmus
   again replaces *iracundia* in the Vulgate with *ira*.
4 Cf OLD s.v. *iracundia* 1: 'proneness to anger, hot temper, irascibility.'
5 Cf LSJ s.v. παροργισμός: 'provocation.'
6 to whom ... vengeance] Added in *1519*
7 For ... own devil.] Added in *1522*. The reference is to Diego López Zúñiga;
   see H.J. de Jonge *Apologia ad annotationes Stunicae* ASD IX-2 210:758–71n.
   Erasmus' interpretation is doubtful; see Lincoln *Ephesians* 302–3 who
   surveys the evidence for taking the passage as referring to the devil.
8 my translation] Added in *1527*
9 Chrysostom ... slanderer.] Added in *1535*. See Chrysostom *Hom in Eph*
   14.1 PG 62 101.

4:27 [ER *neque detis* 'do not give']

[VG] *nolite dare* 'give not'; μήτε δίδοτε, that is, 'do not give.'[1]

   1 For the difference in the two renderings see Brown *Novum Testamentum*
     528:27(1)n. In the *1516* edition the following passage occurred here: *et
     diabolo verti poterat calumniatori* 'and he was able to overthrow the devil,
     the false accuser.'

4:28 [ER *manibus* 'with his hands']

[VG] *manibus suis* 'with his own hands'; ταῖς ἰδίαις χερσίν, that is, 'with
his own hands,' although here he is continually accustomed to translate ἴδιον and ἑαυτοῦ by the same pronoun *suus* 'his.' Some manuscripts
do not add the *suis*, nor does Ambrose.[1]

   1 Ambrosiaster *Comm in Eph* 4:28. The reference is to manuscripts of the
     Vulgate; see Brown *Novum Testamentum* 528–9:28(2)n.

4:28 [ER VG] *quod bonum est* 'what is good.'

This can be read as a paren-
thesis,[1] 'what is good,' 'which is a good thing' or 'let him work a good
thing,' that is 'let him gain his living not from a shameful activity but
an honourable one.'

   1 Parenthesis (Latin *interpositio*) is the insertion of a verbal unit that inter-
     rupts the normal flow of the syntax (Quintilian 9.3.23).

4:28 [ER *ei qui opus habuerit* 'to him who will have need']

[VG] *necessitatem patienti* 'to him that suffers need'; τῷ χρείαν ἔχοντι,
that is, 'to one having need.' [Paul] offers[1] this admonition on account
of some who teach that we are not obligated to help a neighbour except
in need. They understand need to be when it is absolutely certain that
the neighbour will die unless we give what he is lacking.[2] And yet they
think that it is right for someone to ask for the return of whatever has

been donated in this way if the one who received it is able to repay. To such anxieties have we reduced the overabundant charity of the gospel. Jerome reads 'to him who is indigent.'³ Also, the Greek is ἵνα ἔχῃ μεταδιδόναι [4:28], that is, 'in order that he can share.'⁴ For ἔχω when added to infinitive verbs is sometimes used for *possum* 'I am able.'⁵

1 [Paul] offers ... who is indigent.'] Added in 1527
2 On Erasmus' distinction between what is necessary (ἀνάγκη) and what is needed (χρεία) see his annotation on Rom 12:13 ('sharing in the needs of the saints').
3 Jerome *Comm in Eph* 2 (on 4:28) PL 26 (1884) 544C
4 Erasmus' point here is that the conjunction ἵνα introduces a clause expressing purpose. Modern English translations render the latter part of verse 28 as follows: 'that he may have to give to him that needs' (AV), 'so that he may be able to give to those in need' (RSV), 'that he may have something to share with those in need' (NIV).
5 As LSJ notes s.v. ἔχω A.III.C, when followed by an aorist infinitive the verb may mean 'have means or power to do,' 'to be able.'

4:29 [ER *omnis sermo spurcus* 'all foul speech']
[VG] *sermo malus* 'evil speech'; λόγος σαπρός, that is, 'foul speech' or¹ 'malicious.'² He does not have in mind, I believe,³ speech that is trivial or superfluous, but obscene or depraved. Theophylact noted the emphasis of the Greek term⁴ although in the Gospels the evangelist, speaking about the evil tree,⁵ used the same term.

1 or ... term] Added in 1519
2 OLD defines *spurcus* as 'dirty, filthy, foul' and as 'morally polluted, foul, disgusting.' The word does not occur elsewhere in Erasmus' translation of the New Testament.
3 I believe] Added in 1522
4 Theophylact *Expos in Eph* 4:24 PG 124 1100A
5 Matt 7:17–18; cf Matt 12:33, Luke 6:43

4:29 [ER *ad aedificationem, quoties opus est* 'for edification, whenever there is need']
[VG] *aedificationem fidei* 'the edification of the faith.' I read in the Greek manuscripts¹ τῆς χρείας, that is 'of need,' not 'of faith.' Jerome testifies that he corrected it to 'for the edification of the opportunity,'² but in the Latin manuscripts 'faith' is read instead of 'opportunity' because it sounds better. And St Ambrose reads in this way.³ Theophylact⁴ also makes mention of the word χρείας [need]. Chrysostom⁵ likewise reads χρείας. I⁶ do not see, however, what the cacophony is in 'opportunity' or, as I would prefer, 'need.' For 'opportunity' in Latin has a different

meaning from χρεία, nor does 'opportunity' have any connection with the verb *oportet* [ought, need]. From this passage it is possible to infer that Jerome in this epistle follows what he himself had corrected, and yet in no other epistle are there more differences from what the Vulgate reads. Where, therefore, are they who turn heaven and earth upside down because some doubt whether the Vulgate edition is by Jerome?[7] That he wrote these commentaries after the correction of the New Testament is proved by his book *On famous writers* in which he mentions his commentaries on the epistles to the Galatians, to Titus, to Philemon.[8] Moreover, [he wrote the commentary on Ephesians after] the revision of the New Testament, although he makes no mention of this work, as[9] he was likely to do unless he had written these commentaries after the publication of the catalogue *On famous men*. Some craftsman or other will perhaps answer here that the reason was forgetfulness or that the Spirit did not want this.[10]

1 in the Greek manuscripts] Added in *1519*. On the variants in the Old Latin and Vulgate texts see Brown *Novum Testamentum* 529:29(4)n.
2 Jerome *Comm in Eph* 2 (on 4:29) PL 26 (1884) 546A
3 Ambrosiaster *Comm in Eph* 4:29
4 Theophylact ... word χρείας.] Added in *1519*. See Theophylact *Expos in Eph* 4:29 PG 124 1100A.
5 Chrysostom ... χρείας.] Added in *1535*. See Chrysostom *Hom in Eph* 14.2 PG 62 103.
6 I ... want this.] Added in *1527*
7 Erasmus is probably thinking of Pierre Cousturier (c 1475–1537). He was a member of the Carthusian order at Vauvert (near Paris) who rejected all new versions and translations of the Bible, and between 1525 and 1531 he was engaged in bitter exchanges with Erasmus. Among other things, Cousturier argued that Jerome's last work was the revision of the New Testament. For Erasmus' response to Cousturier see *Apologia adversus Petrum Sutorem* (LB IX 737–804, especially 758e–760c). On Cousturier's life and writings see *Contemporaries* I 352–3.
8 Jerome *De viris illustribus* 135 PL 23(1845) 717A–B. On the questionable accuracy of Erasmus' argument here see the note by M. van Poll-van de Lisdonk in ASD VI-9 237:104–5n.
9 as ... men] Added in *1535*
10 The *1527* edition has the following passage here: *apparet autem Hieronymum extrema senectute hos commentarias aedidisse.* 'It appears, moreover, that Jerome published these commentaries in extreme old age.'

4:30 [ER *in diem* 'unto the day']

[VG] *in die* 'on the day'; εἰς ἡμέραν, that is, 'unto the day.'

4:31 [ER *et tumor et ira* 'rage and anger']

[VG] *ira et indignatio* 'anger and indignation'; θυμὸς καὶ ὀργή, that is, 'ferocity and anger.' θυμός¹ properly speaking is an impulse of a mind that is stirred up and boiling over.

    1 θυμός ... boiling over.] Added in 1519. See Brown *Novum Testamentum* 529:31(2)n on both the word order in the Vulgate and Erasmus' effort to find a Latin equivalent for the Greek θυμός. Erasmus' term *tumor*, which is here translated somewhat freely as 'rage,' is literally a swelling either of a part of the body or, in the present case, of an emotion.

4:32 [ER *invicem alius in alium comes* 'in turn pleasant to one another']

[VG] *invicem benigni* 'kind to one another'; χρηστοί [kind, pleasant]. Jerome thinks that 'pleasantness' is a more accurate translation than 'kindness' so that it forms a contrast with bitterness and moral harshness.¹ For people who are especially pleasant and charming are said to be χρηστολόγοι [smooth speakers].² For, strictly speaking, kindness pertains to giving, that is, to generosity.³

    1 Jerome *Comm in Eph* 3 (on 4:32) PL 26 (1884) 550A
    2 LSJ defines χρηστολόγος as 'giving fair words, speaking plausibly.'
    3 See Brown *Novum Testamentum* 530:32(3)n for Erasmus' treatment of the Greek adjective in this passage and elsewhere.

4:32 [ER VG] *misericordes* 'merciful'; εὔσπλαγχνοι [tender hearted]. This pertains not only to mercy but to every feeling of devotion, as though one were to say 'good bowels.' For Sacred Scripture uses the bowels to mean feelings.¹

    1 Eg 2 Cor 6:12 στενοχωρεῖσθε δὲ ἐν τοῖς σπλάγχνοις ὑμῶν, which Erasmus rendered as *sed angusti estis in visceribus vestris* 'you are restricted in your own affections' (RSV). The adjective εὔσπλαγχνος occurs elsewhere in Scripture only in 1 Pet 3:8, where Erasmus also translated it as *misericordes* ('compassionate' NIV).

4:32 [ER *largientes vobis invicem* 'bestowing generously on yourselves']

[VG] *donantes invicem* 'giving one another'; χαριζόμενοι ἑαυτοῖς, that is, 'bestowing to yourselves,' so that you understand that any benefit you have conferred on others is done for your good and your gain rather than of him who received. Thus Jerome.¹ For² giving has not been used here for condoning or forgiving, but χαριζόμενοι, that is, 'bestowing' or 'gladly giving.' Ambrose³ reads and interprets 'giving' to mean 'forgiving' and 'pardoning sin.' And Paul of course used the same verb

χαρίζεσθαι [to bestow] in the Second Epistle to the Corinthians [2:10]:
'For if I forgave anything,' etc. Here[4] too Chrysostom and[5] Theophylact[6]
followed this meaning. Therefore, if this meaning, which is my own
preference, pleases, ἑαυτοῖς would have to be translated 'yourselves in
turn'; so that we mutually forgive one another's errors. For this too
pertains to mercy.

1 Jerome *Comm in Eph* 3 (on 4:32) PL 26 (1884) 550B
2 For] Added in *1519*
3 Ambrose ... to mercy.] Added in *1519*. See Ambrosiaster *Comm in Eph* 4:32.
4 Here ... Therefore] Added in *1527*
5 Chrysostom and] Added in *1535*. See Chrysostom *Hom in Eph* 16.2 PG 62
   114.
6 Theophylact *Expos in Eph* 4:32 PG 124 1101A

4:32 [ER *largitus est vobis* **'having been given to you'**]
[VG] *donavit vobis* **'he gave to you'**; ἡμῖν, that is, 'us,' first person, although the Greek manuscripts vary.[1]

1 For details see Brown *Novum Testamentum* 530–1:32(8)n, and Metzger 538.

From the Fifth Chapter

5:2 [ER *in odorem bonae fragrantiae* **'for an odour of good fragrance'**]
[VG] *in odorem suavitatis* **'for an odour of sweetness'**; εἰς ὀσμὴν εὐωδίας,
that is, 'for an odour of perfume' or 'of good[1] fragrance.' Jerome in the
preface [to the book] of Zechariah translated 'of good fragrance.'[2]

1 'of good] Added in *1522*. Omitted in *1516* and *1519*, the adjective 'good'
   may have been influenced by Valla *Annot in Eph* 5 (I 877), who considered
   the simple phrase 'odour of fragrance' too strained. Evidently Erasmus
   thought that the adverb εὐ ('well, good') in the compound εὐωδία gave
   him licence to add *bonae* 'good' to the Latin text. Weber 1813 reads *in
   odorem suavitatis*; modern translations interpret the phrase metaphori-
   cally: 'a fragrant offering and sacrifice' (RSV), 'an offering and sacrifice
   whose fragrance is pleasing' (NEB).
2 Jerome *Comm in Zech* II praefatio CCL 76A 795:136–7

5:3 [ER *ne nominetur quidem* **'let it not be even named'**]
[VG] *nec nominetur* **'let it not be named'**; μηδὲ ὀνομαζέσθω, that is, 'let it
not even be named.'[1]

1 Erasmus is influenced here by Lefèvre, who has the rendering *ne quidem
   nominetur* (*Pauli epistolae* fol 38 verso). On the force of 'not even' in μηδέ
   see Smyth 2391. See Brown's note *Novum Testamentum* 531:3(2)n.

5:4 [ER *aut obscoenitas aut stultiloquium* 'or obscenity or foolish talking']
[VG] *aut turpitudo aut stultiloquium* 'or filthiness or foolish talking.'[1]
The Greek in this passage does not have a repeated 'or,' but an 'and.'
Even[2] so I do approve the change the Translator has made.[3] For while
the meaning is the same, the style is better. But if it is right for the
Translator to make changes whenever[4] it seemed good to him, what pre-
vents the same thing from being done whenever it seems reasonable?

> 1 Erasmus preferred *obscoenitas* 'obscenity' to *turpitudo* 'filthiness' pre-
>   sumably because the former refers to speech, the latter to conduct. L&S
>   defines *obscoenitas* as 'moral impurity, foulness, unchastity, lewdness,'
>   and *turpitudo* as 'baseness, shamefulness, disgrace, dishonour, infamy.'
>   Cf modern English translations of the phrase here: 'filthiness, nor foolish
>   talking' (AV), 'filthiness nor silly talk' (RSV), 'obscenity, foolish talk' (NIV).
> 2 Even ... reasonable?] Added in 1519
> 3 The Greek reads 'or obscenity and foolish talking.' Erasmus assumes that
>   the Translator changed the Greek 'and' to the Latin 'or.'
> 4 The repetition *quoties quoties* ('whenever') in the editions from 1519 to
>   1535 appears to be a printer's error.

5:4 [ER *aut urbanitas* 'or facetiousness']
[VG] *aut scurrilitas* 'or scurrility'; εὐτραπελία, that is, 'wittiness' or
'charm.'[1] In the philosophers it has a positive connotation.[2] [Paul]
means an urbanity that is buffoonish and unworthy of a serious man.
Jerome thinks those jokes too, which are told only to get a laugh, are
unworthy of people who are truly Christian.[3] He brings in from the
Hebrew Gospel the saying, 'Never laugh except when you look on
your brother in love.'[4] For my part, just as I tolerate any kind of joke
provided it is learned and seasoned with wit, so I do not put up with
certain people who,[5] whenever they want to appear witty, twist something from Scripture to fit their own foolishness. I[6] see that this kind
of tasteless festivity gives immense pleasure to certain monks and
even some priests who, if they happen to be eager to attack someone,
twist the *Song of Mary* (commonly called the *Magnificat*) or the Hymn
commonly called the *Te Deum* into a spiteful insult by changing a few
words. Such jokes rightly are appealing to those who are pleased by the
Catholicon,[7] *Mammaetractus*[8] and the most tasteless glosses of that kind,
and who are delighted by the most frigid petty questions so that they
are the same at every turn, no less ridiculous when they tell jokes, that
is, when a camel dances,[9] as when they discuss serious matters.

'Thanksgiving,' which follows, is in Greek εὐχαριστία.[10] St Jerome understands this word to mean graciousness or grace.[11] In Hebrew 'graciousness' and 'giving thanks' are said with the same word. [Jerome] thinks the

text in Proverbs runs as follows: γυνὴ εὐχάριστος ἐγείρει ἀνδρὶ δόξαν, that is, 'a grateful woman obtains glory for her husband.'[12] For the other translators – Aquila,[13] Theodotion[14] and Symmachus[15] – render χαροπός, that is, 'gracious,' not εὐχάριστος. The point is that the speech of Christians is to be free from scurrilous jokes, but is seasoned with a certain grace of its own. But I leave this to be pondered by the reader. I do not completely approve Jerome's comment on this passage, especially[16] when the Greek texts do not support it. Ambrose interprets εὐχαριστία to mean 'a word used in praising God.'[17]

1 Valla *Annot in Eph* 5 (1 878). LSJ s.v. εὐτραπελία 2 notes that the word here has a pejorative connotation; cf BDAG 'coarse jesting, risqué wit.'

2 Cf Aristotle *Eudemian Ethics* 3.7 (1234a4–23) for the positive connotation; *Nicomachean Ethics* 2.7 (1108a24) and 4.8 (1128a12) and *Rhetoric* 2.12 (1389b11–12) for the pejorative sense. See Lincoln *Ephesians* 323–4.

3 Jerome *Comm in Eph* 3 (on 5:3–4) PL 26 (1884) 552C–D

4 The apocryphal *Gospel of the Hebrews* is a lost gospel dating perhaps to the second century AD. Jerome, whose commentary on Eph 5:4 preserves the fragment quoted by Erasmus, reports (*Comm in Matt* 2:12) that many Nazarenes and Ebionites believed that the *Gospel of the Hebrews* was the original Gospel of Matthew. The standard modern edition of the *Gospel of the Hebrews* is by W. Schneemelcher, *New Testament Apocrypha, Vol 1: Gospels and Related Writings. Revised Edition* (London 1991), 134–72; for an evaluation of Jerome's testimony concerning this gospel see 142–9.

5 who] Added in *1519*

6 I ... serious matters.] The remainder of this paragraph was added in *1519*. In the treatise, *de Lingua*, on the proper use of the tongue, Erasmus records an incident involving an unnamed monk who derived pleasure from hearing obscenities introduced into a liturgical formula (CWE 29 392–3).

7 The *Catholicon* (from the Greek word for 'universal'), or *Summa grammaticalis quae vocatur Catholicon*, was a biblical dictionary and encyclopedia compiled by Johannes Balbus in 1286, and used throughout the Middle Ages. It first appeared in print in 1460. Erasmus repeatedly criticizes the value of reading the *Catholicon* and *Mammaetractus*; see *Antibarbari* CWE 23 36, *De conscribendis epistulis* CWE 25 24. On the *Catholicon* as medieval textbook see Robert Black *Humanism and Education in Medieval and Renaissance Italy* (Cambridge 2001) 95.

8 The *Mammaetractus* (or *Mammetrectus, Mammetrecton, Mammotrectus super Bibliam*) was composed by the Franciscan monk, Johannes Marchesinus, who lived sometime between 1300 and 1466 AD (P.S. Allen *The Age of Erasmus* [Oxford 1914] 26). This book contained a wide range of content, including a glossary on the text of the Vulgate, commentary on the legends of the saints, and many detailed and even trivial comments intended to be of use to students of the church.

9 Erasmus explains the saying 'when a camel dances' in *Adagia* II vii 66: 'when a man tried to do something, but ungracefully ... they used to say it was a camel dancing' (CWE 34 33).

10 εὐχαριστία is the reading in modern editions of the New Testament.
    Modern translations render the words as 'thanksgiving' (RSV), 'thanking
    God' (NEB).
11 Jerome *Comm in Eph* 3 (on 5:3–4) PL 26 (1884) 553A–B.
12 Cf the LXX of Proverbs 11:16, which has the same reading.
13 Aquila, a Jewish proselyte of the early second century AD, made a very lit-
    eral rendering of the Hebrew Bible into Greek. His version was included
    in the *Hexapla* of Origen.
14 Theodotion (second century AD) translated the Old Testament into Greek.
    His version is placed in Origen's *Hexapla* after that of the Septuagint.
15 Symmachus is known to us almost solely from the fragments of his Greek
    translation of the Hebrew Bible incorporated into Origen's *Hexapla*.
    Possibly of Jewish origin, he lived perhaps in the late second and early
    third centuries AD. The fragments have been edited by F. Field *Origenis
    Hexaplorum quae supersunt; sive veterum interpretum Graecorum in totum
    vetus testamentum fragmenta* 2 vols (Oxford 1867–71).
16 especially ... to God'] Added in *1519*
17 Ambrosiaster *Comm in Eph* 5:4

5:4 [ER *quae non conveniunt* 'which are not suitable']
    [VG] *quae ad rem non pertinet* 'which is not to the point';[1] τὰ οὐκ ἀνή-
    κοντα, that is 'not fitting' or 'which are not suitable' as[2] he translates else-
    where so that the reference is to the person: one kind of speech befits
    the buffoon, another befits the servant of Christ. If one must joke, the
    joke should be decorous. We see that some jokes were exchanged be-
    tween Paul the Hermit[3] and Anthony,[4] [and] that Hilarion said many
    witty things.[5] But jokes of this kind do not arouse silly laughter but ring
    with the praise of God.

    1 Following Valla's note *Annot in Eph* 5 (I 878) that the Greek τὰ οὐκ ἀνήκο-
        ντα is plural, Erasmus altered the Vulgate's *pertinet* ('is to the point') to
        conveniunt ('are not suitable').
    2 as ... praise of God] Added in *1519*
    3 the Hermit] Added in *1527*
    4 See Jerome *Vita sancti Pauli eremitae* 9–11 PL 23 (1845) 25A–26B. For a sum-
        mary of this work and its influence see Stefan Rebenich 'Inventing an
        Ascetic Hero: Jerome's *Life of Paul the First Hermit*' in *Jerome of Stridon. His
        Life, Writings and Legacy* ed A. Cain and J. Lössl (Surrey 2009) 13–27.
    5 See Jerome *Vita sancti Hilarionis* 12 PL 23 (1845) 34B. For a depiction of this
        work see J.N.D. Kelly *Jerome* (New York 1975) 172–4.

5:5 [ER *hoc scitis* 'you know this']
    [VG] *scitote intelligentes* 'know, understanding [that]'; ἐστὲ γινώσκο-
    ντες, that is, 'be of understanding,' although some manuscripts have
    ἴστε, that is, 'know,' so that the doubling [of the verbs] creates inten-
    sity.[1] Ambrose[2] and Jerome[3] follow the first reading. πλεονέκτης,[4] which

Cyprian translates 'cheater,'⁵ I translate 'greedy person.' St Jerome observes with respect to the word πλεονεκτεῖν that it is derived from πλέον [more] and ἔχειν ['to have' – thus 'to have more'] and is used when someone occupies another's property.⁶ Accordingly a little above he understands the words 'Let no one circumvent his brother in business'⁷ to refer to adultery and here he thinks πλεονεξία can refer to fornication.⁸

1 Modern editions of the New Testament read ἴστε γινώσκοντες, and English translations render accordingly; eg 'for be very sure of this' (NEB). *Congeminatio* 'the doubling' refers to the rhetorical device of *geminatio*, which 'consists in the repetition of the same word or word group in one place in the sentence, usually at the beginning of the sentence' (Lausberg §616).
2 Ambrose ... reading.] Added in *1519*. See Ambrosiaster *Comm in Eph* 5:5.
3 Jerome *Comm in Eph* 3 (on 5:5) PL 26 (1884) 553B
4 πλεονέκτης ... greedy person.'] Added in *1535*
5 Cyprian *Epistulae* 55.27 CSEL 3/2 645:2
6 Jerome *Comm in Eph* 2 (on 4:17) PL 26 (1884) 538A. Jerome does not discuss the etymology of πλεονεκτεῖν given by Erasmus; LSJ defines the word as 'have or claim more than one's due.'
7 1 Thess 4:6
8 In *1519 fornicatione* 'fornication' was replaced by *stupor* 'drunkenness.' Jerome *Comm in Eph* 3 (on 5:5) PL 26 (1884) 554B

5:5 [ER *qui est simulacrorum cultor* 'who is a worshipper of images']
[VG] *quod est idolorum servitus* 'which is servitude of idols'; ὅς ἐστιν εἰδωλολάτρης, that is, 'who¹ is a worshipper of idols.' Jerome reads 'one who serves idols.'² Here³ the Translator renders λατρείαν [service] sometimes as 'worship,' sometimes as 'obedience,' sometimes as 'servitude.' Augustine in the tenth book of *The City of God* observes that the servitude by which one not his own master is called δουλεία [slavery], but the worship with which we generally worship God is called λατρεία [servitude] in Sacred Scripture.⁴

1 For Erasmus' Greek text which reads 'who' not 'what' as in the Vulgate see Metzger 539.
2 Jerome *Comm in Eph* 3 (on 5:5) PL 26 (1884) 553B and 554B. Jerome actually reads *quod est idolis serviens* 'which is one serving idols.'
3 Here ... Sacred Scripture.] Added in *1519*
4 Augustine *De civitate dei* 10.1 CCL 47 272:39–44. In his text of Rom 1:9 and the annotation there ('whom I serve,' CWE 56 33–4) Erasmus alters the Vulgate's *servio* 'I serve' to *colo* 'I worship.'

5:5 [ER VG] *in regno Christi et dei* 'in¹ the kingdom of Christ and of God.' He seems in this way² to be calling the Father God as though Christ were not God. I have mentioned this elsewhere, that it is customary in apostolic language to signify the Father whenever he names God absolutely, although it is clear from very many passages that the apostles also call Christ God.[3]

   1 'in ... Christ God.] This annotation was added in 1519.
   2 Ie by distinguishing Christ and God
   3 In his commentary on Rom 1:7 ('from God our Father and the Lord Jesus Christ') Erasmus points out that it is characteristic of 'apostolic language' to ascribe deity to God the Son as well as God the Father (CWE 56 31–2); see also his annotation on 2 Cor 2:15 'bonus odor sumus deo' (ASD VI-8 350:381–9).

5:6 [ER *venire solet ira* 'the wrath commonly comes']
[VG] *venit ira* 'comes the anger'; ἔρχεται [comes]. *Venit*[1] in this place[2] is the present tense or at least the future. For[3] it cannot be the past tense. In my opinion it is more correct to take it as a present tense so that we understand that because of such speech divine wrath is accustomed to rage against children who are unwilling to obey or refuse to listen to authority.

   1 *venit* can be either present tense, 'comes' or 'is coming,' or past tense, 'came'; ἔρχεται can indicate either present or future time. For Erasmus' use of the auxiliary verb *solet* 'is accustomed to' to emphasize continuing or repeated action see Brown's note *Novum Testamentum* 532:6(4)n. On the neo-Latin use of *solet* / *solebat* see J. Trapman '*Solet* instead of *Solebat* in Erasmus and other Neo-Latin Authors' *Humanistica Lovaniensia* 44 (1995) 197–201.
   2 place] Added in 1519
   3 For ... authority.] Added in 1519

5:6 [ER *in filios inobedientes* 'upon the disobeying children']
[VG] *in filios diffidentiae* 'upon the children of unbelief'; ἀπειθείας, that is, 'of disobedience' or 'of disbelief,' as I have mentioned previously.[1] Jerome thinks it is more correctly translated by 'incapable of being persuaded,' in relation to those whom we call intractable.[2] It[3] is odd that a word pleased Jerome which is scarcely known to Latin ears. Cyprian in the letter to Epictetus reads 'upon the children of stubbornness.'[4] But then again, I have already mentioned frequently that feature of Hebrew speech[5] in which they call a stubborn child a child of stubbornness.[6]

   1 See Eph 2:2 above. In his annotation on Rom 11:32 ('for God has shut all things') Erasmus also notes that ἀπειθεία 'disobedience' may be rendered by 'unbelief.'
   2 Jerome *Comm in Eph* 3 (on 5:6) PL 26 (1884) 555B–C. The word Jerome uses here, *insuasibilitas*, does not occur in classical Latin.
   3 It ... ears.] Added in 1527

4 Cyprian ... stubbornness.] Added in 1519. See Cyprian *Epistulae* 43.6 CSEL
3/2 595:18–19.
5 From 1519 to 1527 a note in the margin read *colos sermonis Hebraei* 'the
tone of Hebrew speech.'
6 For the Hebrew idiom rendered into Latin by the genitive of quality see
the annotation on Eph 2:12 ('foreigners to the testaments') n2 above.

5:7 [ER *consortes illorum* 'their partners']
[VG] *participes eorum* 'partakers with them'; συμμέτοχοι, that is, 'fellow
partakers,' that is, 'Do not be partakers of evils with them.'¹ He is talking about the fruits of impiety. He² does not want them to be partakers
of these fruits with the impious so that one part of the participation
concerns the subject, the other part the person. Jerome annotated this
carefully and at great length.³ To my mind whoever is a partaker has
to be both a partaker of some thing and a partaker with someone. He
added that in Sacred Scripture the word 'partaker' is used in a good
sense, 'fellow partaker' in a bad sense. I⁴ do not know whether this is a
constant rule. Certainly in the third chapter⁵ [Paul] used 'fellow partakers' in a good sense when he speaks about gentiles who were converted
to Christ, συμμέτοχοι τῆς ἐπαγγελίας αὐτοῦ, that is, 'fellow partakers of the
promise.' A man who is a saint ought not to be criticized, but this is a remarkable lapse of memory. First, he orders that this distinction be carefully observed and says that he does not remember reading the word
'fellow partaker' in Sacred Scripture except in a bad sense although he
himself in [his commentary] on the third chapter of this epistle carefully
indicates that the addition of the prefix *con-* in these words, *concorporales*
and *comparticipes* sounds harsh to Latin ears, but nevertheless ought not
to be omitted because in Sacred Scripture neither jots nor tittles are without mystery. It seemed worthwhile to mention this so that those who are
eager to profit in these matters may tolerate human lapses more mod-
estly when this happened to a man so well exercised in divine books.

1 As Brown (*Novum Testamentum* 532–3:7[3]n) notes, Erasmus prefers the
more emphatic pronoun which connects with 'sons' in verse 6 and con-
trasts with 'unto the Lord' in verse 8.
2 He ... bad sense.] Added in 1519
3 Jerome *Comm in Eph* 3 (on 5:7) PL 26 (1884) 555C–556A
4 I ... books.] Added in 1527
5 Eph 3:6

5:9 [ER *nam fructus spiritus* 'for the fruit of the Spirit']
[VG] *fructus enim lucis* 'for the fruit of the light.' The Greek is 'for
the fruit of the Spirit,'¹ ὁ γὰρ καρπὸς τοῦ πνεύματος. However, the Latin
manuscripts and the agreement of the interpreters and² the sequence

itself of the language are opposed to this reading. For[3] the mention of light comes first, 'but you are now light in the Lord. Walk as children of the light' [5:8]. Theophylact reads and interprets fruit of the light.[4] Chrysostom[5] seems to have read 'of the Spirit.' Likewise there follows, 'and have no fellowship with the unfruitful works of darkness' [5:11].

1 Erasmus has the same wording as Valla and Lefèvre.
2 and ... language] Added in *1527*
3 For ... works of darkness.'] Added in *1527*. For the history of the biblical text see Brown *Novum Testamentum* 533:9(2)n. Erasmus appears to commend the Vulgate reading; perhaps he thought that the word 'light' crept in here under the influence of 'light' in verse 8, and of the imagery of darkness and light in verses 7–14. Also in his paraphrase on this text Erasmus appears to favour the reading 'light' *Paraphrasis in Ephesios* CWE 43 342–3.
4 Theophylact *Expos in Eph* 5:9 PG 124 1108A
5 Chrysostom ... Spirit.'] Added in *1535*. See Chrysostom *Hom in Eph* 18.1 PG 62 121.

5:10 [ER *acceptum Domino* 'acceptable to the Lord']
[VG] *beneplacitum deo* 'well pleasing to God.' The Greek has 'the Lord.'[1]

1 For the text of the Vulgate see Brown's note at *Novum Testamentum* 533:10(2)n. Though Erasmus does not mention it here, probably through an oversight, Ambrosiaster reads 'to God,' and Lefèvre 'to the Lord.' English translations vary: 'what is acceptable to the Lord' (AV), 'what pleases the Lord' (NIV).

5:11 [ER *quin ea potius etiam arguite* 'but rather rebuke them']
[VG] *magis autem redarguite* 'but rather refute.'[1] The conjunction 'and,' καί, has been omitted. And 'refute' for 'rebuke.' Ambrose reads 'scold,'[2] but 'rebuke' ἐλέγχετε would be more suitable. For the light itself of a good life rebukes and brings out the foul deeds of darkness even if there is no scolding. Mindful, therefore, of the metaphor[3] [Paul] added 'but rather rebuke.' For one rebukes who reprehends and wins, and one rebukes who exposes. And the words which follow 'but all things are made manifest by the light'[4] demand that we read 'rebuke' for 'expose' rather than 'scold.' And[5] yet here too Ambrose reads 'they are scolded,' just as he read earlier and explicated 'scold.' To[6] this extent Theophylact sides with me.

1 Erasmus adds *ea* 'them' to make the link with 'works' earlier in 5:11 more explicit, and chooses 'rebuke' for its broader range of meaning.
2 Ambrosiaster *Comm in Eph* 5:11
3 On metaphor see the annotation on Gal 4:24 ('through allegory spoken') n6.
4 Cf Eph 5:13.
5 And ... scold.'] Added in *1527*. Cf Ambrosiaster *Comm in Eph* 5:13.
6 To ... me.] Added in *1519*. See Theophylact *Expos in Eph* 5:11–12 PG 124 1108B.

5:13 [ER *nam quicquid* 'for whatever']

[VG] *omne enim quod* 'for all that'; τὸ φανερούμενον [that which makes manifest]. Because the participle is middle or passive, the words are ambiguous. For the meaning can be 'whatever is manifested is light' or 'whatever makes manifest is light.' However, it appears that it ought to be read as active rather than passive. If the attachment of the article to the participle, not the noun, did not move me, I would interpret in this way: 'That which manifests all things is light' (τὸ πᾶν φανερούμενον, φῶς ἐστιν). For whatever conceals is night and darkness; light uncovers and reveals it. From the holy life of the godly and the preaching of the truth all things which differ from this are made visible. Now,[1] however, we have πᾶν γὰρ τὸ φανερούμενον φῶς ἐστιν. Theophylact[2] with Chrysostom[3] interprets it as a passive and explains that as soon as a sin is exposed and uncovered, it turns from darkness into light. And[4] I followed this. Jerome[5] reads 'shown,' but the Translator who also expressed the tense structure rendered it more accurately. Again[6] it is clear from this passage and the next that the Vulgate translation is not by Jerome.

1 Now ... into light.] Added in 1519
2 Theophylact *Expos in Eph* 5:13 PG 124 1108C–D
3 with Chrysostom] Added in 1535. See Chrysostom *Hom in Eph* 18.1 PG 62 122.
4 And ... this.] Added in 1522
5 Jerome ... by Jerome.] Added in 1527. See Jerome *Comm in Eph* 3 (on 5:13) PL 26 (1884) 558A.
6 Cf Erasmus' annotation on Gal 3:7 ('know therefore').

5:14 [ER *expergiscere qui dormis* 'awake you who sleep']

[VG] *surge qui dormis* 'arise you who sleep.'[1] Jerome denies that Paul's citation is found anywhere in Sacred Scripture;[2] he thinks it was either taken from apocryphal writings or uttered by Paul himself in a prophetic spirit. However,[3] it is strange that this scruple is not mentioned by the Greeks.[4]

1 See Erasmus' translation in the annotation on Rom 13:11 ('to rise from sleep'). Cf Brown's note *Novum Testamentum* 535:14(2)n.
2 Jerome *Comm in Eph* 3 (on 5:14) PL 26 (1884) 558B–C
3 However ... Greeks.] Added in 1519
4 In *Hyperaspistes* 2 Erasmus offers the following interpretation of this text: '"Get up" and "rise" are expressions of impelling grace; "Christ will shine upon you" of consolation and promises.' For the context see CWE 77 409.

5:14 [ER *et illucescet tibi* 'and will give you light']

[VG] *et illuminabit te* 'and will enlighten you'; καὶ ἐπιφαύσει σοι ὁ Χριστός, that is, 'and Christ will give you light,' or 'Christ will dawn for you,' as

Saint Jerome translates and corrects.[1] But the comment he does make
is that some have the reading ἐφάψεται and not ἐπιφαύσει, that is, 'touch
upon,' and they want it to appear that this was said by Christ, hanging
on the cross, to Adam, buried nearby, who, touched by the blood of the
redeemer, will have life again, all of which is far-fetched and smacks of
Jewish fables. And[2] still Jerome testifies that he was present at a sermon
in which this interpretation was received with marvellous applause
from the people.[3] I myself heard [an interpretation] of the Hebrew letter *syn*, which in English means 'sin,' found in the middle of the name
Jesus and likewise about the three cases, *Jesus, Jesu, Jesum*, which they
interpret from the final letters to mean the sum, the ultimate, and the
middle.[4] And yet I see that Ambrose read pretty much[5] in this way,[6]
though[7] otherwise differing somewhat from our reading. For he reads
in this way, 'Rise from the dead and you will touch Christ.' Augustine[8]
likewise in his commentary on Psalm 3 reads 'And Christ will touch
you.' Both[9] readings are mentioned in the Greek commentaries[10] which
circulate under the name of Chrysostom though they give greater
approval to the reading which we follow, and it certainly is more in
accordance with the preceding words, 'Have no fellowship with the
unfruitful works of darkness' [5:11] and 'all that is made manifest is
light' [5:13]. Moreover, blessed Thomas' comment is not implausible,
that the Apostle did not take this passage from the Apocrypha nor did
he utter it in the manner of a prophet, but with the addition of some
words of his own he explicated a passage in Isaiah 60[:1]: 'Arise, be enlightened, O Jerusalem, for your light is come and the glory of the Lord
is risen upon you.' Those who sleep are told to rise, and those who are
buried and cannot see the light of the world [are told] to arise.[11]

1   Jerome *Comm in Eph* 3 (on 5:14) PL 26 (1884) 558A. OLD defines *illucesco*
    as 'to begin to grow light, dawn, break,' and *illumino* as 'to give light to,
    illuminate.' Cf the reading *inluminabit* (Weber 1813).
2   And ... middle.] Added in *1527*
3   Jerome *Comm in Eph* 3 (on 5:14) PL 26 (1884) 559A
4   For a discussion of the interpretations of the name 'Jesus' in the early
    church see ASD IX-2 79.
5   pretty much] Added in *1535*
6   Ambrosiaster *Comm in Eph* 5:14
7   though ... in this way] Added in *1527*
8   Augustine ... you.'] Added in *1519*. See Augustine *Enarrationes in Psalmos*
    3.9 CCL 38 12:34–5.
9   Both ... to arise.'] Added in *1535*
10 Chrysostom *Hom in Eph* 18.1 PG 62 122
11 Thomas Aquinas *Super Eph lect* cap 5 lectio 5.300

5:15 [ER *videte igitur* 'see then']

[VG] *videte itaque fratres* 'see therefore, brothers.' The word 'brothers' is not in the Greek.[1]

> 1 For the reading 'brothers' in the Vulgate see Brown *Novum Testamentum* 535:15(1)n.

5:15 [ER *circumspecte ambuletis* 'that you walk circumspectly']

[VG] *caute ambuletis* 'that you walk cautiously'; ἀκριβῶς, that is, carefully and accurately, being no doubt in so much light.[1] Hence he said it well, 'See, because it is not possible to discern in the dark.'

> 1 As Brown (*Novum Testamentum* 535:15[2]n) notes, Erasmus apparently preferred *circumspecte* to *caute* because the former is more fitting in the context of the light imagery in this passage.

5:16 [ER *redimentes occasionem* 'redeeming the occasion']

[VG] *redimentes tempus* 'redeeming the time'; ἐξαγοραζόμενοι, as if merchandising and buying.[1] And 'time' here means 'occasion' or 'opportunity' which he wants bought by the expenditure of other things, τὸν καιρόν [time].[2]

> 1 The Greek verb ἐξαγοράζω 'to buy' is derived from the word for marketplace.
> 2 καιρός means time in the sense of the opportune or right moment. Cf Col 4:5 where Erasmus translates the Greek term by *opportunitas* 'opportunity.'

5:16 [ER *mali sint* 'are evil']

[VG] *mali sunt* 'are evil'; πονηραί. This particular word is ambiguous, referring to affliction and to wickedness inasmuch[1] as it is derived from πόνος, 'toil.' For the matter is toilsome and deceitful.

> 1 inasmuch ... deceitful] Added in *1519*

5:17 [ER *voluntas domini* 'the will of the Lord']

[VG] *voluntas dei* 'the will of God.' The Greek has 'Lord' τοῦ κυρίου instead of 'God.'[1]

> 1 For the reading *dei* 'God' see Brown *Novum Testamentum* 535:17(2)n.

5:18 [ER *in quo luxus est* 'wherein excess is']

[VG] *in quo est luxuria* 'wherein is extravagance'; ἀσωτία, that is, 'excess.'[1] I have mentioned this lest someone take *luxuria* here to mean 'lust' as people commonly do. I do not see why Lefèvre prefers 'unhealthiness' here in place of 'luxury' as if Paul's intention, like a physician, is to have us physically healthy by avoiding drunkenness.[2] For[3] while I grant that ἄσωτοι [abandoned people] is derived from the verb σεσώσται,[4] that is, 'he has been saved' with the addition of an alpha privative and the removal of a sigma, it cannot, however, signify insalubrity and it is nowhere found used in this sense in Greek authors. The nation of the débauchées [asoti] was called this in Greek because they were utterly dissolute, so persistently engaged in drinking parties that they never saw the sun rising or setting.[5] Plato, beside countless others, mentions them.[6] Also the verb ἀσωτεύομαι, I am awash in excess, which Athenaeus used in the eighth book of his *Deipnosophists*.[7] Now the word, which in my opinion does not refer absolutely to wine but to the whole segment of the utterance which precedes: 'Do not get drunk with wine in which,' that is, in which thing and in which inebriation from wine, 'is excess.' Furthermore[8] what [Paul] here calls ἀσωτία, elsewhere he termed ἀσέλγεια [licentiousness].[9] Nor would it be altogether absurd if someone sometimes uses 'luxury' for the vice of lust on account of the relationship among such vices as drinking, drunkenness, dancing, and lust. Still I think it impudent for Thomas to try to twist the notion that luxury is said especially about the immoderate use of sexual activity, to the point that he even rejects his favourite Augustine who in the books to which he gave the title *Confessions* wrote, 'Luxury is eager to be invited to satiety and abundance.'[10] He untied this knot in this artful way: 'As the principal and proper meaning of temperance concerns the touching of delightful things, and moreover consequently is said through some similarity of certain other materials, so luxury principally concerns the sexual pleasures that very greatly and especially undo a person's mind. But secondarily it is said of some other things that pertain to excess.'[11] I have repeated Thomas' words up to this point. Now lest we make excessive demands because he backed away so easily from the views of Augustine, who had an intimate knowledge of the propriety of the Roman language, who has ever said that temperance was primarily concerned with the pleasures of touch when it is in fact the control over all the feelings? But granted that lust is a completely uncontrolled feeling, is the leading part of this evil located in touch and not rather in the eyes, in speech, in the mind? Secondly, is the term luxury transferred to any kind of excess? Will someone who has an immoderate love of money be called luxurious or someone who is extremely frugal be called luxurious? And yet these are forms of excess. Finally if Euclio[12] falls in love but offers no gifts will he be called luxurious? And yet [Thomas] confirms this opinion from the authority of the *Glossa*[13] on Galatians 5 [:19] which says that luxury is some kind of excess. It is odd that he did not bring in this passage of Paul when he cites a passage from *Proverbs* [20:1] '"Wine is a luxurious thing,' but the use of wine pertains to drink; therefore," etc.[14] He explicates this knot successfully enough. The third knot is difficult. 'Luxury,' he says, 'is called the appetite for lustful pleasure,' etc. Although he cites no authority, he here imagines that 'lustful pleasure' is to be taken for sexual pleasure. Although Augustine testifies that 'lust' is frequently taken for any kind of emotion at all which does not obey the reason (a ruler's execution of an innocent person is lust),[15] nevertheless, as Augustine admits, speech usage sometimes employs this term[16] appropriately for sexual activity, but no approved author has ever written [about sex] as 'luxury.' Even sillier than this is what [Aquinas] interjects between the antitheses and the solution. 'It is said in the book *On True Religion*[17] about luxurious people: "Who sows in the flesh reaps corruption from the flesh."[18] But sowing of the flesh is done through sexual pleasures, therefore, luxury pertains to these pleasures.'[19] First, I appeal to the sober reader, did Paul there have sexual pleasure in view and not rather the Law of Moses, and if he did have it in view, did he have it properly in view? But if he had in view the impious love of all visible things, how does this support Thomas who wants 'luxury' to be the proper term for sexual pleasure? At this point he introduces Isidore to us; he thinks luxurious is said for dissolute as if derived, I suspect, from *luxari* [to revel] or *laxare* [to loosen].[20] But Venus most of all dissolves the mind; therefore, 'luxury' pertains to sex. And yet Thomas had not proposed this but whether it was appropriately applied to this. Lastly, what is Thomas' subject here except the right word for a vice? But where ought a term to be sought other than from Latin authors? To what end was it necessary to twist 'luxury' to this subject since *libido* [lust] and *impudicia* [unchastity] are well known Latin words? And nevertheless as though the matter were now settled, he subdivides 'luxury' into all the forms of lust. I am not attacking Thomas, but clearly I pity those who learn nothing else and I am less dissatisfied with myself because I have not wasted much of my life on such authors.[21]

---

1 BDAG renders ἀσωτία as 'debauchery, dissipation, profligacy.'

2 Lefèvre *Pauli epistolae* fol 39 recto and 171 verso. Erasmus treats the etymology of ἀσωτία also in his *Apologia ad Fabrum* CWE 83 103.

3 For ... *Deipnosophists*.] Added in *1519*

4 The LB edition has this verb in the infinitive, σέσωσθαι, which does not agree with Erasmus' Latin translation *servatus est* 'he has been saved.'

5 From Cicero *De finibus* 2.8.23; cf Seneca *Epistles* 122.2.

6 Plato *Laws* 743B. For a survey of the use and meaning of the adjective in Greek and Roman literature see Arthur Stanley Pease, *M. Tulli Ciceronis De Natura Deorum* III 77 1173.

7 Athenaeus *Deipnosophistae* 8.359C

8 Furthermore ... such authors.] Added in *1522*

9 Cf Eph 4:19, Gal 5:19, Rom 13:13 etc.

10 Augustine *Confessions* 2.6.13 CCL 27 24:32–3, where he reads *luxuria satietatem atque abundantiam se cupit vocari.*

11 Thomas Aquinas *Summa theologiae* pars secunda secundae, quaestio 153

12 Euclio is the old man in Plautus's *Aulularia* who is notorious for stinginess.

13 For the *Glossa Ordinaria* see the annotation on Gal 4:25 ('for it is joined to what is now Jerusalem') n9.

14 The full citation is: 'It says in Proverbs 20, "Wine is a luxurious thing," but the use of wine pertains to the pleasure of food and drink; therefore it appears that luxury concerns these delights especially.'

15 Augustine *De civitate dei* 14.16 CCL 48 438:1–4

16 That is, *libido* 'lust'

17 Augustine *De vera religione* 3.4 CCL 32 190:63–4

18 Thomas Aquinas *Summa theologiae* pars secunda secundae, quaestio 153

19 Erasmus is quoting Augustine via Aquinas; see *De vera religione* 3.4 CCL 32 190:63–4.

20 Isidore of Seville *Etymologies* x, 160: 'voluptuous (*luxuriosus*) as if dissolute (*solutus*) with pleasure (*voluptas*)'

21 Erasmus frequently engages the biblical scholarship of Thomas Aquinas. In general, Erasmus bestows either criticism or faint praise on Aquinas, often chiding him for offering interpretations that are contrived, superfluous, not based on a knowledge of the original Greek text, or, as here, distorted. For a survey of Erasmus' critical treatment of Aquinas' exegesis see Rummel 78–80, who offers the following evaluation of Erasmus' criticism in this note: 'The patronizing tone adopted here serves of course only to underline the gravity of Aquinas' faults' (79).

5:18 [ER *sed impleamini spiritu* 'but be filled with the spirit']
[VG] *implemini spiritu sancto* 'be filled with the Holy Spirit.'[1] The Greek is 'but be filled with the spirit.' 'Holy'[2] is in neither the Greek nor in Ambrose[3] nor in Jerome[4] nor in the older manuscripts[5] as indicated[6] by both of the manuscripts from Constance; there is only 'spirit'[7] ἐν πνεύματι. He contrasted this to the drunkenness caused by wine, a subtle[8] reality to a crude one.

1 The subjunctive *impleamini* is the reading in Erasmus' Latin version and in his text of the Vulgate, but beginning in *1519* the text of the cue phrase and of his translation in the annotation is the imperative *implemini*.

2 'Holy' ... only 'spirit'] Added in *1519*

3 Ambrosiaster *Comm in Eph* 5:18

4 Jerome *Comm in Eph* 3 (on 5:18) PL 26 (1884) 561A

5 Evidently the manuscripts in St Paul's Library. See the annotation on Gal 2:2 ('who seemed something') n14.

6 as indicated ... Constance] Added in *1527*. For more information on the manuscripts from Constance see the annotation on Gal 1:3 ('from God our Father') n3 and CWE 56 xii.

7 For this reading see Brown *Novum Testamentum* 535:18(3)n.

8 a subtle ... crude one] Added in *1535*. By 'subtle' Erasmus means 'spiritual' and by 'crude' a material or physical state. So too Erasmus' paraphrase
on this text: 'be filled with the unfermented wine of the Holy Spirit. For
this is a happy inebriation' *Paraphrasis in Ephesios* CWE 43 344.

5:19 [ER *per psalmos* 'through psalms']

[VG] *in psalmis* 'in psalms.' The 'in' is redundant, ψαλμοῖς.¹ Nor is it 'in
your hearts,' but 'in your heart.' But 'psalm' and 'hymn' are both Greek
words. The former means 'song,' the latter 'praise,' properly of God.²
[Paul] contrasted these with drunken songs.

1 'In' is found in some Greek manuscripts but not those used by Erasmus.
See Brown *Novum Testamentum* 535:19(2)n.

2 Ψαλμός is a loan-word from the Hebrew Old Testament that means 'song
of praise' (BDAG); the Greek word ὕμνος means a hymn sung in honour of
a divinity.

5:21 [ER *cum timore dei* 'with the fear of God']

[VG] *in timore Christi* 'in¹ the fear of Christ.' I have now frequently
mentioned that *in timore* 'in fear' has the same meaning as though he
had said 'through fear.'² Jerome thinks this phrase can be understood as
if it were the proposed genus, which is then divided into its individual
species, namely, wives be submissive to husbands, slaves to masters,
children to parents.³

1 'in ... parents.] This annotation was added in *1522*.

2 Eg Brown *Novum Testamentum* 28:17(1) on Rom 1:17

3 Jerome *Comm in Eph* 3 (on 5:21) PL 26 (1884) 563C–D

5:22 [ER *subditae sitis* 'submit yourselves']

[VG] *subditae sint* 'let [the women] be submissive.' Be submissive, ὑπο-
τάσσεσθε 'submit yourselves.'¹ Jerome² says that this phrase 'let be submissive' is not added in the Greek manuscripts but the words depend
grammatically upon the preceding item, 'being subject to one another
in fear' [Eph 5:21]. Namely, 'women submissive to men,' etc. Be that as
it may, the verb is found today in the Greek manuscripts, added as it
appears to make the sense clearer and to read the clause independently
as the case requires.

1 Erasmus' Greek manuscripts have the second person plural middle
imperative. Other Greek manuscripts, with the Vulgate, have the third
person plural imperative. See Brown *Novum Testamentum* 536–7:22(2)n.

2 Jerome ... requires.] Added in *1522*. See Jerome *Comm in Eph* 3 (on 5:22–3)
PL 26 (1884) 564A.

5:23 [ER *qui salutem dat corpori* 'who gives salvation to the body']
[VG] *ipse salvator corporis* 'he is the saviour of the body'; καὶ αὐτός
ἐστιν, that is, 'and he himself is the saviour of the body.'[1] The pronoun
'his' is not added in the Greek nor[2] in Ambrose[3] nor in Jerome.[4]

1 For Erasmus' Greek text see Brown *Novum Testamentum* 537:23(8)n.
2 nor ... Jerome] Added in *1519*
3 Ambrosiaster *Comm in Eph* 5:23
4 Jerome *Comm in Eph* 3 (on 5:22–3) PL 26 (1884) 564C

5:26 [ER *per verbum* 'through the word']
[VG] *in verbo vitae* 'in the word of life.' 'Life' is not added in the Greek
nor in Ambrose or Jerome.[1]

1 *vitae* 'of life' is not found in any Greek manuscript, nor in Ambrosiaster
Comm in Eph 5:23 or Jerome *Comm in Eph* 3 (on 5:22–3) PL 26 (1884) 564C.
It appears to be an addition that was made late in the transmission of the
Vulgate, probably in the Carolingian period.

5:27 [ER *ut adhiberet* 'that he might bring forth']
[VG] *ut exhiberet* 'that he might present'; ἵνα παραστήσῃ αὐτὴν ἑαυτῷ, that
is, 'that he might join her to himself.' And 'glorious,' ἔνδοξον, is immediately added, then τὴν ἐκκλησίαν, that is, 'namely the church.'

5:27 [ER *sancta et irreprehensibilis* 'holy and blameless']
[VG] *sancta et immaculata* 'holy and without blemish'; καὶ ἄμωμος, that
is, 'blameless.' However,[1] I do not condemn 'without blemish.'

1 However ... blemish.'] Added in *1522*. Erasmus' translation 'blameless'
was criticized by Zúñiga; see *Apologia ad annotationes Stunicae* ASD IX-2
202, which perhaps prompted the addition in *1522*. Erasmus' translation
is, however, closer to the meaning of the Greek word than the Vulgate's
'without blemish.'

5:28 [ER *sic ... viri* 'so ... men']
[VG] *ita et viri* 'so also men.' The 'also' is redundant.

5:28 [ER *ut sua ipsorum corpora* 'as their very own bodies']
[VG] *ut corpora sua* 'as their own bodies'; ὡς τὰ ἑαυτῶν σώματα, that is,
'as their very own bodies.'[1]

1 The Vulgate *ut corpora sua* reflects the Greek text of some manuscripts; see
Brown *Novum Testamentum* 539:28(4)n.

5:30 [ER *corporis eiusdem* 'of *his* body']

[VG] *corporis eius* 'of his body.' It is also possible to read *eiusdem* emphatic '*his*' for *eius* 'his,' αὐτοῦ.[1]

> 1 Compare the use of *idem* 'the same' in Eph 5:23 above.

5:31 [ER *huius rei gratia relinquet* 'for this reason (a man) will leave']

[VG] *propter hoc relinquet* 'on account of this [a man] will leave'; ἀντὶ τούτου, that is, 'for this' or 'in place of that.' St Jerome also observed that ἀντὶ τούτου 'for this' was said by Paul for ἕνεκεν τούτου 'for this reason,'[1] which pretty much means as if one were to say 'in place of father and in place of mother.' [Paul] took this testimony from Genesis, chapter 2[:24] but in his own fashion plucking what seemed appropriate to the present passage. For omitting the pronoun 'his' twice he put only 'father and mother.' Then he passed over the middle,[2] 'and will cleave to his wife,' and attaches what follows, 'and they will be two into one flesh,'[3] because this is more effective than 'to cleave,' namely that one person is made from two.

> 1 Jerome *Comm in Eph* 3 (on 5:31) PL 26 (1884) 568B–C
> 2 This statement is puzzling since the clause is in Erasmus' Greek text and in his translation.
> 3 In the editions from 1516 to 1527, the passage read *et erunt duo in carne una* 'and there will be two in one flesh,' before being changed to *carnem unam* 'into one flesh.'

5:31 [ER *et adiungetur* 'and will be joined']

[VG] *et adhaerebit* 'and will cleave'; καὶ προσκολληθήσεται, that is, 'will be fastened,'[1] a word[2] which does not lack an emphasis. And it is not the dative case, but a prepositional phrase 'to his wife.'[3]

> 1 Cf LSJ s.v. προσκολλάω: 'glue on or to'; passive, 'to be stuck to, stick, or cleave to.'
> 2 a word ... emphasis] Added in 1527
> 3 For the variant readings in the Greek text see Brown *Novum Testamentum* 540:31(2)n and Lincoln *Ephesians* 351–2.

5:31 [ER *una caro* 'one flesh']

[VG] *in carne una* 'in one flesh'; εἰς σάρκα μίαν, that is, 'into one flesh,' which means 'one human will be made from two,' in keeping with a special feature of the Hebrew language which sometimes calls the whole human being 'flesh,' sometimes humans themselves 'souls.'[1] In the same way you will often find in Greek δέμας [body] put for the person.[2] But I have talked about this elsewhere and[3] likewise about the figure of speech by which those who are one flesh are said to be into one flesh.

1 In his annotation on Matt 19:5 (*et dixit: propter hoc dimittit homo*) Erasmus
notes that the whole man is sometimes referred to as 'flesh' or 'soul.' He
ascribes this feature to Hebraism also in his annotation on Matt 24:22 (*nec
est fieret salva*).

2 δέμας is frequently used by poets and tragedians to represent the whole
person (ASD VI-9 255:380–1n).

3 and ... into one flesh] Added in 1522
For Erasmus' defence against Lee's objection that he did not follow
Jerome's *in una carne* see *Responsio ad annotationes Lei* 1 CWE 72 119.

5:32 [ER *mysterium hoc* 'this mystery']

[VG] *sacramentum hoc* 'this **sacrament'**; μυστήριον, that is, 'mystery.'[1]
I wanted this fact to be known to those who use this passage to make
matrimony one of the seven[2] sacraments according[3] to a special and ex-
act meaning of this word.[4] That matrimony is a sacrament should not be
doubted because[5] it is likely that this tradition has reached down to us
continually from the apostles or at least the holy fathers though[6] this was
doubted in the past by orthodox scholastics; indeed a different opinion
met approval. For the objections of some are that no mention of matrimony was made by Dionysius who set out to discuss the sacraments of
the church with careful interpretations of their individual rites and ceremonies;[7] secondly, that nowhere was matrimony called a sacrament in
the many books in which Jerome disputes about matrimony,[8] nor was
the name 'sacrament' given to matrimony even by Augustine[9] who was
quite close to Jerome in this position and even wrote about the good of
marriage, and that even more strange than these no mention was ever
made of the term 'sacrament' in the works of Jovinian who was the cham-
pion of matrimony. For if it had been made, this passage ought to have
been touched on by Jerome in his refutation of that one's books especially
since he does this so meticulously. And Jovinian above all had need of
this weapon when he makes marriage equal to celibacy. For it could be
argued that if matrimony is a sacrament and virginity is not, the high status of matrimony wins hands down.[10] These and such arguments, I say,
are easily taken apart by the learned. I would not have said these things
as though I were calling into doubt whether matrimony is a sacrament,
whose[11] high status I greatly favour, but because it[12] does not seem that an
effective inference can be made from these words of the Apostle. But the
adversative especially, 'but I,' sufficiently indicates that this great mystery pertains to Christ and the church, not to a husband and wife.[13] For
a sacrament is not great in the fact that a man is joined to a wife which is
customarily done even among pagans. St Augustine[14] means this, if I am
not mistaken, in his explication of Psalm 118 when he says, 'Two will be
in one flesh, which great sacrament Paul expounds when he says, "I mean

in Christ and in the church."' However, he clearly explains in his book to
Valerius about marriage where he says, 'The Apostle said this great sacrament in Christ and in the church. Therefore, what is great in Christ and in
the church is a very small thing in individual men of any kind and their
wives, but nevertheless a sacrament of inseparable union.'[15] Paul used a
stylistic effect in the first Epistle to the Corinthians [10:29]: 'On account
of the conscience,' then to exclude any mistake, he adds, 'Conscience, I
say, not yours but the other's.'[16] Then, as I had begun to say, the Greek
word in this passage does not mean 'sacrament' such as the church calls
the seven sacraments, but something hidden and secret. Paul uses this
word often and about topics which are far away from the nature of the
sacraments. Writing to the Thessalonians he speaks of 'the mystery of
iniquity.'[17] Again[18] in First Corinthians 13[:2] where we read 'And if ... I
should know all mysteries.' Augustine in the [epistle] *To Valentinus about
Grace and Free Will* reads, 'And if I shall know all sacraments,' as if there
is no difference between mystery and sacrament.[19] The ancients called an
oath or a religious obligation a sacrament, because I believe these were
carried out with certain secret ceremonies. And[20] this place was the object
of two attacks. I have answered one of them, the other treated the subject
in such a way that he does not deserve any response.[21] For I do not deny
that matrimony is a sacrament, but I want the question explored whether
from the present passage it can be taught that it is properly be called a
sacrament as baptism is called a sacrament.

1 In translating μυστήριον as *mysterium* Erasmus is following Lefèvre *Pauli
 epistolae* fol 39 verso. As H.J. de Jonge points out, the translation *mysterium* occurred in the Italian branch of the Old Latin translation, and was
 cited by Ambrosiaster and Jerome, among others (ASD IX-2 211:772n).
2 seven] Added in *1519*
3 according ... word] Added in *1522*
4 In medieval theology Ephesians 5:32 was an important proof text for
 the sacramental status of marriage, which had been confirmed at the
 Council of Florence in 1439. Erasmus, as early as 1514 when he wrote the
 Christiani hominis institutum (*Carmina* CWE 85 96–7), held that marriage
 was a divine sacrament. See also Erasmus' treatise on marriage, *Christiani
 matrimonii institutio* (1526 ASD V-6 68:217–70:243). In this note, however,
 Erasmus' point is to show that the sacramental view of marriage, though
 correct, cannot be founded upon the use of μυστήριον in this text, because
 it is applied to the relationship between Christ and the church. See further
 John B. Payne *Erasmus, His Theology of the Sacraments* (Richmond 1971)
 109–25; and H. Pabel 'Exegesis and Marriage in Erasmus' Paraphrases' in
 Holy Scripture Speaks ed H. Pabel and M. Vessey (Toronto 2002) 177–9.
5 because ... whether matrimony is a sacrament] Added in *1519*. Erasmus
 composed this lengthy addition in response to the criticism by Edward
 Lee (fols LXVII verso – LXIX verso). Erasmus further defended himself at
 length in his *Responsio ad annotationes Lei* 2 CWE 72 296–303.

6 though ... approval] Added in *1522*

7 See the annotation on 1 Cor 7:39 (*liberata est a lege, cui autem vult, nubat*).

8 Eg Jerome *Adversus Jovinianum* PL 23 (1845) 221–96

9 Augustine *De bono coniugali* 24 PL 40 394

10 hands down] Added in *1535*. This is an allusion to *Adagia* I v 60, which refers to obtaining everyone's votes (*omnium calculis*). Therefore, the high status of matrimony is uncontested.

11 whose ... favour] Added in *1522*

12 it ... the apostle] In *1516*, this passage read *hoc loco non magnopere colligatur* 'from this place it is not especially inferred.'

13 For a modern argument to this effect see Lincoln *Ephesians* 382–3.

14 Saint Augustine ... mystery of iniquity.'] Added in *1519*. See Augustine *Enarrationes in Psalmos* sermo 29.9 CCL 40 1767:30–2.

15 Augustine *De nuptiis et concupiscentia* 1.21.23 PL 44 427

16 The word here translated by 'style' is *color*, 'the partisan nuance of the true state of affairs' (Lausberg §1061).

17 See 2 Thess 2:7.

18 Again ... ceremonies.] Added in *1527*

19 Augustine, *De gratia et libero arbitrio* 17.34 PL 44 902

20 And ... sacrament.] Added in *1522*

21 The two critics are presumably Edward Lee and Diego López Zúñiga. See *Responsio ad annotationes Lei* 2 CWE 72 296–303; *Apologia ad annotationes Stunicae* ASD IX-2 210–12. Sancho Carranza de Miranda (d 1531), professor of theology at Alcalá, defended Zúñiga's criticism of the translation of μυστήριον as 'mystery' in his *Opusculum in quasdam Erasmi Roterodami annotationes* (1522); Erasmus responded in his *Apologia ad Caranzam* (1522). For a discussion of their relationship see Erika Rummel *Erasmus and his Catholic Critics* (Nieuwkoop 1989) 156–8, and Alejandro Coroleu 'Anti-Erasmianism in Spain' in *Biblical Humanism and Scholasticism in the Age of Erasmus* ed E. Rummel (Leiden 2008) 73–92.

5:32 [ER *de Christo* 'about Christ']

[VG] *in Christo* 'in Christ.' [The Greek is] 'unto Christ and unto the church.' I am well aware that in Greek the accusative case sometimes has the same force as the dative. It can, however, mean here 'about Christ and about the church.' For [the preposition 'unto'] is used in this sense by the Greeks in titles, εἰς Ἑρμῆν 'About Hermes,' and εἰς Ἀπόλλωνα 'About Apollo.'[1]

1 About Apollo.'] Added in *1522*

5:33 [ER *quanquam et vos singulatim hoc praestate ut suam quisque uxorem diligat tanquam se ipsum* 'and yet you individually do this: that each love his own wife as himself']

[VG] *et vos singuli unusquisque suam uxorem sicut seipsum diligat* 'let[1] every one of you in particular love his wife as himself.' This kind of speech does not agree with the rules of grammar either in Greek or in

Latin. However, it would not be difficult to heal this inconvenience as follows: 'And yet you too individually do this: that each loves his wife as himself.'[2]

1 'let ... himself.'] This annotation was added in 1519. As at Rom 12:5 and 1 Cor 14:31, so too here Erasmus replaces the adjective *singuli* (for καθ'εἷς) with the adverb *singulatim* 'singly, individually.'

2 Erasmus is uncomfortable with the shift from the plural subject *vos* to the singular in *diligat* here; he expands the translation so as to produce a dependent substantive clause introduced by *praestate ut* 'do this: that.' See also Brown *Novum Testamentum* 541:33(3)n.

5:33 [ER *uxor autem ut revereatur* 'and the wife that she reverence']
[VG] *uxor autem timeat* 'and let the wife fear.' The Greek is 'that she fear,' ἵνα φοβῆται, that is, 'that she reverence.' For St Jerome thinks the verb φοβεῖσθαι 'to fear' can be understood in this [latter] way.[1]

1 Jerome *Comm in Eph* 3 (on 5:33) PL 26 (1884) 570D–571A. Evidently Erasmus prefers the gentler *revereor* 'to regard, respect, honour' (L&s) to *timeo* 'to fear, be afraid of, apprehend, dread' (L&s).

From the Sixth Chapter

6:1 [ER VG] *in domino* 'in[1] the Lord.' This phrase is not added in Ambrose or in the commentaries, quite possibly [it was] omitted accidentally.[2] Jerome[3] points to a two-fold distinction. For this phrase, 'in the Lord,' can be referred either to the verb 'obey' or to the noun 'parents.' For parents in the Lord are those who beget us for Christ with holy teaching. Those who obey their parents out of love for Christ are obeying them in the Lord, so long as the parents do not teach things that are unholy. Those who obey teachers of this latter sort do not obey in the Lord. The prior distinction to which Jerome refers would be more likely if the article had been added, γονεῦσι τοῖς ἐν κυρίῳ 'parents, those in the Lord.'[4] But that would then exclude the natural parents about whom Paul is certainly speaking here.

1 'in ... accidentally.] This annotation was added in 1522.

2 Some early manuscripts omit the words ἐν κυρίῳ; perhaps, as Metzger 541–2 observes, the words were deleted to forestall giving the impression of a restricted command.

3 Jerome ... speaking here.] Added in 1535. See Jerome *Comm in Eph* 3 (on 6:1) PL 26 (1884) 571A–B.

4 Erasmus means that the presence of the word 'those' would make the phrase 'in the Lord' directly modify 'parents.' For this 'particularizing' force of the article see Smyth 1119–20.

6:2 [ER *in promissione* 'with a promise']

[VG] *in repromissione*[1] 'with[2] a promise.' Some read 'first' and 'with a promise' in combination. It is not absolutely first because in the Decalogue the law about honouring parents occupies the fourth place, but 'first with a promise' because only to this [law] is a reward attached: 'that it may be well with you and you may be long-lived.' Jerome[3] does not altogether approve of this solution because a promise is attached to the second commandment too, 'showing mercy unto thousands' [Exod 20:6], and he subjoins another solution, that we understand the first commandment to be the entire Decalogue because this Law was the first one granted to the Hebrews after the departure from Egypt. Not even this explanation satisfied him because it would imply that the promise was attached to all the commandments. In fact, Paul attributes this [promise] to this commandment as though special to it. The argument brought up by more recent scholars is not much stronger:[4] that this is the first commandment of the second table. In the first table they are taught the things that look to the worship of God, and there are four of these; in the second table those matters [are taught] which pertain to neighbours, and in this arrangement the commandment about honouring one's parents occupies the first position. This distinction, however, is not based upon Sacred Scripture, but is the explanation of more recent theologians. In my opinion it could be said that the promise that was added to this commandment alone was not that general promise which is made frequently to those who keep God's commandments, but an appropriate and particular one. For it is fitting that one who is devoted to those from whom one received life will enjoy it gladly and for a long time. However, to the second commandment threats also are added, and the mercy which is promised pertains generally to all the precepts of the Law. The words of the Decalogue are as follows: 'I am the Lord, your God, a jealous God who visits the iniquity of the fathers upon the children, to the third and fourth generation of them that hate me, and showing mercy to thousands to them that love me and keep my commandments' [Exod 20:5]. This from the Decalogue. Here, moreover, the language is general, all 'who keep my commandments.' In the other commandment the promise is special and as if said for it alone, 'that it may be well for you.' Jerome also makes the following observation, that the Apostle omitted the final words of the testimony he cites from Exodus; for there the words are 'that you may be long-lived upon the land which the Lord God will give you' [Exod 20:12]. The Apostle deliberately passed over the last part of these words so that the Jews would not believe that they should hope for another land through the Messiah. For when Moses brought that law they had not yet reached the land flowing with milk and honey [Exod 3:8]. We see that Scripture everywhere nourishes the unformed people with earthly promises, of which the chief one was the promise of a very fertile land. Hence one can take the Apostle's statement here that this command-ment was 'the first with a promise' in this way, that not just any promise is understood, but that one by which the Jews were specially being led. Moreover, mention of this occurs for the first time in this command-ment. Nor is it necessary that with Jerome we take refuge in allegory. For Augustine teaches that temporal rewards for some good deeds are paid by God even to the ungodly, like devotion to parents, for example.[5] But if a happy long life in this world does not befall all who cultivate devotion to their parents, it is not at all necessary to comprehend ev-ery event without exception under the general proclamation. However, Paul did not say 'it will be well for you and you will be long-lived,' but 'that it may be well for you and you may be long-lived.' For God may be moved by such duties to give prosperity of material goods and life, but He is not obligated to do so. Chrysostom, and in agreement with him Theophylact,[6] indicate that 'first with a promise' was said for the reason that the other commandments in Exodus 20 only forbid evils, 'you will not worship strange gods, you will not take the name of your God in vain, you will not do work on the Sabbath, you will not kill, you will not commit adultery, you will not steal, you will not bear false witness against your neighbour, you will not covet property, not a wife' [20:3, 5], etc.[7] But he who abstains from acts that are forbidden, escapes penalty but does not deserve any reward. But when he says 'honour father and mother,' he is not forbidding evil action, but orders doing good; a reward is owed to this person. According to this explanation the command about honouring parents is not only first with a promise, but also the only one. They rightly observe that this alone suits adoles-cent children because that time of life compared to the others is eager to live long and pleasantly.

1 *repromissione* is the reading in Jerome and some manuscripts of the Vulgate. However, Erasmus and the 1527 Vulgate read *promissione* '[a simple] promise' whereas *repromissio* denotes a legal promise to do or un-dertake something. L&s defines *repromissio* as 'a counter-promise.' Weber (1814) reads *promissione*.
2 'with ... pleasantly.] This annotation was added in 1522, but thoroughly re-vised in 1535. The text in 1522 and 1527 read simply, 'Jerome intimates that this phrase was not commonly found in all manuscripts but was added in some in order to explain the question of how this commandment is here called the first when in Exodus it is the fifth. Although Jerome mentions such matters so many times, nevertheless, some people turn heaven and earth upside down, when I do something similar in one or two places.'

3 Jerome *Comm in Eph* 3 (on 6:1) PL 26 (1884) 571C–572A
4 Eg Thomas Aquinas *Super Eph lect* cap 6 lectio 1.339; ASD VI-9 261:457n refers to the *Glossa Ordinaria*, on which see the annotation on Gal 4:25 ('for it is joined to what is now Jerusalem') n9.
5 Augustine *Enarrationes in Psalmos* 79.14 CCL 39 1119:26–35
6 Theophylact *Expos in Eph* 6:1–2 PG 124 1121A–B
7 Chrysostom *Hom in Eph* 21.1 PG 62 149–50

6:3 [ER VG] *et sis longaevus* **'that you may be long-lived';** καὶ ἔσῃ, that is 'and you will be.' However, there is an ambiguity in this text. The verb[1] can be read as an independent clause or it can be governed by the 'that,' so that the conjunction 'that' denotes the result of the action, 'if you do this, you will be.'[2]

1 The verb can ... will be.'] Added in *1527*
2 See F. Blass and A. Debrunner *A Greek Grammar of the New Testament and Other Early Christian Literature* trans and rev (from the 9th – 10th German edition, incorporating supplementary notes of A. Debrunner) Robert W. Funk (Chicago and London 1961) §369 (2), on the combination of subjunctive and indicative.

6:4 [ER *patres* **'Fathers'**]
[VG] *et vos, patres* **'And you, fathers.'** The 'you' is redundant. In the Greek the 'you' is understood.[1]

1 For Erasmus' Latin text see Brown *Novum Testamentum* 541:4(1)n.

6:4 [ER *per eruditionem et correptionem* **'through instruction and correction'**]
[VG] *in disciplina et correptione* **'in the discipline and correction';** ἐν παιδείᾳ καὶ νουθεσίᾳ, that is, 'through learning,' or 'by training and admonition.'[1] For this word pleases St Jerome more[2] because it is gentler than 'correction' which is the word Ambrose used.[3] However,[4] I do not quite understand from where the word 'conversation' crept into the books first printed by my friend Froben.[5] The reading in them is 'in the discipline and the conversation of the Lord.' Both Greek words are ambivalent: παιδεία sometimes means 'instruction,' sometimes 'castigation.' It is derived from the word for child.[6] νουθεσία means 'admonition' and 'scolding' or 'correction.' It is said[7] from the fact that you put and introduce into someone's mind what he ought to do or[8] ought to have done.[9]

1 As in many other places, so too here Erasmus understands the Greek ἐν 'in' to have instrumental sense. See the annotation on Gal 1:6 ('into the grace of Christ') n10.
2 Jerome *Comm in Eph* 3 (on 6:4) PL 26 (1884) 574A. The 1527 Vulgate read *in disciplina et correctione*; the modern edition of the Vulgate reads *in disciplina et correptione* (Weber 1814). Erasmus' preference for *eruditio* to *disciplina* reflects his gentler approach to the rearing of children.

3 Ambrosiaster *Comm in Eph* 6:4
4 However ... of the Lord.'] Added in *1522*
5 Erasmus is referring to his 1516 edition of Jerome; see M. van Poll-van de
  Lisdonk ASD VI-9 263:507–9n.
6 According to LSJ παιδεία means 'rearing of a child; training, teaching.'
7 In *1516* the singular *dictum* was used. Later editions used *dicta*.
8 or ... done] Added in *1535*
9 Cf LSJ s.v. νουθετέω: 'put in mind; admonish, warn, rebuke.'

6:5 [ER *qui domini sunt iuxta carnem* 'who are your masters according
to the flesh']
[VG] *dominis carnalibus* 'your fleshly masters'; τοῖς κυρίοις κατὰ σάρκα,
that is, 'masters according to the flesh.'¹ But [the Translator] was right
to change this to avoid an ambiguity so that no one would make 'according to the flesh' modify 'to serve.'²

  1 Modern editions read τοῖς κατὰ σάρκα κυρίοις.
  2 'To serve' seems to be Erasmus' substitution for 'to obey.'

6:6 [ER VG] *non ad oculum servientes* 'not as serving to the eye.' The word
in Greek is a compound noun, μὴ κατ᾽ ὀφθαλμοδουλείαν,¹ as if one were to
say, 'not according to eye-service' if² someone is eager to translate word
for word.

  1 LSJ defines ὀφθαλμοδουλεία as 'eye-service.' In his apology against Lefèvre,
    Erasmus notes that his translation *ad oculum servitio* 'subjection to the
    eye' *Pauli epistolae* fol 39 verso, misses the force of 'according to' in κατά,
    Apologia ad Fabrum CWE 83 101.
  2 if ... word for word] Added in *1519*

6:6 [ER *velut hominibus placere studentes* 'as if eager to please men']
[VG] *hominibus placentes* 'pleasing men.' Here too it is a compound
word, ἀνθρωπάρεσκοι,¹ much pleasanter than the Latin circumlocution,
but the Translator could not find a word. It means as if one were to say
'man-pleasers,' those who are eager to win approval from men rather²
than from God.

  1 LSJ defines ἀνθρωπάρεσκος as 'man-pleaser.' As Brown notes (*Novum
    Testamentum* 543:6[2]n), Erasmus' translation conveys a sense of intent
    rather than effect.
  2 rather ... God] Added in *1519*

6:7 [ER *cum benevolentia* 'with benevolence']
[VG] *cum bona voluntate* 'with a good will'; μετ᾽ εὐνοίας, that is, 'with
benevolence.'¹ It is strange why the Translator thought this had to be
changed. I² am not wholly in agreement with Augustine's view, which

he infers from this statement, that slaves ought not to demand freedom from Christian masters because the law of Moses wanted all slaves to be set free every seventh year.[3] However, I do not deny that what he said is true. For Paul is here talking about pagan masters, not just Christian ones. For[4] he wishes the Christian slave to serve his master faithfully out of love for Christ, just as he wants Christian citizens to obey the commands of their idolatrous princes. Even if it is not right for slaves to demand that [Mosaic] liberty, still it seems unchristian for Christian masters not to grant to their slaves what the [Mosaic] Law, which is much harsher than the law of Christ, granted to theirs.[5] On the contrary, it seems a disgrace that among Christians the terms 'master' and 'slave' should even be heard. For since baptism makes everyone brothers, how is it fitting for a brother to be called 'slave' to a brother? Let[6] this much be granted to one to whom it seems to be a part of civil law, not just gospel law, according to which a slave obeys his master from the heart, the master in return treats the slave as a brother in Christ.[7]

1 *benevolentia* and *bona voluntas* are essentially synonymous, both mean 'good will.' But according to Brown *Novum Testamentum* 543:7(1)n, Erasmus uses *benevolentia* to translate Greek εὔνοια, human good will, and *bona voluntas* for Greek εὐδοκία, God's good will.
2 I ... to a brother?] Added in *1519*
3 Augustine *Enarrationes in Psalmos* 124.7 CCL 40 1840:1–1842:60
4 For ... princes.] Added in *1535*
5 The Mosaic law for the manumission of slaves occurs in Deut 15:12; slaves were to be manumitted every seventh year.
6 Let ... in Christ.] Added in *1527*
7 For the position of slaves in early Christian churches see Lincoln *Ephesians* 415–20. For a treatment of the household codes for the treatment of slaves in Eph 6:5–9 see J. Albert Harrill *Slaves in the New Testament: Literary, Social and Moral Dimensions* (Minneapolis 2006) 87–117.

6:7 [ER *servientes domino* 'serving the Lord']
[VG] *servientes sicut domino* 'serving as to the Lord.' The adverb 'as' is redundant and is not added by Ambrose.[1] For[2] [Paul] means that this service which is given to ungodly or capricious masters is given not to men but to Christ for the love of whom the slave[3] endures the tyranny of a human lest he impose some trifling offence on the gospel. The[4] ὡς [as] is added in Chrysostom, but it is not at all clear from his commentary what he read.[5] Theophylact's comment suggests rather that the ὡς was not added;[6] otherwise it would have been necessary to say 'serving as to the Lord and not as to men.' We are said to serve the one from whom we expect a reward, and, therefore, the Apostle shortly adds, 'each person will receive from the Lord the good he has done.'

1 For the Greek text see Brown's note *Novum Testamentum* 543:7(2)n.
2 For ... the gospel.] Added in *1527*
3 slave] Added in *1535*
4 The ... he has done.'] Added in *1535*
5 Chrysostom *Hom in Eph* 22.1 PG 62 156
6 Theophylact *Expos in Eph* 6:7 PG 124 1125A

6:9 [ER VG] *remittentes minas* **'forbearing threats'**; ἀνιέντες τὴν ἀπειλήν, that is, 'relaxing threats,' which means being less brutal and less given to threatening. For he wants them to be less domineering than[1] pagan masters are to their slaves.

1 than ... to their slaves] Added in *1527*

6:9 [ER *scientes quod et vester ipsorum dominus est* **'knowing that even your own master is'**]
[VG] *quia et illorum et vester dominus* **'that the Lord of both them and you is'**; εἰδότες ὅτι καὶ ὑμῶν αὐτῶν ὁ κύριός ἐστιν ἐν οὐρανοῖς, that is, 'knowing that your very own master is in heaven' so[1] that the sense is 'because you know that you also have a master in heaven whom you ought to fear.' Ambrose[2] and Jerome[3] seem to have read ὑμῶν τε καὶ αὐτῶν, that is, 'your as well as their,' so that one understands that both have the same master.[4]

1 so ... to fear'] Added in *1519*
2 Ambrosiaster *Comm in Eph* 6:9
3 Jerome *Comm in Eph* 3 (on 6:9) PL 26 (1884) 576B
4 For the variants in the Greek text see the note in ASD VI-3 343-44. Modern editions read ὅτι καὶ αὐτῶν καὶ ὑμῶν ὁ κύριός.

6:10 [ER *fratres mei* **'my brothers'**]
[VG] *fratres* **'brothers.'** The pronoun 'my' is added in the Greek, ἀδελφοί μου. However, neither Ambrose nor Jerome adds 'brothers.' He would have translated τὸ λοιπόν [finally] better by 'what remains.'[1]

1 The Vulgate reads *De caetero* 'About the rest.' For Erasmus' treatment of the Greek phrase see ASD VI-3 210, on 1 Cor 4:2, and the annotation on Gal 6:17 ('concerning the other matter').

6:11 [ER *induite totam armaturam dei* **'Put on the full armour of God'**]
[VG] *induite vos armaturam dei* **'Put you on the armour of God'**; πα-νοπλίαν [panoply]. This one word denotes whatever pertains to arming a soldier for battle, as if one were to say all the arms which pertain to man. Hence a little further on St Jerome[1] observes that it ought not to have been translated by the word 'arms' which the Greeks call ὅπλα,

but by 'the complete arms' πανοπλία.[2] Ambrose reads 'totality of arms.'[3]
Cyprian[4] somewhere translates 'complete weaponry.'

1 Jerome *Comm in Eph* 3 (on 6:11) PL 26 (1884) 576D–577A. This passage is
not completely relevant. Perhaps Erasmus was referring to Jerome *Comm
in Eph* 3 (on 6:13) PL 26 (1884) 583A–B and 583D.
2 LSJ defines πανοπλία as a 'suit of armour,' and thus it includes all pieces
of armour and weapons. Cf BDAG 'the complete equipment of a heavy-
armed soldier.' For a fuller discussion of the spiritual armour see
Enchiridion CWE 66 30–46.
3 Ambrosiaster *Comm in Eph* 6:13
4 Cyprian ... weaponry.'] Added in 1527. See Cyprian *Epistulae* 58.8 CCL 3C
331:199.

6:11 [ER *adversus assultus* 'against the assaults']
[VG] *adversus insidias* 'against the ambushes'; μεθοδείας, the same
word which he had earlier translated by 'craftiness.'[1] Ambrose reads
'against the nations,'[2] but I think the manuscript has been corrupted.
Perhaps[3] *rationes* [methods] had been written, for μέθοδος [method][4] is
a *ratio* [method], but of attacking something. It is μεθοδεία [deception]
if someone attacks another from ambush. Jerome reads and interprets[5]
'against the schemes of the devil,'[6] although here he could have translated 'slanderer' for 'devil.'[7]

1 See Eph 4:14. *Assultus* means 'a leaping towards, attack, charge' (L&S).
Weber 1814 maintains the Vulgate *insidias*; cf also modern English translations of μεθοδεία here: 'devices' (NEB), 'wiles' (RSV).
2 Ambrosiaster *Comm in Eph* 6:11. On the textual variants in Ambrosiaster
see M. van Poll-van de Lisdonk ASD VI-9 267:562n, who notes that some
codices read <*machi*> *nationes*.
3 Perhaps ... something.] Added in 1522
4 LSJ defines μέθοδος as 'a following after, pursuit; trick, ruse,' and μεθοδεία
as 'craft, wiliness.'
5 and interprets] Added in 1522
6 Jerome *Comm in Eph* 3 (on 6:11) PL 26 (1884) 577A and 577D
7 LSJ defines διάβολος as 'slanderer' or 'enemy,' and hence 'Satan' (cf eg 2
Tim 3:3, Titus 2:3). Erasmus suggests that Jerome could have translated
the Greek more precisely by *calumniator* ('a false or vexatious accuser,'
OLD).

6:12 [ER *lucta* 'wrestling']
[VG] *colluctatio* 'wrestling'; ἡ πάλη, that is 'wrestling.'[1]

1 Erasmus may have preferred the simple form *lucta* to the compound *colluctatio* as being closer to the Greek word (thus ASD VI-3 545). *Lucta* was
also the rendering by Lefèvre *Pauli epistolae* fol 39 verso.

6:12 [ER *mundi dominos* 'the world's masters']

[VG] *mundi rectores* 'the rulers of the world'; κοσμοκράτορας, that is, 'masters of the world.' Jerome thinks that this word, obviously new and never found elsewhere, was first invented by Paul in order that he might accommodate new words to the explanation of new realities.[1] The Greek[2] word is a compound noun and for this reason the genitive 'this darkness' combines with it more readily. Tertullian[3] in the fifth book of his *Against Marcion* translates κοσμοκράτορας by *munditenentes* 'holders of the world'; Hilary on the Psalms translates *mundipotentes* 'world powers,' a quite elegantly fashioned compound word.[4]

> 1 Jerome *Comm in Eph* 3 (on 6:12) PL 26 (1884) 582A. This is not completely correct, as the word κοσμοκράτωρ occurred previously in classical literature (ASD VI-9 267:569n).
> 2 The Greek ... more readily.] Added in *1519*
> 3 Tertullian ... compound word.] Added in *1527*. See Tertullian *Adversus Marcionem* 5.18.12 CCL 1 720:1.
> 4 Hilary of Poitiers *Tractatus super Psalmos* 59.14 CCL 61 191:14. For Hilary see the annotation on Gal 6:11 ('with what letters').
> Lefèvre *Pauli epistolae* fol 39 verso transliterated the Greek as *cosmocratoras*.

6:12 [ER *tenebrarum seculi huius* 'of the darkness of this world']

[VG] *tenebrarum harum* 'of this darkness.' The Greek is τοῦ σκότους τοῦ αἰῶνος, that is, 'of the darkness of this world.'[1]

> 1 For the variants in the Greek text see Brown's note in *Novum Testamentum* 545–6:12(6). Modern editions leave out τοῦ αἰῶνος 'of this world.'

6:12 [ER *adversus spirituales astutias in caelestibus* 'against the spiritual schemings in the heavenly places']

[VG] *contra spiritualia nequitiae in caelestibus* 'against[1] the spirits of wickedness in the heavenly places.' Lefèvre observes that 'in the heavenly places' can be taken to mean 'against the celestial beings.'[2] In my own judgment the rationale of the Greek language in no way allows this. Now that he sternly rages against superstitious astrologers and prognosticators there, though we grant that this was not done without reason, it was certainly not done in the appropriate place.[3] Moreover, he said that 'spirits of wickedness' was said for 'spiritual wickednesses' or better 'schemings,' for the Greek is πονηρίας.[4] Ambrose in the twelfth chapter of *On Paradise* inverts the text so that he illustrates the sense, 'against the wickedness of the spirits which are in celestial places.'[5]

> 1 'against ... places.'] This entire annotation was added in *1519*. L&S defines *astutia* as 'cunning, slyness, subtlety, craft.'

2 Lefèvre *Pauli epistolae* fol 39 verso (translation); fol 173 recto (commentary). Erasmus does, however, adopt Lefèvre's rendering *adversus* ('against') and consequently altered the genitive singular *nequitiae* into accusative plural *astutias*.

3 In his response to the criticism of Lefèvre, Erasmus points out that the Greek 'in the heavenly places' cannot be read to mean 'against those dwelling in heaven' (*Apologia ad Fabrum* CWE 83 100–1).

4 'Schemings' is Erasmus' word, not Lefèvre's. But Erasmus is off the mark here. Πονηρία, like Latin *nequitia*, means in moral terms 'wickedness'; in the plural, however, it can mean 'wicked schemes or tricks.'

5 Ambrose *De paradiso* 12.55 CSEL 32/1 313:10–11

6:13 [ER *et omnibus peractis stare* 'and having done all to stand']
[VG] *et in omnibus perfecti stare* 'to stand in all things perfect.' The Greeks read as follows, καὶ ἅπαντα κατεργασάμενοι στῆναι, that is, 'after everything has been done or perfected to stand,' which means 'to stand after you have completed everything.' Jerome reads and explicates 'having worked all things to stand.'[1] Cyprian[2] likewise in the sixth Epistle of the fourth book: 'So that,' he says, 'when you have completed everything, gird your loins and stand,' etc. As the soldier does everything to resist the enemy and to protect his own life, so we who shall struggle constantly with spirits must do everything. Now[3] as I judge that it is not much trouble to have pointed out these particular things, so I do not think it is safe either to be ignorant of or to neglect these little details. For if a theologian philosophizes here to me in a verbose and elaborate speech about those who stand perfectly or those who stand imperfectly, will he not rouse a laugh in those who know Greek, and not at all wrongly? Chrysostom[4] observes that it is not the simplex verb ἐργασάμενοι, that is, 'after you have done,' but κατεργασάμενοι, that is, 'after you have perfected everything.' The Apostle continues with his metaphor[5] from war. The fortifications of soldiers are numerous: to surround with a moat, to raise up a rampart, to fortify the camp with palisades, to get their weapons ready, to hold off the enemy. When all these things are actively completed, it remains to stand ever prepared for battle. For victory brings to many carefree leisure; with a change of fortune carefree leisure turns the victors into the vanquished. The Apostle shows what he meant by military vigilance in what shortly follows: 'Stand, therefore, having your loins girt' etc. Thomas interprets 'all things' to mean in prosperity and in adversity, and from the mention of the word 'perfect' he makes a twofold perfection, one according to the journey of the pilgrim, the other according to the fullness of the homeland.[6] I admit that these things are correctly said, but they are hardly in place here. I suspect that

the Latin manuscripts have been corrupted here and that the Translator had translated, 'so that with everything perfected you can stand.' For I do not think that he read κατειργασμένοι [to have completed].[7]

1 Jerome *Comm in Eph* 3 (on 6:13) PL 26 (1884) 583A–B
2 Cyprian ... stand,' etc.] Added in *1519*. See Cyprian *Epistulae* 58.8 CCL 3C 331:200.
3 Now ... wrongly?] Added in *1519*
4 Chrysostom ... κατειργασμένοι.] Added in *1535*. See Chrysostom *Hom in Eph* 22.3 PG 62 159.
5 For metaphor see the annotation on Gal 4:24 ('through allegory spoken') n6.
6 Ie heaven. So the pilgrim or wayfarer is the person en route to heaven. Thomas Aquinas *Super Eph lect* cap 6 lectio 4.360.
7 For the text of the Vulgate see Brown's note *Novum Testamentum* 546:13(5)n.

6:14 [ER *state igitur lumbis circumcinctis baltheo* 'stand therefore, having your loins girt with the belt']
[VG] *state ergo succincti* 'stand therefore having girt'; περιζωσάμενοι, that is, 'having girt up' or 'having girt around,' that is, 'protected.'[1] For in warfare this part of the body is generally protected by a belt covered with metal plates, and the Apostle is alluding to it now.[2] In his commentary on this passage St Jerome[3] recalls the leather belt with which it is said John the Baptist was girdled [Matt 3:4], and then he mentions the spiritual belt. Compare the adage taken from military life, 'He has lost his money-belt.'[4] Feet and shins are armoured for battle although the lawyers deny that boots are included in the word 'arms.' Ambrose points to a two-fold use of girdle, one whereby it draws up clothing to free a man for action, and another whereby it protects the belly's tender parts.[5] It seemed a good idea to add this because I gather the term 'waist-band' meets with more approval from the learned than does 'belt.'[6]

1 According to L&S *circumcingo* means 'to enclose around, surround,' while *succingo* (in the Vulgate) means 'to gird below or from below.' In choosing the verb with the prefix *circum* 'around,' Erasmus wished to preserve the force in the Greek περί 'around.' Erasmus' *lumbis* 'loins' (ablative of respect) renders the Greek ὀσφῦν (accusative), which does not recur in the Latin of the Vulgate. The modern Vulgate reads *state ergo succincti lumbos vestros* ('stand, therefore, having girded your loins').
2 For a fuller description of the spiritual arming see Erasmus' paraphrase on this verse, *Paraphrasis in Ephesios* CWE 43 353. The image of *militia Christi* was the basis for Erasmus' *Enchiridion*, and in it he alludes to Eph 6:10–20; see CWE 66 30, 37.
3 St Jerome ... 'belt.'] Added in *1535*. See Jerome *Comm in Eph* 3 (on 6:14) PL 26 (1884) 584C–D.
4 See *Adagia* I v 16.
5 It is not known to which Ambrose Erasmus is referring (ASD VI-9 271:613–15n).

6 M. Van Poll-van de Lisdonk ASD VI-9 271:612–26n suggests Erasmus
   may be referring to Lazare de Baïf, whose treatise, *On Matters of Clothing*
   (1526), he had consulted for the *Adagia*. On de Baïf see *Contemporaries* II
   87–8.

6:16 [ER *iacula mali illius* 'the darts of the evil one']
[VG] *tela nequissimi* 'the missiles of the most wicked one'; βέλη τοῦ
πονηροῦ, 'the missiles of the evil one' or 'that[1] wicked one.'

   1 'that] Added in 1527. Presumably Erasmus preferred *iacula* (cognate with
      iacio 'to hurl') to *tela* because he derived βέλος from βάλλω 'to throw.'

6:17 [ER *galeamque salutaris* 'and the helmet of salvation']
[VG] *galeam salutis* 'the helmet of salvation'; τοῦ σωτηρίου, that is, *salutaris* 'of salvation.'[1] This[2] is Jerome's reading in his commentary. And
the verb is not 'take up' but 'take' δέξασθε[3] [receive].

   1 Erasmus replaced the feminine noun *salus* (L&S 'a sound and whole
      condition') with the neuter *salutare* (L&S 'welfare, prosperity'), perhaps to
      reflect the neuter noun σωτήριον.
   2 This ... commentary.] Added in 1522. See Jerome *Comm in Eph* 3 (on 6:17)
      PL 26 (1884) 586B.
   3 δέξασθε] Added in 1522

6:18 [ER *et ad hoc ipsum vigilantes* 'and watching thereunto']
[VG] *et in ipso vigilantes* 'and in the same watching'; καὶ εἰς αὐτὸ τοῦτο,
that is, 'and watching to this very end,' as[1] Ambrose reads. It is unclear
in the Greek whether this phrase refers to the spirit or to the subject-
matter because[2] in Greek πνεῦμα [spirit] is a neuter gender.

   1 as ... reads] Added in 1522. See Ambrosiaster *Comm in Eph* 6:18.
   2 because ... gender] Added in 1535

6:18 [ER *cum omni sedulitate* 'with all diligence']
[VG] *in omni instantia* 'in all instance'; ἐν πάσῃ προσκαρτερήσει. On this
see above.[1] Ambrose reads 'perseverance.'[2]

   1 See the annotation on Rom 13:6 ('serving to this very end') CWE 56
      352. L&S renders *sedulitas* as 'assiduity, application, zeal, earnestness.'
      According to LSJ προσκαρτέρησις means 'perseverance, patience.'
   2 Ambrosiaster *Comm in Eph* 6:18

6:19 [ER *cum libertate* 'with freedom']
[VG] *cum fiducia* 'with confidence'; ἐν παρρησίᾳ.[1] Strictly speaking, this is
freedom and boldness of speech, which[2] Ambrose translates 'openly.'[3]

   1 LSJ defines παρρησία as 'outspokenness; frankness' and 'freedom of speech.'

2 which ... 'openly'] Added in 1522
3 Ambrosiaster *Comm in Eph* 6:19

6:19 [ER *ut notum faciam* 'that I may make known']
[VG] *notum facere* 'to make known.' Why not, 'that I may make known'?

6:20 [ER *in catena* 'in chains']
[VG] *in catena ista* 'in these chains.' 'These' is redundant. It is neither in Ambrose nor in Jerome,[1] and[2] not even in the very old manuscripts, namely those of St Paul's and St Donatian's[3] with[4] the support of the two manuscripts from Constance.

1 Jerome *Comm in Eph* 3 (on 6:20) PL 26 (1884) 587A
2 and ... St Paul's] Added in 1519. For a description of the manuscripts of St Paul's, to which Erasmus had access for the second edition, see the annotation on Gal 2:2 ('who seemed something') n14.
3 and St Donatian's] Added in 1522. For the manuscript of St Donatian see the annotation on Gal 3:1 ('in front of the eyes of whom') n16.
4 with ... from Constance.] Added in 1527. For more information on the manuscripts from Constance see the annotation on Gal 1:3 ('from God our Father') n3 and CWE 56 xii.

6:20 [ER *ut in eo libere loquar* 'that therein I may speak freely']
[VG] *in ipso audeam* 'therein I may be bold'; ἵνα παρρησιάσωμαι [that I may be bold and open]. In explaining this verb Ambrose says, 'that therein I may talk with open freedom as I ought to speak.'[1] But it is not *ita* [therefore], but *ut* [in order that], ἵνα παρρησιάσωμαι, that is, 'that I may be bold.'

1 Ambrosiaster *Comm in Eph* 6:20. Cf BDAG s.v. παρρησιάζομαι 1: 'express oneself freely, speak freely, openly, fearlessly.' Modern English translations have 'that I may declare it boldly' (RSV), 'and may boldly and freely make known' (NEB).

6:21 [ER *dilectus frater* 'a beloved brother']
[VG] *charissimus frater noster* 'our dearest brother'; ἀγαπητός, that is 'beloved,' which is what Jerome reads.[1] Here [the Translator] as if of set purpose translates 'dearest.'

1 Jerome *Comm in Eph* 3 (on 6:21–2) PL 26 (1884) 587D

6:22 [ER *ut cognosceretis de rebus nostris* 'that you might know about our affairs']
[VG] *ut cognoscatis quae circa nos sunt* 'that you may know the things concerning us'; τὰ περὶ ἡμῶν, that is, 'the things that are about us,' which means 'about our affairs' and 'our condition.'

6:23 [ER *a deo patre* 'from God the Father']
[VG] *a deo patre nostro* 'from God our Father.' 'Our' is not added in the
Greek nor in Jerome[1] nor in Ambrose and not[2] in the manuscript from
St Paul's. Both[3] manuscripts from Constance lend their support.

    1 Jerome *Comm in Eph* 3 (on 6:23) PL 26 (1884) 588B
    2 and not ... St Paul's] Added in *1519*. For a description of the manuscripts
      of St Paul's see the annotation on Gal 2:2 ('who seemed something') n14.
    3 Both ... support.] Added in *1527*

6:24 [ER *cum sinceritate* 'in sincerity']
[VG] *in incorruptione* 'in[1] incorruption'; ἐν ἀφθαρσίᾳ [in immortality].
Elsewhere he usually translates this word correctly as 'immortality';
here it means 'integrity' and 'sincerity' of a mind that is free from every corruption of the vices.[2] Jerome disapproves of those who apply
ἀφθαρσίαν [incorruption] solely to bodily chastity.[3] Chrysostom and[4]
Theophylact agree with me in their interpretations.[5] They[6] also make
the point that the preposition ἐν 'in' here has the same meaning as διά
'through.' For Christ is loved in this way if we keep ourselves unstained
from this world. The 'amen'[7] at the end of this Epistle is not added in
Ambrose nor is it possible to conjecture from his commentary what he
read.[8]

    1 'in ... interpretations.] This annotation was added in *1519*.
    2 This interpretation, which is followed by AV, RSV, and NIV, is found in
      some modern commentators; see Lincoln *Ephesians* 467. In his annotation
      on Rom 2:7 ('to those seeking life') Erasmus wondered 'whether *incor-*
      ruptio [incorruption] is a Latin word' CWE 56 77; the word occurs first in
      Tertullian and Augustine (L&S).
    3 Jerome *Comm in Eph* 3 (on 6:24) PL 26 (1884) 588C–D
    4 Chrysostom] Added in *1535*. See Chrysostom *Hom in Eph* 24.4 PG 62 174.
    5 Theophylact *Expos in Eph* 6:24 PG 124 1137B–C
    6 They ... this world.] Added in *1535*
    7 The 'amen' ... he read.] Added in *1522*
    8 Ambrosiaster *Comm in Eph* 6:24. On the textual tradition see Metzger 543.

ANNOTATIONUM IN EPISTOLAM PAULI APOSTOLI
AD EPHESIOS FINIS

The End[1] of the Annotations on the Epistle of the Apostle Paul to the
Ephesians

    1 The End ... Ephesians] *1516*; in *1519*, *1522*: *Finis Epistolae Pauli ad Ephesios*,
      'The End of the Epistle of Paul to the Ephesians.' In *1527*: *Annotationum in*
      epistolam ad Ephesios finis, 'The end of the Annotations on the epistle to the
      Ephesians.' In *1535*: omitted.

WORKS FREQUENTLY CITED

SHORT-TITLE FORMS FOR ERASMUS' WORKS

INDEX OF BIBLICAL AND APOCRYPHAL
REFERENCES

INDEX OF CLASSICAL REFERENCES

INDEX OF PATRISTIC, MEDIEVAL, AND
RENAISSANCE REFERENCES

INDEX OF GREEK AND LATIN WORDS CITED

GENERAL INDEX

WORKS FREQUENTLY CITED

Allen   P.S. Allen, H.M. Allen, and H.W. Garrod eds *Opus epistolarum Des. Erasmi Roterodami* (Oxford 1906–47) 11 vols plus index by B. Flower and E. Rosenbaum (Oxford 1958)

Allen and Greenough   *Allen and Greenough's New Latin Grammar for Schools and Colleges* ed J.B. Greenough, G.L. Kittredge, A.A. Howard, and Benjamin L. D'Ooge (Boston 1931), cited by section number

Ambrosiaster *Comm in Gal*   *Ambrosiastri qui dicitur commentarius in epistulas Paulinas. Pars* III: *In epistulam ad Galatas* ed Henry Joseph Vogels CSEL 81/3 (Vienna 1969). In the notes, references include chapter and verse.

Ambrosiaster *Comm in Eph*   *Ambrosiastri qui dicitur commentarius in epistulas Paulinas. Pars* III: *In epistulam ad Ephesios* ed Henry Joseph Vogels CSEL 81/3 (Vienna 1969). In the notes, references include chapter and verse.

ASD   *Opera omnia Desiderii Erasmi Roterodami* (Amsterdam 1969–   )

Augustine *Expos Gal*   *Epistulae ad Galatas Expositionis liber unus* CSEL 84 ed Johannes Divjak (Vienna 1971). In the notes, references include page and line number.

AV   *The Holy Bible ... Authorized King James Version* (London 1611; repr 1969)

BDAG   *A Greek-English Lexicon of the New Testament and Other Early Christian Literature*, 3rd ed revised and edited by Frederick William Danker based on Walter Bauer's *Griechisch-deutsches Wörterbuch zu den Schriften des Neuen Testaments und der frühchristlichen Literatur* 6th edition, ed Kurt Aland and Barbara Aland with Viktor Reichmann, and on previous English editions by W.F. Arndt, F.W. Gingrich, and F.W. Danker (Chicago 2000)

Bentley *Humanists*   Jerry H. Bentley *Humanists and Holy Writ: New Testament Scholarship in the Renaissance* (Princeton 1983)

Brown *Novum Testamentum*   Andrew J. Brown *Novum Testamentum ab Erasmo recognitum* ASD VI-3

CCL   *Corpus Christianorum series Latina* (Turnhout 1953–   )

Chrysostom *Comm in Gal*   John Chrysostom *Commentarius in epistulam ad Galatas* PG 61 611–82

Chrysostom *Hom in Eph*   John Chrysostom *In epistulam ad Ephesios homiliae* PG 62 9–176

Contemporaries	*Contemporaries of Erasmus: A Biographical Register of the Renaissance and Reformation* ed Peter G. Bietenholz and Thomas B. Deutscher (Toronto 1985–7) 3 vols
CSEL	*Corpus scriptorium ecclesiasticorum Latinorum* (Vienna 1866–)
CWE	*Collected Works of Erasmus* (Toronto 1974–)
Jerome *Comm in Gal*	Eusebius Hieronymus *Commentarii in epistulam Pauli Apostolo ad Galatas* CSEL 77A ed Giacomo Raspanti (Turnhout 2006)
Jerome *Comm in Eph*	Eusebius Hieronymus *Commentariorum in epistolam ad Ephesios libri tres* PL 26 467–590 (Paris 1884)
Lausberg	H. Lausberg *Handbook of Literary Rhetoric* trans M.T. Bliss, A. Jansen, and D.E. Orton, ed D.E. Orton and R.D. Anderson (Leiden 1998)
LB	*Desiderii Erasmi Roterodami opera omnia* ed Jean Lelerc (Johannes Clericus) (Leiden 1703–6; repr 1961–2) 10 vols
Lefèvre *Pauli epistolae*	Jacobus Faber Stapulensis *S. Pauli epistolae XIV ex Vulgata, adiecta intelligentia ex Graeco, cum commentariis* (Paris 1512; facsimile ed Stuttgart-Bad Cannstatt 1978)
Lightfoot	J.B. Lightfoot *The Epistle of Paul to the Galatians* (Cambridge, 1865; repr Grand Rapids, MI 1900)
Lincoln *Ephesians*	Andrew Lincoln *Ephesians* (Dallas 1990)
L&S	Charlton T. Lewis and Charles Short *A Latin Dictionary* (Oxford 1879; repr 1975)
LSJ	*A Greek-English Lexicon* compiled by Henry George Liddell and Robert Scott, revised and augmented by Sir Henry Stuart Jones, 9th ed with supplement (Oxford 1968)
Metzger	Bruce M. Metzger *A Textual Commentary on the Greek New Testament* 2nd rev edition (Stuttgart 1994)
NEB	*The New English Bible, With the Apocrypha* (Oxford 1970)
OLD	*Oxford Latin Dictionary* ed P.G.W. Glare (Oxford 1982)
PG	*Patrologiae cursus completus … series Graeca* ed J.-P. Migne (Paris 1857–86; repr Turnhout) 161 vols. Indexes F. Cavallera (Paris 1912); T. Hopfner (Paris 1928–36) 2 vols
PL	*Patrologiae cursus completus … series Latina* ed J.-P. Migne, 1st ed (Paris 1844–55, 1862–5; repr Turnhout) 217 vols plus 4 vols indexes. In the notes, references to volumes of PL in which column numbers in the first edition are different from those in later editions or reprints include the date of the edition cited.

Pseudo-Oecumenius   Pseudo-Oecumenius *Commentarii in epistulam Pauli ad*
   Comm in Gal   *Galatas* PG 118 1089–1166

Pseudo-Oecumenius   Pseudo-Oecumenius *Commentarii in epistulam Pauli ad*
   Comm in Eph   *Ephesios* PG 118 1165–1256

RSV   *The Holy Bible, Revised Standard Version* 2nd ed (Nashville
                      1971)

Rummel   Erika Rummel *Erasmus' 'Annotations' on the New Testament:
                      From Philologist to Theologian* (Toronto 1986)

Smyth   Herbert Weir Smyth *A Greek Grammar for Colleges* revised
                      Gordon M. Messing (Cambridge, MA 1980 [1956]), cited by
                      section number

Souter   Alexander Souter *Pelagius' Expositions of Thirteen Epistles
                      of Paul* Texts and Studies 9 (Cambridge 1922–31) 3 vols; I
                      Introduction (1922); II *Text and Critical Apparatus* (1926); III
                      Pseudo-Jerome Interpolations (1931)

Theophylact *Expos*   Theophylact *Expositio in epistulam ad Galatas* PG 124 951–1032
   in Gal

Theophylact *Expos*   Theophylact *Expositio in epistulam ad Ephesios* PG 124
   in Eph   1031–1138

Thomas Aquinas   St Thomas Aquinas *Super epistolas S. Pauli lectura: Super
   Super Gal lect   epistolam ad Galatas lectura* ed Raffaele Cai OP 8th ed revised
                      (Rome and Turin 1953)

Thomas Aquinas   St Thomas Aquinas *Super epistolas S. Pauli lectura: Super
   Super Eph lect   epistolam ad Ephesios lectura* ed Raffaele Cai OP 8th ed revised
                      (Rome and Turin 1953)

Valla *Annot in Gal*   Laurentius Valla *Annotationes in epistolam Pauli ad Galatas* in
                      Opera omnia (Basel 1540; repr Turin 1962) 2 vols, I 875–6

Valla *Annot in Eph*   Laurentius Valla *Annotationes in epistolam Pauli ad Ephesios*
                      in *Opera omnia* (Basel 1540; repr Turin 1962) 2 vols, I 876–8

Weber   *Biblia sacra iuxta vulgatam versionem* ed Robertus Weber with
                      Bonifatius Fischer OSB et al, 4th ed (Stuttgart 1994)

SHORT-TITLE FORMS OF ERASMUS' WORKS

Titles following colons are longer versions of the same, or are alternative titles.
Items entirely enclosed in square brackets are of doubtful authorship.
For abbreviations, see Works Frequently Cited.

Adagia: Adagiorum chiliades 1508 (Adagiorum collectanea for the primitive form,
    when required) LB II / ASD II-4, 5, 6 / CWE 30–6

Acta: Academiae Lovaniensis contra Lutherum *Opuscula* / CWE 71

Adagia: Adagiorum chiliades 1508, etc (Adagiorum collectanea for the primitive
    form, when required) LB II / ASD II-1–9 / CWE 30–6

Admonitio adversus mendacium: Admonitio adversus mendacium et obtrectationem
    LB X / CWE 78

Annotationes in Novum Testamentum LB VI / ASD VI-5–10 / CWE 51–60

Antibarbari LB X / ASD I-1 / CWE 23

Apologia ad annotationes Stunicae: Apologia respondens ad ea quae Iacobus Lopis
    Stunica taxaverat in prima duntaxat Novi Testamenti aeditione LB IX / ASD IX-2

Apologia ad Caranzam: Apologia ad Sanctium Caranzam, or Apologia de tribus
    locis, or Responsio ad annotationem Stunicae … a Sanctio Caranza defensam
    LB IX / ASD IX-8

Apologia ad Fabrum: Apologia ad Iacobum Fabrum Stapulensem LB IX / ASD IX-3 /
    CWE 83

Apologia ad prodromon Stunicae LB IX / ASD IX-8

Apologia ad Stunicae conclusiones LB IX / ASD IX-8

Apologia adversus monachos: Apologia adversus monachos quosdam Hispanos
    LB IX

Apologia adversus Petrum Sutorem: Apologia adversus debacchationes Petri
    Sutoris LB IX

Apologia adversus rhapsodias Alberti Pii: Apologia ad viginti et quattuor libros A.
    Pii LB IX / ASD IX-6 / CWE 84

Apologia adversus Stunicae Blasphemiae: Apologia adversus libellum Stunicae
    cui titulum fecit Blasphemiae et impietates Erasmi LB IX / ASD IX-8

Apologia contra Latomi dialogum: Apologia contra Iacobi Latomi dialogum
    de tribus linguis LB IX / CWE 71

Apologia de 'In principio erat sermo': Apologia palam refellens quorundam seditio-
    sos clamores apud populum ac magnates quo in evangelio Ioannis verterit
    'In principio erat sermo' (1520a); Apologia de 'In principio erat sermo' (1520b)
    LB IX / CWE 73

Apologia de laude matrimonii: Apologia pro declamatione de laude matrimonii
    LB IX / CWE 71

Apologia de loco 'Omnes quidem': Apologia de loco taxato in publica professione
    per Nicolaum Ecmondanum theologum et Carmelitanum Lovanii 'Omnes
    quidem resurgemus' LB IX / CWE 73

Apologia qua respondet invectivis Lei: Apologia qua respondet duabus invectivis
    Eduardi Lei *Opuscula* / ASD IX-4 / CWE 72

Apophthegmata LB IV / ASD IV-4 / CWE 37–8

Appendix de scriptis Clichtovei LB IX / CWE 83

Appendix respondens ad Sutorem: Appendix respondens ad quaedam Antapologiae
  Petri Sutoris   LB IX
Argumenta: Argumenta in omnes epistolas apostolicas nova (with Paraphrases)
Axiomata pro causa Lutheri: Axiomata pro causa Martini Lutheri   *Opuscula* /
  CWE 71

Brevissima scholia: In Elenchum Alberti Pii brevissima scholia per eundem
  Erasmum Roterodamum   ASD IX-6 / CWE 84

Carmina   LB I, IV, V, VIII / ASD I-7 / CWE 85–6
Catalogus lucubrationum   LB I / CWE 9 (Ep 1341A)
Christiani hominis institutum, carmen LB V
Christiani matrimonii institutio   LB V / ASD VI-6 / CWE 69
Ciceronianus: Dialogus Ciceronianus   LB I / ASD I-2 / CWE 28
Colloquia   LB I / ASD I-3 / CWE 39–40
Compendium vitae   Allen I / CWE 4
Conflictus: Conflictus Thaliae et Barbariei   LB I / ASD I-8
[Consilium: Consilium cuiusdam ex animo cupientis esse consultum]   *Opuscula* /
  CWE 71

De bello Turcico: Utilissima consultatio de bello Turcis inferendo, et obiter enarratus
  psalmus 28   LB V / ASD V-3 / CWE 64
De civilitate: De civilitate morum puerilium   LB I / ASD I-8 / CWE 25
Declamatio de morte   LB IV
Declamatiuncula   LB IV
Declarationes ad censuras Lutetiae vulgatas: Declarationes ad censuras Lutetiae
  vulgatas sub nomine facultatis theologiae Parisiensis   LB IX / ASD IX-7 / CWE 82
De concordia: De sarcienda ecclesiae concordia, or De amabili ecclesiae concordia
  [on Psalm 83]   LB V / ASD V-3 / CWE 65
De conscribendis epistulis   LB I / ASD I-2 / CWE 25
De constructione: De constructione octo partium orationis, or Syntaxis   LB I /
  ASD I4
De contemptu mundi: Epistola de contemptu mundi   LB V / ASD V-1 / CWE 66
De copia: De duplici copia verborum ac rerum   LB I / ASD I-6 / CWE 24
De delectu ciborum scholia   ASD IX–1 / CWE 73
De esu carnium: Epistola apologetica ad Christophorum episcopum Basiliensem
  de interdicto esu carnium (published with scholia in a 1532 edition but not in
  the 1540 Opera)   LB IX / ASD IX-1 / CWE 73
De immensa Dei misericordia: Concio de immensa Dei misericordia   LB V / ASD V-7 /
  CWE 70
De libero arbitrio: De libero arbitrio diatribe   LB IX / CWE 76
De philosophia evangelica   LB VI
De praeparatione: De praeparatione ad mortem   LB V / ASD V-1 / CWE 70
De pueris instituendis: De pueris statim ac liberaliter instituendis   LB I / ASD I-2 /
  CWE 26
De puero Iesu: Concio de puero Iesu   LB V / ASD V-7 / CWE 29
De puritate tabernaculi: Enarratio psalmi 14 qui est de puritate tabernaculi sive
  ecclesiae christianae   LB V / ASD V-2 / CWE 65

De ratione studii LB I / ASD I-2 / CWE 24
De recta pronuntiatione: De recta latini graecique sermonis pronuntiatione LB I /
    ASD I-4 / CWE 26
De taedio Iesu: Disputatiuncula de taedio, pavore, tristicia Iesu LB V / ASD V-7 /
    CWE 70
Detectio praestigiarum: Detectio praestigiarum cuiusdam libelli Germanice scripti
    LB X / ASD IX-1 / CWE 78
De vidua christiana LB V / ASD V-6 / CWE 66
De virtute amplectenda: Oratio de virtute amplectenda LB V / CWE 29
[Dialogus bilinguium ac trilinguium: Chonradi Nastadiensis dialogus bilinguium
    ac trilinguium] *Opuscula* / CWE 7
Dilutio: Dilutio eorum quae Iodocus Clichtoveus scripsit adversus declamationem
    suasoriam matrimonii / *Dilutio eorum quae Iodocus Clichtoveus scripsit* ed Émile
    V. Telle (Paris 1968) / CWE 83
Divinationes ad notata Bedae: Divinationes ad notata per Bedam de Paraphrasi
    Erasmi in Matthaeum, et primo de duabus praemissis epistolis LB IX / ASD IX-5

Ecclesiastes: Ecclesiastes sive de ratione concionandi LB V / ASD V-4–5 / CWE 67–8
Elenchus in censuras Bedae: In N. Bedae censuras erroneas elenchus LB IX /
    ASD IX-5
Enchiridion: Enchiridion militis christiani LB V / CWE 66
Encomium matrimonii (in De conscribendis epistolis)
Encomium medicinae: Declamatio in laudem artis medicae LB I / ASD I-4 /
    CWE 29
Epistola ad Dorpium LB IX / CWE 3 (Ep 337) / CWE 71
Epistola ad fratres Inferioris Germaniae: Responsio ad fratres Germaniae Inferioris
    ad epistolam apologeticam incerto autore proditam LB X / ASD IX-1 / CWE 78
Epistola ad gracculos: Epistola ad quosdam imprudentissimos gracculos LB X /
    Ep 2275
Epistola apologetica adversus Stunicam LB IX / ASD IX-8 / Ep 2172
Epistola apologetica de Termino LB X / Ep 2018
Epistola consolatoria: Epistola consolatoria virginibus sacris, or Epistola consolatoria
    in adversis LB V / CWE 69
Epistola contra pseudevangelicos: Epistola contra quosdam qui se falso iactant
    evangelicos LB X / ASD IX-1 / CWE 78
Euripidis Hecuba LB I / ASD I-1
Euripidis Iphigenia Aulidensis LB I / ASD I-1
Exomologesis: Exomologesis sive modus confitendi LB V / CWE 67
Explanatio symboli: Explanatio symboli apostolorum sive catechismus LB V /
    ASD V-1 / CWE 70
Ex Plutarcho versa LB IV / ASD IV-2

Formula: Conficiendarum epistolarum formula (see De conscribendis epistolis)

Hyperaspistes LB X / CWE 76–7

In Nucem Ovidii commentarius LB I / ASD I-1 / CWE 29
In Prudentium: Commentarius in duos hymnos Prudentii LB V / ASD V-7 / CWE 29

In psalmum 1: Enarratio primi psalmi, 'Beatus vir,' iuxta tropologiam potissimum LB V / ASD V-2 / CWE 63
In psalmum 2: Commentarius in psalmum 2, 'Quare fremuerunt gentes?' LB V / ASD V-2 / CWE 63
In psalmum 3: Paraphrasis in tertium psalmum, 'Domine quid multiplicate' LB V / ASD V-2 / CWE 63
In psalmum 4: In psalmum quartum concio LB V / ASD V-2 / CWE 63
In psalmum 22: In psalmum 22 enarratio triplex LB V / ASD V-2 / CWE 64
In psalmum 33: Enarratio psalmi 33 LB V / ASD V-3 / CWE 64
In psalmum 38: Enarratio psalmi 38 LB V / ASD V-3 / CWE 65
In psalmum 85: Concionalis interpretatio, plena pietatis, in psalmum 85 LB V / ASD V-3 / CWE 64
Institutio christiani matrimonii LB V / ASD V-6 / CWE 69
Institutio principis christiani LB IV/ ASD IV-1 / CWE 27

[Julius exclusus: Dialogus Julius exclusus e coelis] *Opuscula* ASD I-8 / CWE 27

Lingua LB IV / ASD IV-1A / CWE 29
Liturgia Virginis Matris: Virginis Matris apud Lauretum cultae liturgia LB V / ASD V-1 / CWE 69
Loca quaedam emendata: Loca quaedam in aliquot Erasmi lucubrationibus per ipsum emendata LB IX
Luciani dialogi LB I / ASD I-1

Manifesta mendacia ASD IX-4 / CWE 71
Methodus (see Ratio)
Modus orandi Deum LB V / ASD V-1 / CWE 70
Moria: Moriae encomium LB IV / ASD IV-3 / CWE 27

Notatiunculae: Notatiunculae quaedam extemporales ad naenias Bedaicas, or Responsio ad notulas Bedaicas LB IX / ASD IX-5
Novum Testamentum: Novum Testamentum 1519 and later (Novum instrumentum for the first edition, 1516, when required) LB VI / ASD VI-2, 3, 4

Obsecratio ad Virginem Mariam: Obsecratio sive oratio ad Virginem Mariam in rebus adversis, or Obsecratio ad Virginem Matrem Mariam in rebus adversis LB V / cwe 69
Oratio de pace: Oratio de pace et discordia LB VIII
Oratio funebris: Oratio funebris in funere Bertae de Heyen LB VIII / CWE 29

Paean Virgini Matri: Paean Virgini Matri dicendus LB V / CWE 69
Panegyricus: Panegyricus ad Philippum Austriae ducem LB IV / ASD IV-1 / CWE 27
Parabolae: Parabolae sive similia LB I / ASD I-5 / CWE 23
Paraclesis LB V, VI / ASD V-7
Paraphrasis in Elegantias Vallae: Paraphrasis in Elegantias Laurentii Vallae LB I / ASD I-4
Paraphrasis in Matthaeum, etc LB VII / ASD VII-6 / CWE 42–50
Peregrinatio apostolorum: Peregrinatio apostolorum Petri et Pauli LB VI, VII

Precatio ad Virginis filium Iesum   LB V / CWE 69
Precatio dominica   LB V / CWE 69
Precationes: Precationes aliquot novae   LB V / CWE 69
Precatio pro pace ecclesiae: Precatio ad Dominum Iesum pro pace ecclesiae   LB IV,
   V / cwe 69
Prologus supputationis: Prologus in supputationem calumniarum Natalis Bedae
   (1526), or Prologus supputationis errorum in censuris Bedae (1527)   LB IX / ASD
   IX-5
Purgatio adversus epistolam Lutheri: Purgatio adversus epistolam non sobriam
   Lutheri   LB X / ASD IX-1 / CWE 78

Querela pacis   LB IV / ASD IV-2 / CWE 27

Ratio: Ratio seu Methodus compendio perveniendi ad veram theologiam (Methodus
   for the shorter version originally published in the Novum instrumentum
   of 1516)   LB V, VI
Responsio ad annotationes Lei: Responsio ad annotations Eduardi Lei   LB IX /
   ASD IX-4 / CWE 72
Responsio ad Collationes: Responsio ad Collationes cuiusdam iuvenis gerontodidas-
   cali   LB IX / CWE 73
Responsio ad disputationem de divortio: Responsio ad disputationem cuiusdam
   Phimostomi de divortio   LB IX / ASD IX-4 / CWE 83
Responsio ad epistolam Alberti Pii: Responsio ad epistolam paraeneticam Alberti Pii,
   or Responsio ad exhortationem Pii   LB IX / ASD IX-6 / CWE 84
Responsio ad notulas Bedaicas   LB X
Responsio ad Petri Cursii defensionem: Epistola de apologia Cursii   LB X / Ep 3032
Responsio adversus febricitantis cuiusdam libellum   LB X

Spongia: Spongia adversus aspergines Hutteni   LB X / ASD IX-1 / CWE 78
Supputatio: Supputatio errorum in censuris Bedae   LB IX
Supputationes: Supputationes errorum in censuris Natalis Bedae: contains
   Supputatio and reprints of Prologus supputationis; Divinationes ad notata Bedae;
   Elenchus in censuras Bedae; Appendix respondens ad Sutorem; Appendix de
   scriptis Clithovei   LB IX / ASD IX-5

Tyrannicida: Tyrannicida, declamatio Lucianicae respondens   LB I / ASD I-1 /
   CWE 29

Virginis et martyris comparatio   LB V / ASD V-7 / CWE 69
Vita Hieronymi: Vita divi Hieronymi Stridonensis   *Opuscula* / CWE 61

Index of Biblical and
Apocryphal References

This index lists the citations and allusions made by Erasmus, but not those added by the translator for explanation or illustration.

Genesis

1:2	171 n16
2:24	208
9:4	24 n23
15:3	69 n14
21:10	82 n3
49:20	69 n12

Exodus

3:8	214
20:3	214
20:5	213, 214
20:6	213
20:12	213

Deuteronomy

15:12	217 n5
21	56
27:26	54 n3

Psalms

3	201
4:4	187 n1
4:5	187 n1
8:7	132 n1
10	178
22:27	161
68	172
68:18	xvi, 172, 172 n2
81	150
118	209
119	105 n3

Proverbs

11:16	195 n12
20:1	204, 205 n14

Isaiah

2:3	79
54:1	xvi, 82 n1, 82 n3
60:1	201

Matthew

3:4	222
5:22	46 n7, 147 n9
7:17–18	189 n5
11:13	37 n23
12:33	189 n5
13:33	87 n8
14:17	37 n24

Mark

10:46	69 n11
14:36	68 n5

Luke

1:28	116, 116 n2
2:4	161
6:43	189 n5
13:21	87 n8
16:8	136 n4
16:16	37 n23

Acts

5:36	22, 23 n17

9	15	2:9	22, 24, 136 n4
9:36	69 n13	2:14	37 n30
12:1–2	18 n5	2:15	41 n1
13:10	10 n2	3:29	63
15:10	31, 147 n11	4:1	65 n1
15:36–40	38 n34	4:18	102
16:1–3	26 n3	5:2	84
21:24	38	5:7	46
		5:19	205 n9
Romans		5:25	106 n1
1:4	7 n4, 7 n11, 113 n3,	6:7	102
	136 n4	6:13	74
1:7	3 n3		
1:17	55 n2	**Ephesians**	
1:26	136 n4	1:7	136
2:20	65 n1	1:9	153 n2, 154 n1,
6:10	42 n1		157 n3
6:11	135 n3	1:11	121
8:2	28 n2	1:18	118
8:15	68 n5, 113 n1	1:22	120
8:17	70 n7	2:1	139 n3
13:6	223 n1	2:2	135, 136 n6, 197 n1
13:13	205 n9	2:8	xiv, 142 n2
15:8	63 n1	3:3	154 n1, 157 n3
16:25–7	9 n9, 165 n10	3:6	198 n5
		3:12	159
1 Corinthians		4:14	219 n1
1:12	63 n1	4:17	63 n1
7:8	63 n1	4:19	205 n9
10:29	210	4:22	185 n1
13:2	210	4:23	180
15:50	63 n1	4:27	187
15:54	103 n2	4:28	189
		4:30	126 n4
2 Corinthians		5:7	155 n7
2:8	57 n3	5:8	199
2:10	192	5:11	199, 201
6:12	191 n1	5:13	199, 201
11:23–7	108 n4	5:21	206
11:26	13 n2	5:32	153 n2
12:26	25 n3		
		Colossians	
Galatians		2:4	63 n1
1:13	20 n1	2:8	65
1:16	15, 21 n2	2:14	147 n14
2:2	23 n7	2:20	65, 148 n16
2:6	22, 23 n8	2:21	66 n8

1 Thessalonians
4:3–6   183
4:6   196 n7

2 Thessalonians
2:7   211 n17

1 Timothy
1:9   98 n4
1:17   103 n2

Hebrews
5:12   66

1 Peter
3:8   191 n1

Gospel of the Hebrews
                194 n4

Index of Classical References

Apuleius *Metamorphoses* 13 n1
Aristotle
– *Eudemian Ethics* 194 n2
– *Metaphysica* 81 n5
– *Nicomachean Ethics* 194 n2
– *Physica* 66 n5
– *Rhetoric* 194 n2
Athenaeus *Deipnosophistae* 205 n7

Cicero
– *De finibus* 183 n5, 204 n5
– *De inventione* 43 n1
– *De natura deorum* 204 n
– *De officiis* 183 n5
– *Pro Caecina* 69 n7
– *Rhetorica ad Herennium* 43 n1, 69 n7
– *Tusculan Disputations* 183 n5
Columella 87 n4

Demosthenes *In Defence of Ctesiphon* 46 n4
Diogenes Laertius *Vitae Philosophorum* 171 n9

Euripides
– *Hecuba* 23 n6
– *Iphigenia Aulidensis* 21 n4, 76 n6

Hesychius *Lexicon* 46 n5, 175 n5, 187 n4
Homer *Odyssey* 52 n2
Horace *Satires* 51 n3

Plato *Laws* 204 n6
Plautus
– *Aulularia* 205 n12
– *Captivi* 107 n1
Plutarch *Moralia* 144 n1

Quintilian 7 n4, 51 n2, 69 n7, 93 n8, 99 n7, 110 n5, 118 n3, 120 n1, 162 n13, 165 n6, 188 n1

Seneca *Epistles* 204 n5

Terence
– *Adelphi* 145 n4
– *Eunuchus* 183 n7
Theophrastus *De causis plantarum* 80 n4

Virgil
– *Aeneid* 51 n3, 171 n12
– *Eclogues* 58 n5
– *Georgics* 58 n5, 171 n4, 171 n11

Index of Patristic, Medieval, and Renaissance References

References are to the notes. Individual entries are not given for passages from the commentaries on Galatians and Ephesians most frequently quoted by Erasmus, namely, those of Ambrosiaster, John Chrysostom, Theophylact, and Valla.

Ambrose of Milan
– *De Abraham* 147 n4
– *Exhortatio virginitatis* 122 n3
– *De paradiso* 221 n5
Ambrosiaster
– *Commentarius in epistulam ad Ephesios* passim
– *Commentarius in epistulam ad Galatas* passim
Aquinas. *See* Thomas Aquinas
Augustine. *See also* Pseudo-Augustine
– *Confessions* 205 n10
– *Contra adversarium legis et prophetarum* 79 n10, 79 n12, 89 n9, 149 n2
– *Contra duas epistulas Pelagianorum* 78 n10
– *Contra Faustum Manichaeum* 79 n12, 89 n9, 140 n3, 140 n4, 142 n2, 148 n1, 148 n4, 149 n2, 150 n4
– *Contra litteras Petiliani* 168 n2
– *De agone Christiano* 37 n16
– *De bono coniugali* 211 n9
– *De civitate dei* 59 n5, 79 n10, 79 n12, 96 n3, 98 n5, 174 n1, 177 n5, 179 n4, 196 n4, 205 n15
– *De diversis quaestionibus* 98 n3
– *De genesi contra manichaeos* 96 n5
– *De gratia et libero arbitrio* 164 n12, 211 n19
– *De mendacio* 40 n8
– *De nuptiis et concupiscentia* 211 n15
– *De praedestinatione sanctorum* 107 n4, 116 n1

– *De sermone domini in monte (secundum Matthaeum)* 13 n6
– *De trinitate* 76 n3, 78 n5
– *De vera religione* 205 n17, 205 n19
– *Enarrationes in psalmos* 149 n2, 150 n3, 179 n3, 201 n8, 211 n14, 215 n5, 217 n3
– *Epistulae* 37 n26, 40 n6 (twice), 96 n7, 164 n7, 173 n4
– *Epistulae ad Galatas expositio liber unus* 4 n4, 4 n10, 5 n3, 6 n3, 10 n4, 11 n10, 23 n1, 25 n6, 37 n9, 37 n14, 43 n2, 44 n1, 49 n3, 50 n3, 60 n1, 62 n3, 63 n2, 64 n4, 68 n3, 69 n9, 70 n4, 71 n3, 72 n5, 74 n3, 78 n10, 83 n5, 86 n8, 86 n1, 89 n7, 90 n2, 91 n1, 96 n6, 102 n3, 105 n8, 106 n6, 107 n3
– *Retractionum libri duo* 98 n5

Chrysostom. *See* John Chrysostom
Cyprian *Epistulae* 136 n2, 196 n5, 198 n4, 219 n4, 222 n2

Eusebius *Historia Ecclesiastica* 37 n20

Glossa Ordinaria 81 n9, 85 n3, 85 n4, 205 n13, 215 n4

Hilary of Poitiers
– *De Trinitate* 185 n3
– *Tractatus super psalmos* 105 n3, 220 n4

Irenaeus *Contra haereses* 24 n28
Isidore of Seville *Etymologies* 205 n20

Jerome
– *Adversus Helvidium de Mariae
  virginitate perpetua* 161 n2, 162 n14
– *Adversus Jovinianum* 46 n2, 94 n8,
  211 n8
– *Comentarii in Ezechielem* 97 n2
– *Commentarius in epistulam ad Ephesios*
  111 n2 (x2), 112 n2 (x2), 113 n1, 113 n2,
  113 n4, 114 n3, 114 n4, 115 n5, 116 n1,
  116 n4, 117 n2, 117 n3, 118 n2, 119 n1,
  120 n6, 120 n7, 121 n2, 121 n3, 122 n1,
  123 n3, 124 n1, 124 n4, 127 n2, 128 n1,
  128 n2, 129 n4, 130 n2 (x2), 131 n2,
  132 n2, 133 n2, 134 n3, 135 n2, 135 n4,
  136 n4, 138 n2 (x2), 139 n1, 140 n2,
  141 n1, 141 n5, 143 n2, 143 n3, 147 n1,
  147 n12, 148 n1, 151 n1, 151 n3,
  152 n2, 152 n3, 152 n4, 153 n2, 153 n3,
  154 n4, 155 n3, 155 n6, 156 n2, 157 n2,
  157 n3, 158 n1, 158 n2, 159 n2, 159 n3
  (x2), 159 n5, 160 n2, 160 n5, 161 n1,
  161 n2, 162 n2, 164 n4, 164 n9, 165 n2,
  171 n3 (x2), 171 n6, 171 n7, 171 n8,
  171 n10, 171 n14, 173 n1, 173 n2,
  174 n3, 175 n6, 176 n12, 176 n15,
  178 n1, 178 n2, 181 n1 (x2), 183 n2,
  184 n3, 185 n1, 185 n2, 189 n3, 190 n2,
  191 n1, 192 n1, 194 n3, 195 n11, 196 n3,
  196 n6, 196 n8, 196 n2, 197 n2, 198 n3,
  200 n2, 200 n5, 201 n1, 201 n3, 205 n4,
  206 n2, 206 n3, 207 n1, 207 n4, 208 n1,
  212 n1, 212 n3, 215 n2, 215 n3, 218 n3,
  219 n1, 219 n6, 220 n1, 222 n1, 222 n3,
  223 n2, 224 n1 (x2), 225 n1, 225 n3
– *Commentarius in epistulam ad Galatas*
  2 n2, 4 n6, 5 n2, 5 n5, 7 n5, 7 n8, 8 n2,
  9 n10, 10 n1, 10 n5, 10 n7, 11 n9,
  12 n1, 12 n2, 13 n3, 15 n1, 16 n5,
  16 n13, 17 n2, 18 n3, 18 n5, 20 n1,
  21 n1, 23 n12, 23 n13, 25 n2, 25 n5,
  27 n2 (twice), 36 n5, 37 n11, 37 n17,
  37 n18, 37 n21, 40 n4, 41 n2, 41 n3,
  43 n1, 44 n3, 45 n7, 46 n2, 47 n7,
  49 n10, 50 n2, 51 n2, 52 n1, 52 n2,
  54 n7, 55 n3, 56 n2, 56 n3, 56 n4,
  56 n5, 56 n6, 57 n2, 58 n3, 58 n4,
  59 n2, 61 n5, 62 n3, 62 n1, 63 n1,
  63 n4, 64 n2, 66 n7, 68 n3, 69 n8,
  69 n15, 70 n2, 71 n1, 72 n2, 72 n4,
  73 n2, 75 n2, 76 n1, 78 n2, 80 n2,
  82 n1, 83 n4, 84 n3, 85 n1, 85 n7,
  86 n2, 87 n3, 88 n2, 88 n3, 90 n1,
  90 n2, 91 n2, 93 n1, 93 n4, 94 n4,
  95 n1, 95 n3, 96 n8, 98 n1, 100 n2,
  102 n5, 102 n10, 104 n2, 106 n2,
  107 n2, 152 n4
– *Commentariorum in Zechariam
  prophetam libri duo* 192 n2
– *De viris illustribus* 97 n6, 190 n8
– *Dialogus adversus Pelagianos* 40 n2,
  55 n2, 61 n1
– *Epistolae* 37 n25, 56 n6, 155 n4
– *Interpretatio libri Didymi Alexandrini
  de spiritu sancto* 126 n2
– *Liber quaestionum hebraicarum
  in Genesim* 69 n14
– *Vita sancti Hilarionis* 195 n5
– *Vita sancti Pauli eremitae* 195 n4

John Chrysostom
– *Commentarius in epistulam ad Ephesios*
  passim
– *Commentarius in epistulam ad Galatas*
  passim
– *Epistolae* 37 n26
Justinian *Constitutio tanta* 66 n6

Lactantius
– *De justitia* 129 n7
– *Divinarum institutionum* 129 n7
Lee, Edward *Annotationes in annotationes
  Erasmi* 4 n3, 67 n3
Lefèvre d'Etaples, Jacques *Pauli epistolae*
  passim
Luther, Martin *Assertio omnium
  articulorum Martini Lutheri* 138 n7

Nicholas of Lyra *Postilla ad loc. Biblia
  sacra* 179 n4

Origen
– *Commentarius in epistulam beati Pauli
  ad Romanos* 28 n2

- *Hexapla* 54 n4, 54 n5, 54 n6, 195 n13, 195 n15
- *Homilia in numeros* 162 n7

Pelagius *Commentaria in epistulam ad Ephesios* 147 n13
Peter Lombard *Sententiae* 51 n5
Pseudo-Augustine *De trinitate et unitate dei* 67 n6
Pseudo-Oecumenius
- *Commentarii in epistulam Pauli ad Ephesios* 153 n4, 183 n4
- *Commentarii in epistulam Pauli ad Galatas* 37 n19, 38 n1, 38 n4, 49 n14, 53 n3, 78 n7, 83 n3

Ruechlin, Johann *De rudimentis Hebraeicis* 5 n2

Tertullian
- *Adversus Hermogenem* 13 n1
- *Adversus Marcionem* 9 n13, 87 n4, 123 n7, 150 n2, 220 n3
- *De praescribendis haereticis* 5 n4
- *De resurrectione carnis* 13 n1, 103 n3

Theophylact
- *Expositio in epistulam ad Ephesios* passim
- *Expositio in epistulam ad Galatas* passim
Thomas Aquinas
- *Summa theologiae* 205 n11, 205 n18
- *Super epistolam ad Ephesios lectura* 134 n8, 162 n4, 179 n5, 201 n11, 215 n4, 222 n6
- *Super epistolam ad Galatas lectura* 14 n2, 16 n3, 37 n22, 81 n10
Titelmans, Frans *Responsio ad collationes* 45n13

Valla, Lorenzo
- *Annotationes in epistolam Pauli ad Ephesios* passim
- *Annotationes in epistolam Pauli ad Galatas* passim

Zúñiga, Diego López
- *Opusculum in quasdam Erasmi Roterodami annotationes* 211 n21
- *Annotationes contra Erasmum Roterodamum* 99 n5

Index of Greek and Latin Words Cited

This selective index includes those words that Erasmus undertakes to explain in his annotations. For Greek conjunctions and prepositions see grammar in the General Index.

GREEK WORDS

ἀγαπητός 116, 224
ἀδοκέω 21
ἀεργός 84
ἄζω 187
ἄθεος 144
ἀθετέω 57
αἰσχύνη 75
ἀκούω 19
ἀκριβῶς 202
ἀκρογωνιαῖος 150
ἀκυρόω 57, 59
ἀληθεύω 177
ἀλληγορέω 76
ἁμαρτία 134
ἄμωμος 112, 207
ἀναδίπλωσις 68, 70
ἀνάθεμα 21
ἀνακεφαλαιόω 120
ἀνακεφαλαίωσις 120
ἀναλγησία 182–3
ἀναπληρός 99
ἀναστατόω 89
ἀνασταυρόω 95
ἀνατίθημι 20–1
ἀνθρωπάρεσκος 216
ἀνόητος 44
ἀπείθεια 197
ἀπέχω 39
ἀπεχθάνομαι 39

ἀπαλγέω 182–3
ἀποκάλυψις 12
ἀποκαταλλάσσω 148
ἀπολαμβάνω 67
ἀπορέω 75
ἀπόστολος 2
ἀργός 84
ἀρραβών 127
ἀσέλγεια 203
ἄσιος 187
ἀσωτία 202–3
ἄσωτος 203
αὐξάνω 177–8
ἁφή 178
ἀφθαρσία 225

βασκαίνω 45, 46
βαστάζω 101

γίγνομαι 66–7
γνωρίζω 117
γνῶσις 129
γράμμα 104
γράφω 48, 153

δεισιδαιμονία 144
δέσμιος 151
διαθήκη 56–7, 58, 77
διαφέρω 64
διδάσκαλος 73
δοκέω 21–2, 26

δόξα 115
δουλεία 196
δύναμις 131, 136, 162
δωρεάν 43

ἐγκλείω 73
ἐγκόπτω 46
ἐκβάλλω 73
ἐκκακέω 73, 103, 159
ἐκκλείω 73
ἐλαχύς 156
ἐλέγχω 199
ἐνέργεια 28, 29 n3, 131, 179
ἐνεργέω 51, 122, 135
ἐνέχυρον 127
ἐνίστημι 3
ἑνότης 174
ἐντελέχεια 28
ἐντροπή 75
ἐξαγοράζω 67
ἐξαποστέλλω 66
ἐξουσία 136
ἐπιτέλλω 50
ἐπιφαύσκω 200–1
ἐπιχορηγέω 51
ἐργάζομαι 221
εὐαγγέλιον 28, 52, 125
εὐδοκία 114, 119, 122, 217 n1
εὐλογέω 53
εὐπροσωπέω 105
εὔσπλαγχνος 191
εὐτραπελία 193
εὐχαριστία 193–4

ζηλωτής 14
ζυμόω 87
ζωή 181

θέλημα 136
θυμός 191

ἱστορέω 17

κατάρα 53, 55
καταργέω 84, 184
καταρτίζω 97, 173
καταρτισμός 173
κατεργάζομαι 221–2

κενόδοξος 97
κληρόω 122
κληρονομέω 93 n1
κλῆρος 122
κλίμα 19
κοσμοκράτωρ 220
κυβεία 174–5, 177
κυβεύω 174
κυκεία 174
κυριότης 131

λατρεία 196
λόγος 101
λοιπός 106–7, 218
λύω 145

μακαρισμός 72
μακροθυμία 93, 94, 167, 168 n6
μεθοδεία 176, 219
μεθοδεύω 176
μέθοδος 219
μέλος 180
μέρος 180
μεσίτης 60–1
μεσότοιχον 145
μεταστρέφω 9
μετατίθημι 5
μυκτήρ 102
μυκτηρίζω 102
μυστήριον 118, 152, 157, 209–10
μῶμος 112

νήπιος 63, 64, 65, 174

νουθεσία 215
νοῦς 180

οἰκοδομέω 42
οἰκονομία 120, 152
οἰκονόμος 64
ὀρθοποδέω 35, 39–40
ὁρίζω 113
ὅσιος 187
οὐδέ 26
οὕτως 4

πάθημα 95
παιδαγωγός 61

πάλη 219
παμποίκιλος 158
πανοπλία 218–19
παράπτωμα 134
παρεισάκτος 24
παρίστημι 74–5
πάροικος 149
παροργισμός 187
παρρησία 159, 223
παρρησιάζωμαι 224
πας 122, 133, 169–70, 174, 177
πατριά 161
πατρικός 14
πείθω 10–11
πειρασμός 71–2
πεισμονή 86
πέμπω 66
περθέω 12
πέρθω 12
περιζώννυμι 222
περισσεύω 118
περιτέμνω 83
περιφέρω 174
πέτρος 40–1
πηλίκος 103–4
πιστεύω 125
πλάνη 176, 177
πλεονεκτέω 183, 196
πλεονεξία 184
πληρόω 133
πλήρωμα 132, 133
πλοῦτος 118, 156
πνεῦμα 103, 135, 184, 198–9
ποιέω 145
πολυποίκιλος 158
πονηρός 3, 202
πορθέω 12
πρήθω 12
προανατίθημι 14, 20
προγραφή 47
προελπίζω 123, 124
προευαγγελίζωμαι 52
πρόθεσις 119
προθέσμιος 65
προλαμβάνω 97
προορίζω 113
προορισμός 119

προσαγωγή 149
προσανατίθημι 14–15, 20, 26–7
προσκολλάω 208
προστίθημι 60
πρόσωπον 30
προτίθημι 60
πώρωσις 182

σκλήρωσις 182
σπουδάζω 168
στέγω 96
στείχω 79
στήκω 83
στίξ 79
στίχος 79, 96
στοιχεῖον 65–6, 79, 96
στοιχέω 96, 106
σύγχρονος 13
σύγχυσις 75
συμβιβάζω 178
συμμέτοχος 198
συμπολίτης 149
συμφέρω 21
συναπάγω 39 n2
συναρμολογέω 151, 178
σύνδεσμος 168
συνηλικιώτης 13
σύσσωμα 155
συστοιχέω 79–80
συστοιχία 80
σφραγίζω 126
σώζω 203

ταπεινοφροσύνη 167

υἱοθεσία 67, 113
ὕμνος 206
ὑπερβάλλω 163
ὑποταγή 25

φανερόω 200
φθόνος 92–3
φιλαργυρία 183
φιλοχρηματία 183
φοβέω 212
φόνος 92–3
φορτίον 101, 101 n1

φρεναπατάω   100
φύραμα   87

χαρίζω   59, 191–2
χαριτόω   115–16
χρεία   189–90
χρηστολόγος   191
χρηστός   191

ψαλμός   206

LATIN WORDS

accipio   11, 67
acquiesco   14–15, 26
actor   64
addido   27
aemulor   73 n2, 74
aequalis   13
affectus   95
agnitio   129
agnosco   174
aliquid   21–2
allegoria   76
alter   98
ambulo   39–40, 106
anathema   10
armatura   218–19
arrabo   127
audio   19
autem   139

beatitudo   72
benedico   53
benedictio   53

catechizo   101
cliens   161
clientela   161
coaetaneus   13
commissura   178–9
comparticeps   155, 198
conferro   14–15, 20–1
confirmo   57
confundo   75
conspersio   87
convivifico   133–4

curator   64

delictum   134
depono   184–5
devasto   12
disco   11–12
do   90
dominatio   131

efficax   28
elementum   65–6, 96
exclude   73
exoro   12
expugno   12, 20
exsecratio   56

facio   66–7
fascinare   45, 84–5
fiducia   159
figmentum   142

genero   78
gens   29
genus   13
gratifico   115–16

implano   100
impostura   176
impudicia   204
incedo   39–40, 96, 106
includo   73
indolentia   182–3
indormio   50
indubito   50
infimus   156
inimicitia   145
instauro   97, 120
instruo   97
inverto   9
investigabilis   156
iracundia   187

libido   204
longanimitas   93, 167
loquor   104
lumbus   222
luxuria   202–4

luxus 202–4

magnanimitas 167
maledictio 55
maledictum 53, 55–6
massa 87
mediator 60–1
modo 11
mons 77–8
mundipotens 220
munditenens 220
mysterium 152, 153, 157 n3, 210 n1

neque 62
nimium 139
nunc 10–11

opero 28, 84
oporteo 190
opportunitas 189–90
oppugno 12
opus 142
oro 12

paedagogus 61
parens 161
parentela 161
paternitas 161
patientia 167
peccatum 134–5
persequor 105
persuadeo 12
pignus 127
planus 100
prae 48
praescribo 47–8
predestino 113

pro 48
prodo 48
proferro 48
proloquor 48
promulgo 48
proscribo 47–8
proscriptio 47–9
prostare 48

quia 18

ratio 101, 219
recapitulo 120
reverto 9–10
rideo 102

sacramentum 118, 209
scientia 163
scribo 104
semen 58
sensus 180
stultus 44
suadeo 10, 12
sum 42 n1

testamentum 58, 77–8
timor 206
transferor 5
transpono 5
tutor 64

vasto 12
venio 197
video 21–2, 104
virtus 131

General Index

accommodation, principle of 35, 44 n4,
57–8, 71
Aldine. *See* Bible: editions of
Alexander, bishop of Constantinople
37 n28
allegory. *See under* Scripture
ambiguity. *See under* Scripture
Ambrose of Milan: not distinguished
from Ambrosiaster xii, xvii; Erasmus'
edition of xvii–xix, 101 n1; interpretation of Eph 6 221; on the abrogation
of the Law 146
Ambrosiaster: identified with Ambrose
of Milan xii, xvii–xviii, xviii n14; errs
in interpretation 173; interpretation
of Greek 195, 222
Anselm of Canterbury 81 n9
Apollinaris, bishop of Laodicea 37 n27
apostle(s): meaning of the word in
Greek and Hebrew 2; false 7–8, 107;
called by God 14 n1, 17; equality
among 15–16; conflict between 30–8
Aquila, translator of the Bible 54 n4,
56n2, 82, 195n13
Aser, meaning of name 68
Asso, C. 'Maarten Dorp and Edward
Lee' 4 n3, 176 n9
Athanasius, Theophylact's commentary
falsely attributed to 9 n7, 112
Athenaeus, author of the
Deipnosophistae 205 n7
Augustine of Hippo: dispute with
Jerome 31–2; views of: on Peter's
behaviour in Antioch 31, 34, 36 n1;
on the dispensations 33–4; on

allegory 76, 78; on lust 203–4; on
luxury 203–4; on marriage 209; on
devoted parents 214; on slavery
216–17; interpretations of: (Eph 5:18)
203–4; (Gal 3:1) 47–8; (Gal 5:12) 88;
(Gal 5:14) 90–1

Balbus, Johannes, medieval compiler
of the *Catholicon* 194 n7
baptism 210, 217
Barhanina, Hebrew instructor 56 n6
Bartimaeus, meaning of name 68
Basel. *See under* manuscripts
Béda, Noël 110 n6
Bentley, J.H. *Humanists* 125 n7, 128 n2
Bible. *See also* manuscripts; Scripture
– editions of: Complutensian Polyglot
99 n5, 125 n7; Aldine 124 n6. *See also*
Marcion
– textual criticism of 16 n4, 81 n9,
179 n4, 190 n7. *See also under*
Erasmus, original works, *Annotationes*
– translations of 54 n4, 54 n5, 190 n7,
195 n13, 195 n15
Black, R. *Humanism and Education*
194 n7
Blass, F. and A. Debrunner *Greek
Grammar of the New Testament* 29 n2,
144 n2, 215 n2

Christ: God's calling through 6;
teaching of piety by 10; Paul's calling
by 20; portrayed to the Galatians 47;
proscription of 47–8; became sin 56;
promises and benefits in 63, 68, 83–4;

name of 95; Paul as servant of 107;
divine and human nature of 111;
Christians as forming the body of
113–14, 133; as head 120–1, 132,
178–9; 'Christ' compared with 'God'
128, 196–7; Law abrogated by 146;
as cornerstone 150; Paul as prisoner
of 151–2; all things created in 157,
159; surpassing love of 163; relationship to church of 209–10. *See also* Jesus
Chrysostom. *See* John Chrysostom
church: as tiny flock 12; Paul's persecution of 12; identified with heavenly
Jerusalem 80; excommunication from
97; Christ as head of 132; foundation
of 172; duties within 173; sacraments
of 209; as bride of Christ 209–10
Cephas, identified with Peter 32;
meaning of the name 40–1
Cicero 43 n1, 69 n7, 183 n5, 204 n5
Colet, John 23 n13
Complutensian Polyglot. *See* Bible:
editions of
conjunctions. *See under* grammar
Constance. *See under* manuscripts
Cyprian of Carthage xii, 34, 100 n5, 136,
136 n2, 137, 196, 196 n5, 197, 198 n4,
219, 219 n4, 221, 222 n2

Denniston, J.D. *Greek Particles* 184 n2
Dickey, E. *Ancient Greek Scholarship*
187 n4
Didymus of Alexandria 34, 37 n29, 126,
126 n2, 126 n4
Donatian. *See under* manuscripts
Dorp, Martin ix, 4 n3, 176 n9

Ephesus, chief city of Asia Minor 110
Erasmus: conflict with Luther xiv,
91 n6, 115 n7, 138 n7; his copy of the
Vulgate xv n10; editions of the New
Testament: xi–xii, xv n10, 3 n3, 4 n3,
8 n7; editions of the *Annotations*:
xi–xii, xiv, xviii, 4 n3, 162 n12,
165 n12; purpose of his *Annotations*
xiv–xvi, xvi n11, xvii n12
– commends the Vulgate 5, 10, 20, 44,
63, 181, 187, 193, 200, 216

– criticizes the Vulgate 3, 11, 15, 19 n5,
47, 55, 66, 69, 83–4, 85, 93, 100, 136,
141, 145, 152, 161, 184, 216
– views of: on figures of speech 6; piety
10; ceremonies 10, 38, 44, 54, 65–6,
154; the apostolic conflict 31–6, 38; on
Paul's affliction 71; on exclusion from
the Christian community 73; on
significance of number in lists 94; on
predestination 113, 119, 120 n7; on
knowledge of Greek 126; on joking
194, 195; on luxury 202–4; on
marriage 209–10
Erasmus, original works
– *Adagia* (I v 16) 222 n4; (I v 60)
211 n10; (I viii 22) 102 n1; (II ii 10)
126 n5; (II vii 66) 194 n9
– *Annotations*: quotations from or
allusions to specific annotations:
on Acts (10:38) 166 n3; 1 Cor (7:39)
211 n7, (12:6) 122 n4; on 2 Cor (2:15)
128 n1, 197 n3, (12:7) 72 n4, (12:26)
25 n3; on Eph *passim*; on Gal *passim*;
on Luke (16:8) 136 n4; on Mark
(14:36) 68 n5; on Matt (3:16) 49 n16,
(19:5) 209 n1, (24:22) 109 n1; on Rom
(1:1) 2, 14n1, (1:3) 67 n3, (1:4) 7 n4,
7 n11, 15 n2, 36 n3, 113 n3, 136 n4,
153 n4, (1:7) 3 n3, 128 n1, 197 n3,
(1:11) 111 n2, (1:14) 44 n2, (1:17) 55n2,
55 n4, 114 n2, 172 n 4, (1:25) 111 n1,
(1:26) 136 n4, (1:29) 93 n6, 94 n11, (2:4)
94 n7, (2:6) 185 n2, (2:7) 225 n3, (2:20)
64 n2, 65 n1, (3:3) 84 n2, (3:4) 106 n1,
(3:10) 18 n1, (4:17) 8 n2, (5:6) 185 n2,
(6:1) 42 n1, (6:11) 135 n3, (7:5) 95 n2,
(8:8) 3 n2, (8:15) 68 n5, 113 n1, (8:18)
100 n3, (8:21) 103 n1, (8:28) 114 n1,
119 n5, 185 n2, (8:38) 3 n3, (9:3) 10 n1,
(9:7) 18 n1, (10:2) 14 n1, (11:6) 124 n6,
(11:16) 87 n5, (11:22) 94 n7, (11:25)
153 n2, (11:32) 197 n1, (11:33) 156 n1,
(12:6) 185 n2, (12:13) 30 n1, 189 n2,
(12:14) 89 n9, (13:6) 223 n1, (13:9)
121 n7, (13:11) 200 n 1, (15:4) 94 n7,
153 n1, (15:7) 23 n6, 45 n13, (15:28)
126 n1, (16:5) 9 n9, 111 n4, (16:25–7)
165 n10; on 1 Tim (1:9) 98 n4

– *Apologia ad annotations Stunicae* 9 n7, 16 n11, 99 n5, 112 n1, 131 n1, 145 n3, 188 n7, 207 n1, 211 n21
– *Apologia ad Caranzam* 211 n21
– *Apologia ad Fabrum* 175 n4, 204 n2, 216 n1, 221 n3
– *Apologia adversus monachos* 37 n29
– *Apologia adversus Petrum Sutorem* 190 n7
– *Christiani hominis institutum* 210 n4
– *Christiani matrimonii institutio* 210 n4
– *Ciceronianus* 14 n1
– *Declarationes ad censuras Lutetiae vulgatas* 61 n3
– *De conscribendis epistulis* 194 n7
– *De libero arbitrio* 115 n7, 122 n2
– *De lingua* 194 n6
– *Ecclesiastes* 43 n1, 69 n7, 77 n6, 86 n2, 93 n8, 99 n7, 162 n13, 165 n6
– *Enchiridion* 219 n2, 222 n2
– letters (Ep 182) 13 n1; (Ep 315) 11 n8; (Ep 373) 3 n3, 23 n13, 49 n16; (Ep 456) 16 n4; (Ep 710) 110 n6; (Ep 1189) 140; (Ep 1223) 49 n16; (Ep 1309) 140 n4; (Ep 1316) 3 n3; (Ep 1761) 3 n3; (Ep 1841) 38 n32; (Ep 1858) 3 n3
– *Hyperaspistes* 44 n3, 50 n4, 61 n2, 77 n7, 91 n6, 138 n3, 138 n7, 200 n4
– *Life of Jerome* 164 n16
– *Paraphrasis in Ephesios* 117 n3, 158 n1, 168 n1, 171 n2, 172 n4, 199 n3, 206 n8, 222 n2
– *Paraphrasis in Galatas* 3 n3, 14 n1, 17 n2, 44 n2, 49 n2, 81 n13, 111 n4
– *Paraphrasis in Lucam* 114 n4, 119 n1
– *Peregrinatio Apostolorum Petri et Pauli* 17 n1
– *Responsio ad annotationes Lei* 4 n3, 20 n1, 37 n10, 114 n2, 121 n4, 144 n1, 162 n11, 209 n3, 211 n21
– *Supputatio* 38 n32

faith xiv, 35, 41, 42, 47–8, 50, 53, 55, 58, 61, 84–5, 115 n7, 124, 129–30, 146–7, 173–4, 189
figures of speech 6, 56, 76, 208. *See also* rhetoric

Galatians: origin of name 5; character and origins of 7, 40, 44; Paul's concern for 38, 75; coarse 57, 58
Geanakoplos, D.J. *Greek Scholars in Venice* 46 n5
God: the one who calls 6; Paul as apostle called by 14; shows no partiality 26, 62; worked effectively in Peter 28; testing of 31; not to be mocked 102; determining judgment of 114, 119; bestows the Holy Spirit 127; prayer as conversing with 128; distinct from Christ 128, 196–70; philosophical knowledge of 129; rich in mercy 139–40; clement 142; omnipotent 165, 169–70
grace xiv, 5–6, 7 n5, 31, 33, 38, 43, 47, 59, 79, 111, 115–16, 117, 122 n2, 138, 140, 142, 152, 193
grammar: sentence structure xvi, xix, 26, 58, 134 n11, 152 n1, 154, 169; importance of 124, 160. *See also* rhetoric
– adjective: genitive functions as a noun 150
– adverb: force of 16 n8, 29, 70 n1, 158 n1, 165, 192 n1, 212 n1
– compound words: verbs 28, 50, 100, 105, 153 n1, 181, 208; adjectives 158; nouns 192 n1, 216, 220
– conjunctions: added or omitted 18, 19, 21–2, 24, 26 n3, 28, 39, 42, 49, 93, 95, 115, 132, 166 n4, 199; superfluous 18 n1, 49, 50, 139; significance of 'double conjunction' 139 n2; significance of: γάρ 141, 142; δέ 24, 92, 95, 141; ἵνα 105, 189 n4, 212, 224; καί 62, 88, 139; ὅτι 18 n1, 54, 143; τε 218; ὡς 52 n1, 57, 207, 217
– definite article: omission of 103, 212; function of 116 n2, 185; before noun 158, 181
– nouns (cases of): dative to express instrument 39, 104, 134; advantage 90, 111, 132; end or purpose 143; genitive absolute 150
– participles: participle with force of relative clause 21, 24, 133, 200

– prepositions: often omitted 18, 140, 146; varied use of 58; superfluous 146; significance of: ἀντί 208; ἀπό 77, 83–4, 134 n11; διά 20, 139, 157, 158, 171, 171 n9, 182, 225; εἰς 29, 58, 61, 100, 103, 113, 117, 120 n1, 127, 148, 152, 172, 177, 190, 192, 208, 211; ἐκ 3, 21, 55, 165 n5, 171; ἐν 19, 42, 74, 77, 80, 90, 110, 111–12, 115, 116, 118, 119, 121, 129, 133, 136, 142, 146–8, 153, 158, 168–70, 171–2, 174, 179, 183, 184, 185, 187 n1, 212, 215, 218, 223, 225; ἐν ᾧ 123; ἐπι 121, 143 n1, 170; κατά 30, 41, 44, 65, 95, 101, 114, 119, 131, 133, 135, 158, 169, 177, 185, 216; μετά 187; παρά 24; περί 107, 222 n1, 224; πρό 48, 112, 113 n4, 123–4; πρός 17, 26, 74, 173, 176; σύν 95, 149 n1; ὑπέρ 132, 152 n2, 165; ὑπό 53, 58, 65, 132, 143
– pronouns: force of the relative in particular contexts 19, 77–8, 113–14, 140, 143, 148, 159, 166, 167, 177, 180; personal for reflexive 119, 207; superfluous 135, 184, 208; demonstrative for definite article 145; singular with plural antecedent 160; intensive pronoun used adverbially 188
– verbs: force of imperfect and aorist 39, 42, 131, 148, 152; past tense as present 51, 113, 125, 172; singular with plural neuters 77–8, 223; purpose and result 162, 189, 215; doubling of 195; sudden change of singular to plural 211–12
– imperative: infinitive for imperative 74; form of 99, 206
– indicative: perfect = habeo + participle 19, 181; confused with imperative 52; translation of Greek future 53, 99, 197 n1
– infinitive: after verbs of wishing 9, 75, 105; in place of imperative 74, 185
– subjunctive: expresses potentiality 148; confused with indicative 215 n2

Hagar, meaning of name 77–8
Harrill, J. Slaves in the New Testament 217 n7

Hebion 56
Hebrew: special nuance of 2; pun upon 5; peculiar idiom of 28–9, 51, 143, 144, 147, 187, 197, 208; cited according to Jerome 41, 172; original Hebrew cited 58, 114, 201; loan-word adopted in Greek 68, 206 n2
Heine, R. Commentaries of Origen and Jerome 95 n1
Hesychius 45, 46 n5, 174, 175 n5, 187 n4
Hexapla. See Origen: Hexapla of
Hilarion 195
Hilary of Poitiers 44, 104, 105n3, 185, 186, 220
Hoffmann, M. Rhetoric and Theology 77 n6
Hugh of St Cher 16 n4
Hunter, D.G. 'The Significance of Ambrosiaster' 3 n3

idiom
– Greek: reflects Hebrew 5, 208; reflected in Latin 16 n2, 18 n1, 20, 66 n1, 67, 68 n1, 92 n1, 131 n1, 139 n2, 146, 153 n1, 168 n1, 180 n1, 207 n1, 211, 221 n2, 222 n1, 223 n1; idioms identified 18 n1, 25, 50, 135, 139
– Hebrew: reflected in New Testament usage: noun for adjective 29, 143, 197, 198 n6; noun for pronoun 143; 'in' for instrument 147, 148 n15, 148 n1, 187 n1, 215; idioms identified 51, 166, 209 n1
– Latin: translator adopts Latin idiom 150; Erasmus adopts Latin idiom 150; idioms identified 206, 215
Irenaeus 23, 24 n28

James, identity of 17
Jerome: knowledge of Hebrew 2 n2, 56 n6; commended by Erasmus 5, 51, 69, 73, 88, 116, 123, 198; censured by Erasmus 22, 65, 104, 160, 163, 194, 214; differs with Augustine 31; conflict with Augustine 31–6, 39; Galatian people described by 44; taught by Barhanina 56; distinguished from Pseudo-Jerome, 81 n12; and the

Origenist controversy 125; on Paul's ignorance of Greek 129, 155, 160; on Stoicism 169–70; commentary on Ephesians 190; not the translator of the Vulgate 190, 200; on joking 193; on marriage 209. *See also under* Hebrew

Jerusalem: various spellings and meanings of 78; identified with the church 80; Johann Eck 110 n6

Jesus: portrayed to the Galatians 47; relation to God the Father 113; ancient interpretations of the name 201. *See also* Christ

Jews: interpretations of 9; peculiar language of 10; customs of 17, 31; ceremonies of 23, 65, 70, 146; called 'the circumcision' 29, 143; among the Christians in Antioch 30–3; observing the law 33, 38, 54, 79, 88; Peter's accommodation of 35; believers born as 41; associated with the synagogue 80; addressed by Paul 123–4

Johannes Marchesinus, composer of the *Mammaetractus* 194 n8

John Chrysostom: *Comm in Gal* available for 1535 edition of *Annotations* xii, 8 n6; on allegory 76; interpretations of: (Gal 4:24) 80; (Gal 6:2) 99; (Gal 6:4) 100; (Eph 1:10) 120; (Eph 1:22) 132; (Eph 2:3) 138; (Eph 3:16) 161; (Eph 4:6) 170; (Eph 4:15) 177; (Eph 4:22) 184

Jonge, H.J. de: ed. *Apologia… Stunicae* xviii n15, 8 n7, 15 n2, 49 n16, 99 n5, 112 n1, 145 n3, 188 n7

Jove, meaning of name 169

Judaism: Paul's former life in xiv, 11, 138 n7; combined with Christianity 6–8; Paul's efforts to dissuade believers from 30, 35, 41, 48; gentiles drawn to 33; Peter's relation to 40; apostles living in 123; spiritual life opposed to 151

Kelly, J.N.D. *Jerome* 195 n5

Krans, J. *Beyond What is Written* xv n10, 23 n1; 'Who Coined the Name "Ambrosiaster"?' xviii n14

Krey, P.D.W. and L. Smith, *Nicholas of Lyra* 179 n4

Lausberg, H. *Handbook of Literary Rhetoric* 7 n4, 43 n1, 51 n2, 67 n3, 77 n6, 86 n2, 90 n5, 93 n8, 118 n7, 120 n1, 139 n1, 141 n2, 196 n1, 211 n16

law, Mosaic 31, 32–4, 36 n1, 38, 40, 41, 45, 47, 50, 53, 54, 55, 61, 67, 73, 75, 76, 78, 79, 86, 96, 99, 106, 146–7, 155, 213

Lazare de Baïf, *On Matters of Clothing* 223 n6

Lee, Edward: Erasmus responds to criticism of xiv, 4 n3, 20 n1, 37 n10, 114 n2, 121 n4, 144 n1, 159 n8, 162 n11, 209 n3, 210 n5; critic of Erasmus 4 n3, 63 n3, 116 n2, 121 n4, 211 n21

Lefèvre d'Etaples, Jacques (Stapulensis): relationship with Erasmus 11 n8; reading of Greek New Testament reported by Erasmus 39, 174; Erasmus' criticism of 202, 220

Lubac, H. de: *Medieval Exegesis* 18 n3

Luther, Martin xiv, xiv n7, 91 n6, 138 n7

Macrobius, possible author of *On the Singularity of Clerics* 100 n5

manuscripts, New Testament: from Constance 2, 3 n3, 46, 48, 52, 59, 68, 77, 85, 91, 117, 132, 133, 140, 143, 148, 205, 224, 225; at Basel 8 n7; in St Paul's 25, 46, 91, 205 n5, 224, 225; in St Donatian's 48, 49 n16, 68, 77, 84, 85, 132, 133, 224

Marcion 8, 9 n9, 101, 149, 150 n2

Mary: mother of James 17; mother of Jesus 17; angelic greeting of 116 n1; song of 193

Mathisen, R. 'The Use of Jerome in Gaul' 45 n9

Merk, A. *Novum Testamentum* 138 n1, 145 n1, 154 n5, 177 n4

Mesech, meaning of name 68

Mitchell, S. 'The Galatians: Representation and Reality' 44 n3

Mohrmann, C. *Etudes sur le Latin* 116 n1

Momos, child of the goddess Nyx 112 n1

Monfasani, J. 'Criticism of Biblical
Humanists' 13 n1
Mt Sinai, meaning of name 77

names, ancient interpretations of 18.
See also under individual names
Nicholas of Lyra (Lyranus) 81 n9, 179 n4
Novatian, possible author of *On the
Singularity of Clerics* 100 n5

Oecumenius, Greek scholia mistakenly
attributed to 16. *See also*
Pseudo-Oecumenius
Olin, J. *Erasmus, Utopia* 105 n3
Origen: interpretations favoured by
Erasmus xii, 34; rejected as interpreter by Aquinas 34; Didymus influenced by 37 n29, 126 n2; 'Adamantius'
epithet of 46; *Hexapla* of 54 n4, 54 n6,
195 n13, 195 n14, 195 n15; relationship of commentaries with Jerome
95 n1; influence on Hilary 104;
controversy with Jerome 125 n9;
Rufinus' translation of his *On First
Principles* 125 n9; interpretations of:
(Rom 8) 28; (Gal 5:24) 94–5;
(Eph 1:17) 129

Pabel, H. 'The Authority of Augustine
in Erasmus' Biblical Exegesis' 4 n4
Pabel, H. and M. Vessey *Holy Scripture
Speaks* 172 n2, 210 n4
Pamphilius, translator of Origen's
commentary on Ephesians 95 n1
Parisian Articles 35, 38 n32
Paul, the apostle: confrontation with
Peter xv, 30, 32–5, 38; persecutor of
the church 12; called by God 14; calls
himself a zealot 14; language of
20, 45, 63, 65, 76, 79, 98–9, 110, 172,
191, 210; apostle to the gentiles 28;
pastoral behaviour 31, 36, 43, 44, 56,
61, 71, 188, 203; opposes Mosaic law
59, 84, 151; personal affliction 71;
at a loss 75; use of the Septuagint 82;
epistle to Galatians written by 103–4;
knowledge of Greek 129, 139, 141,
152, 155, 160, 163

Payne, J.B. *Erasmus, His Theology* 210 n4
Pelagius 39, 81 n12, 147 n13
Peter: conflict with Paul xv, 30–6;
known as Cephas 17, 32, 40–1; Paul's
visit with 17; God working in 28;
blamed 38; speech at the synod
of Jerusalem 147
Peter Cousturier (Petrus Sutor) xiv,
171 n17, 190 n7
Peter Lombard 51, 51 n4, 51 n5
Plater, W.E. and H.J. White *Grammar
of the Vulgate* 145 n1
Porsena, Christopher, translator
of Theophylact 8 n7
prayer: a person in 4; instruction
in 101; conversing with God 128
Pseudo-Augustine 67 n6
Pseudo-Jerome 81 n12
Pseudo-Oecumenius 37 n19, 37 n20,
38 n1, 38 n4, 49 n14, 53 n3, 78 n7,
83 n3, 153 n4, 183 n4

Raspanti, G. 'The Significance of
Jerome's Commentary on Galatians'
21 n1
Rebenich, S. 'Inventing an Ascetic'
195 n4
Reeve, A. and M.A. Screech xvi,
xvii n12
rhetoric, devices and figures of: style
(low, middle, high) xvi, 7, 18, 44, 70,
104, 110, 166 n3, 193, 210, 211 n16;
personification 4, 112; hyperbaton 5,
7, 27, 60, 61 n4, 110, 130, 134, 160;
hyperbole 6, 48; opposites 9, 10, 80,
90, 135, 151, 167 (*see also* contrast
and opposition *below*); parenthesis
(= *interpositio*) 26, 28, 140, 141 n2,
188 n1; contrast and opposition 29,
58 n4, 59, 69, 138, 140, 141, 150 n2,
151, 177, 191, 205, 206; *simulatio* 35–7,
92; *ratiocinatio* 43 n1; ellipse 51;
circumlocution 67, 161, 162 n12,
162 n15, 168 n3, 216; repetition 67 n7,
70, 89 n1, 110 n5, 120 n1, 193 n4, 196;
anadiplosis (= ἀναδίπλωσις) 68, 110;
similar word endings 79, 80, 93,
93 n8, 167, 174; *interrogatio* 86 n2;

percontatio 86 n2; emphasis 88, 89, 99,
139, 165, 184 n2, 189, 197 n1, 208;
asyndeton 93; *homoioptoton* 93 n8;
anakephalaiosis (= ἀνακεφαλαίωσις) 120;
recapitulatio 120; anacoluthon 152;
intensification 158, 180 n1, 195;
analogy 161; similitude (= *similitudo*)
162 n13; *interpositio* (*see* parenthesis
above); preface: to *Novum Instrumentum* xii; to *Annotations* (1516) 23 n13;
to Jerome's commentary on Galatians
31; to Rufinus' translation of Origen's
First Principles 125 n9; to Jerome's
commentary on Zechariah 192.
See also figures of speech; idiom
Roussel, B. 'Biblical Paraphrases' 172 n2
Rufinus of Aquileia 124, 125 n9
Rummel, E. *Erasmus and His Catholic
Critics* xiv n6, 4 n3, 11 n8, 99 n5,
114 n2, 211 n21; *Erasmus' Annotations*
xvi n11, xviii n15, 8 n7, 16 n4, 45 n13,
47 n6, 110 n6, 116 n2, 176 n13, 179 n4,
205 n21

Scheck, T. *St. Jerome's Commentaries*
95 n1
Schneemelcher, W. *New Testament
Apocrypha* 194 n4
Schoeck, R.J. 'Erasmus and Valla' 13 n1
scholastics xii, 126 n3; orthodox, 209
Scripture, patristic interpretation of 34;
hermeneutics of xv–xvi, 18; allegory
in 18 n3, 76, 77 n6, 118 n3, 199 n3,
214, 222 n5; special language of 60,
68, 191; ambiguities in Greek text of
Ephesians: (1:14) 127–8; (2:5) 139;
(2:14) 145; (2:15) 146; (3:13) 159; (4:6)
168–9; (5:13) 200; (5:16) 202; (6:3) 215;
(6:5) 216; ambiguities in Greek text
of Galatians: (1:6) 5; (1:14) 13; (3:1) 47;
(4:3) 65; (4:18) 74
Septuagint: Erasmus' use of xvi, 114 n2;
special language of 12, 114; its
readings cited 53, 54, 56, 58, 81, 82,
172; compared with Hebrew by
Erasmus 82; Paul's use of 82
Sider, R. 'Erasmus' Biblical Scholarship'
xi n1; 'Χάρις and Derivatives' 7 n5

sin xiv, 30–1, 34–5, 38, 56, 115, 117,
134–5, 138, 139, 140–1, 187, 200–1
Smith, L. *The Glossa Ordinaria* 81 n9
Souter, A. *Glossary of Later Latin* 100 n7,
102 n3, 142 n3, 162 n11
St Donatian's. *See under* manuscripts
St Paul's. *See under* manuscripts
Symmachus 53, 56, 81, 194

Tabitha, meaning of name 68
Theodotion 53, 56, 82, 194
Theophylact: employed by Erasmus xii;
Archbishop of Ochrida xviii, 8 n7; as
Vulgarius xviii, 8 n7; his commentary
translated by Porsena 8 n7; Erasmus'
report of Greek text read by 46, 48,
59, 60 (twice), 66, 69, 73; his commen-
tary translated 85; rhetorical empha-
sis noted by 89, 189; identified with
Athanasius 112; interpretations of:
(Eph 1:3) 112; (Eph 1:9) 118; (Eph 1:10)
120; (Eph 1:10) 121; (Eph 1:12) 123;
(Eph 1:13) 123–4; (Eph 1:18) 130;
(Eph 1:22) 132; (Eph 1:23) 133;
(Eph 2:3) 138; (Eph 2:5) 140; (Eph 2:15)
146; (Eph 2:21) 151; (Eph 3:5) 154;
(Eph 3:14) 160; (Eph 3:19) 163–4;
(Eph 4:6) 170; (Eph 4:11) 173;
(Eph 4:14) 175; (Eph 4:16) 179;
(Eph 4:19) 184; (Eph 4:21) 184–5;
(Eph 4:32) 192; (Eph 5:9) 199;
(Eph 5:11) 199; (Eph 5:13) 200;
(Eph 6:7) 217; (Eph 6:24) 225;
(Gal 1:19) 17; (Gal 1:20) 18;
(Gal 2:20) 42; (Gal 3:5) 51;
(Gal 3:28) 62; (Gal 4:15) 72;
(Gal 4:24) 77; (Gal 4:25) 80;
(Gal 4:30) 82; (Gal 4:31) 83;
(Gal 5:12) 88; (Gal 5:13) 90;
(Gal 5:25) 96; (Gal 6:1) 98;
(Gal 6:6) 102; (Gal 6:11) 104
Thomas Aquinas: Erasmus' criticism
of 15, 34, 204, 205 n3; summary
of the dispute between Jerome and
Augustine 32–5; view of Paul's
knowledge of Greek 160; Erasmus
recommends interpretation of 201;
ridiculed by Erasmus 203;

interpretations of: (Eph 3:15) 161;
(Gal 1:14) 14; (Gal 4:25) 80
Titelmans, Frans 45 n13
Trapman, J. 'Erasmus on Lying and
Simulation' 36 n1

Valla, Lorenzo: his *Collatio Novi
Testamenti* xii, 13 n1; Erasmus follows
translation of 5 n1, 11 n3, 16 n2,
17 n2, 41 n1, 44 n2, 46 n1, 72 n1,
87 n1, 88 n1, 90 n1, 98 n6, 99 n1,
102 n1, 103 n1, 103 n2, 119 n1, 167 n3,
182 n1; Erasmus' evaluation of 12, 22,
27, 90, 96, 101, 166, 180

Vulgarius, mistakenly identified with
Theophylact xviii, 8 n7

Wengert, T. *Human Freedom, Christian
Righteousness* 142 n3
Westcott, B.F. *Epistle to the Galatians*
181 n3

Zúñiga, Diego López (Stunica): critic
of Erasmus xiv, 16 n11, 99 n5,
110 n6, 134 n3, 207 n1; work on
Complutensian Bible 99 n5; Erasmus
responds to 159 n8, 162 n12, 164 n1,
188 n7, 211 n21

The design of
THE COLLECTED WORKS
OF ERASMUS
was created
by
ALLAN FLEMING
1929–1977
for
the University
of Toronto
Press